The Student Edition of
READY-TO-RUN
ACCOUNTING

The Student Edition of
READY-TO-RUN
ACCOUNTING

Complete general ledger software...
adapted for education

Ronald E. Brunk

Goshen College

Addison-Wesley Publishing Company, Inc.
The Benjamin/Cummings Publishing Company, Inc.

Reading, Massachusetts • Redwood City, California • New York
Don Mills, Ontario • Wokingham, England • Amsterdam • Bonn
Sydney • Singapore • Tokyo • Madrid • San Juan • Milan • Paris

The Student Edition of Ready-to-Run Accounting is published by
Addison-Wesley Publishing Company, Inc. and The Benjamin/
Cummings Publishing Company, Inc. Contributors included:

Alan Jacobs, Executive Editor
Kevin Howat, Sponsoring Editor
Cindy Johnson, Project Manager
Michelle Neil, Development Editor
Kathy O'Neil, Editorial Assistant
Karen Wernholm, Software Production Supervisor
Nancy Benjamin, Production Coordinator
Jean Seal, Cover Designer
Gex, Inc., Compositor

Lotus and 1-2-3 are registered trademarks of Lotus Development
Corporation. IBM, AT, PS/2, PC/XT, and OS/2 are registered trademarks of International Business Machines, Inc.

General Notice: Some of the product names used herein have been
used for identification purposes only and may be trademarks of their
respective companies.

ISBN 0-201-95400-1 (manual)
       0-201-50628-9 (5¼" disk format)
       0-201-50629-7 (3½" disk format)

1 2 3 4 5 6 7 8 9 10-MU-9594939291

Preface

Computerized accounting systems are the norm in business today. And accounting students need to understand computerized systems in order to understand their role as accountants tomorrow. How does an automated system differ from a manual system? How is it similar? What does the computer handle automatically, and what does the accountant control? What advantages does a computerized system offer? The Student Edition of Ready-to-Run Accounting is a powerful automated solution to these issues and more. It builds a tangible link between financial accounting data and the many different kinds of accounting information that can be extracted from it.

Why Ready-to-Run Accounting?

The Student Edition of Ready-to-Run Accounting is the general ledger module of an easy-to-use, very successful commercial accounting system that runs within Lotus 1-2-3, Release 2 or 3*. Originally written by a CPA for his own practice, the Ready-to-Run Accounting system is a complete Lotus 1-2-3 application with its own menus and screen displays. It operates as a dedicated general ledger system, and no prior experience with Lotus 1-2-3 is required. (Its mode of operation will be familiar to Lotus 1-2-3 users, however.)

*The 5¼″ disk format of The Student Edition of Ready-to-Run Accounting requires additional files for use with Lotus 1-2-3, Release 3 and 3.1. These files are available free to registered users from Addison-Wesley. The 3½″ disk format already includes all necessary files for Release 3 installation.

For students learning accounting, The Student Edition of Ready-to-Run Accounting's traditional approach to general ledger accounting makes it easy to compare and contrast its operation with the manual accounting process. It is representative of the systems widely used in business today, and includes many features not found in other student versions. Graphing, budgeting, financial analysis, and report customization are built-in options.

Because The Student Edition of Ready-to-Run Accounting is written in Lotus 1-2-3, it also demonstrates and uses the power of automated systems better than most general ledger software. All data files and reports are immediately accessible through 1-2-3 for additional analysis and reporting. Ready-to-Run links the general ledger to 1-2-3 work undertaken in other classes, and illustrates how one system can serve both external and internal accounting needs. As the demand for more and different kinds of accounting analysis grows, accounting systems will need to be as flexible as Ready-to-Run.

A Manual Written for Students

When I took on the task of writing the manual for The Student Edition of Ready-to-Run Accounting, I was excited about developing a resource that could help beginning accounting students compare automated accounting with the manual system they were learning in the classroom. I had used a number of different software supplements for beginning accounting textbooks but was never satisfied with the flexibility or breadth of those products. Ready-to-Run Accounting presented additional educational opportunities through flexible reporting, financial analysis, and use of Lotus 1-2-3 files. I also felt that the tutorial format used by The Student Edition of Lotus 1-2-3 could help accounting instructors familiarize their students with the capabilities of commercial accounting software without having to teach the software. I have tried to replicate that tutorial approach in this manual. It was written to meet the following objectives:

1. Provide a self-contained introduction to a typical automated accounting system for the beginning student;

2. Present a view of automated accounting that would enhance student understanding of the accounting cycle;

3. Inspire students with the power and potential of the computer as an accountant's tool;

4. Create a flexible learning environment that can be used in a variety of accounting courses.

To accomplish these objectives, The Student Edition of Ready-to-Run Accounting includes:

1. Self-instructional format. Ready-to-Run Accounting is explained from the ground up, in small logical steps that allow the beginning student to master the general ledger system without classroom instruction and with a minimal amount of prior computer experience.

2. Accounting cycle organization. An overview introduces and contrasts Ready-to-Run's structure with the manual process presented in most principles of accounting texts. Labs 1 through 5 then follow the accounting cycle.

3. Unlimited reporting flexibility. Unlike general ledger packages that restrict the user to "canned" reports, Ready-to-Run's data and reports are stored as Lotus 1-2-3 files. Lotus 1-2-3 exercises and labs on financial analysis, graphing, and customizing reports are included to expose students to the options open to the accountant using a system like Ready-to-Run.

4. Varied practice material. Four levels of exercises and four additional practice sets make it easy to tailor The Student Edition of Ready-to-Run Accounting to a principles, financial accounting, intermediate accounting, or accounting information systems course. A continuing case through the lab tutorials provides maximum guidance in learning the software, while the reference section opens the door to more independent systems study.

Organization

This manual is divided into three parts and seven appendixes.

Part One, Getting Started   Getting Started provides a broad overview of the contents and walks the student through setting up and installing the software. It describes how to start and end a session with Ready to-Run, and explains Ready-to-Run's relationship to Lotus 1-2-3.

Part Two, An Overview of Ready-to-Run and Lab Activities

Part Two is the heart of the book. It begins with a hands-on overview that introduces general ledger software, tours RTR menus, screens, and keyboard conventions, and compares Ready-to-Run's operation to the manual accounting process.

Eight interactive lab activities follow. The first five present the functions of RTR that correspond to the accounting cycle:

- setting up a chart of accounts

- entering and posting transactions

- generating a trial balance

- making adjusting entries

- printing audit trail and financial statements

Labs 6 through 8 then introduce capabilities of RTR not found in all general ledger packages:

- generating financial ratios

- graphing data

- creating a budget

- customizing reports

- setting up departmental accounts

Labs 6 through 8 are optional and may be added in the second semester of principles, revisited in a future course, or undertaken independently by the student (perhaps as extra credit).

Each lab activity comprises a tutorial and practice exercises. An ongoing case study integrates the labs, and taken together, they constitute a practice set. Three separate tracks through the lab activities are included:

- Principles of accounting students may set up the books for a sole proprietorship by doing the tutorials and the Walton Electronics exercises.

- Financial and intermediate accounting students may set up the books for a corporation by doing the tutorials and the TWE, Inc. exercises.

- Intermediate accounting students may add written exercises to the TWE, Inc. exercises by completing the ''Going Further'' exercises.

In addition, optional Lotus 1-2-3 exercises are included in most labs for courses at any level where students already have Lotus 1-2-3 experience. More complete information about the uses of the manual in different accounting courses is provided in the Instructor's Manual.

The tutorial portion of each lab requires approximately 45 minutes to complete, not including the exercises. The case study exercise set for each lab varies from 30 to 45 minutes to complete. The actual time will vary from lab to lab, student to student, and instructor to instructor.

Part Three, Reference   Part Three presents a summary guide to Ready-to-Run's operation, its basic skills and menus, and a troubleshooting guide for the novice. Also included are examples of the standard financial reports in Ready-to-Run, descriptions of the Lotus 1-2-3 files that make up RTR, and guidelines for using Lotus 1-2-3 to record transactions that can be uploaded to and incorporated in Ready-to-Run. (These may be useful for students who want to write a 1-2-3 macro program that maintains subsidiary ledgers.)

Appendixes   Appendixes provide a guide to using Lotus 1-2-3's PrintGraph function and additional practice set data. A manufacturing practice set presents accounts and transactions not covered in the labs. Two additional periods of data are provided for Walton Electronics, the sole proprietorship introduced in the lab activities. And data at the intermediate level are provided in an additional corporate practice set.

Acknowledgements

There are several people I would like to thank for helping make The Student Edition of Ready-to-Run Accounting a reality.

Robyn Lawrence, Lehigh University, reviewed manuscript and software, making many useful suggestions, and contributed the financial, intermediate, and Lotus 1-2-3 exercises to the lab activities as well as the intermediate practice set material.

Steve Manus, President of Manusoft Corporation, made several modifications to the Ready-to-Run system to improve its speed and ease of use, and The Student Edition is the beneficiary of his efforts. His dedication to quality and commitment to education yielded many good ideas for the user manual as well.

Michelle Neil, Development Editor, contributed greatly to the clarity and completeness of the manual, and Cindy Johnson, Project Manager, kept the project as a whole directed toward the needs of the accounting student.

Several reviewers participated in reading the manual and testing the software, and I wish to thank them here for their contributions.

Walter Batchelder, University of Alabama
James Borden, Villanova University
Mark Coffey, Western New England College
Rosalind Cranor, Virginia Polytechnic Institute and
  State University
William Cummings, University of Northern Illinois
Sam Hicks, Virginia Polytechnic Institute and
  State University
Phillip May, Wichita State University
Alfred Michenzi, Loyola College
Harold Miller, California Polytechnic State University,
  San Luis Obispo
Gerald Rossen, Lynchburg College

And for student-testing the software and manual, I want to thank Richard Cross, of Bentley College, Wendy Miller, and these Goshen College intermediate accounting students: Ken Anders, Raj Biyani, Wendell Bontrager, Doug Hunsberger, Dean Jantzen, Roger Lehman, and Kathie McClure.

I also want to thank my wife, Carolyn, and my sons, Jevon and Jeremy, for support, encouragement, and extreme patience while I was completing this project. Also, the support of my department chair, Del Good, the assistance of our departmental secretary, Linda Wilfong, and the overnight services of Federal Express were extremely beneficial in meeting tight deadlines.

As I write this, I am aware of the many changes being undertaken in the accounting curriculum, and I look forward to revising and improving The Student Edition of Ready-to-Run Accounting to meet those changing conditions. I would very much like to hear your comments and suggestions as you use the manual and software in class. Please write to me at Goshen College, 1700 So. Main St., Goshen, IN 46526.

Ronald E. Brunk, CPA
December, 1990

Contents

Getting Started

1

Before You Begin

This chapter describes the contents of the Student Edition of Ready-to-Run Accounting package and the typographical conventions used in this manual. You should read this chapter before you use or install Ready-to-Run.

Checking Your Package

Your package for the Student Edition of Ready-to-Run Accounting should contain the following:

- The User's Manual (this book)

- One diskette (either 5¼" or 3½")

- License Agreement (printed on the last page of this manual, opposite the diskette)

- Registration/Warranty Card

The User's Manual

The User's Manual consists of four sections.

Getting Started	Getting Started describes how to install Ready-to-Run, how to start and end Ready-to-Run, and how Ready-to-Run interfaces with Lotus 1-2-3.
An Overview of Ready-to-Run and Lab Activities	The Overview explains the purpose of general ledger accounting software and introduces you to Ready-to-Run's screens and menu structure. The Lab Activities are eight hands-on, interactive labs covering various features of Ready-to-Run, including setting up a chart of accounts, recording transactions, generating financial statements, preparing financial analyses, and budgeting.
Reference	The reference section describes the skills and commands needed to operate Ready-to-Run, provides a reference to the Ready-to-Run menus, includes examples of financial reports generated by Ready-to-Run, and lists the Ready-to-Run data files.

Appendixes   The appendixes provide examples of financial reports generated by Ready-to-Run, practice sets that can be used after you learn how to back up your disks and use Ready-to-Run, how to use Ready-to-Run with Lotus 1-2-3 Release 3, and a brief explanation of how to back up your disks and use Lotus PrintGraph to print graphs generated by Ready-to-Run.

Product Support

Neither Addison-Wesley nor Manusoft Corporation provides phone assistance to students for the Student Edition of Ready-to-Run Accounting. Phone assistance is provided to *registered* instructors adopting the Student Edition.

If you encounter difficulty using the Student Edition software:

- Check the Troubleshooting section in Part 3, Reference.
- Consult the reference section of the User's Manual for information on the commands or procedures you are trying to perform.

If you have to ask your instructor for assistance, describe your question or problem in detail. Write down what you were doing (the steps or procedures you followed) when the problem occurred. Also write down the exact error message, if any.

Typographical Conventions

You issue Ready-to-Run commands by pressing particular keys or sequences of keys. These keys are designated either by symbols (for arrow keys, function keys, and the Return, or Enter, key) or by small caps (for example, ESC). This manual uses the following terminology:

Press: This tells you to strike or press a key. It is used primarily with the arrow keys, the special keys, the function keys, and the Enter key (), to perform an operation. For example, the instruction to press the Enter key would appear as:

Press:

Type: This also tells you to strike or press a key. It is used primarily with the standard typewriter keys to enter information into a worksheet. Keys you type are printed in boldface. For example, the instructions to type the letter A would appear as:

Type: **A**

Move to: This tells you to move the cell pointer to a particular location in the worksheet, usually with the arrow keys. For example, the instruction to move the cell pointer to cell F14 would appear as:

Move to: F14

Select: This tells you to choose a particular menu option. You can choose an option by moving the menu pointer to the command and pressing ⎣⏎⎦ or you can type the first letter or number of the command. The first letter of the command is in bold type to remind you that you can use the second method of selection. For example, the instructions to select the Enter command would appear as:

Select: **E**nter

Key Combinations

When two keys are separated by a - (hyphen), you must press and hold down the first key, press the second key, and then release both keys. For example, the combination CTRL-⎣→⎦ means to press and hold down CTRL, press ⎣→⎦, and then release both keys.

When two keys are separated by only a space, press the first key and release it, then press the second key and release it. For example, the combination END HOME means press END and release it, then press HOME and release it.

2

Installing
Ready-to-Run

This chapter leads you through the steps you should follow before you use the Student Edition of Ready-to-Run Accounting: starting your computer, working with disks, preparing disks, and installing the Ready-to-Run program. The procedures vary depending on the type of system you have: two-diskette or hard-disk. The procedures also vary depending on whether you plan to keep your accounting data on a diskette or on your hard disk.

Preliminaries

You need the following items to install Ready-to-Run:

- The diskette you received with this package

- The DOS system diskette (version 2.0 or higher) or DOS installed on your hard disk

- If you are using a two-diskette system, three blank diskettes with sleeves and labels (to make two working-copy diskettes of your RTR program and to create a data diskette)

- If you are using a hard-disk system, one blank diskette with sleeve and label (to create a data diskette)

- If you are installing Ready-to-Run with Lotus 1-2-3 Release 3 using 5¼" disks, you need an additional disk, which is available from Addison-Wesley at no charge. Order this disk by completing and mailing the coupon at the end of this book.

Working with Disks

Your computer has one or two diskette drives that use either 5¼" or 3½" removable diskettes.

3½" disk

5¼" disk

In addition, your computer may have a fixed (or hard) disk. This is usually a nonremovable unit built into the computer, which can store the contents of many diskettes.

The Student Edition of Ready-to-Run Accounting is packaged on a diskette in either 5¼″ or 3½″ format. Even if you have a hard disk, you will use diskettes to load the program and to store copies of the worksheets and graphs you create.

Whenever you work with diskettes, keep the following in mind:

- Do not touch the exposed areas of a diskette. If you are using a 3½″ diskette, do not handle it with the shutter (the sliding metal door at the bottom center of the diskette) open.

- If you are using a 5¼″ diskette, take care when you write on the diskette label; a sharp point or hard pressure may damage the diskette. Use a felt-tip pen to write on a label that is already on the diskette.

- Always replace a 5¼″ diskette in its sleeve after using it.

- Keep diskettes away from heat, sunlight, smoke, and magnetic fields, such as telephones, televisions, and transformers. Do not use paper clips on diskettes.

- If the drive slot is horizontal, slide the diskette into the drive with the label facing up. The notch on a 5¼″ diskette should be on the left; the metal shutter on a 3½″ diskette should be inserted first. If the drive is mounted vertically, the label on a 5¼″ diskette usually faces left with the notch at the bottom.

- Put the diskette in the drive as far as it will go, but do not force it. If you are using a 5¼″ diskette, you must close the drive door after you insert the diskette.

- Do not remove a diskette while the drive access light is on.

Write-Protecting Diskettes

In addition to environmental hazards, diskettes are vulnerable to human error. Whenever you work with a diskette, you can avoid some accidents by "write-protecting" it. Write-protecting locks the diskette so that you cannot alter or erase the information on it. Write-protecting does not prevent you from running a program from the diskette or retrieving information from it.

The procedure for write-protecting a diskette depends on what kind of diskette you have.

For 5¼″ diskettes, cover the notch on the side of the diskette with a write-protect tab. Put half of the tab over the notch and fold the tab over so it sticks to the other side.

For 3½″ diskettes, there is a small write-protect window in the upper right corner of the diskette. When the window is open, the diskette is protected. If necessary, slide the small plastic tab over to uncover the window.

Starting Your Computer

Before you can prepare diskettes or make copies of your RTR diskettes, you must load DOS, the *disk operating system* that tells the computer how to do basic tasks like copying and formatting diskettes. Your computer should be off when you start this section. If you make a typing error, use BACKSPACE to erase the letters and then type the entry correctly.

> **Note** Step 1 is for two-diskette systems only; skip to step 2 if you are using a hard disk.

1. Insert your DOS diskette in drive A (the upper or left drive). If you are using 5¼″ diskettes, close the drive door.

2. Turn on the computer.

   Some computers also have a separate switch for the monitor; if so, turn it on.

   It may take up to one minute for the small blinking underscore, or *cursor*, to appear in the upper left corner of the screen. When the computer is ready, it may either display the date or ask you to enter it. (On some computers, the date and time are loaded automatically. If so, the operating system prompt appears. If the operating system prompt appears, skip steps 3 and 4.)

3. Enter the date (if necessary) in the form MM-DD-YY and press ⏎.

   For example, if the date is July 16, 1991, type 07-16-91 and press ⏎.

4. Enter the time (if necessary) in HH:MM twenty-four hour format and press ⏎.

For example, if the time is 4:15 p.m., type 16:15 and press ⏎.

If you enter an invalid date or time, DOS prompts you to try again. When you have finished entering the date and time, the operating system prompt appears. This book uses A> for two-diskette systems and C> for hard-disk systems. Your prompt may look somewhat different.

Preparing Your Diskettes

You are now ready to create a working copy of the Ready-to-Run program (if you are using a two-diskette system) or copy the Ready-to-Run program to your hard disk (if you are using a hard-disk system). You will also create a data diskette that you will use in the Lab Activities.

Formatting Blank Diskettes

Before you can use a new diskette, you must format it, or prepare it to hold data. The instructions for formatting a diskette differ slightly depending on what kind of computer you have. Follow the instructions in the section that applies to your computer system.

Two-Diskette System   In this section, you will format three blank diskettes so that they can hold information. You should format only blank diskettes (or diskettes that contain files you do not want, since formatting erases whatever is on the diskette).

Be sure that your *original* Ready-to-Run diskette is not in either drive. If you already know how to format diskettes, do so, then skip to "Labeling the Data Diskette."

First make sure the new blank diskettes are not write-protected. If necessary, remove the write-protect tabs or close the write-protect windows on the diskettes.

Note   If you make a typing error, use BACKSPACE to erase the letters, then retype the entry correctly.

1. Make sure your computer is turned on and the operating system prompt (A>) is displayed on the screen.

2. Insert the DOS diskette in drive A and close the drive door.

3. If the A:> prompt is not on the screen, to make A the current drive,

    Type: **A:**
    Press: ⏎

4. Insert one of the blank diskettes in drive B and close the drive door.

5. Type: **FORMAT B:**
    Press: ⏎

    Your screen displays the message "Insert new diskette for drive B: and strike any key when ready."

6. To begin formatting,

    Press: ⏎

    The message "Formatting..." may appear on the screen, and the lights next to the drive doors go on. Formatting can take as long as a minute. When the process is finished, the lights go out, and the message "Format complete" may appear. (If your version of DOS prompts you to enter a volume label, press ⏎ to skip the volume label.) DOS displays information about available space on the diskette and asks "Format another (Y/N)?"

7. To tell DOS that you want to format another diskette,

    Type: **Y**

    With some versions of DOS, you must also press ⏎.

8. When the message "Insert new diskette for drive B: and strike any key when ready" appears, remove the formatted diskette from drive B and put a label on it to show that it is formatted. Then insert a new blank diskette in drive B, close the drive door, and press ⏎.

    Repeat steps 7 and 8 for the third diskette.

9. To stop formatting after the third diskette, when DOS asks if you want to format another,

Type: **N**

With some versions of DOS, you must also press (⏎).

The system prompt should appear on the screen.

You can now use the formatted diskettes for the working copy of Ready-to-Run and for your data diskette.

Hard-Disk System In this section, you will format one or three blank diskettes so that they can hold information. If you are planning to install the Ready-to-Run program on diskettes, you will need three blank diskettes. If you are planning to install the Ready-to-Run program on the hard disk, you will need one blank diskette.

Be sure that your *original* Ready-to-Run diskette is not in the drive. If you already know how to format diskettes, do so, then skip to "Labeling the Data Diskette."

Before you begin, make sure that the new blank diskettes are not write-protected. If necessary, remove the write-protect tabs or close the write-protect windows on the diskettes.

Note If you make a typing error, use BACKSPACE to erase the letters, then retype the entry correctly.

1. Make sure the C:\ > prompt is on your screen, then,

Type: **FORMAT A:**

Note You *must* include the drive name (A:) in the command, or you can accidentally reformat your hard disk, erasing everything on it.

Press: (⏎)

Your screen should say "Insert new diskette for drive A: and strike any key when ready."

2. Insert a new blank diskette in drive A.

3. To start formatting,

Press: ⏎

The message "Formatting..." may appear on the screen.
The drive indicator light next to the drive door goes on,
and the drive makes a whirring noise. Formatting can take
as long as one minute. When the process is finished, the
light goes out, and the message "Format complete" may
appear. (If your version of DOS prompts you to enter a
volume label, press ⏎ to skip the volume label.) DOS displays information about available space on the diskette
and asks "Format another (Y/N)?"

4. If you need to format a second diskette, in response to the
prompt,

Type: **Y**

With some versions of DOS, you must also press ⏎.

5. When the message "Insert new diskette for drive A: and
strike any key when ready" appears, remove the formatted diskette from drive A, and put a label on it to show
that it is formatted. Then insert a new blank diskette in
drive A, close the drive door, and press ⏎.

If you need to format a third diskette, repeat steps 4 and 5.

6. To stop formatting, when DOS asks if you want to format
another,

Type: **N**

With some versions of DOS, you must also press ⏎.

Labeling the Data Diskette

One of the blank diskettes that you formatted in the previous
section will be your data diskette. Label that diskette "RTR
Data Disk." If you are using 5¼″ diskettes, make sure you use
a felt-tip pen. Later, you will add the name of the company
whose data is contained on this diskette.

> **Note** You cannot use a data diskette for more than one com-
> pany. If you create accounting data for more than one com-
> pany, you must format a blank data diskette for each company.

Problems with Diskettes

If your Ready-to-Run diskette is defective, or if you damage or erase it, see the limited warranty for instructions on returning it for a replacement.

You are now ready to use the Install program.

Installing the Student Edition of Ready-to-Run Accounting

The diskette you received with this package contains the Ready-to-Run files in a compressed state, at least one sample chart of accounts, and some additional data files. To make the RTR files usable and to create a working Ready-to-Run diskette, you must run the Install program. After you run the Install program, you will not use the diskette that came with this package to start Ready-to-Run. You will use the RTR Student Edition Working Diskettes, which the Install program creates, or you will start RTR from your hard disk.

> **Note** If you are using a hard-disk system in a college laboratory, you should ask your instructor if Ready-to-Run has already been installed. If so, you may skip to Chapter 3, "Starting and Ending Ready-to-Run."

Your Hardware Configuration

Before you can install Ready-to-Run, you must determine what type of computer system you will be using to run the program: a two-diskette system or a hard-disk system. The Install program for Ready-to-Run refers to the two-diskette system as a *floppy disk* system.

If you are installing this program on your own computer with a hard-disk system, you need to know whether to store your data files on the hard disk or on diskettes. Check with your instructor regarding which you should do.

Your Lotus 1-2-3 Version

As explained in the next chapter, Ready-to-Run uses Lotus 1-2-3 to perform its operations. Before you install Ready-to-Run, you must know which release of Lotus 1-2-3 you will use. The Student Edition of Ready-to-Run Accounting runs on Lotus 1-2-3 commercial releases 2.0, 2.01, 2.2, 3, and 3.1. It also runs on the Student Edition of Lotus 1-2-3 Release 2.2.

If you are using a hard-disk system, you also need to know the name of the directory containing your Lotus 1-2-3 program files. If you are using a two-diskette system, you must have your Lotus 1-2-3 System disk on hand.

> **Note** If you are using earlier versions of the Student Edition of Lotus 1-2-3, you will *not* be able to use the Student Edition of Ready-to-Run.

If you are using Lotus 1-2-3 Release 2.2, or the Student Edition of Lotus 1-2-3 Release 2.2, you may proceed to "Installing the Ready-to-Run Program" for your type of computer system.

Lotus 1-2-3 Release 3 does not run on a two-diskette system. If you are using Lotus 1-2-3 Release 3, you should follow the instructions for installing on a hard disk. If you are using 5¼" disks, you need an additional disk, available at no charge from Addison-Wesley Publishing Co. Complete and mail the coupon at the end of this book to receive this disk. For instructions on installing this additional disk and other information on running Ready-to-Run with Lotus 1-2-3 Release 3, see the appendix.

Installing the Ready-to-Run Program

The instructions for installing Ready-to-Run differ slightly depending on the kind of computer you have. Follow the instructions in the section that applies to your computer system.

Two-Diskette System This section describes how to start the Install program with a two-diskette system. If you have a hard disk, see the next section, "Hard-Disk System."

Before you start the Install program, make sure you have the following:

- Three blank formatted 5¼" diskettes or two blank formatted 3½" diskettes for your working copy and data

- The original diskette that came with this package

- Your Lotus 1-2-3 System disk

1. Make sure the computer is on and the A> prompt (or the appropriate system prompt) is on the screen.

   If it is not, follow the instructions in "Starting Your Computer."

2. Place the diskette that came with this package in drive A.

3. At the DOS prompt,

   Type: **INSTALL**
   Press: ⏎

4. In a few seconds, the display should say:

   READY-TO-RUN ACCOUNTING
   STUDENT EDITION
   INSTALL ROUTINE

   If the screen says "Bad command or filename":

   Make sure the *original* Ready-to-Run diskette is in drive A. If it is not, remove the diskette that is there, insert the correct diskette, and repeat step 3.

   Check that you typed "install" correctly. If you did not, repeat step 3.

   If the screen says "Abort, Retry, Ignore?":

   If you have the 5¼" version, check that the drive door is closed. If it is open, close it, then type **R** and press ⏎.

   Otherwise, type **A** and start again from step 1. If that does not solve the problem, consult your instructor.

   Under the boxed-in heading on the Install screen, you should see the message:

   (To abort the install at any time press Ctrl + C)

   If at any time you want to stop the Install process and start over, press CTRL-**C**.

   The Install program asks:

   Are you installing RTR on a F)loppy or H)ard disk system?

5. To install Ready-to-Run on a two-diskette system,

Type: **F**

Press: ⏎

The screen now says:

Please enter the disk drive containing the Ready-to-Run diskette:

6. To accept the default drive A, which appears on the screen,

Press: ⏎

The next message is

Please enter the disk drive Ready-to-Run is being installed onto.

7. To accept the default drive B, which appears on the screen,

Press: ⏎

The screen now says:

**Insert a blank diskette into the B: drive.
Strike a key when ready . . .**

8. Be sure that one of your blank formatted diskettes is in drive B, then:

Press: ⏎

The screen now says:

**The RTR Student Edition will now be installed.
Press Ctrl + C to abort the install or any other key to proceed.**

9. If you want to start over, press CTRL-**C**. Otherwise,

Press: ⏎

Several messages appear on your screen as files are transferred from the original Ready-to-Run diskette to your first working diskette. When this process is finished, the following message appears:

**Remove the disk from the B: drive and label it Program Disk #1.
Strike a key when ready . . .**

10. If you are using 3½″ diskettes, do *not* remove the diskette; all of the RTR program files will fit on one diskette. If you are using 5¼″ diskettes, remove the diskette from drive B and label it "RTR Student Edition, Program Disk #1." Remember to use a felt-tip pen to write on the label. Then,

Press: ⏎

The screen should say:

Insert a blank diskette into the B: drive.
Strike a key when ready . . .

11. If you are using a 3½″ diskette, press ⏎. If you are using 5¼″ diskettes, insert the second blank diskette into the B: drive and press ⏎.

The rest of the program files are transferred to your working diskette. When the process is finished, the following message appears:

Remove the disk from the B: drive and label it Program Disk #2.
Strike a key when ready . . .

12. If you are using a 3½″ diskette, remove it and label it "RTR Student Edition Program Disk." If you are using 5¼″ diskettes, remove the diskette and label it "RTR Student Edition, Program Disk #2." Remember to use a felt-tip pen to label 5¼″ diskettes.

The message on the screen should say:

Insert the Lotus 1-2-3 System disk into the B: drive.
Strike a key when ready . . .

Insert the Lotus 1-2-3 System disk you will be using in drive B and

Press: any key

13. The Install program reads your Lotus 1-2-3 System disk and displays a message telling you what release it found. At the bottom of the message are three choices:

1. If this is the correct 1-2-3 release enter 1 to proceed.
2. To install for a different 1-2-3 release enter 2.
3. To abort the install enter 3.

Unless your instructor or lab assistant gives you specific instructions to do otherwise,

Type: 1
Press: ⏎

14.   When you see this message:

Insert Program Disk #1 into the B: drive.
Strike a key when ready . . .

Insert your working copy of Ready-to-Run Program Disk #1 in drive B and

Press: any key

The following message appears:

The Ready-to-Run Accounting Student Edition installation has been completed.
Please store the master disk(s) in a safe place.

If your working diskette is ever damaged, you will have to repeat this installation procedure. Store the original diskette that came with this package in a place where it will not be damaged.

You may now proceed to the next chapter, ''Starting and Ending Ready-to-Run.''

Hard-Disk System   This section describes how to start the Install program with a hard-disk system.

Before you start the Install program, make sure you have the original diskette that came with this package. You must also know the name of the directory that contains your Lotus 1-2-3 program files.

> **Note**   Ready-to-Run will not run from your hard disk unless Lotus 1-2-3 is installed on the same hard disk.

1.   Make sure the computer is on and the C> prompt (or the appropriate system prompt) is on the screen.

If it is not, follow the instructions in the section ''Starting Your Computer.''

2.   Place the diskette that came with this package in drive A.

3. At the DOS prompt,

Type: **A:INSTALL**

Press: ⌷

In a few seconds the screen display should say

READY-TO-RUN ACCOUNTING
STUDENT EDITION
INSTALL ROUTINE

If the screen says ''Bad command or filename'':

Make sure the *original* Ready-to-Run diskette is in drive A. If it is not, remove the diskette that is there, insert the correct diskette, and repeat step 3.

Make sure you typed the command correctly. The first letter should be A followed by a *colon*, then the word ''install.'' If it is not, repeat step 3.

If the screen says ''Abort, Retry, Ignore?'':

If you have the 5¼″ version, check that the drive door is closed. If it is open, close it, then type **R** and press ⌷.

Otherwise, type **A** and start again from step 1. If that does not solve the problem, consult your instructor.

Under the boxed-in heading on the Install screen, you should see the message:

(To abort the install at any time press Ctrl + C)

If at any time you want to stop the Install process and start over, press CTRL-**C**.

The Install program next asks:

Are you installing RTR on a F)loppy or H)ard disk system?

4. To install Ready-to-Run on a hard-disk system,

Press: ⌷ to accept the default of H

The screen now says:

Please enter the disk drive containing the Ready-to-Run diskette:

5. To accept the default drive A, which appears on the screen,

Press:　　⏎

The next message is:

> **Please enter the disk drive Ready-to-Run is being installed onto.**

6. To accept the default drive C, which appears on the screen,

Press:　　⏎

> **Note** If you plan to install Ready-to-Run on a drive other than C, type the letter of that drive before pressing ⏎.

The screen message now says:

> **Ready-to-Run is normally installed into the directory \READY. Press [Enter] to use this directory or [Esc] to enter a different directory path.**
>
> **\READY**

7. To accept the directory \READY, press ⏎. If your hard disk already contains the directory \READY for another use or if your instructor tells you to use a different directory name, press ESC and type the name of the directory you want to use. The directory name must be preceded by a backslash (\). After you have typed the directory name, press ⏎.

If you accepted the default directory, the screen should say:

> **The directory C:\READY will now be created. Press [Esc] to enter a different directory or any key to proceed.**

8. If you entered a different drive and/or directory name, it should be reflected in the message you see. To accept the directory specified in the message,

Press:　　⏎

The screen now says:

The RTR Student Edition will now be installed.
Press Ctrl + C to abort the install or any other key to proceed.

9. If you want to start over, press CTRL-**C**. Otherwise,

Press:　　⟨↵⟩

Several messages appear on your screen as files are transferred from the original Ready-to-Run diskette to the RTR
program directory. When this process is finished, you
should see this message:

Select the desired configuration for the RTR system.
1. Single-user, data files on the hard disk.
2. Single-user, data files on floppy disks.
3. Multi-user, each user's data on the hard disk in a separate
sub-directory
4. Multi-user, each user's data on a separate floppy disk

10. Select either option 1 or option 2. Options 3 and 4 should
be used only by an instructor installing RTR in a computer lab setting.

If your instructor told you to save your data on floppy
diskettes, accept the default of 2.

Press:　　⟨↵⟩

If you want to save your data on the hard disk,

Type:　　**1**
Press:　　⟨↵⟩

If you select 2, the following message appears:

You have selected: Single-user, data on floppy disks
Is this correct? (Y/N)

If you select 1, the message says:

You have selected: Single-user, data on hard disk
Is this correct? (Y/N)

11. If the message is correct, press **Y**; if not, press **N**. If you
press **N**, RTR returns you to the option screen.

If you select 2, skip to step 14.

If you select 1, the screen says

The install program will create a subdirectory of C:\READY to store the General Ledger data files. Press [Enter] to use the default directory or [Esc] to enter a different subdirectory to use.

GL

12. The data files created by Ready-to-Run are stored in a subdirectory of the Ready-to-Run directory. Use the default directory of GL unless your instructor tells you to use a different one. To accept this default name,

Press: ⏎

If you want to enter your own subdirectory name, press ESC, type in the name you wish to use, and then press ⏎.

The following message appears:

The directory C:\READY\GL will now be created. Press [Esc] to enter a different directory or any key to proceed.

13. If you entered a different subdirectory name, the message reflects that name. Press ESC if you want to change the subdirectory name. Otherwise,

Press: ⏎

14. The message on the screen now says:

Enter the directory containing your Lotus 1-2-3 program. (If you do not know it, press Ctrl + C to abort installation, determine the directory containing 1-2-3, and then re-run the install program.)

Lotus 1-2-3 is usually installed in a directory called C:\123. If your Lotus 1-2-3 program is installed on a different drive or in a different directory, substitute your drive or directory in the following instruction:

Type: **C:\123**
Press: ⏎

If you see an error message, check to see that you entered the correct drive or directory and that you typed it correctly.

15. The install program reads your Lotus 1-2-3 program files and displays a message telling you what release it found. At the bottom of the message are three choices:

1. If this is the correct 1-2-3 release enter 1 to proceed.
2. To install for a different 1-2-3 release enter 2.
3. To abort the install enter 3.

Unless your instructor or lab assistant gives you specific instructions to do otherwise,

Type: 1
Press: [↵]

The following message appears:

The Ready-to-Run Accounting Student Edition installation
has been completed.
Please store the master disk(s) in a safe place.

If your working diskette is ever damaged, you will need to repeat this installation procedure. Store the original diskette that came with this package in a place where it will not be damaged.

You may now proceed to the next chapter, "Starting and Ending Ready-to-Run."

3

Starting and Ending Ready-to-Run

This chapter discusses the relationship between Ready-to-Run and Lotus 1-2-3, introduces you to the way Lotus 1-2-3 operates, and tells you how to start and end the Ready-to-Run accounting software.

Ready-to-Run and Lotus 1-2-3

Ready-to-Run accounting software uses the spreadsheet software, Lotus 1-2-3, as its basis. In order to use RTR, you must have Lotus 1-2-3 installed on your computer.

Lotus 1-2-3 is a computerized worksheet, or *spreadsheet*. A spreadsheet works like a giant columnar pad inside the computer. Each Lotus 1-2-3 worksheet contains 8,192 rows and 256 columns. Of course, you can't see the entire worksheet at one time; you can only see a ''window'' on the screen. Figure G-1 is the first window you see when you start Lotus 1-2-3.

This is the mode indicator ———

This is the cell address ———
This entire area is the
control panel ———

Various indicators will appear
on the status line ———

The current date and time
appear here ———

Figure G-1

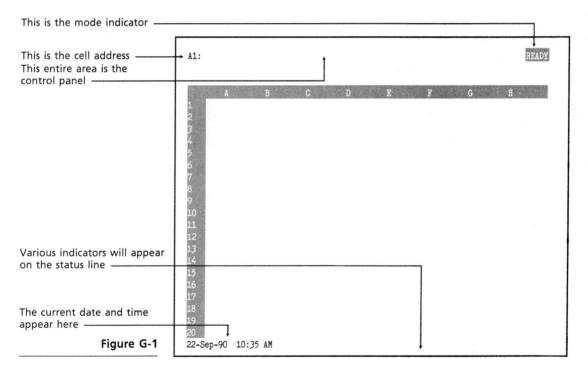

You should know these terms when using 1-2-3:

Cell pointer   The highlighted indicator on the screen. The cell pointer is positioned below the horizontal shaded bar and to the right of the vertical shaded bar.

Cell address	The location of the cell pointer. The alphabetical character(s) represent the column in which the cell pointer rests and the numerical character(s) represent the row in which the cell pointer rests. For example, the cell address F6 refers to column F (the sixth column) and row 6. The current cell address is indicated in the upper left corner of the screen.
Mode indicator	The highlighted indicator in the upper right corner of the screen. When Lotus 1-2-3 starts up, this indicator says ''READY.'' In RTR, this indicator usually says ''R-T-R''; however, sometimes it communicates a message, such as ''WAIT.''
Control panel	The first three lines of the screen. This area contains the cell address and mode indicator. Also, all 1-2-3 and RTR menus appear in the control panel. When a menu appears in 1-2-3 or RTR, it occupies the second and third lines of the control panel. Refer to ''Choosing a Menu Item'' later in this section to learn how to select items from 1-2-3 or RTR menus.
Status line	The bottom row of the screen is called the status line. On the left side of the status line, you should see the current date and time as recorded by the computer. Various indicators may appear on the status line:

CAPS	Appears when you have engaged the CAPS LOCK key on your keyboard.
NUM	Appears when you have engaged the NUM LOCK key above the numeric keypad portion of your keyboard.
CMD	Appears during most of RTR's operations; it indicates that you are using a ''macro-driven'' program.

SCROLL   Appears when you have engaged
the SCROLL LOCK key on your keyboard. Press the SCROLL LOCK key to
disengage it.

CALC   Appears when some RTR programs are running. It indicates
that the Lotus 1-2-3 recalculation
mode has been set to manual.
RTR will make the necessary
recalculations before files are
saved or printed.

Lotus 1-2-3 Command Sequences

Lotus 1-2-3 command sequences in this chapter are offset and
indented. The first letter of each command option is printed in
boldface, indicating that it should be typed or selected. Any
other parts of the command sequence to be typed are also in
boldface. For example, the Lotus 1-2-3 command to retrieve
the file LABELS would be shown as:

/ **F**ile **R**etrieve **LABELS** ⏎

In this case, you would type /**FRLABELS** and then press ⏎.

Starting Lotus 1-2-3

How you start Lotus 1-2-3 depends on the type of computer
system you are using — a two-diskette system or a hard-disk
system.

Two-Diskette System   Before you can start Lotus 1-2-3 on a
two-diskette system, you must have the Lotus 1-2-3 System
disk.

1.   Be sure that the computer is on and the A> prompt (or
the appropriate system prompt) is on the screen. If it is
not, follow the instructions under the heading, ''Starting
Your Computer'' in the previous chapter, ''Installing
Ready-to-Run.''

2.   Place the 1-2-3 System disk in drive A.

3.   At the DOS prompt,

Type: **123**
Press: ⏎

You see the copyright screen for Lotus 1-2-3, then a screen that looks like Figure G-1, shown earlier in this chapter.

If the screen says "Bad command or filename,"

- Make sure the *1-2-3* System disk is in drive A. Drive A should *not* contain your working copy of RTR or any other 1-2-3 diskette. If it does, remove it and insert the 1-2-3 System disk. Then repeat step 3.

- Check that you typed "123" correctly; there should not be hyphens between the numbers. If you didn't type it exactly as indicated, repeat step 3.

If the screen says "Abort, Retry, Ignore?":

- If you are using the 5¼" version, check that the drive door is closed. If it is open, close it, then type **R** and press ⏎.

- Otherwise, type **A** and start again from step 1. If that does not solve the problem, consult your instructor.

Hard-Disk System   On a hard-disk system, you might be able to start Lotus 1-2-3 from a menu on the screen. Otherwise, you must know the name of the subdirectory where the Lotus 1-2-3 program files are located. This subdirectory is usually named 123. The following instructions assume this name and also assume that you are using drive C. If you are using a different drive or directory, you should substitute the appropriate name(s) in the instructions.

1. Make sure that the computer is on and the C> prompt (or the appropriate system prompt) is on the screen.

    If it is not, follow the instructions in "Starting Your Computer" in the previous chapter, "Installing Ready-to-Run."

2. If you are able to start Lotus 1-2-3 from a menu on the screen, do so. Simply select the menu item that says "Lotus 1-2-3." If the screen that appears after the copyright screen does *not* look like Figure G-1 and is entitled "Lotus Access System," press ⏎ to activate the 1-2-3 program. The next screen should look like Figure G-1.

If you cannot start Lotus 1-2-3 from a menu on the screen, change the directory to the one that contains your 1-2-3 program files. To do this,

Type: **CD \ 123**
Press: ⏎

If the screen says "Invalid directory,"

- Make sure that you typed **CD \ 123** exactly as indicated. Note that the third character is a "backslash" and not a "slash." If any portion of your typing is incorrect, repeat step 2.

- Confirm the name of the directory in which your 1-2-3 program files are located. If it is not "123," repeat step 2 using the correct directory name.

3. At the DOS prompt,

Type: **123**
Press: ⏎

You should see a copyright screen for Lotus 1-2-3 and then a screen that looks like Figure G-1.

If the screen says "Bad command or filename,"

- Make sure that you are in the correct directory. You may have ignored the message "Invalid directory" in step 2; if so, repeat step 2.

- Check that you typed "123" correctly; there should not be hyphens between the numbers. If you didn't type it exactly as indicated, repeat step 3.

If your screen does not display Figure G-1 at this point, get assistance from your instructor.

Some Basic 1-2-3 Commands

Before you start to use RTR, you should know some basic Lotus 1-2-3 commands.

The Main menu for Lotus 1-2-3 is accessed by pressing the "/" (slash) key.

Press: /

Your screen should now look like Figure G-2. (If you are using Release 2 or 2.01, the menu item "Add-In" will not appear.)

This line is the Main
menu for 1-2-3 ──────────

This line is the submenu
for Worksheet ──────────

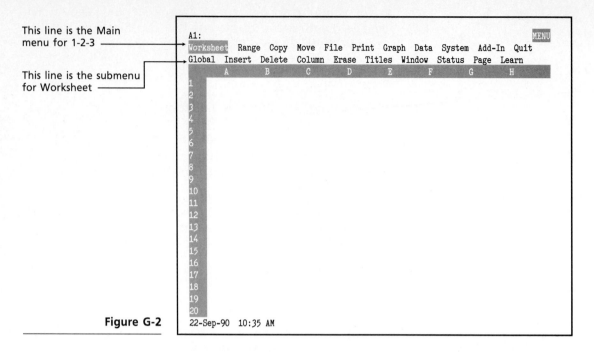

Figure G-2

The options available on the Main menu appear on the second line of the control panel. The third line of the control panel either provides a submenu for the highlighted option or an explanation of the highlighted option. For example, when the Worksheet menu option is highlighted, the third line displays this submenu (in Release 2.2):

Global Insert Delete Column Erase Titles Window Status Page Learn

Use → and ← to highlight other menu options. As you do this, notice that the message in the third line changes.

Most of the Main menu options have submenus. However, when you highlight the Copy, Move, or System option, a description appears on the third line.

Choosing a Menu Item

In Lotus 1-2-3, any menu item can be selected either by highlighting the option and pressing ←┘ or by pressing the first letter of the menu option. For example, the File option can be selected either by highlighting the word File and pressing ←┘ or by pressing the letter **F**.

> **Note** When you press the letter corresponding to a menu item, you do *not* need to press ⏎.

In Lotus 1-2-3 and RTR, the ESC key is your "get-out-of-trouble" key! If you find yourself in a menu or screen where you don't want to be, press ESC until you return to the READY mode in Lotus 1-2-3. When you press ESC in RTR, you will normally back up one menu at a time. Some menus give you a Return or Prior option, which returns you to a previous menu or to the Main menu. If ESC does not take you back one menu in RTR, you must make a selection from the current menu.

You want to return to the READY mode at this point, so:

Press: ESC

You must start 1-2-3 before you can start RTR.

Starting Ready-to-Run

Before you proceed with this section, you must:

- Start up Lotus 1-2-3 as explained in the previous section. (If you are using a two-diskette system, the Lotus 1-2-3 System disk must stay in drive A until the RTR Main menu appears.)

- Determine the type of printer you will use with RTR. The types of printers supported by RTR are listed later in this chapter (in Figures G-6 and G-7). If your printer is not on this list, you must know the printer escape codes for normal and condensed print for your printer. Obtain this information from your instructor.

How you start RTR depends on the type of computer system you are using: two-diskette or hard-disk.

Two-Diskette System

To start RTR in a two-diskette system, you will need your working copy of Ready-to-Run.

1. Place your working copy of RTR in drive B. (If you are using 5¼" diskettes, place Program Disk #1 in drive B.)

2. Issue the following Lotus 1-2-3 command:

     / **File Directory**

The second line of the control panel should read "Enter current directory:" followed by the default directory. If the default directory is B:\, press ⏎. Otherwise,

Type: **B:**
Press: ⏎

3. Issue the following Lotus 1-2-3 command:

/ **F**ile **R**etrieve **AUTO123** ⏎

> **Note** If the Lotus 1-2-3 default directory is B:\, you can start RTR automatically by placing your working copy of RTR in drive B **before** you start up Lotus 1-2-3. Lotus 1-2-3 automatically looks for and retrieves the file AUTO123 on the default directory.

You can make B:\ the Lotus 1-2-3 default directory by following these steps:

1. Issue the Lotus 1-2-3 command sequence:

/ **W**orksheet **G**lobal **D**efault **D**irectory

2. Press: ESC to erase the current default directory
3. Type: **B:**
4. Press: ⏎
5. Select: **Update**
6. Select: **Quit**

Hard-Disk System

The following instructions assume that you are using drive C and the \READY directory for your RTR program files. If either of these is different, alter the instructions to reflect the drive and directory you are using.

> **Note** If you are using a hard-disk system in a college laboratory or are operating Lotus 1-2-3 on a network, check with your instructor regarding the proper procedures for starting RTR.

1. Issue the following Lotus 1-2-3 command:

   / **File Directory**

   The second line of the control panel should read ''Enter current directory:'', followed by the default directory. To change the directory to the one that contains your RTR program,

   Type: **C:\READY**
   Press: ⏎

2. Issue the following Lotus 1-2-3 command sequence:

   / **File Retrieve AUTO123** ⏎

> **Note**   If you are using a hard-disk system, you should always use these procedures or those given to you by your instructor to start RTR. If you are running RTR on your own hard-disk system and do not use Lotus 1-2-3 for any other purpose, you may want to make RTR start automatically when you start Lotus 1-2-3. Follow the steps in the ''Basic Skills'' chapter of the Reference section, under the heading ''Making RTR Boot Automatically.''

The RTR Configuration Screen

When you start RTR for the first time, you will see the screen shown in Figure G-3. The first time RTR is loaded, it runs a utility program that allows you to confirm or change your hardware configuration. (On this and future screens, the top and bottom lines of the screen are omitted from the figures in the text unless they contain important information.)

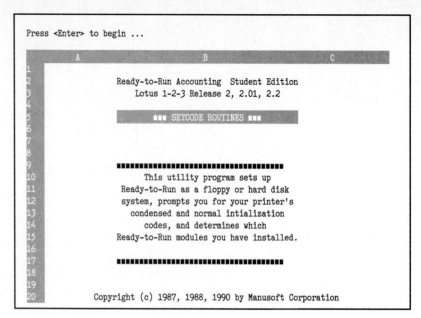

```
Press <Enter> to begin ...

        A                    B                    C

1
2               Ready-to-Run Accounting  Student Edition
3                  Lotus 1-2-3 Release 2, 2.01, 2.2
4
5                      ▪▪▪ SETCODE ROUTINES ▪▪▪
6
7
8
9      ▪▪▪▪▪▪▪▪▪▪▪▪▪▪▪▪▪▪▪▪▪▪▪▪▪▪▪▪▪▪▪▪▪▪▪▪▪▪▪▪
10                   This utility program sets up
11            Ready-to-Run as a floppy or hard disk
12            system, prompts you for your printer's
13             condensed and normal intialization
14                  codes, and determines which
15            Ready-to-Run modules you have installed.
16
17     ▪▪▪▪▪▪▪▪▪▪▪▪▪▪▪▪▪▪▪▪▪▪▪▪▪▪▪▪▪▪▪▪▪▪▪▪▪▪▪▪
18
19
20       Copyright (c) 1987, 1988, 1990 by Manusoft Corporation
```

Figure G-3

As instructed by the second line of the control panel,

Press: ⏎

The screen shown in Figure G-4 appears. This screen is also accessible from the RTR Main menu using the Configure command. On this screen you can change the settings displayed on the screen. Review the first four lines of the screen and confirm or change them before you run the Student Edition of Ready-to-Run.

On a two-diskette system, this H would be an F

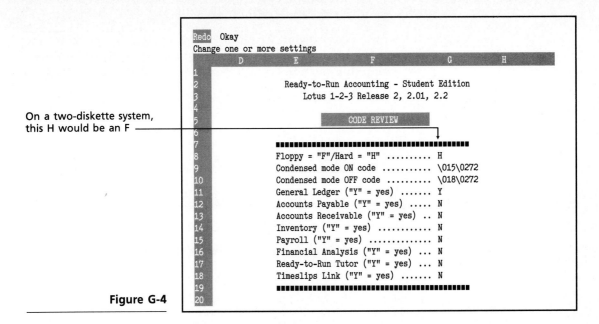

```
Redo  Okay
Change one or more settings
          D          E          F          G          H

1
2                Ready-to-Run Accounting - Student Edition
3                     Lotus 1-2-3 Release 2, 2.01, 2.2
4
5                          CODE REVIEW
6
7          ■■■■■■■■■■■■■■■■■■■■■■■■■■■■■■■■■■■■■■■■■■
8          Floppy = "F"/Hard = "H" .......... H
9          Condensed mode ON code .......... \015\0272
10         Condensed mode OFF code ......... \018\0272
11         General Ledger ("Y" = yes) ....... Y
12         Accounts Payable ("Y" = yes) ..... N
13         Accounts Receivable ("Y" = yes) .. N
14         Inventory ("Y" = yes) ............ N
15         Payroll ("Y" = yes) .............. N
16         Financial Analysis ("Y" = yes) ... N
17         Ready-to-Run Tutor ("Y" = yes) ... N
18         Timeslips Link ("Y" = yes) ....... N
19         ■■■■■■■■■■■■■■■■■■■■■■■■■■■■■■■■■■■■■■■■■■
20
```

Figure G-4

The first line reflects the system you indicated when you ran the Install program: hard- or floppy-disk. The next three lines assume that you are using an Epson or Epson-compatible printer and that the General Ledger module is installed. If you are not using an Epson or Epson-compatible printer, you must change the printer setting.

You may need to ask your instructor whether the printer you are using is Epson-compatible before you proceed. If you are using an Epson or Epson-compatible printer, you can confirm the codes and proceed. To confirm the codes that are displayed,

Select: **Okay**

Then proceed to ''Entering a System Password.''

To change the type of printer you are using, follow the instructions in the following section.

Changing the Printer Codes

If you are not using an Epson or Epson-compatible printer, you must select your printer from a listing that RTR displays. From the menu in Figure G-4,

Select: **R**edo

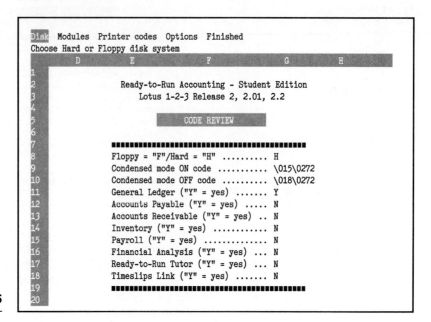

Figure G-5

```
Disk  Modules  Printer codes  Options  Finished
Choose Hard or Floppy disk system
              D           E           F           G           H
1
2                   Ready-to-Run Accounting - Student Edition
3                      Lotus 1-2-3 Release 2, 2.01, 2.2
4
5                             CODE REVIEW
6
7      ■■■■■■■■■■■■■■■■■■■■■■■■■■■■■■■■■■■■■■■■■■■■■■
8      Floppy = "F"/Hard = "H" .......... H
9      Condensed mode ON code .......... \015\0272
10     Condensed mode OFF code ......... \018\0272
11     General Ledger ("Y" = yes) ....... Y
12     Accounts Payable ("Y" = yes) ..... N
13     Accounts Receivable ("Y" = yes) .. N
14     Inventory ("Y" = yes) ............ N
15     Payroll ("Y" = yes) .............. N
16     Financial Analysis ("Y" = yes) ... N
17     Ready-to-Run Tutor ("Y" = yes) ... N
18     Timeslips Link ("Y" = yes) ....... N
19     ■■■■■■■■■■■■■■■■■■■■■■■■■■■■■■■■■■■■■■■■■■■■■■
20
```

You should now see the screen shown in Figure G-5. To change the printer codes,

Select: **P**rinter codes

You now see the screen shown in Figure G-6, which lists some of the printers for which the codes are already built into RTR. Note that row 5 contains an option to manually enter your printer codes; you use this option if your printer is not on the list.

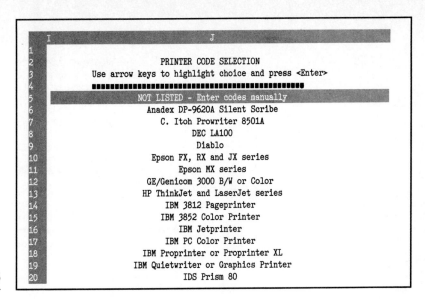

Figure G-6

To see an additional listing of printers,

Press: PGDN

The second Printer Code Selection screen, shown in Figure G-7, appears. This screen lists the remaining printers supported by RTR. You can return to the previous screen by pressing PGUP.

Locate the name of the printer that you will be using. Use ⬇ and ⬆ to highlight that printer name. Then:

Press: ⏎

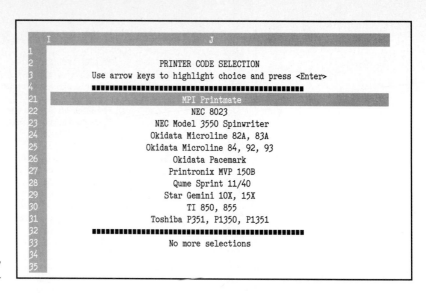

If your printer is not listed on one of these screens, ask your instructor which item to select or to help you with manually entering the printer codes you need.

RTR returns you to the screen shown in Figure G-5. The codes displayed on rows 9 and 10 should correspond to the printer you selected.

To continue with the initial start-up of RTR and confirm the hardware configuration codes,

Select: **F**inished
Select: **O**kay

Entering a System Password

If you are saving your data on a floppy disk, be sure your data disk is in your A drive.

RTR allows you to use a password to gain access to the program. This ''system'' password does not protect your data files; it only restricts access to the RTR program. (In Lab 1, you can enter a ''data'' password to protect your data files.) The screen shown in Figure G-8 appears with the instructions to ''Enter new system access PASSWORD.'' If your instructor has instructed you to use a *system* password, enter it now. If you do not want to use a password, simply press ⏎.

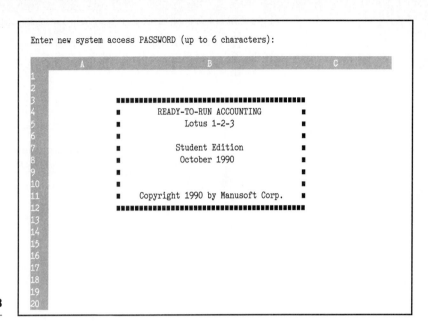

Figure G-8

```
Enter new system access PASSWORD (up to 6 characters):

          A                    B                    C
 1
 2
 3          ■■■■■■■■■■■■■■■■■■■■■■■■■■■■■■■■■■■■■■
 4          ■          READY-TO-RUN ACCOUNTING          ■
 5          ■               Lotus 1-2-3                  ■
 6          ■                                            ■
 7          ■               Student Edition              ■
 8          ■               October 1990                 ■
 9          ■                                            ■
10          ■                                            ■
11          ■       Copyright 1990 by Manusoft Corp.     ■
12          ■■■■■■■■■■■■■■■■■■■■■■■■■■■■■■■■■■■■■■
13
14
15
16
17
18
19
20
```

If you choose to use a password, please note that it is limited to six characters. It can be less than six characters but not more than six characters. The password may appear on the screen as you type it. After you have entered the password, you will be asked to confirm it by retyping it. If you do not type it the second time exactly the same as the first time, the password will not be recorded. After the first time you enter the password, you will not be able to see it when you type it.

> **Note** If you choose to use a password, you *must* remember what it is in order to start RTR from this point on. You will also be allowed to add the password — or change it — each time you start RTR. To change it, however, you must know the original password.

The Ready-to-Run Main Menu

You should now see the RTR Main menu in Figure G-9. RTR uses the same type of menus as Lotus 1-2-3: the menu options appear on the second line of the control panel and the submenus or description for the highlighted option appear on the third line. You select RTR menu options the same way you select 1-2-3 menu options: highlight the option and press ⏎ or press the first letter of the menu option.

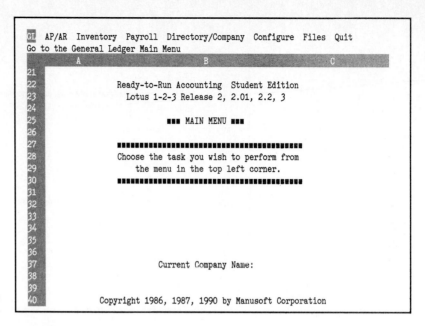

GL AP/AR Inventory Payroll Directory/Company Configure Files Quit
Go to the General Ledger Main Menu
        A   B   C

            Ready-to-Run Accounting Student Edition
               Lotus 1-2-3 Release 2, 2.01, 2.2, 3

                       ■■■ MAIN MENU ■■■

        ■■
             Choose the task you wish to perform from
                  the menu in the top left corner.
        ■■

                  Current Company Name:

        Copyright 1986, 1987, 1990 by Manusoft Corporation

Figure G-9

The commercial version of RTR can link several subsidiary modules — namely, Accounts Receivable/Accounts Payable, Inventory, and Payroll. These items appear on the RTR Main menu, but they are not included in the Student Edition of Ready-to-Run.

The Configure option on the Main menu returns you to the SETCODE routine, which you used to name the type of printer you are using. Use it only if you need to change any of the codes that are now set.

Except for the Quit option, the rest of the options on the RTR Main menu are explored in ''An Overview of RTR,'' which opens the Lab Activities section of this book.

Starting Ready-to-Run from Now On

Each time you start RTR, use the same procedure. However, notice that RTR asks you to confirm your hardware configuration only the first time you start the program. Follow the procedure outlined earlier for your type of computer system.

If you decided to use a system password, you will be asked to enter the system password each time you start RTR. You must type it exactly as you typed it when you entered it for the first time. After you enter the correct password, RTR asks if you want to change it. If you do not want to change it, press ⏎ to go to the RTR Main menu.

If you decided not to use a system password, press ⏎ when prompted for the password. RTR then asks if you want to change the password. If you do not want to change it, press ⏎ to go to the RTR Main menu.

Ending Ready-to-Run

To end Ready-to-Run, from the RTR Main menu:

Select: **Q**uit

The screen shown in Figure G-10 appears. The three menu options on this screen are:

Return   Returns you to the RTR Main menu in case you inadvertently selected Quit from that menu.

Lotus   Allows you to exit from RTR but remain in the Lotus 1-2-3 program. Use this option only if you know how to use Lotus 1-2-3 for other applications.

If you inadvertently select this command, issue the following Lotus 1-2-3 command sequence to exit from Lotus 1-2-3 to the DOS prompt:

/ **Q**uit **Y**es

To return to RTR from the Lotus 1-2-3 program, issue the following Lotus 1-2-3 command sequence:

/ **F**ile **R**etrieve **AUTO123** ⏎

Quit   Returns you to the DOS prompt.

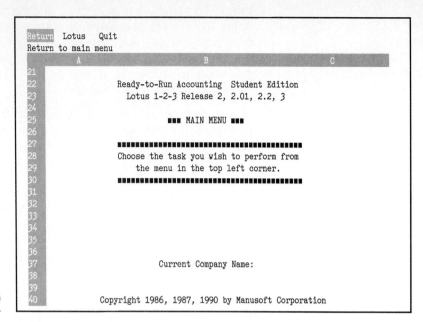

Since you are now ready to exit to DOS,

Select: **Q**uit

The DOS prompt appears. If you are using a two-diskette system, you may need to replace the 1-2-3 System disk in drive A with the DOS diskette to return to the DOS prompt.

> **Note**   *Always* quit RTR and Lotus 1-2-3 and return to the DOS prompt before turning off your computer.

An Overview of Ready-to-Run and Lab Activities

An Overview of Ready-to-Run

Objectives

In this overview, you will explore:

- General ledger accounting software

- Getting around in Ready-to-Run

- Ready-to-Run's menus

General Ledger Accounting Software

In your accounting class, you are learning how to process accounting information using a manual accounting system. To complete an accounting cycle using a manual accounting system, you must:

1. Analyze transactions to determine their financial impact on the company. You must decide which accounts to debit and which accounts to credit.

2. Record transactions in a general journal, or record them in special journals. Each special journal contains a particular type of transaction. The amounts debited must equal the amounts credited.

3. Post transactions by transferring data from the various journals to the ledger. The ledger contains a summary of the transactions affecting each element of the financial statements.

4. Prepare a trial balance, which is a periodic listing of accounts and their balances. The trial balance verifies that total debits equal total credits.

5. Prepare adjusting entries that reflect the expiration of costs, revenue earned, or costs incurred because of the passage of time. Adjusting entries are required in the accrual method of accounting to record revenue and expense in the proper period.

6. Post adjusting entries and prepare an adjusted trial balance.

7. Prepare financial statements, such as the Balance Sheet, the Income & Retained Earnings Statement, and the Statement of Cash Flows.

8. Close the accounting period by recording in the journal and posting to the ledger entries that zero out revenue and expense accounts, preparing them to record transactions for the next period, and transferring net income for the period to a capital account.

9. Prepare reversing entries for certain adjusting entries, recording them in the journal and posting them to the ledger.

In some manual systems, the steps from trial balance through the preparation of financial statements are accomplished using a *worksheet*. A worksheet enables you to prepare financial statements before adjusting entries are recorded and posted. Thus, users of financial statements can have earlier access to the information they need for decision-making.

Features of Computerized Accounting Systems

A computerized accounting system mechanizes many steps performed in the accounting cycle:

- Recording transactions
- Posting transactions
- Trial balance
- Posting adjusting entries
- Preparing financial statements
- Closing
- Posting reversing entries

A computer cannot analyze events to determine which accounts to debit and which accounts to credit in the accounting records. Similarly, a computer cannot examine supporting documentation, a trial balance, or the general ledger to determine how to adjust the accounts to properly reflect an accrual basis. These steps require the judgment and expertise of an accountant.

Recording Transactions   In a computerized accounting system, you use the computer to record transactions. You enter data using the computer keyboard. A general ledger accounting software package displays on the screen a summary of the data you are entering. Sometimes, the software helps you prepare journal entries by listing debits on the left and credits on the right of the screen. However, it is not much faster to enter transactions into a computer than to record them manually in a journal. In both cases, the entries must be recorded with appropriate account titles, numbers, debit amounts, and credit amounts.

Posting Transactions On the other hand, posting transactions and preparing reports in a computerized accounting system can save a lot of time. To post transactions, you sort and classify recorded transactions according to the categories needed to prepare financial statements.

For example, you record all transactions affecting cash in the Cash account. In a manual system, you must post each transaction (or a monthly total from a special journal) to the Cash account by hand. Then you must subtotal the Cash account to determine the ending balance. On a computerized general ledger accounting software system, you enter an account number and title when you record each debit and credit. Then, instead of manually transferring data to a ledger, you can instruct the computer to automatically sort all of the debits and credits affecting Cash (in the example given) and provide a subtotal of those transactions.

Preparing Financial Statements To prepare financial statements in a manual system, you must transfer account titles and balances from the general ledger to the appropriate reporting format. You may have to combine and summarize some accounts before you compute subtotals according to generally accepted accounting principles. In a computerized system, you set up the chart of accounts so that financial statements can be prepared automatically. You designate each new account as an asset, liability, capital, revenue, or expense account when you create it. As a result, the computer lists the balance of that account in the correct place on the financial statements.

The content and format of financial statements are programmed into the software according to the rules of accounting. Subcategories for items like current assets, intangible assets, current liabilities, etc., are included in order to prepare classified financial statements. After you create the chart of accounts in a computerized system, you can print financial statements anytime by issuing a Print command to the computer. As you will see in Lab 1, careful planning as you create the chart of accounts saves time in the long run.

Closing Accounts   You can close the revenue and expense accounts in a computerized system much faster than in a manual system. In a manual system, you enter closing entries in the general journal and then post them to the ledger. In a computerized system, the computer knows which accounts are revenue and which are expense. The computer determines which capital account should be credited with the net income — either from information in the initial set-up or by prompting for the entry of an account number during the closing process. Thus, to close the period, you issue the command to close and the computer does everything automatically.

In the closing process, you normally must close some capital accounts, such as Drawing or Dividends, along with the revenue and expense accounts. In most general ledger software systems, you must record a general journal entry to close out these accounts. The computer software will not close them automatically.

Adjusting Entries   You can also record reversing entries automatically in a computerized accounting system by giving the adjusting entries a "flag" that tells the computer whether or not to reverse that entry. For example, when you record an entry, you might see a prompt with the question:

Should this entry be reversed?

If you were recording the entry to accrue salaries payable, you would answer "Yes" and the computer would reverse the adjusting entry automatically after you closed the period. This feature must be built into the accounting software you use to record your accounting information. The Ready-to-Run system does not have this feature. If you record reversing entries in RTR, you must record the reversing entries in the general journal on the first day of the next accounting period. The lab activities in this text do not require you to prepare reversing entries.

Ready-to-Run versus a Manual System

Using the Student Edition of Ready-to-Run Accounting, you can compare the capabilities of a general ledger software package with the manual system you have been using in your accounting class. As a result, you will see how a computerized accounting system reduces the time required to perform record-keeping tasks. Thus, you can spend more time on analysis and assisting in the decision-making process. (The accountant's major tasks are to analyze events before they are recorded in the accounting records and to interpret the financial statements generated by the computer.)

Figure 1 shows how the flow of accounting information in the Ready-to-Run system compares to the flow of accounting information in a manual system.

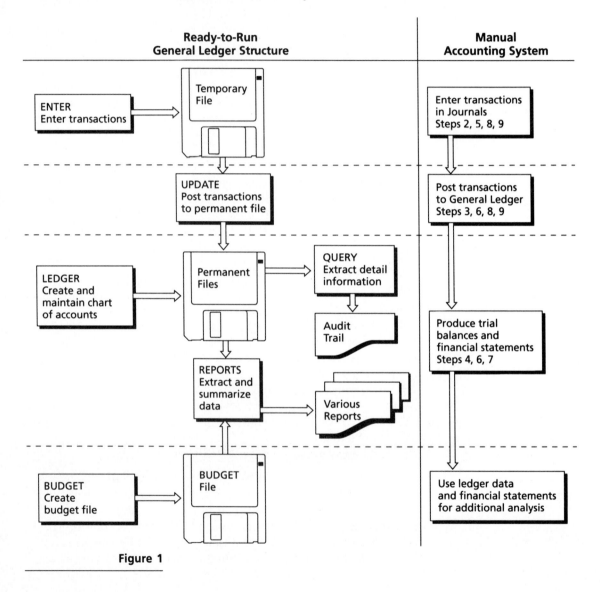

Figure 1

The Ready-to-Run system is shown on the left. The rectangular boxes represent the individual programs within RTR that perform the procedures indicated. The diskettes represent stored data that has been entered using RTR. The symbols that look like the top part of a page represent documents and reports produced by the RTR programs.

On the right, the flow of a manual system is shown as it parallels the RTR system. The nine steps in the accounting cycle outlined earlier in this chapter are indicated at the points where they would occur in the manual process. For example, several steps involve entering transactions in a journal; all of these are shown in the first box on the manual side. The analysis step (step 1) does not appear because it does not require recording, processing, or output.

As you work through the lab activities, a portion of the graphic on the left will be highlighted to show where each lab activity fits into the information flow of the RTR system.

Getting Around in Ready-to-Run

You must have Lotus 1-2-3 in order to use Ready-to-Run. Ready-to-Run is a general ledger accounting software package created using the macro capabilities of Lotus 1-2-3. All the routines contained in the RTR software are run by Lotus 1-2-3 macros. Because of this, you must be familiar with the basic structure of Lotus 1-2-3. Before you continue in this section, be sure you know:

- How to start Lotus 1-2-3

- How to issue Lotus 1-2-3 commands

Refer to ''Starting and Ending Ready-to-Run'' in ''Getting Started'' for a discussion of these topics.

Keyboard Conventions

Most of the time, Ready-to-Run displays a menu that is similar to a Lotus 1-2-3 menu. Figure 2 shows the RTR Main menu. Menus appear on the second and third lines of the screen in the ''control panel'' portion of the screen. The second line lists the available menu items. The third line describes the highlighted menu item. Use $\rightarrow$ and $\leftarrow$ to highlight individual menu items and read the description of those items.

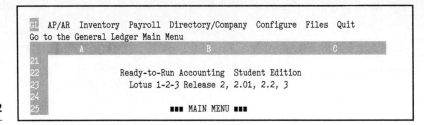

Figure 2

You select menu items from an RTR menu as you do in Lotus 1-2-3: you can either press the first letter of the menu item or highlight the menu item and press ⏎. However, in RTR, you do not have to type the / (slash) character. In some RTR menus, the menu items are numbered, as shown in Figure 3. To select a numbered menu item, press the *number* of the item, not the first letter of the item.

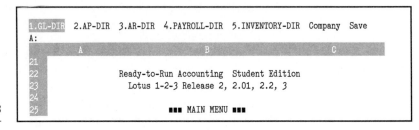

Figure 3

When you enter data into a cell in RTR, you can correct it before you press ⏎. Use the BACKSPACE key to erase the incorrect characters. Then type the correct characters.

When you enter a column of data in Lotus 1-2-3, you can press ⬇ to move the cell pointer to the next cell in the column. This is the equivalent of pressing ⏎ ⬇, but it is more efficient because you can enter the data and position the cell pointer with one key rather than two. This technique also works with other directional keys, such as ➡, ⬆, PGUP, and PGDN. You will use this convention in RTR when you enter beginning balances (Lab 1) and when you enter budgets (Lab 7).

Cursor Movement

On some RTR screens, you must use ⬆, ⬇, ➡, and ⬅ to enter data on the screen. Figure 4 shows the screen you use to enter beginning balances into the chart of accounts. The cell pointer highlights the beginning balance column for the first account. After you enter the balance for that account, you move the cell pointer to the second account by pressing ⬇.

	C	D	E	F
4	Acc #	Account Title	Beg Bal	Period 1
5	100	Cash in Bank	0.00	0.00
6	110	Accounts Receivable	0.00	0.00
7	119	Allow for Doubtful Accts	0.00	0.00
8	120	Merchandise Inventory	0.00	0.00
9	130	Prepaid Rent	0.00	0.00
10	131	Unexpired Insurance	0.00	0.00
11	132	Supplies on Hand	0.00	0.00
12	200	Accounts Payable	0.00	0.00
13	300	Tom Walton, Capital	0.00	0.00
14	400	Sales	0.00	0.00
15	510	Purchases	0.00	0.00

Use up/down keys to select accounts and enter beginning balances
Use + for debits, - for credits - Press <Esc> when done

Figure 4

When you selected your printer in ''Installing Ready-to-Run,'' you used PGUP or PGDN to move up or down an entire screen at a time. You also move about this way in some other RTR operations. For example, Figure 5 shows the screen you use to set up a chart of accounts. When you enter your accounts, they appear on the screen one at a time. To review your work, use PGUP to see the previous screen and PGDN to see the next screen, as indicated in the instructions at the top of the screen.

```
■■   Use up & down arrow keys, pgup, and pgdn to move cell pointer   ■■
■■   {Ins}=Add menu {F2}=Change acct. {Del}=Delete line {F4}=Defaults  ■■
■■   {F5}=Page {F6}=Depts. {F7}=Print samples {F8}=Interrupt {F9}=Done  ■■
```

	Acc #	Account Title	
100	Acc #	Account Title	
101		ASSETS	
102			---------
103		TOTAL ASSETS	0.00
104			
105		LIABILITIES	
106			---------
107		TOTAL LIABILITIES	0.00
108			
109		EQUITY	
110		Net Income	0.00
111			---------
112		TOTAL EQUITY	0.00
113			
114		TOTAL LIABILITIES & EQUITY	0.00

Figure 5

Screen Display

The RTR screen looks like a Lotus 1-2-3 screen, with the horizontal bar along the top containing the column headings and the vertical bar on the left side containing the row numbers highlighted. Some RTR screens use the Lotus 1-2-3 capability of splitting the screen into two sections called *windows*. Sometimes the screen is split vertically and you can choose from a list of items on one side of the screen. Other times, as in Figure 5, the screen is split horizontally and one of the windows contains instructions.

As noted in "Keyboard Conventions," you usually choose items from a menu in RTR. At times, however, you enter data on a screen that does not have a menu. For example, in Figure 5 the window at the top of the screen contains instructions for setting up the chart of accounts. In Lab 1, you will use the keys identified in the instruction window as you add accounts to the chart of accounts.

Other screens in RTR explain the program that you are running. Figure G-3 of "Starting and Ending Ready-to-Run" in the "Getting Started" section showed a screen that explains the SETCODE routines. You will see screens containing explanations when the menu does not give you enough detail about your choices. Figure 6 is another screen that contains an explanation of the program. It is called the File Initialization Routines screen, and it appears when you set up your accounts for the first time.

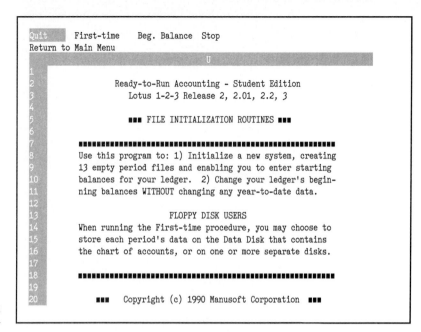

```
Quit      First-time    Beg. Balance  Stop
Return to Main Menu
                          U
 1
 2                Ready-to-Run Accounting - Student Edition
 3                  Lotus 1-2-3 Release 2, 2.01, 2.2, 3
 4
 5               ■■■ FILE INITIALIZATION ROUTINES ■■■
 6
 7        ■■■■■■■■■■■■■■■■■■■■■■■■■■■■■■■■■■■■■■■■■■■■■■■■
 8        Use this program to: 1) Initialize a new system, creating
 9        13 empty period files and enabling you to enter starting
10        balances for your ledger.  2) Change your ledger's begin-
11        ning balances WITHOUT changing any year-to-date data.
12
13                        FLOPPY DISK USERS
14        When running the First-time procedure, you may choose to
15        store each period's data on the Data Disk that contains
16        the chart of accounts, or on one or more separate disks.
17
18        ■■■■■■■■■■■■■■■■■■■■■■■■■■■■■■■■■■■■■■■■■■■■■■■■
19
20           ■■■   Copyright (c) 1990 Manusoft Corporation   ■■■
```

Figure 6

Ready-to-Run Menus

This section lists the menu structure of RTR, with a brief explanation of each menu item. To better understand the menu structure, start RTR before you read this section.

The Ready-to-Run Main Menu

When you start Ready-to-Run, you'll see the Main menu, which was shown in Figure 2. Figure 7 contains a tree diagram that shows the RTR Main menu as the basis of all other RTR menus.

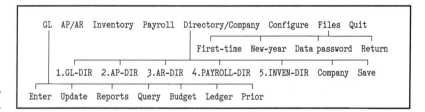

Figure 7

The GL Menu   The GL choice (short for *G*eneral *L*edger) on the RTR Main menu is the one that you will use most frequently during the lab activities.

Select: **GL**

Your screen should now look like Figure 8. The GL submenu appears on the second line.

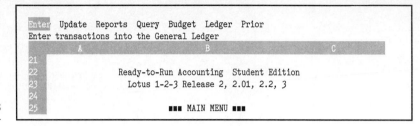

Figure 8

Enter Update Reports Query Budget Ledger Prior
Enter transactions into the General Ledger
         A   B   C
21
22   Ready-to-Run Accounting Student Edition
23   Lotus 1-2-3 Release 2, 2.01, 2.2, 3
24
25   ■■■ MAIN MENU ■■■

This submenu contains the following choices:

Enter Records transactions in RTR. It also allows you to print a list of unposted transactions and to correct errors in unposted transactions.

Update Posts transactions to the ledger. Once you post transactions, you cannot alter them except by recording a correcting entry in one of the journals.

Reports Generates printed general ledger reports.

Query Allows you to review activity in a specific account for the year. Also use Query to print an audit trail of all transactions or a general ledger detail for each account.

Budget Allows you to enter or change budget numbers when you want to prepare financial statements compared to budget.

Ledger Allows you to add or delete accounts from the chart of accounts (after the initial set-up), to change an account title, or to revise beginning balances in your accounts.

Prior Returns you to the RTR Main menu.

You will learn more about these menu options in the lab activities.

AP/AR, Inventory, and Payroll The Main menu items AP/AR (Accounts Payable/Accounts Receivable), Inventory, and Payroll are not used in the Student Edition of RTR. They apply only to the commercial version of the RTR General Ledger program. They are included in the Main menu of the Student Edition so that you see what the Main menu of the commercial version looks like.

A business can purchase individual modules for Accounts Payable/ Accounts Receivable, Inventory, and Payroll that link directly to the General Ledger program. Transactions recorded in these modules can be totaled and transferred to the general ledger to be added to the accounting records and financial statements.

These modules are available to students for an additional fee from Addison-Wesley Publishing Company. If you want to order them, an order form is included at the end of this manual.

Directory/Company   From the RTR Main menu,

Select: **D**irectory/Company

If you are working on a hard-disk system, you should see the submenu shown in Figure 9. Notice that the first five items on this menu are numbered. To select one of them, press the number in front of the menu item. If you are working on a two-diskette system, your menu has only the Company and Save options.

On a two-diskette system, options 1 through 5 do not appear ⟶

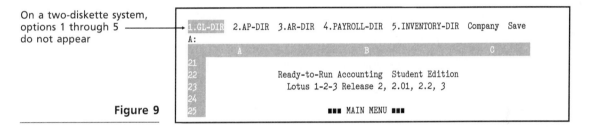

```
1.GL-DIR   2.AP-DIR  3.AR-DIR  4.PAYROLL-DIR  5.INVENTORY-DIR  Company  Save
A:
            A                      B                      C
21
22                  Ready-to-Run Accounting  Student Edition
23                     Lotus 1-2-3 Release 2, 2.01, 2.2, 3
24
25                         ■■■ MAIN MENU ■■■
```

Figure 9

The 1.GL-DIR menu item (for *G*eneral *L*edger-*Dir*ectory) should be highlighted. The third line of the control panel contains the name of the directory you designated for data storage during the installation process. If you are using a hard-disk system and keeping your data files on a floppy disk, the third line reads ''A:''. If you are using a hard-disk system and keeping your data files on the hard disk, it shows the name of the sub-directory you designated during installation. If you accepted the default, the line shows ''C:\READY\GL''.

If you press ⟨←⟩ or 1, you can change the name of the direc-tory where your data files are located. *Do not choose this item unless you want to change the directory.* If you inadvertently press ⟨←⟩ or 1, press ESC to return to the menu.

The Directory/Company menu also allows you to enter a name for your company that will appear on your printed reports. You choose the Company option on the submenu when you want to enter this name. *Do not do this now.* When you begin Lab 1, you will enter the name of the company given in the case study. If you inadvertently select the Company option, press ⏎ or ESC to return to the submenu.

The Save command on this menu saves changes you have made to your data or program files. Since you have not made any changes that you want to keep, you should *not* choose this item now.

As you may have guessed, the other menu options in the Directory/Company menu are active only if you are using the subsidiary modules that RTR provides for Accounts Payable, Accounts Receivable, Payroll, or Inventory.

To return to the RTR Main menu,

Press: ESC

Configure   The Configure option on the RTR Main menu returns you to the SETCODE routine, which you performed in "Starting and Ending Ready-to-Run." Use this option only if you change the type of computer system or printer you are using.

Files   From the RTR Main menu,

Select: Files

The menu displayed in Figure 10 will be in the control panel of your screen. The four menu options are First-time, New-year, Data password, and Return. The Return option takes you back to the RTR Main menu.

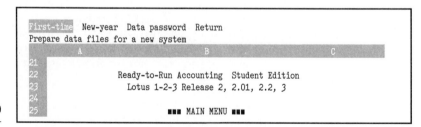

Figure 10

The First-time option allows you to set up a new chart of accounts and enter the beginning balances into the accounts. You will use this option in Lab 1.

The New-year item closes out the files for an accounting year and opens files for a new accounting year. It is covered in Lab 5.

The Data password option allows you to set a password for accessing data files. The RTR program can use *two* passwords. You encountered a password prompt when you started up the RTR program. That is called the *system password*. It allows the person starting RTR to gain access to the program. Some companies may also want to keep their data files protected from unauthorized access. They can add a second password, called the *data password*.

When you select First-time in Lab 1, you will be able to add a data password. You can also add a new data password by selecting Data password from the Files menu. The Data password option also allows you to change a data password after it is set.

You are not going to set up your files now. You will use the Main menu to view another screen. From the Files menu,

Select: **R**eturn

From the Main menu,

Select: **GL**

From the next menu,

Select: **E**nter

You should see the menu in Figure 11, which appears in various places in RTR.

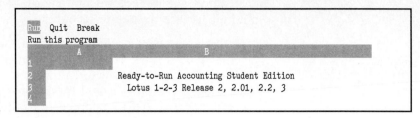

Figure 11

The submenu contains three options: Run, Quit, and Break. These three options work the same way whenever you see this menu.

Run   Runs the program that you have selected. You usually choose Run when you see this menu.

Quit   Returns you to the RTR Main menu. Use this option if you have chosen the menu item incorrectly and want to return to the RTR Main menu.

Break   Breaks you out of the macro routine in RTR. This option does not break out of the program, but it allows you to examine the macros on which RTR is based. *You should never use this option during the lab activities.*

If you inadvertently choose Break, issue the Lotus 1-2-3 command / **F**ile **R**etrieve **AUTO123** to get back into the RTR program.

This time, to return to the RTR Main menu,

Select: **Q**uit

Quit As explained in ''Starting and Ending Ready-to-Run,'' the Quit option displays a menu that allows you to quit to DOS, return to the RTR Main menu, or enter the Lotus 1-2-3 program. To end this session, from the RTR Main menu,

Select: **Q**uit

1

Creating the Chart of Accounts

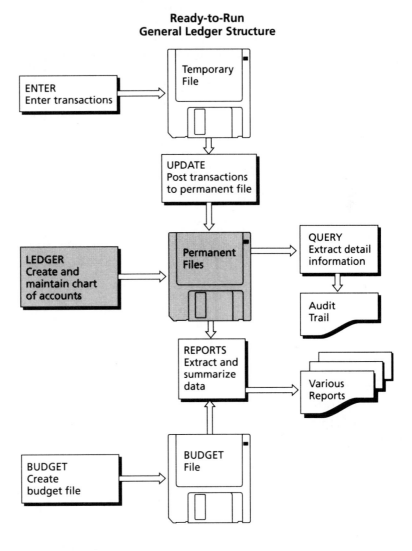

Ready-to-Run
General Ledger Structure

Objectives

In Lab 1, you will learn how to:

- Automatically back up your files while you enter data

- Create a chart of accounts

- Enter beginning balances

Case Study

Tom Walton, a sole proprietor, started a small business selling computer hardware out of his home. At first, he had very little business, so he found it convenient to keep his accounting records on a manual system. However, as news of his aggressive pricing spread, demand increased dramatically. Tom has opened a small shop and started to stock some of the parts that are in high demand. Now he wants to change his records over to a computerized accounting system. He has a small personal computer and has already invested in Lotus 1-2-3 for other applications. Therefore, he decided to purchase the Ready-to-Run general ledger software package, which will run with Lotus 1-2-3. In this lab, you will get his general ledger package up and running and enter his first month's transactions.

Tom has decided to make the transition to a computerized system at the end of his current accounting year. The books have been closed out for 1991 and he is ready to begin recording information for 1992 on his new system.

Because Tom has closed his books for 1991, you should have to enter only the Balance Sheet accounts to make sure everything is balanced and working correctly. However, RTR requires that you add at least one revenue and one expense account. In the exercises at the end of this tutorial, you will add the rest of the Income Statement accounts for Tom's business so that you are ready to enter transactions in Lab 2.

Creating the Balance Sheet Accounts

After you start RTR as explained under "Starting and Ending Ready-to-Run" in "Getting Started," you should see the RTR Main menu, shown in Figure 1-1.

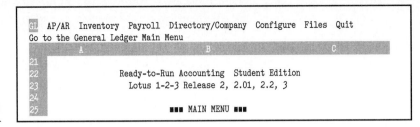

Figure 1-1

You should be familiar with the structure of the Ready-to-Run software after studying the Overview section. Remember that the menus are displayed on the second line of the screen and that you can select each menu item in one of two ways:

1. Move the menu pointer to highlight your choice and then press ⏎.

2. Press the key that corresponds to the first letter of your menu choice.

If you are using a hard-disk system and saving your data on a diskette, be sure your blank data diskette is in drive A before proceeding.

If you are using a two-diskette system, prompts on the second line of the control panel tell you when and where to insert your data diskette.

Recording a Company Name

Before setting up the chart of accounts, record the company name that RTR should print on all reports. Tom's business is called Walton Electronics. To record this name,

Select: **D**irectory/Company

From the Directory/Company menu,

Select: **C**ompany

You now see a prompt on the second line of the control panel telling you to enter the company name.

Type: **Walton Electronics**
Press: ⏎

If you made an error when you entered the name, select **C**ompany, retype the name, and press ⏎.

After you have typed in the name of the company correctly, save this name on your data diskette or directory:

Select: **Save**

If you use a diskette to save your data, the light on the disk drive containing your data diskette comes on briefly as the name of the company is being saved. The name you typed in should appear on the bottom portion of your screen under the heading "Current Company Name."

Preparing to Enter the Chart of Accounts

You should now see the RTR Main menu. To set up your chart of accounts,

Select: **Files**

You should see the Files menu shown in Figure 1-2. The four choices on this menu are explained in the "Ready-to-Run Menus" section of "An Overview of Ready-to-Run." Remember that choosing Return (or pressing the ESC key) takes you back to the RTR Main menu.

Figure 1-2

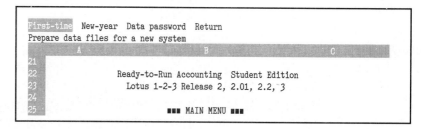

Since you are setting up the files for the first time,

Select: **First-time**

Entering a Data Password   As explained in "An Overview of Ready-to-Run," the RTR system uses two passwords: a *system* password, for which you are prompted when you boot up RTR, and a *data* password, for which you are prompted whenever you want to enter data.

A prompt on the second line of the control panel tells you to enter a data password if you want one. Follow your instructor's directions as to whether to use a data password. Remember that if you use a data password, you *must* remember exactly how you entered it. If you don't, neither you nor your instructor can gain access to your data files.

If your instructor has told you to use a password, enter it now by typing the password and pressing ⏎. A prompt asks you to verify the password by typing it again and pressing ⏎. If you don't type the password the same way both times, RTR does not allow you to proceed, and you have to start again.

After you have set and verified the data password (if you are using one), you must enter it again before going on. Simply retype the password and press ⏎.

If your instructor has told you *not* to use a data password, press ⏎ to proceed.

You should now see the Run/Quit/Break menu, shown in Figure 1-3.

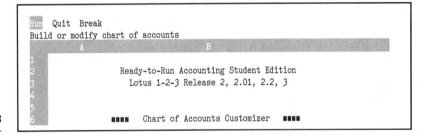

Figure 1-3

Since you want to enter accounts,

Select: **R**un

Using the Automatic Backup System Before you begin to enter data into the RTR system, you see a menu that allows you to choose whether to automatically back up your data files. If you choose Backup, RTR will save your work to disk at a time interval you specify.

All current operations in Lotus 1-2-3 are stored in the temporary memory of the computer. If the computer freezes or the power goes off, you lose all your work from that session and have to redo it. To protect you from losing *all* of your work, RTR has an automatic backup option.

> **Note**   The automatic backup option protects your data only if the power to the computer shuts off while you are entering data. Once you have finished entering data, you must still save all data using the appropriate command.

The automatic backup option menu shown in Figure 1-4 should appear on your screen.

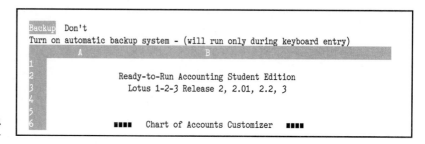

Figure 1-4

If you choose not to use automatic backup, select **D**on't at the backup option menu. You might select **D**on't if you need to make only a few changes in your data and will only take a few minutes to do so. Select **D**on't now if you are using a two-diskette system.

To choose the automatic backup option,

Select: **Backup**

The prompt asks:

How often to back up to disk (in minutes)?:

The length of time you choose determines how often your work will be saved to disk and how much you might lose if your computer fails for any reason. Choose a twenty-minute interval. A shorter backup interval interrupts your data entry too often.

Type: **20**
Press: ⏎

Entering the Chart of Accounts

You should now see the menu displayed in Figure 1-5.

Figure 1-5

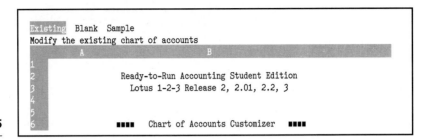

The three menu choices are:

Existing   Use this choice to modify an existing chart of accounts.

Blank   Use this choice to build a new chart of accounts from scratch.

Sample   Use this choice to use or modify a chart of accounts provided by the makers of RTR software.

To build the chart of accounts for Walton Electronics from scratch,

Select: **B**lank

You should now see the chart of accounts entry screen shown in Figure 1-6. Note that the screen is split into two "windows" horizontally. The upper window contains instructions for the keys that you can use to build the chart of accounts. The lower window contains the framework for the chart of accounts.

This is the cell address ⟶

This is the cell pointer ⟶

Figure 1-6

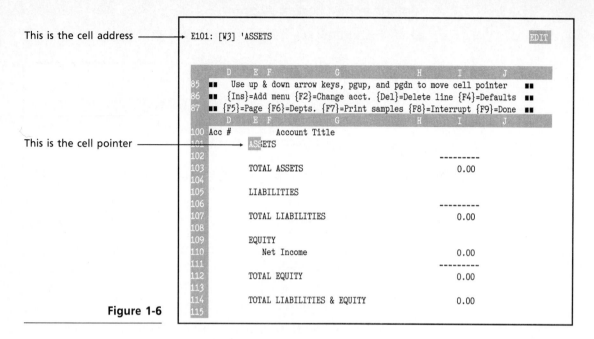

The top line of the control panel in Figure 1-6 shows the location of the cell pointer, which is on the first part of the word ASSETS. Note that the upper left corner of the screen contains the *cell address,* E101. When you are asked to "move to" a designated cell, use the cell address designation in the upper left corner to determine the location of your cell pointer.

Instruction Keys for Entering the Chart of Accounts   The window at the top of the screen contains a list of the nine keys you can use to perform various operations. In addition, the first line of instructions indicates that you can use the (↑), (↓), PGUP, and PGDN keys to move the cell pointer. Remember that the PGUP and PGDN keys move the screen up and down one full screen at a time.

The instructions on your screen for {Ins} and {Del} refer to two keys on the right side of your keyboard. The {Ins} key is usually a separate key that says INS. If you don't have a separate INS key, it is the 0 key on the numeric keyboard, which may also contain the designation INS. The {Del} key is usually a separate key that says DEL. The . (period) key on the numeric keyboard may also contain the designation DEL.

The remaining seven keys shown in the screen instructions are {F2}, {F4}, {F5}, {F6}, {F7}, {F8}, and {F9}. These refer to the "function" keys found either on the left side or at the top of the keyboard. They look like this: (F2), (F4), (F5), (F6), (F7), (F8), and (F9).

These nine keys have the following functions:

INS   Use this to add a summary heading, a new account, a blank line, or a formula.

DEL   Use this to delete a heading line, account line, blank line, or formula line from the chart of accounts.

(F2)   Use this to change a summary heading or the title of an account. If you add departments to your chart of accounts, you can also use it to change the departmental status of an account.

(F4)   Use this to enter the default account numbers for special journals used by RTR. Default account numbers can be added for Checking, Payables, and Receivables accounts.

(F5)   Use this to insert a forced page break into your financial statements.

(F6)   Use this to add departments to the chart of accounts. (This feature will be discussed in Lab 8.)

(F7)   Use this to print a listing of the chart of accounts, a sample income statement, a sample balance sheet, or a listing of the available summary headings.

(F8)   Use this to interrupt the process of entering accounts if you run out of time and want to resume entering accounts at a later time. Pressing (F8) temporarily saves the *program* you are using in a *.HLD file — you must return to it to permanently save your data. If you use (F8) to interrupt the program, the Main menu screen will indicate you have interrupted a program when you restart RTR. You can reenter the interrupted program by selecting the same command sequences you selected to start it.

(F9)   Use this to save the chart of accounts and proceed to entering beginning balances. Also use to abandon the process of entering the chart of accounts without saving your work.

In this lab you will use the INS, F2, F7, and F9 keys.

Entering a New Account

Begin by adding an account named Cash in Bank, which is an asset.

Press: INS

You should now see the menu displayed in Figure 1-7.

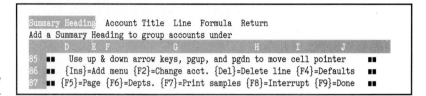

Figure 1-7

```
Summary Heading  Account Title  Line  Formula  Return
Add a Summary Heading to group accounts under
      D    E    F             G              H      I        J
85 ▪▪    Use up & down arrow keys, pgup, and pgdn to move cell pointer  ▪▪
86 ▪▪  {Ins}=Add menu {F2}=Change acct. {Del}=Delete line {F4}=Defaults ▪▪
87 ▪▪  {F5}=Page {F6}=Depts. {F7}=Print samples {F8}=Interrupt {F9}=Done ▪▪
```

The options on this menu are:

Summary Heading	Adds a Summary Heading where you can group accounts.
Account Title	Adds a new account to the chart of accounts.
Line	Adds a blank line.
Formula	Adds a formula to create a subtotal.
Return	Returns to the RTR Main menu.

The Line and Formula options will be discussed in Lab 5 before you print financial statements.

Summary Heading   The Summary Heading option on this menu allows you to group accounts according to certain predetermined categories that are set up in the software. One of the features of the RTR software is financial analysis. Financial analysis provides information to managers regarding the financial condition of a business; this enables managers to compare its performance with that of previous years or with that of other businesses in the same industry.

To perform a financial analysis, certain summary categories must be used. These have been "hard-coded" into the software. You can change the wording of the summary heading, but you cannot change its use in financial analysis.

You can use any Summary Heading more than once in the chart of accounts. You would probably rename it each time you use it. Even though you rename it, the heading is still used as it was originally programmed to be used in financial analysis.

To see how the Summary Heading feature works,

Select: **S**ummary Heading

Your computer beeps, and an error message appears on the second line of the control panel that says,

Cannot ADD at this location:, press <Enter> then move up or down

The INS key will always attempt to insert an account or heading *above* the line highlighted by the cell pointer.

You tried to enter an account above the title ASSETS. This is not permitted by the software, so you received the error message. To clear the message and return to the chart of accounts editing screen,

Press: ⏎

Before you can add a new asset account or summary heading, you must position the cell pointer on the row between the heading ASSETS and the summary line TOTAL ASSETS. To move the cell pointer down one row,

Press: ↓

Now you should be able to add the summary heading for Cash in Bank.

Press: INS
Select: **S**ummary Heading

You should now see the screen shown in Figure 1-8. This screen is split into two vertical windows. The right window contains the Assets Heading List that has been preset in the software. Ready-to-Run displays the Assets Heading List because your cell pointer is located in the ASSETS section in the left window.

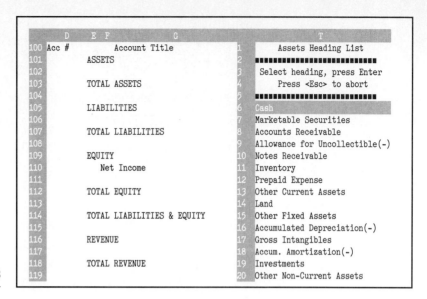

Figure 1-8

The instructions at the top of the window say, "Select heading, press Enter." The cell pointer is highlighting the heading entitled Cash.

Because Tom Walton's business is small, you will not use all of the summary headings in this lab. As Tom's business grows, he can add new summary headings as he needs them.

Make sure the screen shown in Figure 1-8 is on your monitor and the cell pointer is highlighting the asset heading Cash. Then

Press: ⏎

RTR displays the Chart of Accounts editing screen, as shown in Figure 1-9. Below the ASSETS heading in column F, the Cash heading appears, along with a Total Cash line.

```
       D     E F              G              H        I        J
85  ■■    Use up & down arrow keys, pgup, and pgdn to move cell pointer    ■■
86  ■■  {Ins}=Add menu {F2}=Change acct. {Del}=Delete line {F4}=Defaults  ■■
87  ■■  {F5}=Page {F6}=Depts. {F7}=Print samples {F8}=Interrupt {F9}=Done ■■
       D     E F              G              H        I        J
100 Acc #          Account Title
101           ASSETS
102             Cash
103             Total Cash                          0.00
104                                              ---------
105           TOTAL ASSETS                          0.00
106
107           LIABILITIES
108                                              ---------
109           TOTAL LIABILITIES                     0.00
110
111           EQUITY
112             Net Income                          0.00
113                                              ---------
114           TOTAL EQUITY                          0.00
115
```

Figure 1-9

Account Number and Title   You are now ready to add the account named Cash in Bank.

When you added the Cash summary heading, the cell pointer automatically positioned itself on the same row as the total for that summary heading. The new account, Cash in Bank, should be added between the summary heading line and the total for that summary heading. If the cell pointer were positioned on the summary heading line, the new account would be added before the summary heading and would not be included in it. Each time you add a new account to a summary heading category, be sure that the cell pointer is positioned on the total line for that category.

To add the Cash in Bank account,

Press: INS

Each data-gathering account must have an account number and an account title. From the Insert menu,

Select: **A**ccount Title

The computer beeps and the prompt line (the second line of the control panel) asks you to enter the account number.

Type: **100**
Press: ⏎

RTR prompts you to enter the name of the account.

Type: **Cash in Bank**

Press: [↵]

Your screen should look like Figure 1-10. The Cash in Bank account appears between the Cash summary heading and the Total Cash line. Also, the account number appears in the left column of the screen, column D. The C following the account number means that this account is a consolidation account. Since Walton Electronics is not yet using departments, all of its accounts are consolidation accounts and have a C after the account number.

```
     D    E  F           G                H        I       J
85  ■■   Use up & down arrow keys, pgup, and pgdn to move cell pointer    ■■
86  ■■  {Ins}=Add menu {F2}=Change acct. {Del}=Delete line {F4}=Defaults  ■■
87  ■■  {F5}=Page {F6}=Depts. {F7}=Print samples {F8}=Interrupt {F9}=Done ■■
     D    E  F           G                H        I       J
100 Acc #         Account Title
101          ASSETS
102            Cash
103 100C         Cash in Bank            0.00
104            Total Cash                         0.00
105                                             ---------
106          TOTAL ASSETS                         0.00
107
108          LIABILITIES
109                                             ---------
110          TOTAL LIABILITIES                    0.00
111
112          EQUITY
113            Net Income                         0.00
114                                             ---------
115          TOTAL EQUITY                         0.00
```

Figure 1-10

Adding More Accounts

You are ready to add the Accounts Receivable account to the chart of accounts. Tom Walton does not have many customers that buy on account, so he does not need to maintain a subsidiary ledger. If he decides to add this feature, he can purchase the Accounts Receivable/Accounts Payable module for Ready-to-Run.

Every account must be included under a summary heading. Accounts receivable cannot be included in the Cash summary heading. You must add a new summary heading before you add the Accounts Receivable account.

To move the cell pointer to the line above TOTAL ASSETS,

Press: ⬇

To add the new summary heading,

Press: INS
Select: **S**ummary Heading

In the Assets Heading List window, press ⬇ until the heading
Accounts Receivable is highlighted. Then press ⬅.

To add the new account,

Press: INS
Select: **A**ccount Title

When prompted for the account number,

Type: **110**
Press: ⬅

When prompted for the account title,

Type: **Accounts Receivable**
Press: ⬅

Your screen should now look like Figure 1-11.

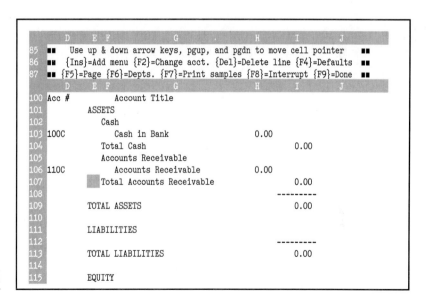

Figure 1-11

Follow the same steps to add the next two accounts. Remember, to add an assets summary heading, you must position the cell pointer above the TOTAL ASSETS line.

Summary Heading	Account No.	Account Title
Inventory	120	Merchandise Inventory
Prepaid Expense	130	Prepaid Insurance

After you add these two accounts, your screen should look like Figure 1-12.

```
     D   E F              G                  H        I         J
85  ■■   Use up & down arrow keys, pgup, and pgdn to move cell pointer    ■■
86  ■■  {Ins}=Add menu {F2}=Change acct. {Del}=Delete line {F4}=Defaults  ■■
87  ■■ {F5}=Page {F6}=Depts. {F7}=Print samples {F8}=Interrupt {F9}=Done  ■■
     D   E F              G                  H        I         J
100 Acc #            Account Title
101       ASSETS
102          Cash
103 100C        Cash in Bank              0.00
104             Total Cash                         0.00
105          Accounts Receivable
106 110C        Accounts Receivable       0.00
107             Total Accounts Receivable          0.00
108          Inventory
109 120C        Merchandise Inventory     0.00
110             Total Inventory                    0.00
111          Prepaid Expense
112 130C        Prepaid Insurance         0.00
113             Total Prepaid Expense              0.00
114                                            ---------
115       TOTAL ASSETS                          0.00
```

Figure 1-12

The next two accounts also fall under the Prepaid Expense summary heading. Position the cell pointer on the Total Prepaid Expense line and:

Press: INS

To enter a second account under the heading Prepaid Expense,

Select: **Account Title**

Enter account number 131, Prepaid Rent. Following the same procedure, add account number 132, Supplies.

Your screen should now look like Figure 1-13.

```
        D     E  F              G                  H          I        J
 85  ██    Use up & down arrow keys, pgup, and pgdn to move cell pointer    ██
 86  ██  {Ins}=Add menu {F2}=Change acct. {Del}=Delete line {F4}=Defaults ██
 87  ██  {F5}=Page {F6}=Depts. {F7}=Print samples {F8}=Interrupt {F9}=Done ██
        D     E  F              G                  H          I        J
100  Acc #            Account Title
101          ASSETS
102            Cash
103  100C        Cash in Bank                    0.00
104            Total Cash                                    0.00
105          Accounts Receivable
106  110C        Accounts Receivable             0.00
107            Total Accounts Receivable                     0.00
108          Inventory
109  120C        Merchandise Inventory           0.00
110            Total Inventory                               0.00
111          Prepaid Expense
112  130C        Prepaid Insurance               0.00
113  131C        Prepaid Rent                    0.00
114  132C        Supplies                        0.00
115            Total Prepaid Expense                         0.00
```

Figure 1-13

Changing an Account Title

Suppose you decide that the title of the last account should be
Supplies on Hand, instead of Supplies. To change the title,

Move to: the row containing the Supplies account (row 114)
Press: [F2]

The prompt line asks if you want to change the account number. It says: ". . .Press <Enter> if okay:." Since you don't
want to change the number,

Press: [⏎]

The prompt line asks whether you want to change the account
title. To change the title,

Type: **Supplies on Hand**
Press: [⏎]

The account title should change to Supplies on Hand.

Entering the Remaining Asset Accounts

The remaining asset accounts are property, plant, and equipment accounts.

Walton Electronics has four property, plant, and equipment accounts. Two of them are used to record the cost of purchased assets, and two are used to record the accumulated depreciation. Enter them into the chart of accounts according to the table below. Move the cell pointer to the line above Total Assets before inserting each new summary heading.

Summary Heading	Account Number	Account Title
Other Fixed Assets	150	Equipment
Other Fixed Assets	151	Furniture
Accumulated Depreciation	155	Accum. Depr. – Equipment
Accumulated Depreciation	156	Accum. Depr. – Furniture

Add each new summary heading and then add the accounts under the summary heading. Note that there are two accounts under each summary heading; add the second account the same way you added Rent and Supplies on Hand.

Tom has decided that he does not like the title of the Other Fixed Assets summary heading. He wants to change it to Property, Plant and Equipment.

Move the cell pointer to the line containing the summary heading Other Fixed Assets.

Press: ⬚F2⬚

RTR prompts you to enter the new summary heading. When you type the new heading, it is too long to fit on the prompt line. Some letters will disappear to the left. Press ⬚↵⬚ to make them all appear in the title.

Type: **Property, Plant & Equipment**
Press: ⬚↵⬚

Note that the description on the total line changes at the same time.

Your screen should now look like Figure 1-14. If you have made any errors, move the cell pointer to the incorrect line and use ⬚F2⬚ to make the necessary changes.

```
         D    E  F              G               H        I        J
    85  ■■    Use up & down arrow keys, pgup, and pgdn to move cell pointer   ■■
    86  ■■  {Ins}=Add menu {F2}=Change acct. {Del}=Delete line {F4}=Defaults ■■
    87  ■■ {F5}=Page {F6}=Depts. {F7}=Print samples {F8}=Interrupt {F9}=Done  ■■
         D    E  F              G               H        I        J
   100  Acc #          Account Title
   109  120C            Merchandise Inventory   0.00
   110             Total Inventory                       0.00
   111             Prepaid Expense
   112  130C            Prepaid Insurance       0.00
   113  131C            Prepaid Rent            0.00
   114  132C            Supplies on Hand        0.00
   115             Total Prepaid Expense                 0.00
   116          Property, Plant & Equipment
   117  150C            Equipment               0.00
   118  151C            Furniture               0.00
   119             Total Property, Plant & Equipment      0.00
   120             Accumulated Depreciation(-)
   121  155C            Accum. Depr. - Equipment  0.00
   122  156C            Accum. Depr. - Furniture  0.00
   123             Total Accumulated Depreciation(-)      0.00
```

Figure 1-14

You can also use the DEL key to eliminate an account and start
over. Position the cell pointer on the row that contains the
account you want to delete and press DEL. You cannot delete a
summary heading if there are accounts listed under it. You
must delete the accounts first.

Entering the Remaining Balance Sheet Accounts

To position the next screen on your monitor,

Press: PGDN

You should now enter the liability and equity accounts. The
procedures are the same as for asset accounts.

The liability accounts should be added under the heading
LIABILITIES. Position the cell pointer immediately above the
row for TOTAL LIABILITIES, and then press INS and select
Summary Heading to add the first summary heading. Ready-to-
Run shows you the Liabilities Heading List.

Here are the liability accounts that you should enter. Remember that every account must be included in a summary heading.

Summary Heading	Account Number	Account Title
Accounts Payable	200	Accounts Payable
Notes Payable	210	Notes Payable
Other Current Liabilities	230	Customer Deposits

The equity accounts should be added under the heading EQUITY. When you add accounts to the EQUITY section, add them *above* the line that says Net Income. Therefore, use ⬇ to position the cell pointer on the row that says Net Income before you press INS and select Summary Heading. Ready-to-Run shows you the Equity Heading List.

Enter the following Equity accounts:

Summary Heading	Account Number	Accounts Title
Paid-in Capital	300	Tom Walton, Capital
Drawing	310	Tom Walton, Drawing

After entering these two accounts, change the summary heading for Paid-in Capital to Owner's Capital.

When you are finished, your screen should look like Figure 1-15.

Figure 1-15

```
        D    E    F          G              H       I       J
 85  ■■    Use up & down arrow keys, pgup, and pgdn to move cell pointer  ■■
 86  ■■  {Ins}=Add menu {F2}=Change acct. {Del}=Delete line {F4}=Defaults  ■■
 87  ■■  {F5}=Page {F6}=Depts. {F7}=Print samples {F8}=Interrupt {F9}=Done  ■■
        D    E    F          G              H       I       J
100  Acc #          Account Title
132  210C           Notes Payable          0.00
133                 Total Notes Payable             0.00
134                 Other Current Liabilities
135  230C           Customer Deposits       0.00
136                 Total Other Current Liabilities  0.00
137                                         ---------
138             TOTAL LIABILITIES                   0.00
139
140             EQUITY
141             Owner's Capital
142  300C           Tom Walton, Capital     0.00
143                 Total Owner's Capital           0.00
144             Drawing (-)
145  310C           Tom Walton, Drawing     0.00
146             Total Drawing (-)                   0.00
```

Adding Income Statement Accounts

Ready-to-Run requires that you add at least one revenue and one expense account before you can record the chart of accounts for the first time. You will add the rest of the revenue and expense accounts in the exercises at the end of this lab.

Press: PGDN

You will see the rest of the headings for the chart of accounts.

Use ⬇ to position the cell pointer above the line that says TOTAL REVENUE. Add the summary heading Sales, and then add account number 400, Sales.

Position the cell pointer above the line that says TOTAL EXPENSES. Add the summary heading Cost of Sales, and then add account number 510, Purchases.

When you are finished, your screen should look like Figure 1-16.

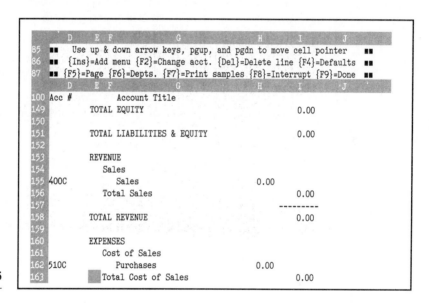

Figure 1-16

Printing Your Chart of Accounts

Before you save your new chart of accounts, print it out to make sure it is correct. You can do this from the chart of accounts editing screen.

Press: F7

You will see the menu shown in Figure 1-17.

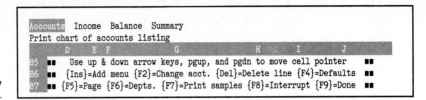

Figure 1-17

The options on this menu are as follows:

Accounts   Prints a chart of accounts listing. Choose this option to print a copy of your chart of accounts. The printout will show the type of account, the summary heading of the account, the account number, and the account title.

Income   Prints a sample detailed income statement. You will use this option in Lab 5 when you prepare financial statements.

Balance   Prints a sample detailed balance sheet. You will also use this option in Lab 5.

Summary   Prints a listing of the summary headings available under each type of account.

All options print a heading with your company name and the current date.

To print a chart of accounts, be sure your printer is on and ready to receive instructions from the computer. Then, from the menu,

Select: **Accounts**

Wait until your printer finishes printing. Then take the printout out of the printer and examine it to see if you entered the chart of accounts correctly. Figure 1-18 shows a correct copy of the chart of accounts. If you want, you can also print the summary account headings by pressing ⬚F7⬚ and selecting Summary.

Type	Sum Head	Acc #	Account Title
1ASSETS	Cash	100	Cash in Bank
1ASSETS	Accounts Receivable	110	Accounts Receivable
1ASSETS	Inventory	120	Merchandise Inventory
1ASSETS	Prepaid Expense	130	Prepaid Insurance
1ASSETS	Prepaid Expense	131	Prepaid Rent
1ASSETS	Prepaid Expense	132	Supplies on Hand
1ASSETS	Other Fixed Assets	150	Equipment
1ASSETS	Other Fixed Assets	151	Furniture
1ASSETS	Accumulated Depreciation (-)	155	Accum. Depr. - Equipment
1ASSETS	Accumulated Depreciation (-)	156	Accum. Depr. - Furniture
2LIABILITIES	Accounts Payable	200	Accounts Payable
2LIABILITIES	Notes Payable	210	Notes Payable
2LIABILITIES	Other Current Liabilities	230	Customer Deposits
3EQUITY	Paid-In-Capital	300	Tom Walton, Capital
3EQUITY	Drawing (-)	310	Tom Walton, Drawing
4REVENUE	Sales	400	Sales
5EXPENSES	Cost of Sales	510	Purchases

Figure 1-18

If you find errors in the chart of accounts, use (↑), (↓), PGDN, or PGUP to locate the item that needs to be corrected. Then use (F2) or DEL to make the corrections.

Updating Your Data Diskette or Directory

You are ready to save the chart of accounts you have created to your data diskette (or data directory if you are using a hard-disk system and saving the data on your hard disk).

Press: (F9)

You see the menu shown in Figure 1-19.

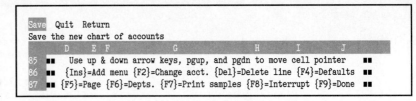

Figure 1-19

The options on this menu are as follows:

Save   Saves the new chart of accounts. Select this
        option when you have entered the new accounts
        and want to proceed to the next step entering
        beginning balances.

Quit   Exits this program *without* saving any changes to
        the chart of accounts. If you choose this option,
        all of the work performed during the session is
        lost. If you select this option, a submenu appears
        asking you to verify that you really want to quit.

Return Returns to Edit mode. Choose this option if you
        pressed (F9) by mistake and want to return to add
        more accounts.

If you are saving your work on diskette, make sure it is in
drive A. Then, to save the new chart of accounts,

Select: **S**ave

It takes some time for the program to save the chart of
accounts to your data diskette. Some computers take more
time than others. When you see the menu in Figure 1-20, you
are ready to enter beginning balances.

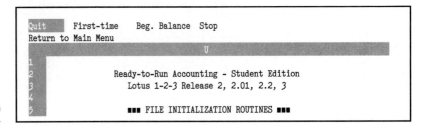

Figure 1-20

Entering Beginning Balances

The options on the menu in Figure 1-20 are:

Quit
: Returns to the Main menu. Use this option to return to the RTR Main menu.

First-time
: Sets up *all* data files for RTR. Use this option only when you set up a system for the first time.

Beg. Balance
: Adjust beginning balances without making any other changes. Use this option if you want to enter or change beginning balances after you set up your accounts for the first time. You cannot use this option if you have not set up your data files for the first time. If RTR cannot find your data files, it will lock you out of this option and tell you to select First-time.

Stop
: Stops execution of Ready-to-Run macros. Use this option to exit the RTR menu and go to Lotus 1-2-3. *Do not choose this option unless you know how to use Lotus 1-2-3.*

Because you are installing the system for the first time,

Select: **F**irst-time

RTR prompts you for your data password. If you are using one, type it and press ⏎, or just press ⏎.

You should see the screen shown in Figure 1-21, listing your chart of accounts. Each account appears on one row. The account number is listed in column C and the account title in column D. You enter beginning balances for each account in column E. Column F has information for period 1. You do not use column F now.

```
      C              D                        E          F
 4  Acc #     Account Title              Beg Bal    Period 1
 5       100 Cash in Bank                   0.00         0.00
 6       110 Accounts Receivable           0.00         0.00
 7       120 Merchandise Inventory         0.00         0.00
 8       130 Prepaid Insurance             0.00         0.00
 9       131 Prepaid Rent                  0.00         0.00
10       132 Supplies on Hand              0.00         0.00
11       150 Equipment                     0.00         0.00
12       151 Furniture                     0.00         0.00
13       155 Accum. Depr. - Equipment      0.00         0.00
14       156 Accum. Depr. - Furniture      0.00         0.00
15       200 Accounts Payable              0.00         0.00
16       210 Notes Payable                 0.00         0.00
17       230 Customer Deposits             0.00         0.00
18       300 Tom Walton, Capital           0.00         0.00
19       310 Tom Walton, Drawing           0.00         0.00
20       400 Sales                         0.00         0.00
                            U
25   Use up/down keys to select accounts and enter beginning balances
26       Use + for debits, - for credits - Press <Esc> when done
```

Figure 1-21

The instructions on this screen are shown in a horizontal window at the bottom of the screen. Notice the instructions and the keys you use:

↑	To move the cell pointer up one row
↓	To move the cell pointer down one row
+	To begin the entry of a debit balance
−	To begin the entry of a credit balance

Entering Beginning Balances

The cell pointer is positioned in column E on the row for Cash in Bank. Walton Electronics has a balance of $21,300 in the bank.

Type: **+21300**
Press: ↓

The screen should now look like Figure 1-22.

```
          C                    D                       E          F
  4  Acc #      Account Title               Beg Bal      Period 1
  5       100 Cash in Bank                  21,300.00        0.00
  6       110 Accounts Receivable                0.00        0.00
  7       120 Merchandise Inventory             0.00         0.00
  8       130 Prepaid Insurance                 0.00         0.00
  9       131 Prepaid Rent                      0.00         0.00
 10       132 Supplies on Hand                  0.00         0.00
 11       150 Equipment                         0.00         0.00
 12       151 Furniture                         0.00         0.00
 13       155 Accum. Depr. - Equipment          0.00         0.00
 14       156 Accum. Depr. - Furniture          0.00         0.00
 15       200 Accounts Payable                  0.00         0.00
 16       210 Notes Payable                     0.00         0.00
 17       230 Customer Deposits                 0.00         0.00
 18       300 Tom Walton, Capital               0.00         0.00
 19       310 Tom Walton, Drawing               0.00         0.00
 20       400 Sales                             0.00         0.00
                                   U
 25  Use up/down keys to select accounts and enter beginning balances
 26    Use + for debits, - for credits - Press <Esc> when done
```

Figure 1-22

Keep the following in mind when you enter beginning balances.

- When you enter an amount in Lotus 1-2-3 or RTR, you do not enter dollar signs or commas. They are automatically entered by the program. You must, however, enter a period when cents are involved.

- Instead of pressing ⏎ ↓ after you type the balance, you can press only ↓. This is the equivalent of pressing ⏎ ↓ in either Lotus 1-2-3 or RTR; it positions the cell pointer at the next cell ready for entry.

The cell pointer is now positioned on the row for the Accounts Receivable account. The balance outstanding in accounts receivable is $36,280.

Type: **+36280**
Press: ↓

Continue to enter the beginning balances. The following accounts have debit balances:

Merchandise Inventory	$33,500
Prepaid Insurance	1,800
Prepaid Rent	1,000

Supplies on Hand	650
Equipment	16,500
Furniture	7,200

The following accounts have credit balances. Remember to enter these balances with a minus (−). Note that two accounts, Notes Payable and Tom Walton, Drawing, do not have beginning balances. After you enter the balance for Accounts Payable, press ⬇ once more to bypass Notes Payable, and then enter the balance for Customer Deposits.

Accum. Depr. − Equipment	$ 825
Accum. Depr. − Furniture	900
Accounts Payable	24,050
Customer Deposits	1,500
Tom Walton, Capital	89,955

If you enter a balance on a line that should not have a balance, move the cell pointer to that row and enter 0 to correct it.

There are never any beginning balances for the income statement accounts. RTR maintains files for a complete fiscal year; therefore, you cannot enter beginning balances for income statement accounts.

Correcting Beginning Balances

You have entered all the beginning balances. The instructions at the bottom of the screen tell you what to do now.

Press: ESC

Your computer beeps and an error message appears on the prompt line. It says that your ledger is out of balance.

Press: ⏎

The cell pointer returns to the column with the beginning balances so that you can correct your error.

You examine Tom's manual records and discover that the balance in Merchandise Inventory should be $32,500 instead of $33,500. Move the cell pointer to the row for the Merchandise Inventory account.

Type: **+32500**
Press: ⏎

Now that you have corrected this error, you are ready to move on.

Press: ESC

The menu in Figure 1-23 should appear. If your computer beeps, your ledger is still out of balance. Use Figure 1-23 to check the amounts you entered and correct any error. Credit balances on the screen should have parentheses around them. Be sure that you have entered them correctly. When your accounts balance and you press ESC, you see the menu shown in Figure 1-23.

```
Done  Re-enter  Abort
Okay to save beginning balances as entered
       C           D                    E          F
4   Acc #      Account Title        Beg Bal     Period 1
5        100 Cash in Bank           21,300.00       0.00
6        110 Accounts Receivable    36,280.00       0.00
7        120 Merchandise Inventory  32,500.00       0.00
8        130 Prepaid Insurance       1,800.00       0.00
9        131 Prepaid Rent            1,000.00       0.00
10       132 Supplies on Hand          650.00       0.00
11       150 Equipment              16,500.00       0.00
12       151 Furniture               7,200.00       0.00
13       155 Accum. Depr. - Equipment  (825.00)     0.00
14       156 Accum. Depr. - Furniture  (900.00)     0.00
15       200 Accounts Payable      (24,050.00)      0.00
16       210 Notes Payable              0.00        0.00
17       230 Customer Deposits      (1,500.00)      0.00
18       300 Tom Walton, Capital   (89,955.00)      0.00
19       310 Tom Walton, Drawing        0.00        0.00
20       400 Sales                      0.00        0.00
                          U
25     Use up/down keys to select accounts and enter beginning balances
26          Use + for debits, - for credits - Press <Esc> when done
```

Figure 1-23

Saving Beginning Balances

The options on this menu are:

Done   Saves beginning balances as entered. Choose this option to proceed.

Re-enter	Continue to adjust beginning balances. Choose this option if you want to reenter beginning balances.
Abort	Quit file maintenance without saving any changes. Choose this option only to start over. You will have to enter all balances again from the beginning. RTR will not save any of them.

To save your work,

Select: **D**one

The RTR program creates all of the files needed to maintain the accounting records for Walton Electronics. It takes some time to do this.

The RTR program keeps a separate file on your data diskette to hold the transactions for each period in the accounting year. Ready-to-Run creates empty files for each period so that they are ready to receive data when you enter transactions. RTR creates 13 period files. The thirteenth period can be used in one of two ways:

1.   Some companies operate their accounting cycle on a four-week period instead of a calendar month. They have 13 periods in a year instead of 12.

2.   A company may use the thirteenth period files to record year-end adjustments resulting from an audit of the company's accounting records.

If you are saving your data on a diskette, RTR prompts you to insert a diskette for each period's file. The following message appears on the prompt line:

If needed, insert a blank disk for Period *n* into A: – <Enter>

This message appears for each of the 13 periods. You do not need a separate diskette for each period because you are not going to enter that many transactions. Leave your data diskette in the drive specified and press ⏎ each time you are prompted to do so. RTR will store the files for all 13 periods on one diskette.

> **Note** If you are saving your data on a hard disk, you will not see the 13 messages. RTR automatically creates all 13 files in your default directory.

When RTR finishes creating the files, you see the RTR Main menu again.

Adding Accounts to the Chart of Accounts

When you showed Tom Walton the printout of the chart of accounts you created, he realized that at the end of the current period he will need two more liability accounts: Interest Payable and Salaries Payable. He asked you to add these before you add the remaining revenue and expense accounts.

Do *not* use the Files option from the RTR Main menu to change the existing chart of accounts. If you use the Files option, the beginning balances you entered are zeroed out and you must reenter them.

From the RTR Main menu, select the general ledger program, which is designated by the letters GL on the menu.

Select: **GL**

You should see the GL menu in Figure 1-24.

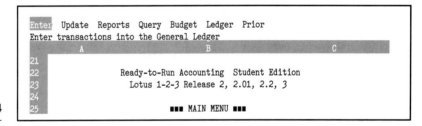

```
Enter  Update  Reports  Query  Budget  Ledger  Prior
Enter transactions into the General Ledger
          A                    B                    C
21
22              Ready-to-Run Accounting   Student Edition
23              Lotus 1-2-3 Release 2, 2.01, 2.2, 3
24
25                       ■■■ MAIN MENU ■■■
```

Figure 1-24

To change the existing chart of accounts, select the Ledger option from the GL menu.

Select: **L**edger

The Ledger option allows you to change either the chart of accounts or the beginning balances or to return to the Main menu. These three options should appear on the menu line, as in Figure 1-25.

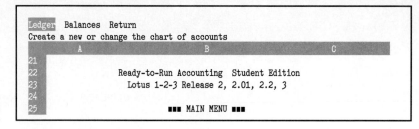

Figure 1-25

```
Ledger  Balances  Return
Create a new or change the chart of accounts
           A                          B                          C
21
22                    Ready-to-Run Accounting  Student Edition
23                    Lotus 1-2-3 Release 2, 2.01, 2.2, 3
24
25                         ■■■ MAIN MENU ■■■
```

To change the chart of accounts from this menu, choose Ledger again.

Select: **Ledger**

Follow the same steps you used to build the chart of accounts:

1. Enter your data password.

2. Select **R**un from the menu in Figure 1-3.

3. Select **B**ackup from the menu in Figure 1-4 to use automatic backup (unless you are using a two-diskette system).

4. Type **20** and press ⏎ to select a 20-minute backup period.

You should see the menu shown in Figure 1-5. To select the chart of accounts you already created,

Select: **E**xisting

Your screen should now display the Chart of Accounts editing screen. Press PGDN twice to get to the correct screen for entering the two new accounts.

The two new accounts go under a new summary heading, Accrued Liabilities. Insert the new heading between Notes Payable and Other Current Liabilities. Position the cell pointer on the cell containing the heading Other Current Liabilities. To add the new summary heading,

Press: INS
Select: **S**ummary Heading

Then move the cell pointer to the summary heading Accrued Liabilities and press ⏎.

Now insert the two new accounts:

Account Number	Acount Title
220	Interest Payable
225	Salaries Payable

Use $\boxed{\text{F7}}$ to print a copy of the changed chart of accounts, to make sure you entered the new accounts correctly.

If you are working on a two-diskette system, your data diskette should be in drive A. Save the changed chart of accounts.

Press: $\boxed{\text{F9}}$
Select: **S**ave

You should see the RTR Main menu again. You are now ready to proceed to the exercises, where you will add the remaining revenue and expense accounts.

Exercises

How to Use the Lab Exercises

The Walton Electronics exercises form a sole-proprietorship case study for Principles of Accounting students. The TWE, Inc. exercises form a corporation case study for Financial Accounting and more advanced students. The Lotus 1-2-3 exercises, which appear in later labs, are intended for students who know how to use Lotus 1-2-3.

If your instructor assigns the Walton Electronics exercises, complete the Walton Electronics exercises at the end of every lab. If your instructor assigns the TWE, Inc. exercises, complete the TWE, Inc. exercises at the end of every lab.

If your instructor asks you to follow a case study for a different company, you must use a different diskette or directory from the one you use for the labs. You cannot store the data for more than one company on a diskette or in a directory.

Walton Electronics

1. Add the following accounts to the Walton Electronics chart of accounts under the heading REVENUE, *after* the Sales summary heading.

Summary Heading	Acct. No.	Account Title
Deductions from Revenue	410	Sales Discounts
Deductions from Revenue	415	Sales Returns & Allowances

2. Add the following accounts to the chart of accounts under the heading EXPENSES.

Summary Heading	Acct. No.	Account Title
Cost of Sales	515	Purchases Discounts
Cost of Sales	520	Purchases Returns & Allowances
Cost of Sales	550	Freight-in
Selling Expense	600	Sales Salaries Expense
Selling Expense	610	Delivery Expense
Selling Expense	620	Advertising Expense
Other General & Admin.	700	Office Salaries Expense
Other General & Admin.	705	Rent Expense
Other General & Admin.	710	Supplies Expense
Other General & Admin.	715	Insurance Expense
Other General & Admin.	720	Utility Expense
Other General & Admin.	725	Telephone Expense
Other General & Admin.	730	Postage Expense
Depreciation Expense	740	Depr. Exp. – Equipment
Depreciation Expense	745	Depr. Exp. – Furniture

3. Change the summary heading Other General & Admin. to Other Operating Expenses.

4. Add the following account under the heading NON-OPERATING ITEMS:

Summary Heading	Acct. No.	Account Title
Interest Expense (Revenue)	800	Interest Expense

5. Print a new Chart of Accounts.

6. Update your data files for the new accounts.

TWE, Inc.

1. Follow steps 1-4 for Walton Electronics.

2. In a discussion with Tom Walton, you learn that Tom has recently incorporated his business. First, change the company name to TWE, Inc. Then you need to make some changes to the chart of accounts. Add the following LIABILITY and EQUITY accounts.

Summary Heading	Acct. No.	Account Title
Other Current Liabilities	240	Dividends Payable
Common Stock	315	Common Stock, $2 par
Common Stock	330	Add'l Paid-in Capital — Common
Retained Earnings	360	Retained Earnings
Common Dividends	370	Common Dividends Declared

3. Update your data files for the new accounts.

4. Enter and save the following new account balances (use the GL Ledger Balances command sequence):

Common Stock, $2 par	$40,000 (credit)
Add'l Paid-in Capital — Common	45,000 (credit)
Retained Earnings	4,955 (credit)
Tom Walton, Capital	0

5. Make the following changes in the chart of accounts.

a. Eliminate the following accounts from the chart of accounts:

Tom Walton, Capital

Tom Walton, Drawing

b. Eliminate the following summary headings from the chart of accounts:

Owner's Capital

Drawing

6. Print a new chart of accounts.

7. Print a list of all the summary headings using the Summary menu option.

8. Update your data files for the new accounts.

Going Further

9. Which of the four corporate accounts added in TWE, Inc. exercise 2 replaces the following proprietorship accounts?

   a. Tom Walton, Capital

   b. Tom Walton, Drawing

10. When the beginning balances were entered, the RTR software automatically checked whether total debits equaled total credits. In a manual accounting system, how would such a check be made?

11. Refer to the list of summary headings and indicate which summary heading would be most appropriate for each of the following accounts. Also indicate whether the account would normally have a debit or credit balance.

   a. Factory Buildings

   b. Paid-in Capital in Excess of Par on Common

   c. Patents

   d. Revenue Received in Advance

   e. Bonds Payable (due in 5 years)

   f. Dividends Received

   g. Loss on Sale of Equipment

   h. Short-term Investment in IBM Stock

   i. Premium on Bonds Payable

   j. Property Taxes Payable

   k. Work-in-Process

   l. Finished Goods Inventory

Entering Non-Cash Transactions

**Ready-to-Run
General Ledger Structure**

ENTER Enter transactions →	Temporary File	
	↓	
	UPDATE Post transactions to permanent file	
	↓	
LEDGER Create and maintain chart of accounts →	Permanent Files	→ **QUERY** Extract detail information ↓ Audit Trail
	↓	
	REPORTS Extract and summarize data	→ Various Reports
	↑	
BUDGET Create budget file →	**BUDGET** File	

Objectives

In Lab 2, you will learn how to:

- Set up default account numbers

- Enter payables transactions

- Enter receivables transactions

- Enter general journal transactions

- Add an account to the chart of accounts while entering transactions

- Print unposted transactions

- Fix errors in unposted transactions

- Post transactions to the permanent period file

Preparing to Enter Transactions

You are now ready to begin entering transactions for Walton Electronics. Remember that the computer cannot analyze transactions. Before you can enter transactions into RTR, you must analyze each one and decide which account (or accounts) to debit and which account (or accounts) to credit.

Special Journals

RTR uses special journals to record transactions. You may have studied this topic in your accounting class. A special journal groups all transactions of one class. In a manual system, using a special journal speeds up the recordkeeping process by allowing you to post totals rather than individual transactions to an account. For example, a Cash Disbursements Journal is used to record the checks written by the company during a given month. At the end of the month, the total of all the checks written is posted as one credit to Cash in Bank. If the transactions were recorded in the General Journal, there would be a credit to Cash in Bank for each check. Thus, in a manual system, a special journal saves a significant amount of time.

In a computerized system, the special journal also saves time. When you record checks in a special journal on the computer, you do not need to record the credit to Cash in Bank for each one. You tell the software to credit Cash in Bank for *all* checks. This is known as assigning a *default* account.

RTR uses four special journals and one general journal.
The special journals are:

Checks	Records all transactions that involve a credit to Cash in Bank.
Deposits	Records all transactions that involve a debit to Cash in Bank.
Payables	Records all transactions that involve Accounts Payable, except those transactions that also involve Cash in Bank.
Receivables	Records all transactions that involve Accounts Receivable, except those that also involve Cash in Bank.

The Enter Menu

To begin entering transactions, from the RTR Main menu,

Select: **GL**

You see the General Ledger menu shown in Figure 2-1.

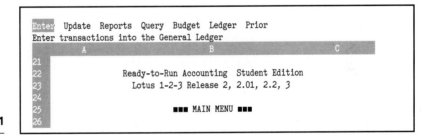

Figure 2-1

To enter transactions,

Select: **E**nter

You should see the Run/Quit/Break menu, which you saw
when you created the chart of accounts. Below the menu is
the Transaction Entry screen, shown in Figure 2-2.

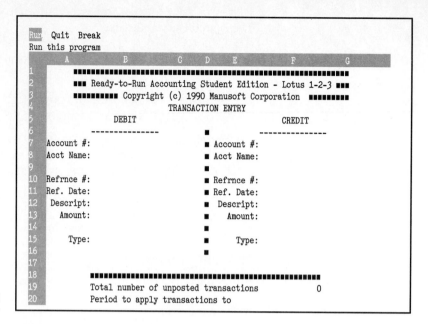

Figure 2-2

To run the Enter program,

Select: **R**un

You should see the automatic backup menu. Select **B**ackup to choose the automatic backup option. Type **20** and press ⏎ to select a 20-minute backup period.

The next message on the prompt line is:

Enter period to post:

Because you are recording the transactions for the first period of Walton Electronics's new year,

Type: **1**
Press: ⏎

The screen displays the menu shown in Figure 2-3.

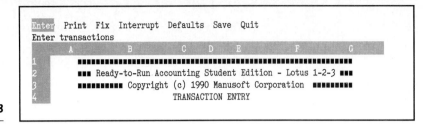

Figure 2-3

The options on this menu are:

Enter — Choose this option to enter new transactions.

Print — Choose this option to print a listing of all unposted transactions. Use the listing to check for errors before you post.

Fix — Choose Fix to correct or delete unposted transactions after you review the printed listing of unposted transactions.

Interrupt — Temporarily interrupts the Enter program. Choose Interrupt if you must stop entering transactions before you are finished. RTR saves a file containing the Enter program; it does not save the entries you made to a separate file. When you restart RTR, a message on the opening screen tells you that you have interrupted the Enter program. If you select the same commands you would select to start the Enter program normally, you are returned to the program at the point you left off.

Defaults — Choose Defaults to tell RTR which account numbers to use as defaults for each of the special journals.

Save — Choose Save when you have finished entering transactions and want to save them to the temporary unposted data file.

Quit — Choose Quit only if you have made too many errors and want to start over. The message "BE CAREFUL!" on the prompt line alerts you to the fact that you will lose the transactions you have entered in that session at the computer. This option does *not* allow you to delete previously saved transactions. You must use the Fix command to do that.

Setting Up Default Account Numbers

Before you can enter transactions, you must tell RTR which account is your checking account, which is accounts payable, and which is accounts receivable. From the Enter menu,

Select: **Defaults**

You should see the menu shown in Figure 2-4. The four choices on this menu are Checking, Payables, Receivables, and Save. The first three options let you enter the default account numbers, and the fourth lets you save the default account numbers to your data files.

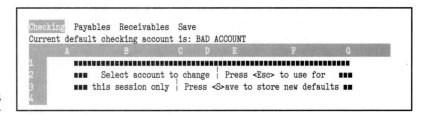

Figure 2-4

Default Checking Account   The menu highlight is on Checking, and the third line of the control panel states:

Current default checking account is: BAD ACCOUNT

Since you have not told RTR which account is your checking account, you see the BAD ACCOUNT message. To enter a default checking account number,

Select: **Checking**

The menu shown in Figure 2-5 appears. To tell RTR which account is the checking account, you can either enter the number (if you know it), or you can ask RTR to show you a listing of the chart of accounts and then select the one you want by pointing to it.

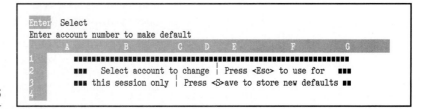

Figure 2-5

Since you know that the account number for Cash in Bank is 100, choose the Enter command.

Select: **Enter**

The following message appears on the prompt line:

Enter account number:

Type: **100**
Press: ⌨︎

You should see the following message on the prompt line:

Account selected is: Cash in Bank – Okay? (Y/N):

Confirm that you selected the correct account. If you selected the wrong account, type **N** and press ⌨︎. Then enter the correct account number at the prompt. If you selected the correct account,

Type: **Y**
Press: ⌨︎

The third line of the control panel should now read:

Current default checking account is: Cash in Bank

Default Payables Account   Now enter the default payables account number.

Select: **Payables**

To see a list of the chart of accounts,

Select: **Select**

The screen shown in Figure 2.6 should appear. Use ⬇︎ to highlight the account number for Accounts Payable. Then press ⌨︎.

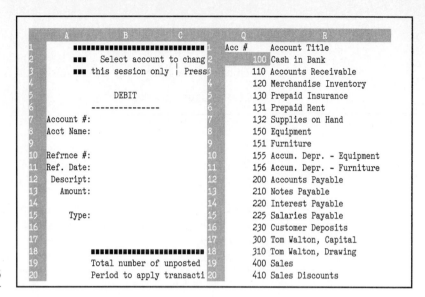

Figure 2-6

Because you chose the account number from a list instead of typing it in, RTR does not ask you to confirm it.

The default account for Receivables is Accounts Receivable. Use the procedure you just learned to tell RTR what the default account is.

When you finish, save these default account numbers to your data disk,

Select: **Save**

Entering Payables Transactions

Now that you have entered the default account numbers, you are ready to enter some payables transactions.

Select: **Enter**

The menu shown in Figure 2-7 should appear at the top of the screen. This is the Journal Selection menu. The items on this menu correspond to the four special journals (Checks, Deposits, Payables, Receivables, and the general journal). As you highlight each menu item, you will see a description of the highlighted journal on the third line.

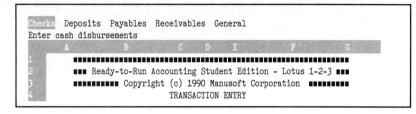

Figure 2-7

This menu does not have a Return option. If you get to this menu by mistake, use the Lotus 1-2-3 method to back out of it: Press the ESC key. You should return to the Enter menu.

Entering a Merchandise Purchase with Freight

Tom Walton's first payable transaction in January is a receipt of merchandise from Rebco Computer on January 3. It is accompanied by invoice number Z4928, dated January 2, 1992, in the amount of $5,090. Freight of $90 is included in the total and the terms are 2/10, net 30. Tom records purchases using the gross method.

Analysis of this transaction indicates that you should make the following entry:

Debit Purchases (#510)	$5,000	
Debit Freight-in (#550)	$90	
Credit Accounts Payable (#200)		$5,090

To record this transaction, select the Payables command from the Journal Selection menu.

Select: **P**ayables

The screen shown in Figure 2-8 should appear. This is the Payables entry screen. Note that the left side of the screen is titled "PURCHASE(S)" and the right side of the screen is titled "BILL." The standard double-entry procedure that you learned in your accounting class is in effect here. The total of the debit amounts must equal the total of the credit amounts. If they do not, you cannot finish the entry. You will enter all detail items on the left side of the screen; the account shown on the right side of the screen will be credited with the total of all the detail items.

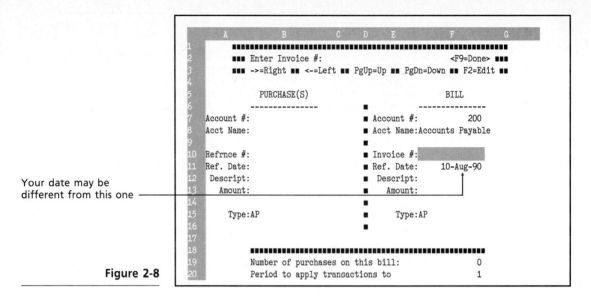

Your date may be different from this one

Figure 2-8

Completing the Right Side Row 7 on the right side of the screen shows the account number 200, and row 8 shows the account name Accounts Payable. These were retrieved from the information you entered regarding the default account numbers. You can change the account number that is credited by pressing ⬆ and entering a different account number in cell F7. Do not do that now. In this case you want the default account number to be credited.

In row 15 on both sides of the screen the heading Type: is followed by the letters AP. These letters were automatically recorded by RTR when you selected the Payables command from the Journal Selection menu. If you select a different special journal or the general journal, RTR records a different type code. RTR uses the type code to sort and print the transactions for each journal.

The cell pointer is positioned on cell F10, beside the label Invoice #. In row 2 at the top of the screen the instruction for this cell says: "Enter Invoice #."

Type: **Z4928**
Press: ⏎

> **Note** Do not use the Lotus 1-2-3 method of entry (pressing ⏎ when you enter transactions). The Lotus 1-2-3 macros in the transaction entry program control the entry screen, and you will lose the data you enter if you press ↓ (or any arrow key) instead of ⏎.

The invoice number appears in cell F10, and the cell pointer is positioned on cell F11. The date in this cell is probably not the date associated with the transaction. It should be the date on your computer's internal clock. Normally, it is the current date. However, you should record the transaction with the date the merchandise is received.

The prompt on row 2 tells you to enter the date in this cell. The prompt also tells you to enter the date in the format mm/dd/yy. Because the merchandise was received on January 3, 1992, the date should be entered as 1/3/92.

Type: **1/3/92**
Press: ⏎

RTR reformats the date so that it looks like this: 03-Jan-92. RTR uses a Lotus 1-2-3 date format to record the date of the transaction. All dates on the screen and on your printed journals appear in this format.

The cell pointer is now positioned on cell F12 for the description. The description should be the name of the company from which the merchandise was purchased.

Type: **REBCO COMPUTER**

Enter the name of the company in capital letters to give your journals and ledgers a more uniform appearance. You may find it easier to turn on the CAPS LOCK key so that the text you enter will be in capital letters. You can leave CAPS LOCK on while you continue to enter transactions.

Press: ⏎

Completing the Left Side   When you press ⏎, the cell pointer does not move down to the Amount cell. It moves to the left side of the screen to the Account #: cell, because RTR allows you to have more than one debit per payable. As you enter debits, the program totals them and enters the total in the credit to Accounts Payable. The RTR entry screen is *self-balancing.* You cannot have total debit amounts that do not equal total credit amounts.

RTR also automatically enters the same date and description on the left side of the screen as on the right side. You can change the date or description if you need to. Normally, however, all the debits and credits for one transaction have the same date and description.

Row 2 prompts "Enter Account to debit:". Note that row 2 also says "<F10=Help>". Whenever the cell pointer is in the cell labeled Account #:, the F10 key is your Help key. It allows you to select the account number you want from a listing of the chart of accounts.

Press: F10

You will now see the screen shown in Figure 2-9. The screen is split into two vertical windows. In the right window, the chart of accounts appears so that you can select the account you want to debit. This screen is similar to the split screen you saw when you entered the default account numbers using the Select command.

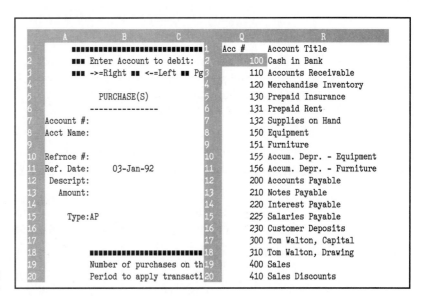

Figure 2-9

The account you want is Purchases.

Move to: The cell containing the account number for Purchases (You may need to use the PGDN key to find the Purchases account.)

Press: ↵

The transaction entry screen is restored, and the account number and title for the Purchases account appear on rows 7 and 8 of the left side.

The cell pointer is positioned on the cell labeled Refrnce #:. This cell records an internal reference number that identifies this transaction, such as a purchase order or receiving report number. Tom does not use either of these because his operation is so small. Bypass this cell.

Press: ⏎

The cell pointer is positioned on the date cell on the left side of the screen. Since you do not want to change the date or the description,

Press: ⏎

The cell pointer is positioned on the Amount: cell on the left side of the screen. Enter the amount to be debited to Purchases.

Type: **5000**
Press: ⏎

> **Note** When you enter an amount in RTR, you do not need to enter a dollar sign or commas. If the dollar amount is even (that is, if there are no cents), you do not need to enter the period and the cents.

The menu at the top of Figure 2-10 appears.

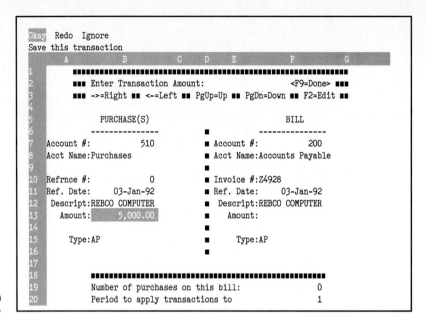

Figure 2-10

The menu offers you three choices:

Okay   Choose this if the transaction is okay as it is entered. You are confirming only the entry that appears on the left side of the screen.

Redo   Choose this if the transaction has an error in one of the fields. This option allows you to go back over the rows and change the incorrect one.

Ignore   Choose this if you want to ignore this transaction and start over. The menu that appears is the same that appears when you choose Okay. However, when you choose Ignore, the transaction is not saved.

If the entry on your screen matches Figure 2-10,

Select: **O**kay

If it doesn't, select **R**edo and fix whichever row needs to be fixed. When you press ⏎ after the Amount: row, you will see the Okay/Redo/Ignore menu again. Select **O**kay to continue.

You should see the screen in Figure 2-11. Note that the $5,000 amount has been automatically added to the credit amount on the screen and the number of purchases on this bill, at the bottom of the screen, has changed to 1.

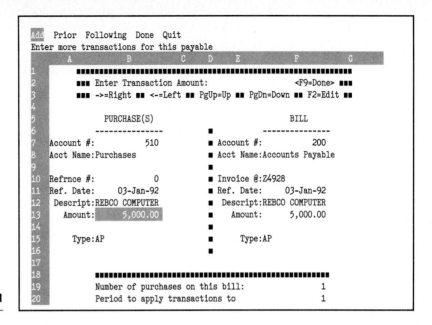

```
Add   Prior  Following  Done  Quit
Enter more transactions for this payable
         A        B        C      D    E        F        G
 1    ■■■■■■■■■■■■■■■■■■■■■■■■■■■■■■■■■■■■■■■■■■■■■■■■■■■■■■■■■■■■
 2       ■■■ Enter Transaction Amount:              <F9=Done> ■■■
 3       ■■■ ->=Right ■■ <-=Left ■■ PgUp=Up ■■ PgDn=Down ■■ F2=Edit ■■
 4
 5              PURCHASE(S)                          BILL
 6           ---------------      ■       ---------------
 7    Account #:           510    ■ Account #:           200
 8    Acct Name:Purchases         ■ Acct Name:Accounts Payable
 9                                ■
10    Refrnce #:             0    ■ Invoice @:Z4928
11    Ref. Date:   03-Jan-92     ■ Ref. Date:   03-Jan-92
12    Descript:REBCO COMPUTER     ■ Descript:REBCO COMPUTER
13       Amount:     5,000.00     ■    Amount:     5,000.00
14                                ■
15       Type:AP                  ■       Type:AP
16                                ■
17
18    ■■■■■■■■■■■■■■■■■■■■■■■■■■■■■■■■■■■■■■■■■■■■■■■■■■■■■■■■■
19    Number of purchases on this bill:          1
20    Period to apply transactions to            1
```

Figure 2-11

There are five choices on this menu. Use them to perform the following functions:

Add	Enter another debit for this payable.
Prior	Go back to a previous debit for this payable to view or correct it.
Following	Go forward to a subsequent debit for this payable to view or correct it.
Done	Save this payable as it is now entered.
Quit	Quit the payable entry process without saving *any* entries. If you choose this item, RTR asks you to confirm that you really want to quit.

Because you must debit a second account (Freight-in) for this payable,

Select: **Add**

The cell pointer returns to the Account #: row on the left side. Last time, you used (F10) to help you find the account for the debit. This time, simply enter the account number.

Type: **520**
Press: (⏎)

If you followed the instructions and are looking at the screen, you should see that you entered an incorrect account number. The account number should have been 550. Remember that you will have a chance to confirm the debit, so leave the incorrect number and proceed with the rest of the entry.

The reference number, date, and description rows do not change. The only other change is the amount.

Press: ⏎ ⏎ ⏎
Type: **90**
Press: ⏎

The Debit Confirmation screen appears. To correct the account number,

Select: **Redo**

The cell pointer moves to the Account #: row.

Type: **550**
Press: ⏎

The account name should read Freight-in. Instead of pressing ⏎ four times to see the Debit Confirmation menu, tell RTR that you have completed your changes:

Press: F9

The Debit Confirmation menu appears.

Select: **Okay**

The Entry Confirmation menu appears. Since you have entered all the debits for this payable,

Select: **Done**

The menu in Figure 2-12 appears.

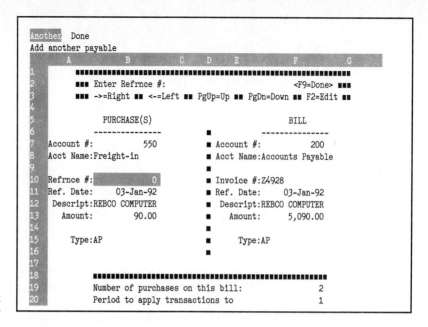

Figure 2-12

```
Another  Done
Add another payable
         A        B        C     D      E        F        G
  1  ■■■■■■■■■■■■■■■■■■■■■■■■■■■■■■■■■■■■■■■■■■■■■■■■■■■■■■■■■■■■■
  2      ■■■ Enter Refrnce #:                      <F9=Done> ■■■
  3      ■■■ ->=Right ■■ <-=Left ■■ PgUp=Up ■■ PgDn=Down ■■ F2=Edit ■■
  4
  5            PURCHASE(S)                      BILL
  6            ---------------          ■      ---------------
  7  Account #:           550           ■ Account #:          200
  8  Acct Name:Freight-in               ■ Acct Name:Accounts Payable
  9                                      ■
 10  Refrnce #:              0           ■ Invoice #:Z4928
 11  Ref. Date:    03-Jan-92            ■ Ref. Date:    03-Jan-92
 12   Descript:REBCO COMPUTER           ■  Descript:REBCO COMPUTER
 13     Amount:        90.00            ■     Amount:      5,090.00
 14                                      ■
 15       Type:AP                        ■        Type:AP
 16                                      ■
 17
 18  ■■■■■■■■■■■■■■■■■■■■■■■■■■■■■■■■■■■■■■■■■■■■■■■■■■■
 19  Number of purchases on this bill:            2
 20  Period to apply transactions to             1
```

The two options on this menu are:

Another   Choose if you want to add another payable.

Done   Choose if you have finished entering payables for this computer session.

Because you want to add a second payable,

Select: **A**nother

Entering a Non-Merchandise Payable

Frequently, companies receive invoices that are not for merchandise. These invoices should also be recorded as payables.

Walton Electronics received invoice number QT3342 for $891 from Today's Advertising Agency. It is dated January 7, 1992, and is for ads to appear in magazines during the month of January.

Analyzing this transaction yields the following journal entry:

Debit Advertising Expense (#620) $891

Credit Accounts Payable (#200) $891

Because you told RTR that you wanted to add another payable, the cell pointer is positioned at the Invoice #: cell, waiting for you to indicate the invoice number. Watch the screen and think about what you are doing as you perform the following steps:

Type: **QT3342**
Press: ⏎
Type: **1/7/92**
Press: ⏎
Type: **TODAY'S ADVERTISING**
Press: ⏎
Type: **620**
Press: ⏎
Press: ⏎ ⏎ ⏎
Type: **891**
Press: ⏎

Your screen should match Figure 2-13. If you have made an error, select **R**edo and make changes. If you need to change something on the right side of the screen, use → to move to the right side. Then use ↑ or ↓ to move to the row you want to change.

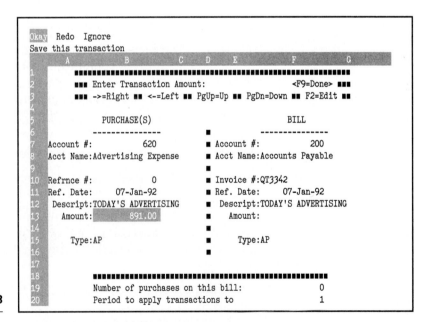

```
Okay  Redo  Ignore
Save this transaction
          A          B          C     D     E          F          G
1
2        ■■■ Enter Transaction Amount:                 <F9=Done> ■■■
3        ■■■ ->=Right ■■ <-=Left ■■ PgUp=Up ■■ PgDn=Down ■■ F2=Edit ■■
4
5               PURCHASE(S)                          BILL
6               ---------------        ■            ---------------
7        Account #:         620        ■ Account #:         200
8        Acct Name:Advertising Expense ■ Acct Name:Accounts Payable
9                                      ■
10       Refrnce #:           0        ■ Invoice #:QT3342
11       Ref. Date:     07-Jan-92      ■ Ref. Date:     07-Jan-92
12       Descript:TODAY'S ADVERTISING  ■ Descript:TODAY'S ADVERTISING
13         Amount:        891.00       ■   Amount:
14                                      ■
15          Type:AP                    ■      Type:AP
16                                      ■
17
18       ■■■■■■■■■■■■■■■■■■■■■■■■■■■■■■■■■■■■■■■■■■■■
19       Number of purchases on this bill:          0
20       Period to apply transactions to            1
```

Figure 2-13

When everything is correct,

Select: **Okay**

This payable has only one debit. To save it,

Select: **Done**

There is one more type of payables transaction to enter.

Select: **Another**

Entering a Merchandise Return

In December, Walton Electronics received $500 worth of
damaged merchandise from Venus Systems. Tom sent for
authorization from Venus before sending it back. The authorization came on January 9, and he returned the merchandise
the same day. Debit Memo #442 was sent with the merchandise.

Analyzing this transaction yields the following journal entry:

> Debit Accounts Payable (#200) $500
>
> Credit Purchases Returns & Allowances (#520) $500

How can you use the payables journal to record this transaction,
when the right side of the entry is automatically credited to
Accounts Payable? You must trick RTR by entering the amount
on the left side of the screen as a negative amount. This will
yield a debit to Accounts Payable and a credit to Purchases
Returns & Allowances. Again, watch what happens on the entry
screen as you perform the following steps:

Type: **DM442**
Press: ⏎
Type: **1/9/92**
Press: ⏎
Type: **VENUS SYSTEMS**
Press: ⏎
Type: **520**
Press: ⏎
Press: ⏎ ⏎ ⏎
Type: **– 500**
Press: ⏎

Be sure that you type a minus (–) sign before the amount, to
reverse the effect of the entry.

If your screen matches Figure 2-14,

Select: **O**kay

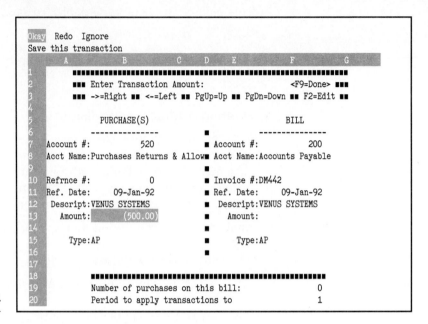

```
Okay  Redo  Ignore
Save this transaction
        A        B        C     D     E         F           G
1  ■■■■■■■■■■■■■■■■■■■■■■■■■■■■■■■■■■■■■■■■■■■■■■■■■■■■■■■■■■■■
2  ■■■ Enter Transaction Amount:              <F9=Done> ■■■
3  ■■■ ->=Right ■■ <-=Left ■■ PgUp=Up ■■ PgDn=Down ■■ F2=Edit ■■
4
5           PURCHASE(S)                        BILL
6        ---------------          ■         ---------------
7  Account #:          520        ■ Account #:          200
8  Acct Name:Purchases Returns & Allow■ Acct Name:Accounts Payable
9                                 ■
10 Refrnce #:            0         ■ Invoice #:DM442
11 Ref. Date:      09-Jan-92       ■ Ref. Date:      09-Jan-92
12 Descript:VENUS SYSTEMS          ■ Descript:VENUS SYSTEMS
13   Amount:       (500.00)        ■   Amount:
14                                 ■
15      Type:AP                    ■      Type:AP
16                                 ■
17
18       ■■■■■■■■■■■■■■■■■■■■■■■■■■■■■■■■■■■■■■■■■■■■■■
19       Number of purchases on this bill:          0
20       Period to apply transactions to            1
```

Figure 2-14

The negative amount on the right side of the screen will be *debited* to Accounts Payable; the negative amount on the left side of the screen will be *credited* to Purchases Returns and Allowances.

This entry has only one debit. Therefore, at the Entry Confirmation menu,

Select: **D**one

Entering a Transaction on Your Own

Try analyzing and entering a transaction on your own.

Select: **A**nother

On January 10, Walton Electronics received an invoice from We-Haul-It, a local delivery company, for delivery of merchandise to one of Walton's customers. The invoice is number VVK94, dated January 10, in the amount of $83.

Analyze this transaction, then record it on the RTR Payables entry screen.

When you finish, your screen should look like Figure 2-15. Use the Redo command if you need to correct anything. If everything is correct, confirm the debit and save the entry.

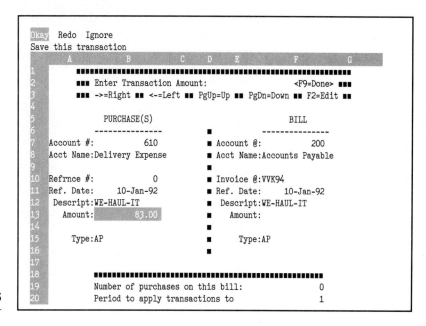

Figure 2-15

Because you have finished entering payables,

Select: **D**one

You should see the Enter menu you saw in Figure 2-3. Row 19 of the screen says: "Total number of unposted transactions," followed by the number 9. Why this number, when you only recorded four transactions? RTR refers to each debit and each credit as a transaction. In the four payables you recorded, there were five debits and four credits. Thus, nine appears as the total number of unposted transactions.

Entering Receivables Transactions

You are now ready to enter some receivables transactions. The process is similar to that of entering payables transactions. However, because almost all receivables involve either Sales or Sales Returns & Allowances, there are fewer types of receivables transactions.

Select: **E**nter

You should see the same Journal Selection menu you saw in Figure 2-7. To record receivables transactions,

Select: **Receivables**

Your screen should now look like the one shown in Figure 2-16. The default receivables account, Accounts Receivable, appears on the left side and the cell pointer is positioned for the invoice number. The left side of the screen is titled INVOICE and the right side is titled REVENUE(S).

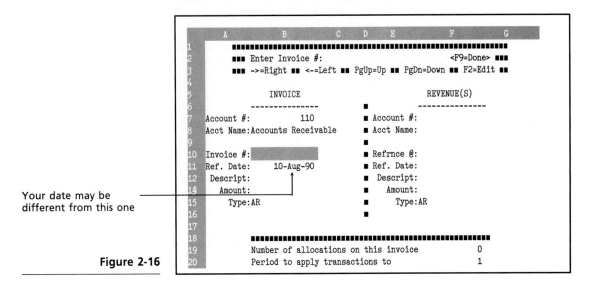

Your date may be different from this one

Figure 2-16

Entering a Sale on Account

On January 6, Walton Electronics sold a computer to Randy's Video Stop on invoice number 2036 for $5,300. To encourage his customers to pay early, Tom allows a discount for early payment. All sales on credit are on terms of 2/10, net 30.

Analyzing this transaction yields the following journal entry:

Debit Accounts Receivable (#110) $5,300

Credit Sales (#400) $5,300

Completing the Left Side   When you record receivables, you enter the left side of the transaction first. To record the invoice number,

Type: **2036**
Press: (⏎)

When you enter a number in the invoice number cell, RTR automatically increments the number by one for each entry after that. Thus, when you enter another invoice in this lab, the screen will automatically say 2037. You can type over this number if you need to change it. You can use this feature to make the data entry faster when you enter the invoices in the exercises.

To record the date (which should be the date of the sale),

Type: **1/6/92**
Press: ⏎

Record the name of the customer in the description field.

Type: **RANDY'S VIDEO STOP**
Press: ⏎

Completing the Right Side   The cell pointer jumps to the right side of the screen. The debit amount is the total of the amounts you enter on the right side of the screen.

Use F10 (Help) to select the Sales account.

Press: F10
Move to: the account number for Sales
Press: ⏎

Bypass the reference number field.

Press: ⏎

Accept the date and description you entered on the left side.

Press: ⏎ ⏎

Enter the amount of the invoice.

Type: **5300**
Press: ⏎

Your screen should match Figure 2-17.

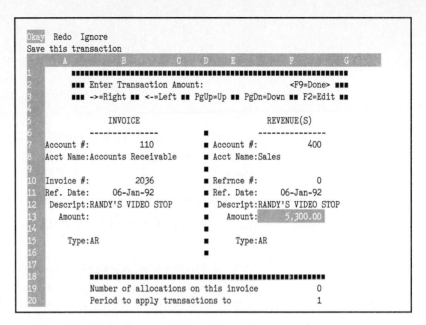

```
Okay  Redo  Ignore
Save this transaction
        A         B        C     D      E          F           G
1    ■■■■■■■■■■■■■■■■■■■■■■■■■■■■■■■■■■■■■■■■■■■■■■■■■■■■■■■■■
2    ■■■ Enter Transaction Amount:                  <F9=Done> ■■■
3    ■■■ ->=Right ■■ <-=Left ■■ PgUp=Up ■■ PgDn=Down ■■ F2=Edit ■■
4
5              INVOICE                        REVENUE(S)
6         ---------------              ■    ---------------
7    Account #:           110          ■ Account #:         400
8    Acct Name:Accounts Receivable     ■ Acct Name:Sales
9                                       ■
10   Invoice #:          2036          ■ Refrnce #:           0
11   Ref. Date:     06-Jan-92          ■ Ref. Date:     06-Jan-92
12    Descript:RANDY'S VIDEO STOP      ■ Descript:RANDY'S VIDEO STOP
13      Amount:                         ■    Amount:     5,300.00
14                                       ■
15      Type:AR                          ■    Type:AR
16                                       ■
17
18        ■■■■■■■■■■■■■■■■■■■■■■■■■■■■■■■■■■■■■■■■■■■■■■■■■■■
19        Number of allocations on this invoice          0
20        Period to apply transactions to                1
```

Figure 2-17

If not, select **R**edo and make corrections. When the screen matches Figure 2-17,

Select: **O**kay

The entry is complete. To save it,

Select: **D**one

To record another receivable,

Select: **A**nother

Entering a Sales Return

On January 8, Walton Electronics received a return of merchandise from Excellent Hardware. The merchandise was sold on December 30, 1991, on invoice 2035. Walton Electronics had approved the return of this merchandise and issued credit Memo number 52 in the amount of $600.

The analysis of this transaction yields the following journal entry:

    Debit Sales Returns & Allowances (#415) $600

    Credit Accounts Receivable (#110) $600

As when you recorded the return of a purchase under payables, you must trick RTR when you record a sales return by entering the amount as a negative amount. Watch what happens on your entry screen as you perform the following steps:

Type: **CM52**
Press: ⏎
Type: **1/8/92**
Press: ⏎
Type: **EXCELLENT HARDWARE**
Press: ⏎
Type: **415**
Press: ⏎
Press: ⏎ ⏎ ⏎
Type: **– 600**
Press: ⏎

Your screen should match Figure 2-18.

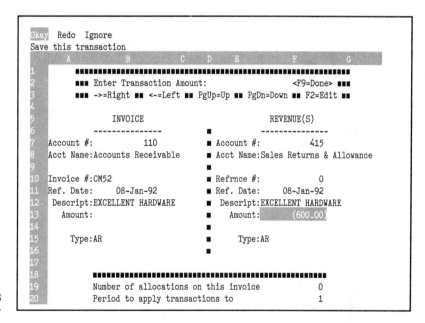

```
Okay   Redo   Ignore
Save this transaction
       A         B         C     D     E       F           G
1     ■■■■■■■■■■■■■■■■■■■■■■■■■■■■■■■■■■■■■■■■■■■■■■■■■■■■
2       ■■■ Enter Transaction Amount:              <F9=Done> ■■■
3       ■■■ ->=Right ■■ <-=Left ■■ PgUp=Up ■■ PgDn=Down ■■ F2=Edit ■■
4
5                   INVOICE                      REVENUE(S)
6                ---------------        ■       ---------------
7     Account #:          110           ■  Account #:          415
8     Acct Name:Accounts Receivable     ■  Acct Name:Sales Returns & Allowance
9                                       ■
10    Invoice #:CM52                     ■  Refrnce #:           0
11    Ref. Date:    08-Jan-92            ■  Ref. Date:    08-Jan-92
12     Descript:EXCELLENT HARDWARE       ■   Descript:EXCELLENT HARDWARE
13      Amount:                          ■     Amount:       (600.00)
14                                       ■
15        Type:AR                        ■       Type:AR
16                                       ■
17
18    ■■■■■■■■■■■■■■■■■■■■■■■■■■■■■■■■■■■■■■■■■■■■■■■■■■■
19        Number of allocations on this invoice        0
20        Period to apply transactions to              1
```

Figure 2-18

If it does not, select **R**edo and make corrections. Otherwise,

Select: **O**kay

To approve the entry and save it,

Select: **D**one

Entering a Receivable Transaction on Your Own

You are now ready to analyze and enter a receivable transaction on your own.

Select: **A**nother

On January 10, Walton Electronics sold computer hardware to Len's Appliance Depot on invoice number 2037 for $12,650.

Analyze this transaction and then record it using the RTR receivables entry screen. When you finish, your screen should look like Figure 2-19. Make sure it is correct, and then accept and save the entry by selecting **D**one.

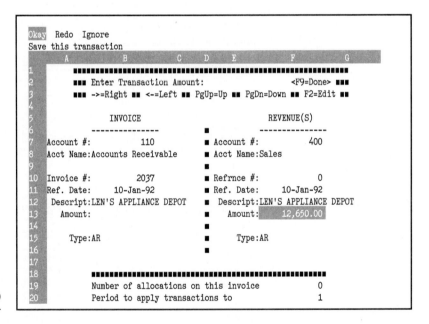

Figure 2-19

To tell RTR you are finished recording receivables transactions,

Select: **D**one

You should see the Enter menu.

Entering General Journal Transactions

Most of Walton Electronics's transactions are recorded in the special journals, but a few must be recorded in the general journal. To get to the Journal Selection menu,

Select: **E**nter

To enter transactions in the general journal,

Select: **General**

The General Journal Selection Method Menu

You should see the menu shown in Figure 2-20. The menu has two options, which correspond to the two methods of recording general journal entries.

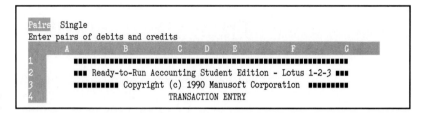

Figure 2-20

Pairs   The Pairs command allows you to enter debits and credits together.

When you choose the Pairs command, you see the screen shown in Figure 2-21. This screen is similar to the payables and receivables entry screens. The debit side is on the left, and the credit side is on the right.

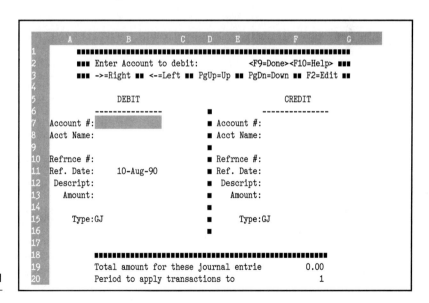

Figure 2-21

You can enter a compound entry — more than one debit or more than one credit. However, it is easier to use this screen only when the number of debits and credits are equal. Also, the total dollar amount of the debits must equal the total dollar amount of the credits before you can exit the screen. (If you selected **P**airs to view this screen, press (F9) twice, select **I**gnore, and then select **Q**uit to return to the Enter menu. Now select **E**nter and then **G**eneral to return to the General Journal Selection Method menu.)

Single The Single command allows you to enter debits and credits individually.

When you choose the Single command, you see the entry screen shown in Figure 2-22. This screen has only one side. You enter credit amounts as negative amounts, and debit amounts as positive amounts. This method of journal entry is easier when you have an unequal number of debits and credits.

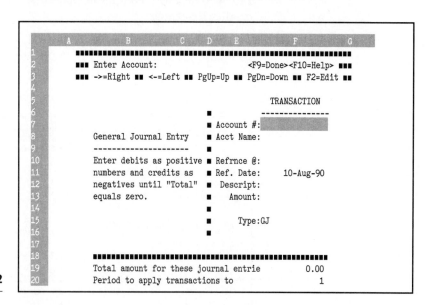

Figure 2-22

When you use this screen, the total amount for the journal entries, displayed on row 19, must equal zero before you can exit from the screen. (If you selected **S**ingle to view this screen on your monitor, press (F9), select **I**gnore and then select **Q**uit to return to the Enter menu. Select **E**nter and then **G**eneral to return to the General Journal Selection Method menu.)

In the labs and exercises in this manual, use the Pairs command when the number of debits equal the number of credits. Otherwise, use the Single command.

Entering a General Journal Transaction

On January 15, Tom Walton purchased a used delivery truck from Del's Motors for $4,800. Del's Motors agreed to accept a note for the delivery truck payable at the end of six months. The interest rate is 12%.

The analysis of this transaction yields the following journal entry:

Debit Trucks (#?)	$4,800	
Credit Notes Payable (#210)		$4,800

Adding an Account

Walton Electronics does not have an asset account for Trucks. You must add this account to the chart of accounts before you can record this transaction. To leave the General Journal Selection Method menu,

Press: ESC

The Enter menu appears on your screen. You must return to the GL menu to add the new account. However, you have entered some transactions that you have not saved. From the Enter menu, save the transactions you have already recorded:

Select: **S**ave

RTR takes a few moments to save, and then the GL menu should appear. On your own, follow the procedure at the end of Lab 1 to add the Trucks account under the Property, Plant & Equipment summary heading. Use account number 152. After you have added the account and saved the changed chart of accounts, RTR returns you to the Main menu.

Completing the General Journal Transaction

To return to the Enter menu,

Select:	**GL**
Select:	**Enter**
Select:	**Run**
Select:	**Backup**
Type:	**20**
Press:	(⏎) to set the backup time at 20 minutes
Type:	**1**
Press:	(⏎) to select the period to post as 1

You should now see the Enter menu.

Select:	**Enter**

To record general journal transactions,

Select:	**General**

Select the Pairs method of entering general journal entries.

Select:	**Pairs**

Completing the Left Side   The screen shown in Figure 2-21 should appear. The cell pointer is positioned on the left side waiting for you to enter the account number to debit.

Type:	**152**
Press:	(⏎)

For the reference number on general journal entries, Walton Electronics uses the letters JE followed by a five-digit number. The first two digits are the year, and the last three digits number the journal entries for that year consecutively. This is the first journal entry for 1992, so the number is 92001.

Type:	**JE92001**
Press:	(⏎)

Enter the date, January 15, just as you did for receivables and payables entries.

For the description on the left side, which will appear in the Trucks account, type a description that reminds Tom what he purchased.

Type:	**DELIVERY TRUCK**
Press:	(⏎)

The amount to be entered is the amount of the purchase price.

Type: **4800**
Press: ⏎

Completing the Right Side   The cell pointer jumps to the right side of the screen ready for you to enter the account to credit. Everything except the account number from the left side of the screen is copied to the right side of the screen. Enter the account to be credited.

Type: **210**
Press: ⏎

The only item that Tom wants you to change on the right side of the screen is the description. He wants the account credited to show the name of the business to which he owes the note.

Press: ⏎ ⏎
Type: **DEL'S MOTORS**
Press: ⏎

The entry is now complete: total debit amount equals the total credit amount. When you are finished, your screen should look like Figure 2-23. If it doesn't, use the arrow keys to move to any cell that needs correcting and correct it.

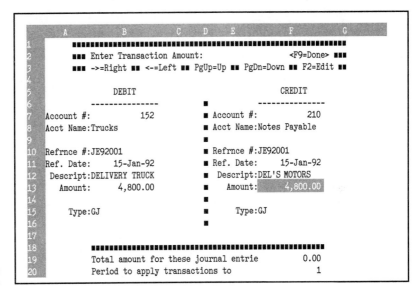

Figure 2-23

To accept the screen as it is displayed,

Press: F9 *or* ⏎

The Okay/Redo/Ignore Confirmation menu appears.

Select: **O**kay

The General Entry Confirmation menu appears.

Select: **D**one

A General Journal Continuation menu appears. It is similar to the Payables Continuation and Receivables Continuation menus. This is the only entry you need to enter. Save it and return to the Enter menu.

Select: **D**one

Printing the Unposted Transactions

The transactions you have entered are saved in a temporary file. They are not yet posted to the accounts for January. You and Tom Walton should review them before you post them. Thus, you need a printed copy of the transactions you have entered.

Be sure that your printer is on and the paper in it is aligned. Then, to print a copy of your unposted transactions, select Print from the Enter menu.

Select: **P**rint

A copy of the unposted transactions should print. When the printout is finished, remove it from your printer and examine it. It should look like Figure 2-24.

Walton Electronics		Unposted GL Transactions				29-Sep-90 - Page 1
	1	<- Period to be posted				
Acc	#	Description	Ref #	Ref Date	SJ	Transaction
	200	REBCO COMPUTER	Z4928	03-Jan-92	AP	(5,090.00)
	550	REBCO COMPUTER	0/Z4928	03-Jan-92	AP	90.00
	510	REBCO COMPUTER	0/Z4928	03-Jan-92	AP	5,000.00
	200	TODAY'S ADVERTISING	QT3342	07-Jan-92	AP	(891.00)
	620	TODAY'S ADVERTISING	0/QT3342	07-Jan-92	AP	891.00
	200	VENUS SYSTEMS	DM442	09-Jan-92	AP	500.00
	520	VENUS SYSTEMS	0/DM442	09-Jan-92	AP	(500.00)
	200	WE-HAUL-IT	VVK94	10-Jan-92	AP	(83.00)
	610	WE-HAUL-IT	0/VVK94	10-Jan-92	AP	83.00
	110	RANDY'S VIDEO STOP	2036	06-Jan-92	AR	5,300.00
	400	RANDY'S VIDEO STOP	0/2036	06-Jan-92	AR	(5,300.00)
	110	EXCELLENT HARDWARE	CM5	08-Jan-92	AR	(600.00)
	415	EXCELLENT HARDWARE	0/CM52	08-Jan-92	AR	600.00
	110	LEN'S APPLIANCE DEPOT	2037	10-Jan-92	AR	12,650.00
	400	LEN'S APPLIANCE DEPOT	0/2037	10-Jan-92	AR	(12,650.00)
	210	DEL'S MOTORS	JE92001	15-Jan-92	GJ	(4,800.00)
	152	DELIVERY TRUCK	JE92001	15-Jan-92	GJ	4,800.00

Figure 2-24

There are six columns on this printout:

Acc #   The account number to be debited or credited.

Description   The description entered on the screen for each debit or credit.

Ref #   The reference number you entered on the screen for each debit or credit. (The invoice numbers 2036 and 2037 are right-aligned in the Ref # column because they were entered as numbers. The other invoice numbers all have at least one letter in them.)

Ref Date   The date you entered on the screen for each debit or credit.

SJ   The journal in which the entry was recorded:

GJ = General Journal

AP = Payables

AR = Receivables

Transaction   The amount of each debit or credit. Credits appear in parentheses.

Fixing Errors in an Unposted Transaction

When he examines the printout of unposted transactions, Tom Walton discovers that the amount of the invoice from Today's Advertising Agency should be $819 instead of $891. He asks you to fix this before you post the transaction.

Your screen should still have the Enter menu on it. To edit unposted transactions,

Select: **Fix**

The menu in Figure 2-25 appears on your screen.

Figure 2-25

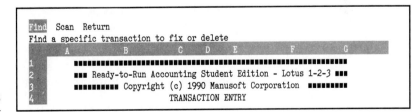

This menu has three options:

Find   Use this option if you know the reference number you want to fix. You will be prompted to enter the reference number.

Scan   Use this option to look through all the transactions to find the one you want to fix or to be sure you have corrected every debit and credit relating to the entry you are correcting.

Return   Use this option to return to the Enter menu.

Although you know the reference number of the item you want to correct, use the Scan command to find it.

Select: **Scan**

Your screen should look like the printed copy of your unposted transactions. One debit or credit appears on each row. The six columns in each row correspond to the six columns on the printout. The cell pointer is positioned in the first column for the first transaction entered.

The transaction you want to correct is the second one, for Today's Advertising. The credit should appear on row 103 and the debit on row 104. Use ⬇ and ➡ to move the cell pointer to row 103, column M.

Your cell pointer should be located over the (891.00) in cell M103. To correct the amount, type it in on the keyboard.

Type: **−819**
Press: ⏎

When you correct a credit amount, you must enter it with a minus sign so the computer can distinguish it from a debit.

Now correct the debit amount.

Press: ⬇

Your cell pointer should be on the 891.00 in cell M104.

Type: **819**
Press: ⏎

Fixing a Date on an Entered Transaction

You also realize that the date for the Today's Advertising transaction should be January 6 instead of January 7.

Use the arrow keys to position the cell pointer on the date column on row 103. To correct the date on an entered transaction, you must use the Lotus 1-2-3 @DATE function. The syntax for the @DATE function is @DATE(year,month,day). You don't need to type the first two digits of the year. When you correct a date this way, you *must* enter the parentheses and commas as specified in the syntax.

Type: **@DATE(92,1,6)**
Press: ⤶

Also correct the date on the debit portion of the entry.

Press: ↓
Type: **@DATE(92,1,6)**
Press: ⤶

You have made all the corrections. The instructions on row 3 say to "Press <Esc> when done."

Press: ESC

The Enter menu appears. Save the general journal transaction you entered and the corrections you made.

Select: **S**ave

After RTR finishes saving, the Main menu appears.

Posting Transactions

Now that you have corrected your unposted transactions, you can record them permanently. To do so, choose the Update command from the GL menu.

Select: **GL**
Select: **U**pdate

You should see another Run/Quit/Break menu.

Select: **R**un

You should see the menu in Figure 2-26.

Figure 2-26

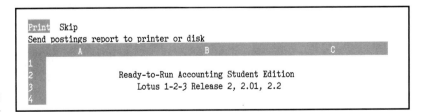

This menu gives you two options:

Print   Prints a report showing the entries that are being posted.

Skip   Posts the transactions without printing a report.

You should print the report as part of your audit trail. The audit trail will be discussed more fully in Lab 4. Before you print, make sure that your printer is turned on and that the paper is aligned.

Select: **Print**

A menu gives you the choice of printing to the printer or to a disk file. Print to the printer.

Select: **Printer**

The mode indicator indicates WAIT while RTR transfers the transactions from a temporary data file into the permanent file for period 1. Observe the messages on the screen as this process takes place. The posting process takes more time on some computers than on others. Do not interrupt the posting process. Your computer sounds a series of beeps when posting is complete.

The RTR Main menu appears when all entries have been posted.

Remove the printouts generated by the posting process from your printer. There should be two of them.

The first printout lists the transactions to be posted for period 1. It should look like Figure 2-27. It is similar to the printout of unposted transactions, but it should show the corrections you made.

```
Walton Electronics        Transactions to be posted - Period 1        29-Sep-90 - Page 1

Acc #       Description           Ref #            Ref Date   SJ   Transaction
    200     REBCO COMPUTER        Z4928            03-Jan-92  AP    (5,090.00)
    550     REBCO COMPUTER        0/Z4928          03-Jan-92  AP        90.00
    510     REBCO COMPUTER        0/Z4928          03-Jan-92  AP     5,000.00
    200     TODAY'S ADVERTISING   QT3342           06-Jan-92  AP      (819.00)
    620     TODAY'S ADVERTISING   0/QT3342         06-Jan-92  AP       819.00
    200     VENUS SYSTEMS         DM442            09-Jan-92  AP       500.00
    520     VENUS SYSTEMS         0/DM442          09-Jan-92  AP      (500.00)
    200     WE-HAUL-IT            VVK94            10-Jan-92  AP       (83.00)
    610     WE-HAUL-IT            0/VVK94          10-Jan-92  AP        83.00
    110     RANDY'S VIDEO STOP            2036     06-Jan-92  AR     5,300.00
    400     RANDY'S VIDEO STOP    0/2036           06-Jan-92  AR    (5,300.00)
    110     EXCELLENT HARDWARE    CM52             08-Jan-92  AR      (600.00)
    415     EXCELLENT HARDWARE    0/CM52           08-Jan-92  AR       600.00
    110     LEN'S APPLIANCE DEPOT        2037     10-Jan-92  AR    12,650.00
    400     LEN'S APPLIANCE DEPOT 0/2037           10-Jan-92  AR   (12,650.00)
    210     DEL'S MOTORS          JE92001          15-Jan-92  GJ    (4,800.00)
    152     DELIVERY TRUCK        JE92001          15-Jan-92  GJ     4,800.00
                                                                  ===========
                                                                         0.00
```

Figure 2-27

The second printout is a summary of amounts posted to each account for period 1, and it should look like Figure 2-28. Since this is the first posting, the Period prior to Postings column contains all zeroes. The net total of all postings for each account is in the Posting column. The Period after Postings column is the total of the first two amount columns.

Retain both these printouts as a permanent record of the posting process.

Acc #	Account Title	Period prior to Postings	Posting	Period after Postings
100	Cash in Bank	0.00	0.00	0.00
110	Accounts Receivable	0.00	17,350.00	17,350.00
120	Merchandise Inventory	0.00	0.00	0.00
130	Prepaid Insurance	0.00	0.00	0.00
131	Prepaid Rent	0.00	0.00	0.00
132	Supplies on Hand	0.00	0.00	0.00
150	Equipment	0.00	0.00	0.00
151	Furniture	0.00	0.00	0.00
152	Trucks	0.00	4,800.00	4,800.00
155	Accum. Depr. - Equipment	0.00	0.00	0.00
156	Accum. Depr. - Furniture	0.00	0.00	0.00
200	Accounts Payable	0.00	(5,492.00)	(5,492.00)
210	Notes Payable	0.00	(4,800.00)	(4,800.00)
220	Interest Payable	0.00	0.00	0.00
225	Salaries Payable	0.00	0.00	0.00
230	Customer Deposits	0.00	0.00	0.00
300	Tom Walton, Capital	0.00	0.00	0.00
310	Tom Walton, Drawing	0.00	0.00	0.00
400	Sales	0.00	(17,950.00)	(17,950.00)
410	Sales Discounts	0.00	0.00	0.00
415	Sales Returns & Allowance	0.00	600.00	600.00
510	Purchases	0.00	5,000.00	5,000.00
515	Purchases Discounts	0.00	0.00	0.00
520	Purchases Returns & Allow	0.00	(500.00)	(500.00)
550	Freight-in	0.00	90.00	90.00
600	Sales Salaries Expense	0.00	0.00	0.00
610	Delivery Expense	0.00	83.00	83.00
620	Advertising Expense	0.00	819.00	819.00
700	Office Salaries Expense	0.00	0.00	0.00
705	Rent Expense	0.00	0.00	0.00
710	Supplies Expense	0.00	0.00	0.00
715	Insurance Expense	0.00	0.00	0.00
720	Utility Expense	0.00	0.00	0.00
725	Telephone Expense	0.00	0.00	0.00
730	Postage Expense	0.00	0.00	0.00
740	Depr. Exp. - Equipment	0.00	0.00	0.00
745	Depr. Exp. - Furniture	0.00	0.00	0.00
800	Interest Expense	0.00	0.00	0.00
		0.00	0.00	0.00

Figure 2-28

Proceed to the exercises, where you will enter additional payables, receivables, and general journal transactions. Remember to choose the same case study — Walton Electronics or TWE, Inc. — that you chose in Lab 1.

Exercises

Walton Electronics

Enter the following transactions for Walton Electronics for the month of January, 1992.

1. Payables transactions:

   a. Merchandise purchased on January 13 from Carron Peripherals. Invoice number HK4821-86, dated January 10, is for $11,602, which includes $752 of freight charges.

   b. A freight bill from We-Haul-It for delivering merchandise to a customer on January 14. The invoice number is VVK99 and is for $44.

   c. Merchandise purchased on January 17 from J. M. Supply. Invoice number B3559, dated January 15, is for $16,890, which includes $540 of freight charges.

   d. Merchandise purchased from Venus Systems on January 23. Invoice number QP69PR, dated January 21, is for $7,300. The invoice does not include freight charges.

   e. A bill from Lodico Communications for long distance charges. Invoice number 6954, dated January 24, is for $558.

   f. Merchandise purchased from Rebco Computer on January 29. Invoice number Z5143, dated January 27, is for $6,550, which includes $250 of freight charges.

   g. A freight bill from We-Haul-It for delivering merchandise to a customer on January 30. The invoice number is VVK114 and is for $135.

   h. Defective merchandise returned to Venus Systems on January 31. Issue Debit Memo number 443 in the amount of $250.

2. Receivables transactions:

   a. Merchandise sold to Bob's Auto Repair on invoice number 2038 on January 13. The amount of the invoice is $2,650.

b. Merchandise sold to Jim's Fitness Clinic on invoice number 2039 on January 16. The amount of the invoice is $5,980.

c. Merchandise sold to Marcia's Flower Shop on invoice number 2040 on January 24. The amount of the invoice is $16,500.

d. Merchandise sold to Corner Drug Store on invoice number 2041 on January 30. The amount of the invoice is $8,500.

e. Credit Memo number 53 issued to Jim's Fitness Clinic for $150 on January 31 because part of the order was not received.

3. General journal transaction:

On January 22, Tom Walton took merchandise that cost the company $1,600 home to set up a personal computer for his children and wife to use. (Reduce Purchases by the cost of the merchandise.)

4. Save and print a listing of the unposted transactions and make corrections if necessary.

5. Post the corrected transactions to the permanent period 1 file, printing out a listing at the same time.

Check figures (after postings):

Accounts Receivable	50,830
Accounts Payable	(48,321)
Sales	(51,580)
Purchases	44,200

TWE, Inc.

1. Enter the payables and receivables transactions in exercises 1 and 2 for Walton Electronics.

2. Consider the following events and enter the appropriate transactions in the journals.

   a. Payables transactions:

   On January 20, Tom Walton purchases a computer from Rebco Computer, for personal use at home. The invoice, numbered Z5062, is dated January 17 and is for $1,062, which includes $78 for freight charges. Walton will pay for the computer in early February from personal funds.

   On January 17, TWE, Inc. purchases supplies from Jason's Office Supplies. The invoice, numbered 299, is dated January 17 and is for $1,890. The terms are Net 30. TWE, Inc. records supplies purchases in an asset account.

   b. Receivables transaction:

   On January 26, TWE, Inc., agrees to supply Jed's Information Services with its monthly requirements of computer discs. Tom Walton will send $280 worth of merchandise on February 4. Jed's will pay for the items after they are received.

   c. General Journal transaction:

   On January 12, Tom Walton, as sole stockholder in TWE, Inc., declares a cash dividend of $2,000, to be paid January 21.

3. Print a listing of unposted transactions and make any corrections necessary.

4. Post the corrected transactions to the permanent period 1 file, printing out a permanent record at the same time.

Going Further

5. Special Journals: RTR uses four special journals: checks, deposits, payables, and receivables. Most textbooks refer to the following special journals: sales, purchases or voucher register, cash receipts, and cash payments (cash disbursements) or check register.

   a. Indicate which of the special journals named in your textbook corresponds to each of the special journals named in RTR.

b. The purchases journal format can consist of either one amount column, if the journal includes only the purchases of merchandise inventory on account, or multiple amount columns, if the journal includes the purchase of any item on account (the latter is true of a voucher register). Is RTR using the equivalent of a one-column or a multiple-column purchases journal? Explain.

c. If TWE, Inc. were in the business of providing haircuts to its customers instead of computer hardware, which of the five journals in RTR (checks, deposits, payables, receivables, or general) would you expect to be used the least throughout the *entire* accounting period? Explain.

6. What is the purpose of an invoice? Who prepares the invoice?

7. If TWE, Inc. used the perpetual instead of the periodic inventory method:

a. How would the accounts used in payables transactions d and h in exercise 1 have differed from what you entered during the exercise?

b. How would the accounts used in receivables transaction d in exercise 1 have differed from what you entered during the exercise?

8. If TWE, Inc. used the "net" method of handling cash discounts offered on sales and offered each of its customers the terms 2/10, net 30, how would the receivables transaction d in exercise 1 have differed from what you entered during the exercise?

3

Entering Cash
Transactions

**Ready-to-Run
General Ledger Structure**

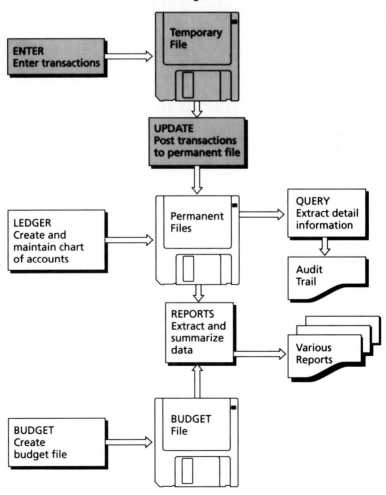

Objectives

In Lab 3, you will learn how to:

- Enter checks in RTR

- Enter deposits in RTR

Tom Walton is ready for you to enter the checks that have been written and the deposits that have been made to the checking account in January. He has provided you with the information you need to record the checks and deposits. You will enter several different types of checks and deposits in the lab activity. In the exercises you will complete the entry of January's checks and deposits for Walton Electronics.

Entering Checks

Load RTR and proceed to the Journal Selection menu as you did in Lab 2.

Entering a Check with One Debit and No Discount

The first check Tom wrote in January paid for supplies he received in December from J. M. Supply. Check number 1553 was written in the amount of $422 on January 2, 1992. The invoice from J. M. Supply was number B3399 for $422. The terms were net 15 and Tom paid it within the time allowed.

You decide that the following debits and credits should be made:

Debit Accounts Payable (#200) $422

Credit Cash in Bank (#100) $422

You are now ready to record this check in RTR.

Select: **Checks**

You should now see the screen shown in Figure 3-1. The entry screen is similar to those you used in Lab 2. The left side is labeled PURCHASE(S) and the right side is labeled CHECK. The label on the left side is somewhat misleading, because in some cases you are paying off accounts payable for previously recorded purchases. When you record payment for these items, the debit must go to Accounts Payable, not Purchases. Continue to consider the left side of the screen the debit side and the right side the credit side.

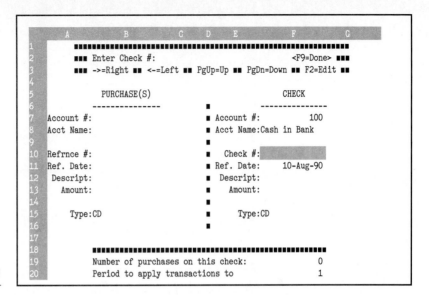

```
       A           B         C       D     E              F               G
 1  ■■■■■■■■■■■■■■■■■■■■■■■■■■■■■■■■■■■■■■■■■■■■■■■■■■■■■■■■■■■■■■■■
 2    ■■■ Enter Check #:                           <F9=Done> ■■■
 3    ■■■ ->=Right ■■ <-=Left ■■ PgUp=Up ■■ PgDn=Down ■■ F2=Edit ■■
 4
 5          PURCHASE(S)                      CHECK
 6          ---------------       ■         ---------------
 7  Account #:                    ■  Account #:            100
 8  Acct Name:                    ■  Acct Name:Cash in Bank
 9                                ■
10  Refrnce #:                    ■   Check #:▓▓▓▓▓▓▓▓▓▓▓▓
11  Ref. Date:                    ■   Ref. Date:      10-Aug-90
12   Descript:                    ■    Descript:
13     Amount:                    ■      Amount:
14                                ■
15       Type:CD                  ■         Type:CD
16                                ■
17
18     ■■■■■■■■■■■■■■■■■■■■■■■■■■■■■■■■■■■■■■■■■■■■■■■■
19       Number of purchases on this check:          0
20       Period to apply transactions to             1
```

Figure 3-1

You enter checks in the same way as you enter payables. The amount of the check on the right side of the screen is the total of the amounts entered as debits on the left side of the screen. Anything subtracted, such as a discount on a purchase, must be entered as a negative amount on the left side of the screen.

The reference number feature in RTR lets you provide additional audit trail information when you record a transaction. For example, when you enter checks in this lab, record the check number as the reference number for the right side of the transaction. If you are paying a payable, enter the number of the invoice you are paying as the reference number on the left side. These reference numbers will appear on the detail listing for the Accounts Payable account, providing you or Tom Walton with information regarding which invoice was paid and on which check number. Since Tom does not maintain a subsidiary record of Accounts Payable, this information can help him or his accountant determine which bills are outstanding. The audit trail is discussed in more detail in Lab 4.

The Type line on the screen contains the initials CD for Cash Disbursements, which is the journal designation.

Follow these steps to enter this check:

Type: **1553**
Press: ⏎
Type: **1/2/92**
Press: ⏎
Type: **J. M. SUPPLY**
Press: ⏎

The cell pointer should now be located in cell B7 on the left side of the screen.

Type: **200**
Press: ⏎
Type: **B3395**
Press: ⏎
Press: ⏎ ⏎
Type: **422**
Press: ⏎

The screen should now look like Figure 3-2.

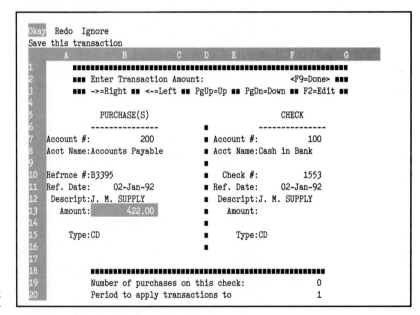

```
Okay   Redo  Ignore
Save this transaction
        A          B          C      D      E         F            G

 1     ■■■■■■■■■■■■■■■■■■■■■■■■■■■■■■■■■■■■■■■■■■■■■■■■■■■■■■■■■■■■■■
 2     ■■■ Enter Transaction Amount:                  <F9=Done> ■■■
 3     ■■■ ->=Right ■■ <-=Left ■■ PgUp=Up ■■ PgDn=Down ■■ F2=Edit ■■
 4
 5              PURCHASE(S)                            CHECK
 6            ---------------           ■           ---------------
 7     Account #:          200          ■  Account #:          100
 8     Acct Name:Accounts Payable       ■  Acct Name:Cash in Bank
 9                                      ■
10     Refrnce #:B3395                  ■    Check #:          1553
11     Ref. Date:     02-Jan-92         ■  Ref. Date:     02-Jan-92
12     Descript:J. M. SUPPLY            ■  Descript:J. M. SUPPLY
13       Amount:        422.00          ■    Amount:
14                                      ■
15       Type:CD                        ■    Type:CD
16                                      ■
17
18     ■■■■■■■■■■■■■■■■■■■■■■■■■■■■■■■■■■■■■■■■■■■■■■■■■■■■■■■■■■■■■■
19     Number of purchases on this check:                  0
20     Period to apply transactions to                     1
```

Figure 3-2

If it doesn't, select **R**edo and make corrections. When the entry is correct,

Select: **O**kay
Select: **D**one   to accept the entry as complete
Select: **A**nother   to tell RTR you want to add another check

Entering a Check for a Payable with a Discount

The second check written in January paid for merchandise received and recorded in December from Rebco Computer. Check number 1554 was written in the amount of $4,724 on January 3. The invoice from Rebco Computer was number Y2095 for $4,820. The terms were 2/10, net 30, so Tom is paying it within the discount period. The invoice price included $20 in postage charges that Tom cannot include when computing the cash discount. Remember that Tom uses the gross method of recording purchases.

You decide that the following debits and credits should be made:

Debit Accounts Payable (#200)	$4,820	
Credit Cash in Bank (#100)		$4,724
Credit Purchases Discounts (#515)		$ 96

Since the check number is numeric, RTR automatically advances the check number to 1554. To accept this check number,

Press: ⏎

Enter the right side of the screen and the debit to Accounts Payable with the following steps:

Type: **1/3/92**
Press: ⏎
Type: **REBCO COMPUTER**
Press: ⏎
Type: **200**
Press: ⏎
Type: **Y2095**
Press: ⏎
Press: ⏎ ⏎
Type: **4820**
Press: ⏎

Your screen should look like Figure 3-3.

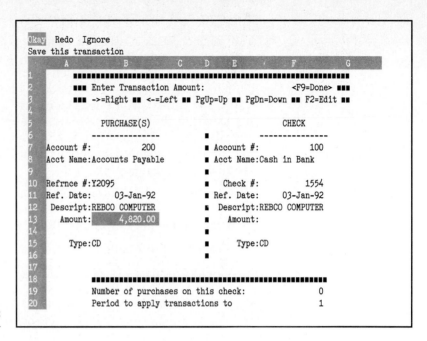

```
Okay  Redo  Ignore
Save this transaction
        A         B         C      D       E          F            G
1  ■■■■■■■■■■■■■■■■■■■■■■■■■■■■■■■■■■■■■■■■■■■■■■■■■■■■■■■■■■■■■■■
2    ■■■ Enter Transaction Amount:                   <F9=Done> ■■■
3    ■■■ ->=Right ■■ <-=Left ■■ PgUp=Up ■■ PgDn=Down ■■ F2=Edit ■■
4
5            PURCHASE(S)                           CHECK
6        ----------------          ■          ----------------
7  Account #:           200        ■  Account #:           100
8  Acct Name:Accounts Payable      ■  Acct Name:Cash in Bank
9                                  ■
10 Refrnce #:Y2095                 ■   Check #:            1554
11 Ref. Date:    03-Jan-92         ■  Ref. Date:    03-Jan-92
12  Descript:REBCO COMPUTER        ■   Descript:REBCO COMPUTER
13    Amount:        4,820.00      ■     Amount:
14                                 ■
15       Type:CD                   ■        Type:CD
16                                 ■
17
18 ■■■■■■■■■■■■■■■■■■■■■■■■■■■■■■■■■■■■■■■■■■■■■■■■■■■■■■■■■■■■
19 Number of purchases on this check:              0
20 Period to apply transactions to                 1
```

Figure 3-3

If it does,

Select: **Okay**

Otherwise, select **R**edo and make corrections. Then select **Okay**.

The check amount appears on the screen as $4,820. But the check was written for $4,724. You must record the discount of $96. To add another entry to the left side of the screen,

Select: **Add**

The cell pointer is located at B7 for the account number.

Type: **515**
Press: ⏎
Press: ⏎ ⏎ ⏎
Type: **−96**
Press: ⏎

Did you remember to put the minus sign (−) in front of the amount? Your screen should look like Figure 3-4.

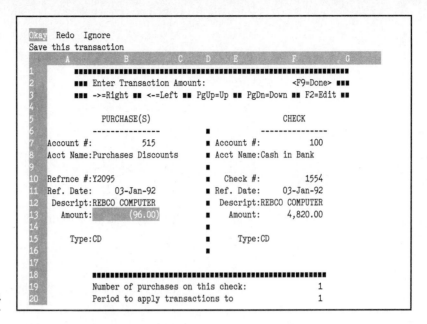

```
Okay  Redo  Ignore
Save this transaction
         A        B         C      D      E        F         G
1  ■■■■■■■■■■■■■■■■■■■■■■■■■■■■■■■■■■■■■■■■■■■■■■■■■■■■■■■
2     ■■■ Enter Transaction Amount:            <F9=Done> ■■■
3     ■■■ ->=Right ■■ <-=Left ■■ PgUp=Up ■■ PgDn=Down ■■ F2=Edit ■■

5           PURCHASE(S)                         CHECK
6           ---------------        ■            ---------------
7  Account #:            515       ■ Account #:            100
8  Acct Name:Purchases Discounts   ■ Acct Name:Cash in Bank
9                                  ■
10 Refrnce #:Y2095                 ■   Check #:           1554
11 Ref. Date:    03-Jan-92         ■ Ref. Date:    03-Jan-92
12  Descript:REBCO COMPUTER        ■  Descript:REBCO COMPUTER
13    Amount:        (96.00)       ■    Amount:      4,820.00
14                                 ■
15      Type:CD                    ■      Type:CD
16                                 ■
17
18  ■■■■■■■■■■■■■■■■■■■■■■■■■■■■■■■■■■■■■■■■■■■■■■■■■■■■■■
19     Number of purchases on this check:           1
20     Period to apply transactions to              1
```

Figure 3-4

If it does,

Select: **Okay**

Notice that the check now totals the correct amount, $4,724.

Select: **D**one

You will record a third check, so

Select: **A**nother

Entering a Check for an Item Expensed Immediately

Check number 1555 was written on January 3 for $300 to the Postmaster to fill the postage meter. For this check, you do not enter a reference number on the left side of the screen. The supporting requisition for the postage, with Tom's signature as authorization, will be attached to a copy of the check.

Analyzing this transaction yields the following journal entry:

Debit Postage Expense (#730) $300

Credit Cash in Bank (#100) $300

Record the check as follows:

Press: 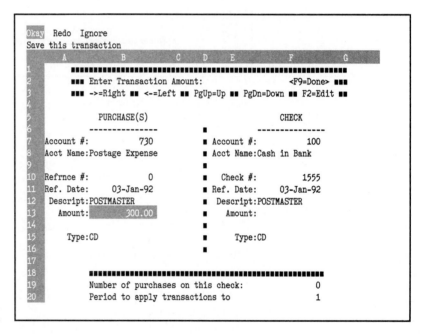 ⏎ to accept the default check number
Press: ⏎ because the date is the same as the previous check
Type: **POSTMASTER**
Press: ⏎

On the left side of the screen,

Type: **730**
Press: ⏎
Press: ⏎ ⏎ ⏎
Type: **300**
Press: ⏎

Your screen should look like Figure 3-5.

```
 Okay  Redo  Ignore
Save this transaction
      A        B         C      D    E        F            G
 1  ████████████████████████████████████████████████████████
 2  ███ Enter Transaction Amount:              <F9=Done> ███
 3  ███ ->=Right ██ <-=Left ██ PgUp=Up ██ PgDn=Down ██ F2=Edit ██
 4
 5          PURCHASE(S)                         CHECK
 6         ---------------       █           ---------------
 7  Account #:           730     █  Account #:           100
 8  Acct Name:Postage Expense    █  Acct Name:Cash in Bank
 9                               █
10  Refrnce #:             0     █    Check #:          1555
11  Ref. Date:     03-Jan-92     █  Ref. Date:     03-Jan-92
12  Descript:POSTMASTER          █  Descript:POSTMASTER
13    Amount:        300.00      █    Amount:
14                               █
15    Type:CD                    █    Type:CD
16                               █
17
18  ████████████████████████████████████████████████████
19  Number of purchases on this check:            0
20  Period to apply transactions to              1
```

Figure 3-5

If it does,

Select: **O**kay
Select: **D**one — since there is only one debit on this check
Select: **A**nother — to enter another check

Entering a Check with Multiple Debits

Every Monday, Tom pays his three employees for the previous week. He has made arrangements with the local bank for the bank to deposit the money directly into their accounts, if he brings the bank a check for the total. On Monday, January 6, he writes check number 1556 to Second City Bank for $1,435. Of this check, $550 is for office salaries and $885 is for sales salaries.

Analyzing this transaction yields the following journal entry:

Debit Sales Salaries Expense (#600)	$ 885	
Debit Office Salaries Expense (#700)	$ 550	
Credit Cash in Bank (#100)		$1,435

Record the check as follows:

Press: ⏎
Type: **1/6/92**
Press: ⏎
Type: **SECOND CITY BANK**
Press: ⏎

On the left side of the screen,

Type: **600**
Press: ⏎
Press: ⏎ (There is no reference for the left side.)
Press: ⏎ ⏎
Type: **885**
Press: ⏎

Examine the screen. If you made an error, select **R**edo and correct it. Otherwise,

Select: **Okay**
Select: **Add**   to add a second debit to the screen

The cell pointer should jump to the top of the left side.

Type: **700**
Press: ⏎
Press: ⏎ ⏎ ⏎
Type: **550**
Press: ⏎

Your screen should look like Figure 3-6.

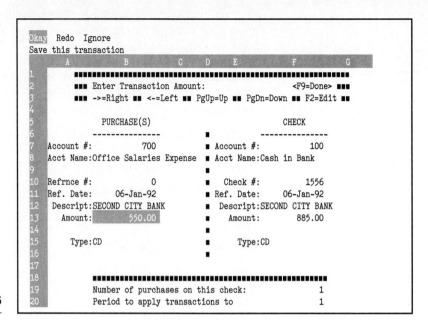

```
Okay   Redo  Ignore
Save this transaction
       A          B          C      D      E          F          G
1      ■■■■■■■■■■■■■■■■■■■■■■■■■■■■■■■■■■■■■■■■■■■■■■■■■■■■■■■■■■■■
2      ■■■ Enter Transaction Amount:                 <F9=Done> ■■■
3      ■■■ ->=Right ■■ <-=Left ■■ PgUp=Up ■■ PgDn=Down ■■ F2=Edit ■■
4
5              PURCHASE(S)                           CHECK
6              ---------------        ■              ---------------
7      Account #:          700        ■ Account #:          100
8      Acct Name:Office Salaries Expense ■ Acct Name:Cash in Bank
9                                     ■
10     Refrnce #:            0        ■   Check #:          1556
11     Ref. Date:    06-Jan-92        ■ Ref. Date:    06-Jan-92
12      Descript:SECOND CITY BANK     ■  Descript:SECOND CITY BANK
13        Amount:        550.00       ■     Amount:        885.00
14                                     ■
15         Type:CD                     ■       Type:CD
16                                     ■
17
18     ■■■■■■■■■■■■■■■■■■■■■■■■■■■■■■■■■■■■■■■■■■■■■■■■■■■■■■■■■
19     Number of purchases on this check:                 1
20     Period to apply transactions to                    1
```

Figure 3-6

If it does,

Select: **O**kay

Select: **D**one   to indicate that you have finished this transaction

You have finished entering checks.

Select: **D**one

Entering Cash Receipts

You are ready to enter cash receipts for Walton Electronics.

Select: **E**nter

From the Journal Selection menu, choose the Deposits command.

Select: **D**eposits

The blank deposits entry screen is shown in Figure 3-7.

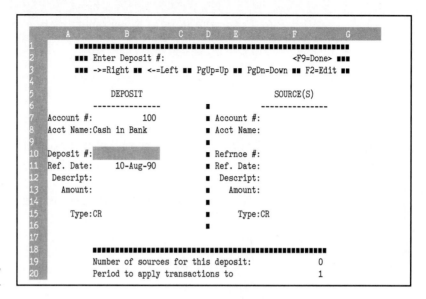

```
         A          B          C      D     E            F              G
1   ■■■■■■■■■■■■■■■■■■■■■■■■■■■■■■■■■■■■■■■■■■■■■■■■■■■■■■■■■■■■■■■■■
2   ■■■ Enter Deposit #:                              <F9=Done> ■■■
3   ■■■ ->=Right ■■ <-=Left ■■ PgUp=Up ■■ PgDn=Down ■■ F2=Edit ■■
4
5            DEPOSIT                            SOURCE(S)
6        ----------------        ■         ----------------
7   Account #:          100      ■  Account #:
8   Acct Name:Cash in Bank       ■  Acct Name:
9                                ■
10  Deposit #:                   ■  Refrnce #:
11  Ref. Date:     10-Aug-90     ■  Ref. Date:
12   Descript:                   ■   Descript:
13    Amount:                    ■    Amount:
14                               ■
15      Type:CR                  ■      Type:CR
16                               ■
17                               ■
18       ■■■■■■■■■■■■■■■■■■■■■■■■■■■■■■■■■■■■■■■■■■■■■■■■■
19       Number of sources for this deposit:        0
20       Period to apply transactions to            1
```

Figure 3-7

The Cash in Bank account is automatically entered as the debit account. The left side of the screen is labeled DEPOSIT and the right side is labeled SOURCE(S). The total of the items on the right side of the screen is automatically entered as the total on the left side. Thus, if you have a subtraction from a credit, such as a discount taken by a customer, it must be entered on the right side as a negative amount. The journal type here is CR, which stands for cash receipts.

Entering a Cash Receipt with No Discount

On January 3, Walton Electronics received a check from Erin's Boutique for $3,200. The invoice paid is number 2026, which was dated December 5, so the discount period was past. (Remember, Tom offers terms of 2/10, net 30 on all invoices.)

Analyzing this transaction yields the following entry:

Debit Cash in Bank (#100) $3,200

Credit Accounts Receivable (#110) $3,200

Tom uses a five-digit reference number for deposits. The first two digits are the year, and the last three digits are a consecutive number beginning with 001. Thus, the first deposit for 1992 is numbered 92001.

Type:	**92001**
Press:	⏎

Enter the date and customer name as follows:

Type:	**1/3/92**
Press:	⏎
Type:	**ERIN'S BOUTIQUE**
Press:	⏎

The cell pointer should now be located at cell F7 at the top of the right side.

Type:	**110**
Press:	⏎

The invoice number being paid is the reference number for a collection on accounts receivable:

Type:	**2026**
Press:	⏎
Press:	⏎ ⏎
Type:	**3200**
Press:	⏎

The screen should look like Figure 3-8. As before, if you need to make corrections, select **R**edo and do so.

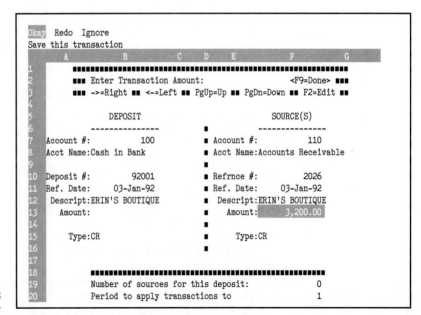

```
Okay  Redo  Ignore
Save this transaction
         A        B         C      D      E          F          G
 1      ■■■■■■■■■■■■■■■■■■■■■■■■■■■■■■■■■■■■■■■■■■■■■■■■■■■■■■■■
 2       ■■■ Enter Transaction Amount:                 <F9=Done> ■■■
 3       ■■■ ->=Right ■■ <-=Left ■■ PgUp=Up ■■ PgDn=Down ■■ F2=Edit ■■
 4
 5               DEPOSIT                         SOURCE(S)
 6              ---------------          ■      ---------------
 7      Account #:          100          ■  Account #:          110
 8      Acct Name:Cash in Bank           ■  Acct Name:Accounts Receivable
 9                                       ■
10      Deposit #:        92001          ■  Refrnce #:         2026
11      Ref. Date:    03-Jan-92          ■  Ref. Date:    03-Jan-92
12       Descript:ERIN'S BOUTIQUE        ■   Descript:ERIN'S BOUTIQUE
13         Amount:                       ■     Amount:     3,200.00
14                                       ■
15          Type:CR                      ■     Type:CR
16                                       ■
17                                       ■
18      ■■■■■■■■■■■■■■■■■■■■■■■■■■■■■■■■■■■■■■■■■■■■■■■■■■■■■■■■
19      Number of sources for this deposit:              0
20      Period to apply transactions to                  1
```

Figure 3-8

When everything is okay,

Select: **Okay**

Since there is not another entry for the right side of this deposit,

Select: **Done**

To enter the next deposit,

Select: **Another**

Entering a Cash Receipt with a Discount

On January 6, Walton Electronics received a check from Granny's Home Cooking for $6,835. This represented payment for invoice number 2030, dated December 28, 1991. The invoice total was $6,970 and included a delivery charge of $220. Granny's paid within the discount period and took a 2% discount on the merchandise total of $6,500. The discount allowed is $135.

Analyzing this transaction yields the following entry:

Debit Cash in Bank (#100)	$6,835	
Debit Sales Discounts (#410)	$ 135	
Credit Accounts Receivable (#110)		$6,970

Deposit reference numbers are numeric; they advance automatically. Accept the reference number 92002.

Press: ⏎
Type: **1/6/92**
Press: ⏎
Type: **GRANNY'S HOME COOKING**
Press: ⏎

The first item on the right side should be the credit to Accounts Receivable.

Type: **110**
Press: ⏎
Type: **2030**
Press: ⏎
Press: ⏎ ⏎
Type: **6970**
Press: ⏎

The screen should look like Figure 3-9.

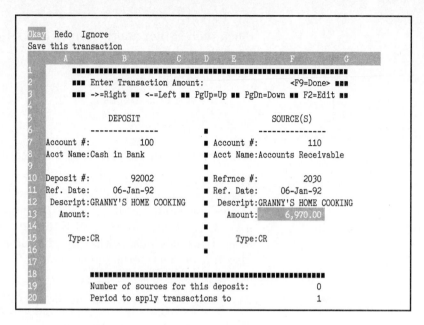

Figure 3-9

Select: **O**kay   to confirm that the screen is okay
Select: **A**dd   to add another entry to the right side of
                    this deposit screen

Record the discount on the right side. Remember to enter the
amount as a negative number.

Type: **410**
Press: ⏎
Press: ⏎ ⏎ ⏎
Type: **– 135**
Press: ⏎

The screen should look like Figure 3-10.

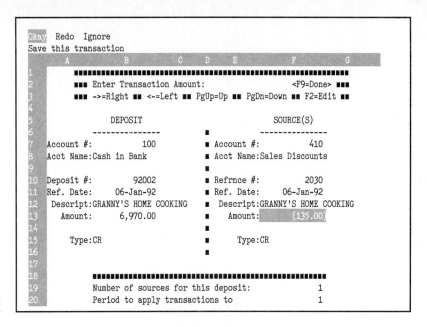

```
Okay  Redo  Ignore
Save this transaction
        A        B        C      D      E        F        G
 1  ■■■■■■■■■■■■■■■■■■■■■■■■■■■■■■■■■■■■■■■■■■■■■■■■■■■■■■
 2     ■■■ Enter Transaction Amount:              <F9=Done> ■■■
 3     ■■■ ->=Right ■■ <-=Left ■■ PgUp=Up ■■ PgDn=Down ■■ F2=Edit ■■
 4
 5             DEPOSIT                         SOURCE(S)
 6         ---------------          ■       ---------------
 7  Account #:           100        ■ Account #:           410
 8  Acct Name:Cash in Bank          ■ Acct Name:Sales Discounts
 9                                  ■
10  Deposit #:         92002        ■ Refrnce #:          2030
11  Ref. Date:    06-Jan-92         ■ Ref. Date:    06-Jan-92
12   Descript:GRANNY'S HOME COOKING ■  Descript:GRANNY'S HOME COOKING
13    Amount:       6,970.00        ■    Amount:        (135.00)
14                                  ■
15      Type:CR                     ■      Type:CR
16                                  ■
17                                  ■
18  ■■■■■■■■■■■■■■■■■■■■■■■■■■■■■■■■■■■■■■■■■■■■■■■■■■■■■■
19     Number of sources for this deposit:          1
20     Period to apply transactions to              1
```

Figure 3-10

Select: **O**kay   to confirm that the screen is okay

Select: **D**one   to indicate you are finished with this deposit

The net amount of the deposit on the left side of the screen should be the amount received from Granny's Home Cooking.

Select: **A**nother   to enter another deposit

Entering a Cash Sale

On January 8, Walton Electronics made a cash sale to Linda's Antiques. Tom uses a different invoice number sequence for cash sales. The invoice number is 1342. Linda gave him a check for the amount of the invoice, which was $6,110. She picked up the merchandise, so there are no delivery charges.

Analyzing this transaction yields the following entry:

Debit Cash in Bank (#100) $6,110

Credit Sales (#400) $6,110

Enter this transaction as follows:

Press:	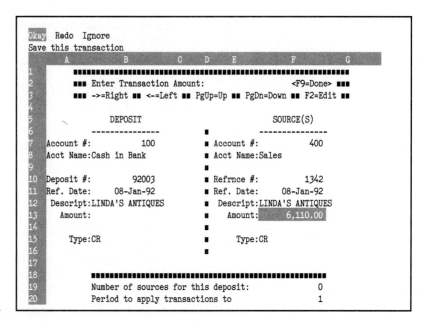 ↵
Type:	**1/8/92**
Press:	↵
Type:	**LINDA'S ANTIQUES**
Press:	↵
Type:	**400**
Press:	↵
Type:	**1342**
Press:	↵
Press:	↵ ↵
Type:	**6110**
Press:	↵

The screen should look like Figure 3-11.

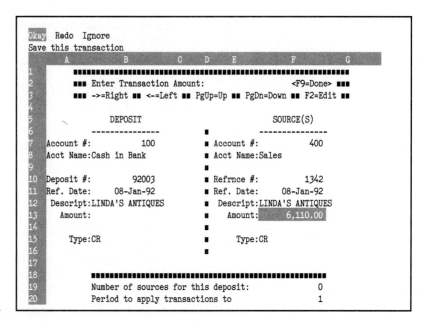

Figure 3-11

```
Okay  Redo  Ignore
Save this transaction
          A          B          C     D     E         F          G
1
2      ■■■ Enter Transaction Amount:                  <F9=Done> ■■■
3      ■■■ ->=Right ■■ <-=Left ■■ PgUp=Up ■■ PgDn=Down ■■ F2=Edit ■■
4
5              DEPOSIT                           SOURCE(S)
6            ---------------         ■         ---------------
7  Account #:           100          ■ Account #:           400
8  Acct Name:Cash in Bank            ■ Acct Name:Sales
9                                    ■
10 Deposit #:         92003          ■ Refrnce #:          1342
11 Ref. Date:      08-Jan-92         ■ Ref. Date:      08-Jan-92
12  Descript:LINDA'S ANTIQUES        ■  Descript:LINDA'S ANTIQUES
13    Amount:                        ■    Amount:       6,110.00
14                                   ■
15     Type:CR                       ■     Type:CR
16                                   ■
17
18      ■■■■■■■■■■■■■■■■■■■■■■■■■■■■■■■■■■■■■■■■■■■■■■■■■
19      Number of sources for this deposit:          0
20      Period to apply transactions to             1
```

Select:	**O**kay	if the screen looks okay
Select:	**D**one	to indicate you are finished recording this deposit

You are now finished entering cash receipts.

Select:	**D**one

Printing and Editing Cash Transactions

As you did in Lab 2, print a copy of the cash transactions you have just entered. Use the Print command from the Enter menu.

Your printed list should look like Figure 3-12. If you need to correct any of your entries, use the Fix command from the Enter menu.

Walton Electronics		Unposted GL Transactions				29-Sep-90 - Page 1
	1 <- Period to be posted					
Acc	#	Description	Ref #	Ref Date	SJ	Transaction
	100	J. M. SUPPLY	1553	02-Jan-92	CD	(422.00)
	200	J. M. SUPPLY	B3395/1553	02-Jan-92	CD	422.00
	100	REBCO COMPUTER	1554	03-Jan-92	CD	(4,724.00)
	515	REBCO COMPUTER	Y2095/1554	03-Jan-92	CD	(96.00)
	200	REBCO COMPUTER	Y2095/1554	03-Jan-92	CD	4,820.00
	100	POSTMASTER	1555	03-Jan-92	CD	(300.00)
	730	POSTMASTER	0/1555	03-Jan-92	CD	300.00
	100	SECOND CITY BANK	1556	06-Jan-92	CD	(1,435.00)
	700	SECOND CITY BANK	0/1556	06-Jan-92	CD	550.00
	600	SECOND CITY BANK	0/1556	06-Jan-92	CD	885.00
	100	ERIN'S BOUTIQUE	92001	03-Jan-92	CR	3,200.00
	110	ERIN'S BOUTIQUE	2026/92001	03-Jan-92	CR	(3,200.00)
	100	GRANNY'S HOME COOKING	92002	06-Jan-92	CR	6,835.00
	410	GRANNY'S HOME COOKING	2030/92002	06-Jan-92	CR	135.00
	110	GRANNY'S HOME COOKING	2030/92002	06-Jan-92	CR	(6,970.00)
	100	LINDA'S ANTIQUES	92003	08-Jan-92	CR	6,110.00
	400	LINDA'S ANTIQUES	1342/92003	08-Jan-92	CR	(6,110.00)

Figure 3-12

When you are sure that your entries are ready to post, save them by using the Save command from the Enter menu.

Posting Cash Transactions

You are ready to post the cash transactions. You should be looking at the RTR Main menu. Select the GL command to return to the General Ledger menu, and then select the Update command. Use the same procedure you used at the end of Lab 2 to post and print out a copy of the posting. The Cash in Bank balance in the Period after Postings column should be $9,264.00.

Exercises

Walton Electronics

1. Record the following transactions for Walton Electronics
   for the month of January, 1992. If no reference is given
   for the left side of the screen for checks or the right side
   of the screen for deposits, bypass that cell.

Checks

a. Check number 1557, dated 1/9/92, to Carron
   Peripherals for invoice number HK4800-79 dated
   12/31/91. The invoice amount is $9,195. Terms are
   2/10, net 30. The invoice includes $195 of freight
   charges. The check amount is $9,015. The cash dis-
   count is $180.

b. Check number 1558, dated 1/9/92, to Venus Systems
   for invoice number QZ74RP dated 12/31/91. The invoice
   amount is $8,600. Terms are 2/10, net 30. A deduction
   was taken for the $500 of merchandise returned. The
   check amount is $7,938. The cash discount is $162.
   (Note: Do not record the return on this check. You
   already recorded a debit memo for that in Lab 2. The
   debit to accounts payable should be for the balance due.)

c. Check number 1559, dated 1/10/92, to Rebco Computer
   for invoice number Z4928 recorded in Lab 2. The check
   amount is $4,990. The cash discount is $100.

d. Check number 1560, dated 1/13/92, for salaries. Record
   this check the same way you recorded check number
   1556 in the lab activity. It is for the same amount.

e. Check number 1561, dated 1/15/92, to Lodico Communications for invoice number 6833 dated 12/20/91. The
   invoice amount is $693, and it was properly recorded
   as a payable in December. Terms are net 15 days. The
   check amount is $693.

f. Check number 1562, dated 1/15/92, to Linda's Antiques
   for a return of defective merchandise from the cash
   sale on 1/8/92. The check amount is $550.

g. Check number 1563, dated 1/16/92, to Jason's Office Supplies for supplies purchased that day. The check amount is $1,095. (Debit Supplies on Hand.)

h. Check number 1564, dated 1/17/92, to Tom Walton for a personal withdrawal. The check amount is $1,800.

i. Check number 1565, dated 1/20/92, for salaries. See check number 1560 above. Again, the amount is the same.

j. Check number 1566, dated 1/23/92, to Carron Peripherals for invoice number HK4821-86 recorded in exercise 1 of Lab 2. Terms are 2/10, net 30. The check amount is $11,385. The cash discount is $217.

k. Check number 11567, dated 1/24/92, to City Power Company for utilities for the month of January. The check amount is $489.

l. Check number 1568, dated 1/27/92, for salaries. See check number 1560 and number 1565 above. The amount is the same.

m. Check number 1569, dated 1/28/92, to We-Haul-It for a statement received for delivery charges during the month of December. The check amount is $320. This was properly included in Accounts Payable in December. Use "STMT" for the reference on the left side of the entry screen.

n. Check number 1570, dated 1/30/92, to Tom Walton for a personal withdrawal. The check amount is $1,800.

o. Check number 1571, dated 1/31/92, to Local Phone Company for telephone charges for the month of January. The check amount is $257.

p. Because of the amount of cash on hand, Tom Walton decided to pay $2,000 against the note for the delivery truck on January 31. Check number 1572 is dated 1/31/92 to Del's Motors. The check amount is $2,000.

Deposits

a. Deposit number 92004 on 1/9/92 from Jim's Fitness Clinic for invoice number 2034, dated 12/31/91, in the amount of $9,450. The cash received is $9,261. The cash discount is $189.

b. Deposit number 92005 on 1/10/92 from Excellent Hardware for invoice number 2035, dated 12/31/91, in the amount of $11,420. In Lab 2, you entered a $600 merchandise return, which is deducted from this invoice amount. The invoice included $320 of freight charges. The cash received is $10,295. The cash discount is $525.

c. Deposit number 92006 on 1/13/92 from Paul's Hardware for a cash sale on invoice number 1343 in the amount of $825.

d. Deposit number 92007 on 1/16/92 from Randy's Video Stop for invoice number 2036, dated 1/6/92 (and recorded in Lab 2), in the amount of $5,300. The cash received is $5,194. The cash discount is $106.

e. Deposit number 92008 on 1/20/92 from A-1 Grocers for invoice number 2028, dated 12/20/91, in the amount of $5,400. (The invoice was properly recorded as a receivable at the end of December.)

f. Deposit number 92009 on 1/23/92 from Bob's Auto Repair for Invoice number 2029, dated 12/22/91, in the amount of $1,840 and for invoice number 2038, dated 1/13/92, in the amount of $2,650. (Invoice number 2029 was properly recorded as a receivable at the end of December.) The cash received is $4,437. The cash discount is $53. Record a separate entry on the right side of the screen for each of the two invoices, using the appropriate reference for each one.

g. Deposit number 92010 on 1/27/92 from Jim's Fitness Clinic for invoice number 2039, dated 1/16/92, in the amount of $5,980. The invoice included $180 for freight. Jim deducted $150 for merchandise not received. The cash received is $5,717. The cash discount is $113. (The exercises in Lab 2 included a credit memo for the $150, which was issued on 1/31/92. Do not record it twice! The credit to Accounts Receivable should be for the invoice amount less the deduction for the return.)

h. Deposit number 92011 on 1/30/92 from Carolyn's Country Store for a cash sale on invoice number 1344 in the amount of $1,128.

2. Print a listing of unposted transactions and make any necessary corrections.

3. Post the corrected transactions to the permanent period 1 file, printing a record of the posting at the same time.

   Check figures (Period after Postings column):

Cash in Bank	4,884.00
Accounts Receivable	(630.00)
Accounts Payable	(8,079.00)

TWE, INC.

1. Record the following transactions for TWE, Inc. for the month of January 1992. If no reference is given for the left side of the screen for checks or the right side of the screen for deposits, bypass that cell.

Checks

   a. Check number 1557, dated 1/7/92, for $1,000 to Tate's Security Systems, as a down payment on a $3,000 security system for the computer storage room. Tom Walton signs a note promising to make two equal monthly payments covering the remaining principal and accrued interest of 12% per year.

   b. Check number 1558, dated 1/9/92, to Carron Peripherals for invoice number HK4800-79 dated 12/31/91. The invoice amount is $9,195. Terms are 2/10, net 30. The invoice includes $195 of freight charges. The check amount is $9,015. The cash discount is $180.

   c. Check number 1559, dated 1/9/92, to Venus Systems for invoice number QZ74RP dated 12/31/91. The invoice amount is $8,600. Terms are 2/10, net 30. A deduction was taken for the $500 of merchandise returned. The check amount is $7,938. The cash discount is $162. (Note: Do not record the return on this check. You already recorded a debit memo for that in Lab 2. The debit to accounts payable should be for the original amount less the debit memo.)

   d. Check number 1560, dated 1/10/92, to Rebco Computer for invoice number Z4928 recorded in Lab 2. The check amount is $4,990. The cash discount is $100.

e. Check number 1561, dated 1/13/92, for salaries. Record this check the same way you recorded check number 1556 in the lab activity. It is for the same amount.

f. Check number 1562, dated 1/15/92, to Linda's Antiques for a return of defective merchandise from the cash sale on 1/8/92. The check amount is $550.

g. Check number 1563, dated 1/16/92, to Frank's Auto Repair for $700 in necessary repairs to ready the used truck, purchased yesterday, for use by TWE, Inc.

h. Check number 1564, dated 1/21/92, for $2,000 to Tom Walton as payment of the cash dividends declared January 12.

i. Check number 1565, dated 1/23/92, for salaries. See check number 1561 above. The amount is the same.

j. Check number 1566, dated 1/24/92, to City Power Company for utilities for the month of January. The check amount is $489.

k. Check number 1567, dated 1/27/92, for salaries. See check number 1561 and 1565 above. The amount is the same.

l. Check number 1568, dated 1/28/92, to We-Haul-It for a statement received for delivery charges during the month of December. The check amount is $320. This was properly included in Accounts Payable in December. Use "STMT" for the reference on the left side of the entry screen.

m. Check number 1569, dated 1/29/92, to Local Phone Company for telephone charges for the month of January. The check amount is $257.

n. Check number 1570, dated 1/30/92, to Carron Peripherals for invoice number HK4821-86 recorded in exercise 1 of Lab 2. Terms are 2/10, net 30, so the payment is not within the discount period. The check amount is $11,602.

o. Check number 1571, dated 1/30/92, to Today's Advertising Agency for invoice number QT3342 received 1/7/92 (recorded during Lab 2 activities) for $819 of magazine ads during January, and invoice number QT3395 received today, for $909 of magazine ads scheduled for February. The check amount is $1,728. Assume that TWE, Inc. records all advertising as a debit to advertising expense. Record a separate entry on the left side of the screen for each of the two invoices.

p. Because of the amount of cash on hand, Tom Walton decided to pay $2,000 against the note for the delivery truck on January 31. Check number 1572 is dated 1/31/92 to Del's Motors. The check amount is $2,000.

Deposits

a. Enter the deposits from Walton Electronics exercise 1.

b. Deposit number 920012 on 1/31/92 from Carmen's Candies in the amount of $425 as a deposit on $2,125 of specially ordered merchandise that will be shipped in a few weeks.

2. Print a listing of unposted transactions and make any necessary corrections.

3. Post the corrected transactions to the permanent period 1 file, printing a record of the posting at the same time.

Going Further

4. Indicate the appropriate journal (payables, receivables, checks, deposits, or general) and the accounts debited and credited for recording each of the following events.

a. TWE, Inc. issues 5% preferred stock with a par value of $50, for $50.20 per share. Six hundred shares are issued.

b. TWE, Inc. suffers $5,000 in uninsured damage to inventory from the first hurricane in the area in more than 20 years.

c. Tom Walton sells half of his shares of common stock to his son, Jim, for $5 per share.

d. TWE, Inc. sets up a $200 petty cash fund on the premises by cashing a check at the bank.

e. TWE, Inc. makes disbursements from the petty cash fund for $43 of supplies and $23 in postage.

f. TWE, Inc. replenishes petty cash by cashing a check for $66 at the bank.

g. TWE, Inc. purchases 1,000 shares of common stock from Jim for $5.10 per share. TWE, Inc. plans to reissue the shares in the future.

h. TWE, Inc. spends $142 on parts and labor to repair a computer it sold to Erin's Boutique. The repair is covered by a one-year warranty offered by the manufacturer. TWE, Inc. will be reimbursed by the manufacturer.

i. TWE, Inc. sells a $2,000 computer to Wendy Watkins. Wendy acquired the computer by charging the amount on her VISA credit card. The bank that issued the VISA card charges TWE, Inc. a fee of 0.5 percent of the amount of the charged sale.

j. TWE, Inc. pays the state the 6 percent sales tax it collected on all sales during the past three months.

k. TWE, Inc. appropriates $28,000 of retained earnings. The state restricts retained earnings for an amount equal to the balance in the treasury stock account.

l. TWE, Inc. declares a 10% stock dividend to be distributed in two weeks. The stock last sold for $28 per share.

5. If you have many transactions to enter into RTR, what order of entering those transactions would maximize the efficiency of the entering process? Explain.

4

Adjusting Entries and Audit Trail

**Ready-to-Run
General Ledger Structure**

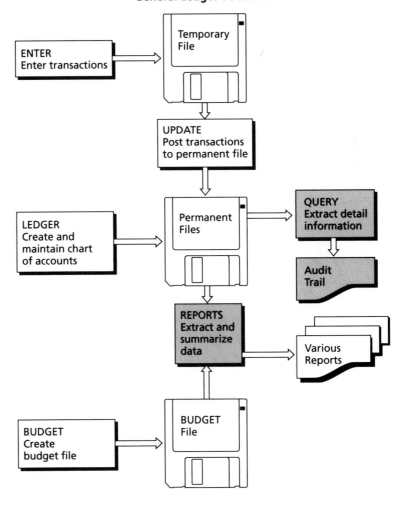

Objectives

In Lab 4, you will learn how to:

- Print a trial balance

- Prepare adjusting entries

- Print journals

- Print and use an audit trail

You have recorded all of the transactions for January in Labs 2 and 3. Tom Walton is ready to print financial statements for the end of January to see how Walton Electronics did. Before he can do this, however, he must make adjustments to the accounts to reflect the accrual basis. He will use a trial balance to determine what adjustments to make.

Using the Trial Balance

After recording and posting transactions, the next step in the accounting cycle is to print a trial balance to make sure that the debits and credits are equal.

In a computerized accounting system, printing a trial balance is simply a matter of telling the computer to print one. Ready-to-Run does not allow you to enter a transaction in which the debits do not equal the credits, so the trial balance is simply a visual assurance that your ledger is in balance. Keep the printed trial balance as part of the permanent record and audit trail.

The Reports Menu

To print a trial balance, first select the Reports command from the GL (General Ledger) menu.

Select: **R**eports

You see the menu shown in Figure 4-1.

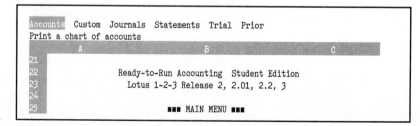

Figure 4-1

This menu has six options:

Accounts   Prints a chart of accounts. This printed chart
             of accounts is different from the one you
             printed when you edited the chart of
             accounts in Lab 1. This report lists the
             account number, the account title, and the
             current balance for each account.

Custom   Prints a custom report. This topic will be
             covered in Lab 8.

Journals   Prints listings of the transaction journals. This
             report is similar in appearance to the printout
             of unposted transactions and the printout of
             transactions to be posted, which you saw in
             Labs 2 and 3.

Statements   Prints standard financial statements. Printing
             the Income Statement and Balance Sheet will
             be covered in Lab 5. Graphing will be covered
             in Lab 6 and budgeting will be covered in
             Lab 7.

Trial   Prints a trial balance.

Prior   Returns to the previous menu, the GL menu.

To print a trial balance,

Select: **Trial**

You see the screen shown in Figure 4-2. The menu on this
screen appears on all the report options. It is a variation of the
Run/Quit/Break menu that you saw earlier, with an additional
command — Adjust. The Adjust command allows you to modify
the report that you are running, save the modifications, and
run the report using the Custom command from the Reports
menu. Customized reports will be covered in Lab 8.

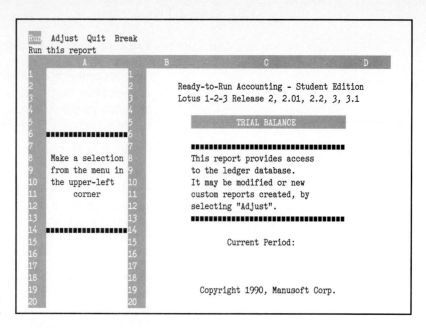

```
Run  Adjust  Quit  Break
Run this report
              A                    B              C                    D
1
2                               2     Ready-to-Run Accounting - Student Edition
3                               3     Lotus 1-2-3 Release 2, 2.01, 2.2, 3, 3.1
4
5                               5
6  ■■■■■■■■■■■■■■■■■■■■■■6            TRIAL BALANCE
7                               7
8   Make a selection 8     ■■■■■■■■■■■■■■■■■■■■■■■■■■■■■■■■■■■■■■
9   from the menu in 9     This report provides access
10  the upper-left   10    to the ledger database.
11      corner       11    It may be modified or new
12                   12    custom reports created, by
13                   13    selecting "Adjust".
14  ■■■■■■■■■■■■■■■■■■■■■■14    ■■■■■■■■■■■■■■■■■■■■■■■■■■■■■■■■■■■■■■
15                   15
16                   16          Current Period:
17                   17
18                   18
19                   19
20                   20        Copyright 1990, Manusoft Corp.
```

Figure 4-2

Another standard feature of the report screens is the vertical window. The left window provides instructions on how to proceed. For example, in Figure 4-2, the left window says: "Make a selection from the menu in the upper-left corner." The right window will display the report you run. Until you run the trial balance, the right window contains information about the report you selected, Trial Balance.

Run the Trial Balance

To run the trial balance report,

Select: **R**un

The following prompt appears:

Enter current period:

To run a trial balance for the first period.

Type: **1**
Press: ⏎

Ready-to-Run processes the trial balance for January. It takes some time to do this. During this time, several messages appear toward the bottom of the right window telling you what RTR is doing. When the processing is complete, you should see the screen shown in Figure 4-3. (If you are completing the TWE, Inc. case study, some of the accounts that appear in the right window will be different.)

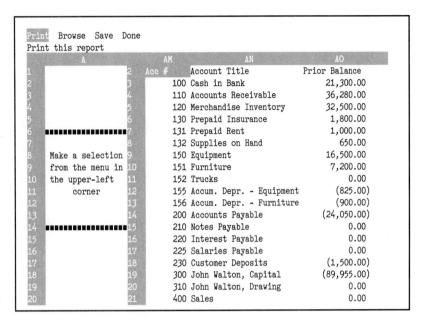

Figure 4-3

The menu you see on this screen is another standard menu that appears for all reports. It has four commands:

Print	Prints the report that appears in the right window.
Browse	Activates the arrow keys so you can look at the report on the screen.
Save	Saves the report to a Lotus 1-2-3 worksheet file. Advanced users can retrieve the worksheet in Lotus 1-2-3 and customize it.
Done	Returns to RTR Main menu.

Browse in the Report

Because of the limited size of the screen, you cannot see the entire report in the right window at one time. The expense accounts are out of sight at the bottom. Also, you cannot see the last three columns to the right: Debits, Credits, and Ending Balance.

The Browse command allows you to move around and look at all of the information in the report. To see how the Browse command works,

Select: **B**rowse

The cell pointer is located on the Acc # column head. The second and third lines of the control panel are blank, and the left window contains the instruction: ''Press the ENTER or ESC key when done.'' Use the arrow keys to move around in the browsing window.

Press: → → → ↓

The cell pointer should now be located in the Debits column for the Cash in Bank account. When you pressed → the third time, the window scrolled to the left, and the Acc # and Account Title columns disappeared from view.

When you look at the screen, you cannot tell the title of the account for the row the cell pointer is on. This is a major disadvantage of using the Browse command if you want to look at a report that takes up as many columns as the trial balance. Use the Browse command to review one or two account balances without printing out the entire report. However, before making adjusting entries, you should print out the entire trial balance.

Press: → → →

When you pressed → the first time, the cell pointer moved to the Credits column; the second time the cell pointer moved to the Ending Balance column. The third time, however, the cell pointer moved to the Acc # column for the next row down. You can't move outside the report using the arrow keys.

Use the arrow keys some more to get a sense of how they work in the browsing screen. The only keys you can use on this screen are →, ←, ↑, ↓, HOME, and END. If you press another key, like TAB or PGDN, you will hear a beep.

When you finish moving around the report, follow the instructions in the left window.

Press: ↵

Print the Trial Balance

The menu shown in Figure 4-3 reappears. To print a copy of the trial balance,

Select: **P**rint

Make sure that your printer is turned on and that the paper is properly aligned.

You should see the menu shown in Figure 4-4. This is another menu that appears whenever you print a report. Choose Wide if you have a wide-carriage printer or Narrow if you have a narrow-carriage printer. If you are not sure, check with your instructor. If you are using a wide-carriage printer but are using paper that is 8½″ wide, choose the Narrow command. In most cases you will choose Narrow.

Select: **N**arrow or **W**ide

Figure 4-4

```
Wide   Narrow
Use a wide-carriage printer (132 columns or greater)
         A              AM              AN              AO
1                       2   Acc #    Account Title      Prior Balance
2                       3            100 Cash in Bank        21,300.00
3                       4            110 Accounts Receivable  36,280.00
4                       5            120 Merchandise Inventory 32,500.00
5                       6            130 Prepaid Insurance     1,800.00
```

You should now see the menu shown in Figure 4-5. This menu asks whether you want to print in condensed (smaller) print or in regular print. The third line of the control panel tells you how many pages it takes to print the report in each print size.

Figure 4-5

```
Condensed   Regular
Report will fit across 1 page(s)
         A              AM              AN              AO
1                       2   Acc #    Account Title      Prior Balance
2                       3            100 Cash in Bank        21,300.00
3                       4            110 Accounts Receivable  36,280.00
4                       5            120 Merchandise Inventory 32,500.00
```

Move the highlight to the Regular command. The message on line 3 indicates that the trial balance report will take two pages in regular print. In condensed print, it takes only one page. Print the trial balance on one page so you can see all of the information more easily.

Select: **C**ondensed

Your printout should look similar to Figure 4-6. (If you are completing the TWE, Inc. case study, your printout will differ slightly.)

Walton Electronics		TRIAL BALANCE			Period 1
Acc #	Account Title	Prior Balance	Debits	Credits	Ending Balance
100	Cash in Bank	21,300.00	58,402.00	53,518.00	26,184.00
110	Accounts Receivable	36,280.00	51,580.00	52,210.00	35,650.00
120	Merchandise Inventory	32,500.00	0.00	0.00	32,500.00
130	Prepaid Insurance	1,800.00	0.00	0.00	1,800.00
131	Prepaid Rent	1,000.00	0.00	0.00	1,000.00
132	Supplies on Hand	650.00	1,095.00	0.00	1,745.00
150	Equipment	16,500.00	0.00	0.00	16,500.00
151	Furniture	7,200.00	0.00	0.00	7,200.00
152	Trucks	0.00	4,800.00	0.00	4,800.00
155	Accum. Depr. - Equipment	(825.00)	0.00	0.00	(825.00)
156	Accum. Depr. - Furniture	(900.00)	0.00	0.00	(900.00)
200	Accounts Payable	(24,050.00)	40,992.00	49,071.00	(32,129.00)
210	Notes Payable	0.00	2,000.00	4,800.00	(2,800.00)
220	Interest Payable	0.00	0.00	0.00	0.00
225	Salaries Payable	0.00	0.00	0.00	0.00
230	Customer Deposits	(1,500.00)	0.00	0.00	(1,500.00)
300	Tom Walton, Capital	(89,955.00)	0.00	0.00	(89,955.00)
310	Tom Walton, Drawing	0.00	5,200.00	0.00	5,200.00
400	Sales	0.00	0.00	59,643.00	(59,643.00)
410	Sales Discounts	0.00	1,121.00	0.00	1,121.00
415	Sales Returns & Allowance	0.00	1,300.00	0.00	1,300.00
510	Purchases	0.00	45,800.00	1,600.00	44,200.00
515	Purchases Discounts	0.00	0.00	755.00	(755.00)
520	Purchases Returns & Allow	0.00	0.00	750.00	(750.00)
550	Freight-in	0.00	1,632.00	0.00	1,632.00
600	Sales Salaries Expense	0.00	3,540.00	0.00	3,540.00
610	Delivery Expense	0.00	262.00	0.00	262.00
620	Advertising Expense	0.00	819.00	0.00	819.00
700	Office Salaries Expense	0.00	2,200.00	0.00	2,200.00
705	Rent Expense	0.00	0.00	0.00	0.00
710	Supplies Expense	0.00	0.00	0.00	0.00
715	Insurance Expense	0.00	0.00	0.00	0.00
720	Utility Expense	0.00	489.00	0.00	489.00
725	Telephone Expense	0.00	815.00	0.00	815.00
730	Postage Expense	0.00	300.00	0.00	300.00
740	Depr. Exp. - Equipment	0.00	0.00	0.00	0.00
745	Depr. Exp. - Furniture	0.00	0.00	0.00	0.00
800	Interest Expense	0.00	0.00	0.00	0.00
		0.00	222,347.00	222,347.00	0.00

Figure 4-6

The printout is the same as the report you saw on the screen using the Browse command. It has six columns: Acc #, Account Title, Prior Balance, Debits, Credits, and Ending Balance. The information in these columns pertains only to period 1. The Prior Balance column contains the beginning balances you entered in Lab 1. The Debits and Credits columns reflect the transactions you entered in Labs 2 and 3. The Ending Balance column totals the Prior Balance, Debits, and Credits. Credit balances in the Prior Balance and Ending Balance columns are shown in parentheses. Do not think of these as negative numbers — the parentheses are used only to distinguish a credit balance from a debit balance.

The Debits and Credits columns are totaled to demonstrate that the entries for the period balance.

You have finished with the Trial Balance.

Select: **Done**

Preparing Adjusting Entries

According to generally accepted accounting principles, accounting financial statements must be prepared on an accrual basis. In a manual accounting system, you record the trial balance on a worksheet. Then you review the balances in each account and determine which adjustments to make for the accrual basis and temporarily record these adjustments on the worksheet. You can extend the worksheet balance in each account to the Income Statement or Balance Sheet columns. This way, you can prepare financial statements before you record adjusting entries in the journal, post them to the ledger, and take a new trial balance.

In RTR, adjusting entries must be prepared using the General Journal. As in most computerized systems, a worksheet is not used. The computer posts and prepares financial statements from the data you enter.

The computer cannot analyze and determine what adjustments must be made. You must review a printed trial balance and decide what adjustments to make. At this point, look over the trial balance. Can you identify accounts that should be adjusted before accrual basis statements are prepared? The rest of this lab and the exercises at the end guide you through the process of making these adjustments.

Adding Accounts to the Chart of Accounts

Sometimes when you review a trial balance you find that accounts must be added to the chart of accounts before an adjustment can be made. In a manual system, you add these accounts at the bottom of the worksheet. In a computerized system, you must add these accounts before you record the adjusting entries.

When Tom Walton purchased the truck, you added a Trucks account to Property, Plant, and Equipment. To record depreciation, you must create corresponding Accumulated Depreciation and Depreciation Expense accounts.

Tom wants to see a breakdown of the calculation of Cost of Goods Sold on the detailed income statement. Therefore, you must also establish accounts in the Cost of Sales section of the chart of accounts for beginning and ending inventory.

Beginning at the RTR Main menu,

Select: **GL**
Select: **Ledger**
Select: **Ledger**

Enter your password and choose **R**un; then choose **B**ackup and set the backup period to 20 minutes. If you save your data on diskette, be sure it is in drive A, then

Select: **Existing**

You should see the chart of accounts editing screen. Add the following accounts. Be sure to insert them so that the account numbers are in numerical order. If you insert an account in the wrong place, use DEL to delete it, then reenter it in the correct location.

Summary Heading	Acct. Number	Account Title
Accumulated Depreciation	157	Accum. Depr. – Trucks
Depreciation Expense	750	Depr. Exp. – Trucks
Cost of Sales	500	Beginning Inventory
Cost of Sales	590	Ending Inventory

To save your work, press ⌨F9 and choose the Save command. You should see the RTR Main menu again.

Entering Adjustments

You use the General Journal to enter adjustments. Select the appropriate commands to record entries in the General Journal using the Pairs command. Use a backup period of 20 minutes. The entries should be recorded in period 1.

When you review the trial balance, the first adjustment you should make involves Prepaid Insurance. The account had no activity in the month of January, but it did have a balance at the beginning of the month. A portion of the prepaid amount must have expired during January. The previous year's records show that Tom paid an annual premium of $2,400 on October 1. Thus, one month's expense is $200. Record that expense for January.

The Debit Side   On the debit side of the screen, select the Insurance Expense account:

Type: **715**
Press: ⌨

Tom wants to continue the numbering sequence you used on regular journal entries. However, instead of using JE before the number, he wants to use AJE to designate the entry as an adjusting journal entry.

Type: **AJE92003**
Press: ⌨

All adjusting entries should be dated as of the last day of the period.

Type: **1/31/92**
Press: ⌨

Type a brief explanation of the adjustment for the description.

Type: **INSURANCE EXPIRED**
Press: ⌨

Enter the amount.

Type: **200**
Press: ⌨

The Credit Side   On the credit side, select the Prepaid Insurance account:

Type: **130**
Press: ⏎

The reference number, date, description, and amount are automatically duplicated on the credit side. To accept the entry and move to the Confirmation menu,

Press: **F9**

Your screen should look like Figure 4-7.

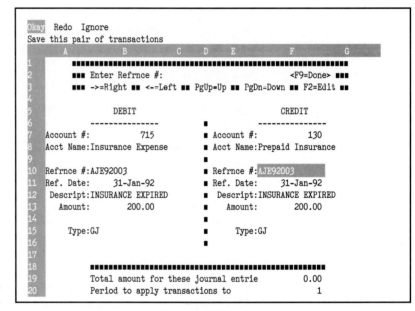

Figure 4-7

To confirm that everything is okay,

Select: **O**kay
Select: **D**one
Select: **A**nother

The second adjustment is for rent expense. Three months' rent was paid on December 1. Prepaid rent has a balance of $1,000, which represents rent for January and February. The rent expense per month is $500.

Record the rent expense for January using AJE92004. After you enter the credit side, your screen should look like Figure 4-8. If it does, confirm the entry, save it, and prepare to enter a third adjustment.

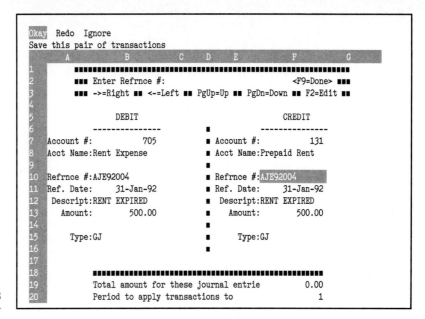

```
Okay  Redo  Ignore
Save this pair of transactions
           A        B         C    D    E           F            G
   1   ■■■■■■■■■■■■■■■■■■■■■■■■■■■■■■■■■■■■■■■■■■■■■■■■■■■■■■■■■■■■■■
   2      ■■■ Enter Refrnce #:                        <F9=Done> ■■■
   3      ■■■ ->=Right ■■ <-=Left ■■ PgUp=Up ■■ PgDn=Down ■■ F2=Edit ■■
   4
   5                 DEBIT                           CREDIT
   6               ---------------     ■           ---------------
   7   Account #:              705     ■ Account #:              131
   8   Acct Name:Rent Expense          ■ Acct Name:Prepaid Rent
   9                                   ■
  10   Refrnce #:AJE92004              ■ Refrnce #:AJE92004
  11   Ref. Date:     31-Jan-92        ■ Ref. Date:     31-Jan-92
  12   Descript:RENT EXPIRED           ■ Descript:RENT EXPIRED
  13      Amount:        500.00        ■    Amount:        500.00
  14                                   ■
  15        Type:GJ                    ■         Type:GJ
  16                                   ■
  17
  18   ■■■■■■■■■■■■■■■■■■■■■■■■■■■■■■■■■■■■■■■■■■■■■■■■■■■■■■■■■■■■
  19      Total amount for these journal entrie          0.00
  20      Period to apply transactions to                   1
```

Figure 4-8

Entering the Inventory Adjustment

To calculate cost of goods sold when using a periodic inventory system, you must make adjustments for beginning and ending inventory. You must remove beginning inventory from the asset account and add it to the cost of goods sold, and you must add the ending inventory to the asset account and subtract it from cost of goods sold.

You should make the required adjustment in two journal entries. The first entry removes the beginning inventory balance from the asset account and transfers it to the Beginning Inventory account in the Cost of Sales section. The second entry records the ending inventory balance in the asset account and enters it as a credit in the Ending Inventory account in Cost of Sales.

Adjusting the Beginning Balance   The trial balance shows a balance of $32,500 in the Merchandise Inventory account, which represents the amount of inventory on hand at the beginning of January. To transfer the beginning inventory to Cost of Sales, select the Beginning Inventory account in the Cost of Sales section:

Type: **500**
Press: ⏎

Type:	**AJE92005**
Press:	⏎
Type:	**1/31/92**
Press:	⏎
Type:	**REMOVE BEG INVEN**
Press:	⏎
Type:	**32500**
Press:	⏎

On the credit side, select the Merchandise Inventory asset account:

Type:	**120**
Press:	⏎
Press:	F9

Your screen should look like Figure 4-9. If it does, confirm the entry, save it, and prepare to enter another entry.

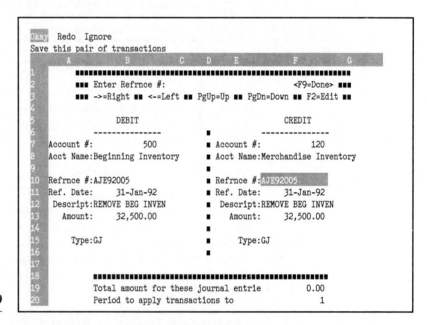

Figure 4-9

Adjusting the Ending Balance Tom Walton took a physical inventory of merchandise on hand at the end of January. He looked up the prices he paid for the inventory and calculated the value of inventory to be $36,485. To record this amount as ending inventory, select the Merchandise Inventory asset account:

Type:	**120**
Press:	⏎

Type:	**AJE92006**
Press:	⏎
Type:	**1/31/92**
Press:	⏎
Type:	**ENTER END INVEN**
Press:	⏎
Type:	**36485**
Press:	⏎

Enter the credit side, crediting account number 590, the Ending Inventory account in the Cost of Sales section. When it is complete, your screen should look like Figure 4-10. If it does, confirm and save your work.

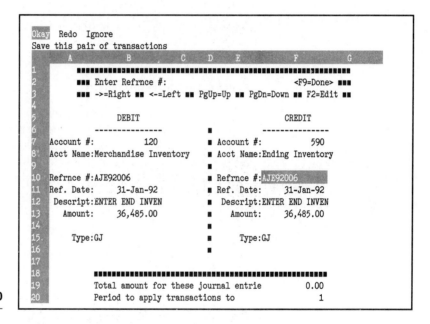

Figure 4-10

From the Another/Done menu, select **D**one to return to the Enter menu.

Because you will enter more adjustments in the exercises, do not print these unposted transactions now. Save them by selecting **S**ave, then return to the RTR Main menu. You will also update (post) all of your adjustments in the exercises.

The Audit Trail

Financial statements are the end result of the accounting process. Accounting records support the numbers that appear in the financial statements. The audit trail is a paper "path" that allows you to trace the numbers in the financial statements through the accounting records to the original transaction.

The ledger provides detailed information about the transactions that make up the balance in each account. By tracing each transaction back to its original journal and thus to the original documents supporting the transaction, Tom can verify that the financial statements reflect properly all the financial events that have been recorded. Thus, the data you entered when you recorded each entry provides part of the support for the financial statements.

You must provide Tom Walton with a permanent record of the transactions you recorded in Labs 2, 3, and 4. One part of that permanent record is the journals. Another part is the ledger.

Printing the Journals

Each transaction in the general ledger (which you will print later in this lab) refers to the journal in which it was posted. To review all the information regarding a transaction, you must refer to that journal. Tom Walton will find it easier to locate a particular transaction if you keep a separate copy of each journal.

Print the journals using the Reports command on the GL menu.

Select: **GL**
Select: **R**eports
Select: **J**ournals
Select: **R**un

At the prompt, enter the current period:

Type: **1**
Press: ⏎

If you are saving your data on diskette, you are prompted to insert your period 1 data disk. Leave the same diskette in drive A and press ⏎. At the next prompt, enter a period name for the report.

Type: **JANUARY 1992**
Press: ⏎

You should see the menu shown in Figure 4-11. The menu contains an option for each of the five journals, plus an option to print all of the journals. There is also a Quit command, which takes you back to the RTR Main menu. The All command from this menu prints *one* listing of the transactions in all the journals, *sorted by date*. It is easier to locate a particular transaction if you print each journal individually.

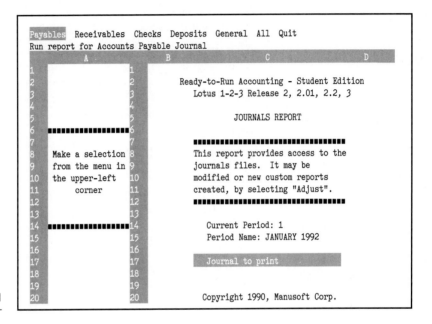

Figure 4-11

Printing the Payables Journal   The screen in Figure 4-11 shows the period you selected and the title for the period that you entered. Choose the Payables journal,

Select: **P**ayables

You should see a menu similar to the one shown in Figure 4-3, except that the last command is Return instead of Done. The Return command returns you to the Journal Choice menu in Figure 4-11, so you can print each of the journals in succession without returning to the RTR Main menu.

You want to print the Payables journal. Make sure your printer is on-line and the paper is properly aligned.

Select: **P**rint
Select: **N**arrow

The menu you should see is similar to the one shown in Figure 4-5. The menu options are the same, but the description line for the Condensed command has a different message. It says:

Report will fit using REGULAR size > > > > > > >

This message tells you that your printout will fit on one page using regular print. Move the highlight to the Regular command. The message on the third line confirms that the report will fit on one page. Use regular print instead of condensed print when the report fits on one page; regular print is easier to read.

Select: **R**egular

The printed journal should look like Figure 4-12. After the journal prints, your screen returns to the Print/Browse-/Save/Return menu.

Select: **R**eturn

```
Walton Electronics                AP JOURNALS REPORT                JANUARY 1992

Acc #    Description              Ref #         Ref Date   SJ    Transaction
  200    REBCO COMPUTER           Z4928         03-Jan-92  AP       (5,090.00)
  510    REBCO COMPUTER           0/Z4928       03-Jan-92  AP        5,000.00
  550    REBCO COMPUTER           0/Z4928       03-Jan-92  AP           90.00
  200    TODAY'S ADVERTISING      QT3342        06-Jan-92  AP         (819.00)
  620    TODAY'S ADVERTISING      0/QT3342      06-Jan-92  AP          819.00
  200    VENUS SYSTEMS            DM442         09-Jan-92  AP          500.00
  520    VENUS SYSTEMS            0/DM442       09-Jan-92  AP         (500.00)
  200    WE-HAUL-IT               VVK94         10-Jan-92  AP          (83.00)
  610    WE-HAUL-IT               0/VVK94       10-Jan-92  AP           83.00
  200    CARRON PERIPHERALS       HK4821-86     13-Jan-92  AP      (11,602.00)
  510    CARRON PERIPHERALS       0/HK4821-86   13-Jan-92  AP       10,850.00
  550    CARRON PERIPHERALS       0/HK4821-86   13-Jan-92  AP          752.00
  200    WE-HAUL-IT               VVK99         14-Jan-92  AP          (44.00)
  610    WE-HAUL-IT               0/VVK99       14-Jan-92  AP           44.00
  200    J. M. SUPPLY             B3559         17-Jan-92  AP      (16,890.00)
  510    J. M. SUPPLY             0/B3559       17-Jan-92  AP       16,350.00
  550    J. M. SUPPLY             0/B3559       17-Jan-92  AP          540.00
  200    VENUS SYSTEMS            QP69PR        23-Jan-92  AP       (7,300.00)
  510    VENUS SYSTEMS            0/QP69PR      23-Jan-92  AP        7,300.00
  200    LODICO COMMUNICATIONS          6954    24-Jan-92  AP         (558.00)
  725    LODICO COMMUNICATIONS    0/6954        24-Jan-92  AP          558.00
  200    REBCO COMPUTER           Z5143         29-Jan-92  AP       (6,550.00)
  510    REBCO COMPUTER           0/Z5143       29-Jan-92  AP        6,300.00
  550    REBCO COMPUTER           0/Z5143       29-Jan-92  AP          250.00
  200    WE-HAUL-IT               VVK114        30-Jan-92  AP         (135.00)
  610    WE-HAUL-IT               0/VVK114      30-Jan-92  AP          135.00
  200    VENUS SYSTEMS            DM443         31-Jan-92  AP          250.00
  520    VENUS SYSTEMS            0/DM443       31-Jan-92  AP         (250.00)
----------------------------------------------------------------------------
                                                                       0.00
```

Figure 4-12

Printing the Other Journals   To print the Receivables journal,

Select:	**R**eceivables
Select:	**P**rint
Select:	**N**arrow
Select:	**R**egular
Select:	**R**eturn

Continue this process by printing the Checks and Deposits journals. Do not print the General Journal at this time. You will print it in exercise 1, after you have posted the adjusting entries.

Review the journals you have printed. They are similar in appearance to the Unposted GL Transactions and Transactions to Be Posted reports you saw in Labs 2 and 3. Retain these journals in a permanent file as part of the audit trail, maintaining a separate file for each journal type. At the end of February, a similar journal report would be added to each file showing the activity in that journal for period 2.

From the Journal Choice menu, select **Q**uit to return to the Main menu.

The Query Program

When you recorded transactions for Tom, you entered the account number and amount, as well as three additional items:

Reference Number

Reference Date

Description

When you printed a copy of the posting, each of these items appeared on that report. These items appeared again when you printed the journals. The ledger that you print for Tom in this section also contains these items. This information provides the audit trail described earlier.

In RTR, you print the ledger or audit trail using the GL menu command called Query. This command also allows you to view the activity of a single account or several specified accounts on the screen. You can also view the activity of one period only, several specified periods, or the entire year.

To learn how to use these features and print an audit trail, from the GL menu:

Select: **Q**uery

The Inquire System screen appears, with the Run/Quit/Break menu. Select **R**un to run the Query program.

The Query program graphs the activity in the account or accounts you select. The menu on your screen, shown in Figure 4-13, allows you to indicate whether your monitor can display graphs and, if it can, whether it is a black-and-white or a color monitor. Check with your instructor to make sure that your monitor can display graphs. This lab assumes that you are using a black-and-white monitor that can display graphs.

Select: **Black/White**

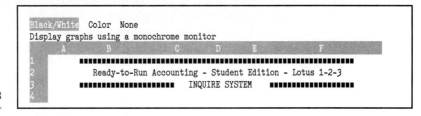

Figure 4-13

A prompt appears in the control panel that says:

Enter last active period (1 to 13):

Type: **1**
Press: ⌐⌐

to indicate that you have only entered activity for period 1.

The menu and screen in Figure 4-14 appear.

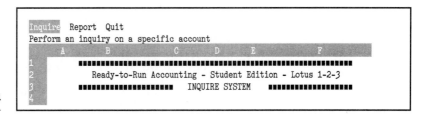

Figure 4-14

The three options on this menu are:

Inquire   Allows you to view, print, or graph information regarding one specific account.

Report   Allows you to select one or more accounts and view, print, or graph the information in the selected accounts.

Quit   Returns you to the RTR Main menu.

Inquiring about Activity in a Single Account   Tom Walton has received the bank statement for January and wants to prepare a bank reconciliation. He needs to see the detailed activity that has been recorded in the Cash in Bank account. Before you provide him with a printout of this activity, review it on the screen to make sure that all the transactions that should have been recorded are there. Use the Inquire command to view the activity in the Cash in Bank account.

Select: **Inquire**

The menu in Figure 4-15 appears. Choose Enter to enter the account number you want or choose Select to select the account from the chart of accounts.

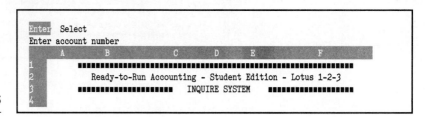

Figure 4-15

The Select option is similar to the help screen in the Ledger program, which allows you to select an account while entering transactions. Since you know the account number of Cash in Bank is 100, select the Enter option.

Select: **Enter**

The prompt in the control panel says:

Enter account number to inquire:

Enter the account number of Cash in Bank.

Type: **100**
Press: ⏎

You should see the menu and screen shown in Figure 4-16. The screen displays a summary of the posted and unposted activity for the Cash in Bank account.

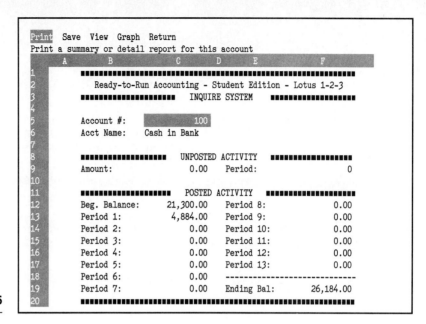

```
Print  Save  View  Graph  Return
Print a summary or detail report for this account
        A          B          C          D          E          F
1  ■■■■■■■■■■■■■■■■■■■■■■■■■■■■■■■■■■■■■■■■■■■■■■■■■■■■■■■■■■■■■
2            Ready-to-Run Accounting - Student Edition - Lotus 1-2-3
3  ■■■■■■■■■■■■■■■■■■■■■■■    INQUIRE SYSTEM    ■■■■■■■■■■■■■■■■■■■■■
4
5  Account #:              100
6  Acct Name:   Cash in Bank
7
8  ■■■■■■■■■■■■■■■■■■■■■■  UNPOSTED ACTIVITY  ■■■■■■■■■■■■■■■■■■■■■
9  Amount:             0.00    Period:                    0
10
11 ■■■■■■■■■■■■■■■■■■■■■■   POSTED ACTIVITY  ■■■■■■■■■■■■■■■■■■■■■
12 Beg. Balance:   21,300.00   Period 8:              0.00
13 Period 1:        4,884.00   Period 9:              0.00
14 Period 2:            0.00   Period 10:             0.00
15 Period 3:            0.00   Period 11:             0.00
16 Period 4:            0.00   Period 12:             0.00
17 Period 5:            0.00   Period 13:             0.00
18 Period 6:            0.00   ----------------------------
19 Period 7:            0.00   Ending Bal:       26,184.00
20 ■■■■■■■■■■■■■■■■■■■■■■■■■■■■■■■■■■■■■■■■■■■■■■■■■■■■■■■■■■■■■
```

Figure 4-16

The menu contains five options:

Print	Prints either the summary screen or a detailed audit trail for the account.
Save	Saves the summary or detailed report for this account to disk.
View	Displays the detailed report for the account on the screen.
Graph	Draws a bar graph of this account's activity. After you view the bar graph, you can choose to save it to print later. You will learn more about graphing in Lab 6. (Graphs saved by RTR are printed by PrintGraph. See the appendix for a detailed explanation of how to use PrintGraph to print a graph.)
Return	Returns to the Query menu.

Viewing the Detailed Report Before you print a detailed report of Cash in Bank for Tom, review it to make sure everything is recorded properly.

Select: **V**iew

The menu that appears has two choices:

All   Runs the detail report for all periods, including unposted transactions.

Select   Allows you to specify one or more periods to include in the report.

If you choose the All command, your computer looks for data in all 13 periods and the unposted transactions file. Then RTR displays the data for each period for which it has data on a separate screen. RTR also displays a separate screen at the beginning for unposted transactions, even if there are no unposted transactions. Because you are interested in viewing only the transactions from period 1 for Cash in Bank, choose the Select command.

Select: **Select**
Type: **1**
Press: ⏎
Select: **Done**

You should see the screen shown in Figure 4-17. The window at the top tells you to use the arrow keys to move around in the report. The PGDN and PGUP keys also work to move you down and up one screen at a time. The HOME key brings you back to the top of the report.

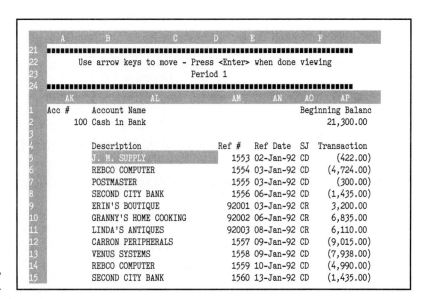

Figure 4-17

Use the arrow keys, PGDN, PGUP, and HOME to move around the screen and look at the report. The information on the report is formatted as it was in the journals you printed. The transactions appear in the report in the order in which you entered them. Credit amounts appear in parentheses and debit amounts appear without parentheses. When you press PGDN two times, you see the total of all transactions for period 1. The ending balance for Cash in Bank for period 1 is two rows below this total.

You cannot change the information on the screen. Because you are in a browse (or view) mode, you can only view it. You can move the cell pointer off the screen to the right or page down past the end of the report, which is actually part of a Lotus 1-2-3 worksheet. However, the rest of the worksheet is blank, and it isn't very interesting. Press HOME to return to the upper-left corner of the report.

When you have finished looking at the report on the screen,

Press: ⏎

RTR returns you to the Query menu. To print a report of the information you have just viewed, or to view a graph of it and perhaps save the graph for printing, you would choose the Inquire command again and reenter the account number for Cash in Bank.

Printing an Audit Trail for a Specific Account

To print a detail report for Cash in Bank that Tom can use to reconcile his bank account, select the Report command from the Query menu.

Select: **R**eport

You should see a menu with three options: Print, Save, and View. These options function the same way as the corresponding commands on the Inquire menu. However, the Graph option is only available through the Inquire menu, as is the Return option. To return to the Query menu, you would press ESC.

The Report option only prints a detailed report. To print the Summary you see on the screen, you must use the Inquire option.

To print a copy of the detailed report for Cash in Bank:

Select: **P**rint

You should see a menu with two options: All and Select. You can choose to print a detailed report of all the accounts in the ledger or a report of selected accounts. Print a detailed report for Cash in Bank that Tom can use to reconcile the bank account:

Select: **Select**

The Enter/Select menu you saw in Figure 4-15 appears. Since you know the number, enter it.

Select: **Enter**
Type: **100**
Press: ⏎

You should see a menu with two options: Another and Done. The Another command allows you to enter additional account numbers to include in your audit trail. If you choose Another, RTR continues to come back to this menu until you choose Done. Because you want to print an audit trail for Cash in Bank only,

Select: **Done**

You should see another menu with two commands: All and Select. This time, you can select the *periods* for your audit trail, as opposed to the *accounts*.

> **Note** If you select the All command from this menu, RTR prints a page for each of the 13 periods and another for unposted transactions, even if no transactions are in the file. Because this wastes a lot of paper, always choose the Select command. You can select as many periods as you want to print. Thus, you can tell RTR to print activity for periods 1 through 4, for example, instead of choosing All.

Select: **Select**

RTR prompts you to enter the period for which you want to print transactions. Notice that you can get a printout of unposted transactions for a given account by entering period 0. Since you want the transactions for period 1,

Type: **1**
Press: ⏎

You should see another menu with two choices: Another and Done. Make sure that your printer is on-line and the paper is properly aligned. Then, since you don't want to include any other periods,

Select: **Done**

RTR prints a detailed report for the Cash in Bank account for period 1. Remove it and look it over. The report should be similar to Figure 4-18 and to what you saw when you used the View command on the Inquire menu. It contains a listing of all the deposits made to the bank account and all the checks written on the bank account. Tom Walton can check this list against the items on his bank statement lists and determine which ones are still outstanding.

```
Walton Electronics            ACCOUNT AUDIT TRAIL            PERIOD 1

Acc #        Account Name                          Beginning Balance
     100     Cash in Bank                                 21,300.00

             Description          Ref #      Ref Date   SJ   Transaction
             J. M. SUPPLY          1553      02-Jan-92  CD      (422.00)
             REBCO COMPUTER        1554      03-Jan-92  CD    (4,724.00)
             POSTMASTER            1555      03-Jan-92  CD      (300.00)
             SECOND CITY BANK      1556      06-Jan-92  CD    (1,435.00)
             ERIN'S BOUTIQUE       92001     03-Jan-92  CR     3,200.00
             GRANNY'S HOME COOKING 92002     06-Jan-92  CR     6,835.00
             LINDA'S ANTIQUES      92003     08-Jan-92  CR     6,110.00
             CARRON PERIPHERALS    1557      09-Jan-92  CD    (9,015.00)
             VENUS SYSTEMS         1558      09-Jan-92  CD    (7,938.00)
             REBCO COMPUTER        1559      10-Jan-92  CD    (4,990.00)
             SECOND CITY BANK      1560      13-Jan-92  CD    (1,435.00)
             LODICO COMMUNICATIONS 1561      15-Jan-92  CD      (693.00)
             LINDA'S ANTIQUES      1562      15-Jan-92  CD      (550.00)
             JASON'S OFFICE SUPPLIES 1563    16-Jan-92  CD    (1,095.00)
             TOM WALTON            1564      17-Jan-92  CD    (1,800.00)
             SECOND CITY BANK      1565      20-Jan-92  CD    (1,435.00)
             CARRON PERIPHERALS    1566      23-Jan-92  CD   (11,385.00)
             CITY POWER COMPANY    1567      24-Jan-92  CD      (489.00)
             SECOND CITY BANK      1568      27-Jan-92  CD    (1,435.00)
             WE-HAUL-IT            1569      28-Jan-92  CD      (320.00)
             TOM WALTON            1570      30-Jan-92  CD    (1,800.00)
             LOCAL PHONE COMPANY   1571      31-Jan-92  CD      (257.00)
             DEL'S MOTORS          1572      31-Jan-92  CD    (2,000.00)
             JIM'S FITNESS CLINIC  92004     09-Jan-92  CR     9,261.00
             EXCELLENT HARDWARE    92005     10-Jan-92  CR    10,295.00
             PAUL'S HARDWARE       92006     13-Jan-92  CR       825.00
             RANDY'S VIDEO STOP    92007     16-Jan-92  CR     5,194.00
             A-1 GROCERS           92008     20-Jan-92  CR     5,400.00
             BOB'S AUTO REPAIR     92009     23-Jan-92  CR     4,437.00
             JIM'S FITNESS CLINIC  92010     27-Jan-92  CR     5,717.00
             CAROLYN'S COUNTRY STORE 92011   30-Jan-92  CR     1,128.00
             - - - - - - - - - - - - - - - - - - - - - - - - - - - - -
             Period Total                                      4,884.00

                                            Ending Balance    26,184.00
             ===============================================================
Report run: 06-Oct-90
```

Figure 4-18

Printing an Audit Trail for All Accounts

When RTR finishes printing the period 1 report for the Cash in
Bank account, it returns to the Query menu.

The General Ledger represents the permanent audit trail record of the activity in all accounts. The General Ledger is the primary supporting document for the financial statements you will prepare in Lab 5. This printed copy of the audit trail corresponds to the General Ledger accounts in a manual system. When you post in a manual system, you provide cross-references in the General Ledger and in the journals that allow you to trace posted amounts back and forth. In a computerized system, the account number in the printed journal allows you to trace the entry to the account in the audit trail, and the journal designation in the audit trail allows you to trace the entry back to the journal.

Printing the General Ledger takes a lot of paper and a long time. Because of this, you should only print the General Ledger once, after you have posted all the transactions for the month. Since you will enter more adjustments in the exercises for this lab, don't print a General Ledger now. Study the steps that follow to learn how to print the General Ledger. When you are asked to print the General Ledger at the end of the exercises, refer to this section for the procedures you need to follow.

To secure a printout of the audit trail, or General Ledger, for all of the accounts in the chart of accounts:

Select: **Report**
Select: **Print**
Select: **All**

You should see a menu that has two options:

Non-Zero   Prints activity for all accounts that have a non-zero beginning balance or that have activity during the period. Use this option most of the time.

Active   Prints activity only for accounts that have activity during the period. For example, the Tom Walton Capital account would not print with this option because it had no activity during January.

Select: **Non-Zero**
Select: **Select**
Type: **1**
Press: ⏎

When you are ready to print the complete audit trail at the end of the lab exercise, be sure your printer is turned on and has a good supply of paper in it. Then select **D**one.

To return to the previous menu, which is the Query menu,

Press: ESC three times

If you start printing by mistake, follow the instructions on the screen and press any key to stop the printing.

When you select Done, the audit trail for January prints. The Cash in Bank account, which you printed earlier, is the first account listed on the audit trail. The rest of the accounts and their activity follow in numerical order.

After the audit trail prints, RTR returns to the Query menu. To return to the RTR Main menu,

Select: **Q**uit

Using the Audit Trail to Trace a Transaction

You can complete this section only after you have printed out the audit trail in the exercises.

Using the audit trail printout, find account number 110, Accounts Receivable. Locate the fourth item on the detail, invoice number 2038 for Bob's Auto Repair. The name of the customer appears in the description column, and the invoice number appears in the Ref # column. The SJ column indicates the source journal for the entry: AR, which stands for Accounts Receivable.

Trace this item back to the receivables journal you printed in the lab activity. The debit to Accounts Receivable for this invoice should be the seventh item listed in that journal. When you refer to the journal, you can also see the corresponding credit for the invoice to account number 400. If you were working with Walton Electronics's original documents, you would be able to locate a copy of invoice number 2038, which would show a copy of the order received from Bob's Auto Repair. The invoice copy should also have evidence attached that Bob's Auto Repair actually received the merchandise.

The audit trail thus provides a way to verify that all recorded transactions are supported by appropriate documentation, part of a company's internal control structure.

Using the audit trail, you can also verify that a transaction has been recorded. For example, in the process of reviewing shipping records and invoices for Walton Electronics, the auditor discovers a shipment to Corner Drug Store on January 30. The shipping record indicates that this sale was recorded on invoice number 2041 and that it was a credit sale. The auditor can use the audit trail to verify that the sale to Corner Drug Store was recorded. Refer to the printout of the audit trail and find that the shipment to Corner Drug Store on January 30 was recorded in both Accounts Receivable and Sales. The receivable entry should appear in account number 110 and the sale should appear in account number 400.

Exercises

Walton Electronics

1. Prepare adjusting entries for Walton Electronics for the following items:

   a. Supplies on Hand at the end of January cost $545. The balance was used during the month of January.

   b. Depreciation for the month of January is as follows:

      Equipment $275

      Furniture   75

      Trucks   100

      Use the same journal entry number as the reference for all three transactions.

   c. Compute interest payable on the note signed on January 15 for half a month. Be sure to calculate interest payable on the full balance — the $2,000 was not paid on the principal until January 31.

   d. A full week's salaries will be paid on February 3. The salary accrual must equal the amount of the check paid for a full week.

   e. Customer deposits against future orders of $1,000 were outstanding at the end of January. Credit the $500 earned to the Sales account.

2. Print a listing of unposted entries and check it for errors. Use the Fix command on the Enter menu to make corrections if necessary.

3. Post the entries to the permanent period 1 file, printing the documentation of the posting process.

4. Print a new copy of the Trial Balance that summarizes all of January's transactions and adjusting entries.

5. Print a copy of the General Journal, which should include the entries made in Lab 2 and the adjusting entries made in this lab.

6. Print the audit trail for Tom Walton showing the activity for all accounts for the month of January. Follow the procedures outlined at the end of the lab activity. Use the audit trail to trace the transactions described at the end of the lab activity.

TWE, Inc.

1. Prepare adjusting entries for TWE, Inc. for the following items. Before making the adjusting entries, add three more accounts to the chart of accounts:

Summary Heading	Account No.	Account Title
Prepaid Expenses	129	Prepaid Advertising
Income Taxes Payable	215	Income Taxes Payable
Income Taxes	850	Income Tax Expense

a. Supplies on Hand at the end of January cost $1,345. The balance was used during the month of January.

b. Depreciation for the month of January is as follows:

Equipment $275

Furniture   75

Trucks   100

Use the same journal entry number as the reference for all three transactions.

c. Compute the interest payable on a note signed on January 7 (24/365 of a year) for the purchase of the security system. Round your adjustment to the nearest dollar.

d. Compute the interest payable on the note signed on January 15 for one-half month. Remember that the $2,000 payment on the principal was not made until January 31.

e. Salaries for the week of January 25 through 31 will be paid on February 3.

f. Some of the advertising paid for on January 30 is scheduled for February.

g. By the end of January, only $1,000 in customer deposits are for future orders. Therefore, any amount above $1,000 should be recognized as sales revenue.

h. $900 in income taxes accrued in the month of January.

2. Print a listing of unposted entries and check it for errors. Use the Fix command on the Enter menu to make corrections if necessary.

3. Post the entries to the permanent period 1 file, printing the documentation of the posting process.

4. Print a new copy of the Trial Balance that summarizes all of January's transactions and adjusting entries.

5. Print a copy of the General Journal, which should include the entries made in Lab 2 and the adjusting entries made in this lab.

6. Print the audit trail for Tom Walton showing the activity for all accounts for the month of January. Follow the procedures outlined at the end of the lab activity. Use the audit trail to trace the transactions described at the end of the lab activity.

Going Further

7. Examine the following journal entries. Indicate an alternative method of recording the original journal entry. Then indicate the appropriate adjusting entry based on the alternative original entry.

a. Postage in Lab 3 on page 148. Assume that $270 of the metered postage has been used.

b. Advertising in Lab 3, TWE, Inc. exercise 1, check #1571.

c. Customer deposit (Carmen's Candies) in Lab 3, TWE, Inc. exercise 1, deposit b.

8. Examine the events in exercise 4 at the end of Lab 3. Indicate the nature of any adjusting entry(ies) that might result from those events.

9. The trial balance is used to detect certain types of errors.

a. What types of errors will a trial balance *not* detect?

b. With the RTR system, the trial balance will automatically balance. Describe why the RTR system automatically balances. What potential danger does this present?

Lotus 1-2-3

1. Sort the journal entries for January.

a. From the Reports menu, save a file consisting of the entries in all the journals (select All from the Journals menu) for period 1. Quit RTR to Lotus 1-2-3.

b. In Lotus 1-2-3, retrieve the file you saved from the GL subdirectory. Clear the window and set the column widths as follows:

Column	Width
A	7
B	25
C	12
D	12
E	4
F	12

c. The transactions are listed by date. Tom Walton wants to review the transactions by customer or supplier. Sort (using the Data menu) the transactions using the description as the primary sort key and the date as the secondary sort key. Print a copy of the sorted transactions.

d. Tom Walton also wants to review the period's activity by account. Provide a printed copy of the debits and credits organized by account and chronologically within each account.

2. Prepare a Lotus worksheet that calculates net income and separates the income statement accounts from the balance sheet accounts.

    a. From the Reports menu, save a file consisting of the trial balance for period 2. Quit RTR to Lotus 1-2-3.

    b. In Lotus 1-2-3, retrieve the file you created from the GL subdirectory. Clear the window and globally set the column widths to 12. Globally format the worksheet to comma with zero decimal places. Then adjust the column widths as follows:

Column	Width
A	7
B	25
C	9

    c. Center the Debits and Credits headings in columns D and E. Add the headings "Income Stmt" and "Bal. Sheet" in columns G and H.

    d. Under the Income Stmt heading, create an @IF statement that enters the balances of the income statement accounts in column G. Under the heading Bal. Sheet, create an @IF statement that enters the balances of the balance sheet accounts in column H.

    e. Insert a line under the last balance in column G. Below the line, use an @SUM statement to total the balances in column G. Insert three blank rows after the last entry in column H. Use another @SUM statement to enter the total of the balances in column G after the last entry in column H. Label this amount "Net (Income) Loss" in column B.

    f. In column H, after the net income amount, insert a line. Below this line, use an @SUM statement to total the balances in column H. (The total of the income statement accounts should be negative if there is net income. The balance sheet column should total zero.)

    g. Print a copy of the worksheet.

5

Financial Statements

**Ready-to-Run
General Ledger Structure**

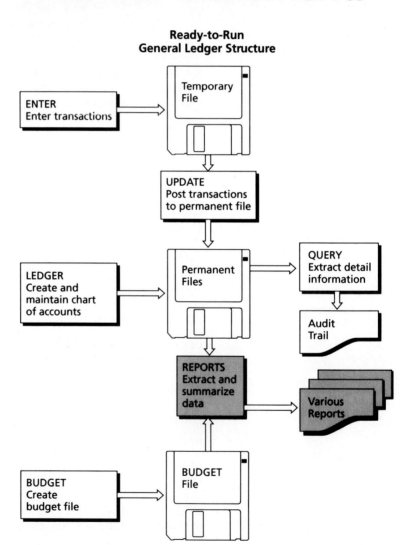

Objectives

In Lab 5, you will learn how to:

- Format classified financial statements
- Print primary financial statements
- Back up data diskettes
- Close the books for an accounting period

Formatting Financial Statements

Tom Walton wants you to print the balance sheet and income statement so that he can see how Walton Electronics performed in the month of January, 1992.

You can use RTR to print financial statements any time after you have set up the chart of accounts. The accounts and their balances appear on the statement within the summary heading to which you assigned them. There would be no subtotals for current assets, net property, plant, and equipment, or current liabilities, for example. The income statement would not have any subtotals either.

Tom wants to see the balance sheet in a classified format, with subtotals for current assets, property, plant, and equipment, and current liabilities, and the income statement in a multiple-step format. To accomplish this in RTR, you must revise the chart of accounts to include lines and formulas for the subtotals.

To make changes to the chart of accounts, go to the Chart of Accounts editing screen. From the RTR Main menu,

Select: **GL Ledger Ledger**

Enter your password, select **R**un and select **B**ackup with a 20-minute backup period.

Select: **Existing**

Your screen should look like Figure 5-1.

```
        D     E   F              G                  H       I         J
 85  ■■    Use up & down arrow keys, pgup, and pgdn to move cell pointer   ■■
 86  ■■  {Ins}=Add acct/heading {F2}=Change acct/heading {Del}=Delete line ■■
 87  ■■  {F5}=Page {F6}=Depts. {F7}=Print samples {F8}=Interrupt {F9}=Done ■■
        D     E   F              G                  H       I         J
100  Acc #            Account Title
101        ASSETS
102            Cash
103  100C        Cash in Bank                      0.00
104            Total Cash                                           0.00
105        Accounts Receivable
106  110C        Accounts Receivable               0.00
107            Total Accounts Receivable                            0.00
108        Inventory
109  120C        Merchandise Inventory             0.00
110            Total Inventory                                      0.00
111        Prepaid Expense
112  130C        Prepaid Insurance                 0.00
113  131C        Prepaid Rent                      0.00
114  132C        Supplies on Hand                  0.00
115            Total Prepaid Expense                                0.00
```

Figure 5-1

Creating a Subtotal for Current Assets

The first subtotal that appears on the classified balance sheet Tom wants you to prepare is Current Assets. To create a subtotal, you must add a blank line to the balance sheet and then enter a formula that calculates the subtotal for you. The formula tells Ready-to-Run which cells to sum to arrive at the correct figure.

The subtotal for Current Assets should be located after the Prepaid Expense section of the balance sheet. You want to create a subtotal that will include all items from Cash through Prepaid Expense.

> **Note** Throughout this lab activity, references are made to row and cell numbers. If you have been completing the exercises for TWE, Inc., your row and cell references will be different. Use the descriptions of the rows and cells in the text, not the row and cell numbers, to position your cell pointer in the correct position.

Use ⬇ to

Move: to the row below Total Prepaid Expense (row 116)
Press: INS
Select: **Line**

Your screen should look like Figure 5-2, with a blank line inserted at row 116 below Total Prepaid Expense.

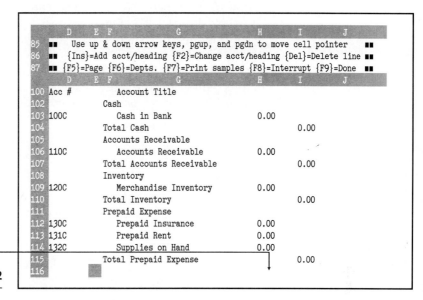

```
        D    E  F              G              H      I      J
85  ■■   Use up & down arrow keys, pgup, and pgdn to move cell pointer    ■■
86  ■■  {Ins}=Add acct/heading {F2}=Change acct/heading {Del}=Delete line ■■
87  ■■  {F5}=Page {F6}=Depts. {F7}=Print samples {F8}=Interrupt {F9}=Done ■■
        D    E  F              G              H      I      J
100 Acc #            Account Title
102              Cash
103 100C            Cash in Bank              0.00
104              Total Cash                          0.00
105              Accounts Receivable
106 110C            Accounts Receivable       0.00
107              Total Accounts Receivable           0.00
108              Inventory
109 120C            Merchandise Inventory     0.00
110              Total Inventory                     0.00
111              Prepaid Expense
112 130C            Prepaid Insurance         0.00
113 131C            Prepaid Rent              0.00
114 132C            Supplies on Hand          0.00
115              Total Prepaid Expense               0.00
116
```

This is the blank line you added

Figure 5-2

Creating the Formula

Now create the formula to subtotal Current Assets:

Press: ⬇
Press: INS
Select: **Formula**

The prompt line asks you for a description for the subtotal.

Type: **Total Current Assets**
Press: ⏎

The cell pointer jumps to column I, which contains the totals of the summary headings. RTR switches to EDIT mode so you can enter a formula into that cell. You want to write a formula that adds up the totals of the accounts that make up current assets. To do this, you must use a Lotus 1-2-3 @function called @SUM. The syntax for the @SUM function is

@SUM(range)

The range is a block of cells. @SUM tells Lotus 1-2-3 to add up all the values in the block of cells indicated by the range. If the values in any of the cells change, the @SUM formula automatically changes the value in the Total Current Assets cell accordingly. Using a formula allows you to revise your balance sheet repeatedly without having to revise the totals.

In Lotus 1-2-3, you can indicate the range two ways: you can type in the range of cells or you can use the "pointing" method to show Lotus 1-2-3 which cells to include in the range. The pointing method is more accurate because you can't make a typing mistake and include the wrong cells. To use the pointing method to sum Walton Electronics' current assets, follow the steps below. If you make a mistake, press ESC until the second line of the control panel is clear. Then repeat the steps.

Type: **@SUM(**

Do *not* press ⏎ at this time. Use ↑ and ← to

Move: to the cell in column H containing the amount Cash in Bank (cell H103)

Your screen should look like Figure 5-3.

Here is the formula
you are entering ⟶ @SUM(H103

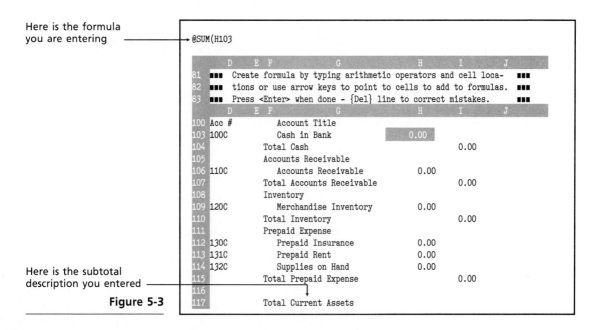

Here is the subtotal
description you entered ⟶

Figure 5-3

```
             D    E  F              G                  H        I       J
       81  ■■■   Create formula by typing arithmetic operators and cell loca-   ■■■
       82  ■■■   tions or use arrow keys to point to cells to add to formulas.  ■■■
       83  ■■■   Press <Enter> when done - {Del} line to correct mistakes.      ■■■
             D    E  F              G                  H        I       J
      100  Acc #          Account Title
      103  100C           Cash in Bank            0.00
      104                 Total Cash                       0.00
      105                 Accounts Receivable
      106  110C           Accounts Receivable     0.00
      107                 Total Accounts Receivable         0.00
      108                 Inventory
      109  120C           Merchandise Inventory   0.00
      110                 Total Inventory                   0.00
      111                 Prepaid Expense
      112  130C           Prepaid Insurance       0.00
      113  131C           Prepaid Rent            0.00
      114  132C           Supplies on Hand        0.00
      115                 Total Prepaid Expense             0.00
      116
      117                 Total Current Assets
```

Type: . (a period, which is used to "anchor" the range)

Press: ⬇️

Your screen should look like Figure 5-4. The cell pointer is expanding to cover the range you want to total.

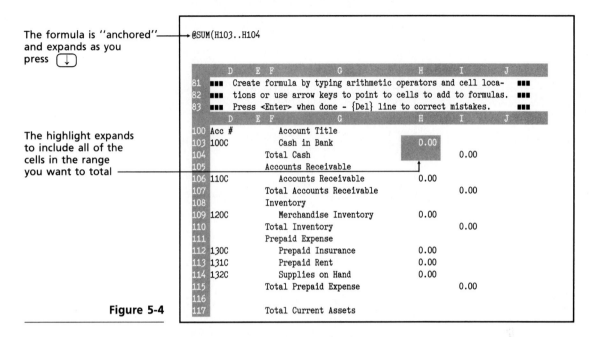

The formula is "anchored" and expands as you press ⬇️

The highlight expands to include all of the cells in the range you want to total

Figure 5-4

Continue pressing ⬇️ until the cell pointer is on the amount for Supplies on Hand (cell H114). Your screen should look like Figure 5-5.

The formula includes a reference to all of the cells you want to total

The range is now complete for the formula and the entire range is highlighted

Figure 5-5

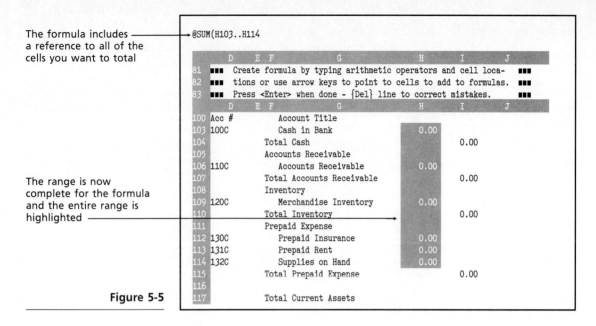

```
@SUM(H103..H114

         D    E F          G                    H       I       J
81  ▪▪▪  Create formula by typing arithmetic operators and cell loca-  ▪▪▪
82  ▪▪▪  tions or use arrow keys to point to cells to add to formulas.  ▪▪▪
83  ▪▪▪  Press <Enter> when done - {Del} line to correct mistakes.     ▪▪▪
         D    E F          G                    H       I       J
100 Acc #          Account Title
103 100C           Cash in Bank                    0.00
104                Total Cash                               0.00
105                Accounts Receivable
106 110C              Accounts Receivable          0.00
107                Total Accounts Receivable                0.00
108                Inventory
109 120C              Merchandise Inventory        0.00
110                Total Inventory                          0.00
111                Prepaid Expense
112 130C              Prepaid Insurance            0.00
113 131C              Prepaid Rent                 0.00
114 132C              Supplies on Hand             0.00
115                Total Prepaid Expense                    0.00
116
117                Total Current Assets
```

Type:)

The right parenthesis completes the @SUM formula. (If you press ⏎ instead of the parenthesis by mistake, RTR allows you to edit your formula to correct it.) The cell pointer jumps back to the cell in which you are entering the formula. Your screen should look like Figure 5-6. If it doesn't, press ESC and start over.

The right parenthesis
completes the @SUM formula ──▶ @SUM(H103..H114)

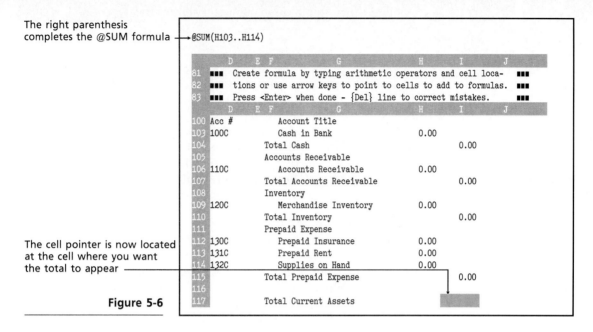

The cell pointer is now located
at the cell where you want
the total to appear ─────────

Figure 5-6

When you finish,

Press: ⏎

The amount 0.00 appears in cell I117. When you print the balance sheet, the total dollar value of the current assets prints in that cell.

> **Note**   All the accounts included in Current Assets must be included in a summary heading for this formula to give an accurate total. If you add an account before Cash in Bank or after Supplies on Hand, you must change the formula. Also, if you insert a new summary heading above Cash or below Prepaid Expense, you must change the formula. To change the formula, use DEL to delete the current formula line, Total Current Assets, and insert a new formula line.

Insert a blank line between the formula line and the beginning of the Property, Plant and Equipment summary heading:

Press: ↓
Press: INS
Select: **Line**

A blank line should appear on the screen below Total Current Assets.

Creating a Net Sales Subtotal

The multiple-step income statement that Tom Walton wants to use requires a subtotal for Gross Margin. To calculate Gross Margin, you must subtract Cost of Goods Sold from Net Sales. A Net Sales subtotal sums total sales and total deductions from sales. Currently, the Total Revenue line does this. If you were to add other operating revenue accounts in the Revenue section in the future, however, you could not continue to use Total Revenue to calculate Gross Margin.

Press: PGDN four times

Before you create the Net Sales subtotal, change the description of the Deductions from Revenue summary heading to Deductions from Sales. Remember that to change the description of a summary heading, you move the cell pointer to the row containing the heading, press (F2), and enter the new summary heading description at the prompt. Do this on your own now. Both the description line and the total line for the summary heading change.

To create the Net Sales subtotal,

Move: to the line above TOTAL REVENUE (row 170)

Use the procedure you learned in the last section to insert a blank line below the Total Deductions from Sales line, and then

Press: (↓)

To insert a formula to combine the Total Sales and Total Deductions from Sales amounts,

Press: INS
Select: **Formula**
Type: **Net Sales**
Press: (↵)

The cell pointer is positioned in column I ready for you to input the formula. Use the Lotus 1-2-3 @SUM formula.

Type: **@SUM(**
Move: to the amount in column H for Sales (cell H164)
Type: **.**
Move: to the amount for Sales Returns & Allowances (cell H168)
Type: **)** to complete the formula

The formula on the second line of the control panel should read @SUM(H164..H168). If it doesn't, press ESC and reenter the formula.

When you finish,

Press:　　(⏎)

Move the cell pointer down one row and insert another blank line between the Net Sales subtotal and the row that contains the line above TOTAL REVENUE.

Creating a Cost of Goods Available for Sale Subtotal

Move to the screen containing the detail for Cost of Sales.

Press:　　PGDN
Move:　　to the row containing the Ending Inventory account (row 183)

Tom Walton wants to see the usual Cost of Goods Sold computation, which includes a Goods Available for Sale subtotal between Freight-in and Ending Inventory. The subtotal should include all of the accounts from Beginning Inventory through Freight-in. Do not insert a blank line before or after the subtotal for Cost of Goods Available for Sale.

Press:　　INS
Select:　　**Formula**
Type:　　**Cost of Goods Avail for Sale**
Press:　　(⏎)

The cell pointer should now be positioned in column I, ready for you to type the formula. You will again use the Lotus 1-2-3 @SUM formula.

Type:　　**@SUM(**
Move:　　to the amount in column H for Beginning Inventory (cell H178)
Type:　　.
Move:　　to the amount in column H for Freight-in (cell H182)

Your screen should look like Figure 5-7.

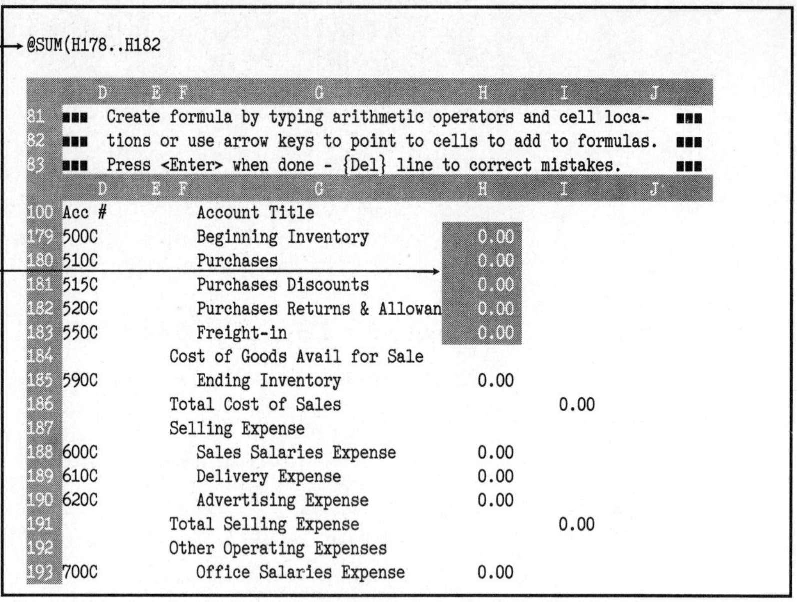

Your formula
should look like this ────────→ @SUM(H178..H182

```
        D     E  F              G                    H        I        J
 81  ███  Create formula by typing arithmetic operators and cell loca-  ███
 82  ███  tions or use arrow keys to point to cells to add to formulas. ███
 83  ███  Press <Enter> when done - {Del} line to correct mistakes.     ███
        D     E  F              G                    H        I        J
100  Acc #              Account Title
179  500C               Beginning Inventory          0.00
180  510C               Purchases                    0.00
181  515C               Purchases Discounts          0.00
182  520C               Purchases Returns & Allowan  0.00
183  550C               Freight-in                   0.00
184                  Cost of Goods Avail for Sale
185  590C               Ending Inventory           0.00
186                     Total Cost of Sales                  0.00
187                     Selling Expense
188  600C               Sales Salaries Expense     0.00
189  610C               Delivery Expense           0.00
190  620C               Advertising Expense        0.00
191                     Total Selling Expense                0.00
192                     Other Operating Expenses
193  700C               Office Salaries Expense    0.00
```

The range for the formula
should look like this ──────────┘

Figure 5-7

The formula @SUM(H178..H182 should appear on the second
line of the control panel. If it doesn't, press ESC and reenter
the formula.

To complete the formula,

Type: **)**
Press: ⏎

Creating a Subtotal for Gross Margin

Now that you have lines for Cost of Goods Sold and Net Sales,
you are ready to create the subtotal for Gross Margin required
in the multiple-step income statement Tom wants to use.

The Gross Margin subtotal will appear on the income statement
immediately below the Cost of Sales subtotal. You want to
draw a line below Total Cost of Sales to show that it is included
in the Gross Margin subtotal. In RTR, you can insert a line
between totals in the chart of accounts and income statement
using the Formula command.

Move: to the row that contains the Selling Expense heading
          (row 187)

Use the Formula command to insert a line after Total Cost
of Sales.

Press: INS
Select: **Formula**
Press: ⏎ to skip entering a label for this line

To enter a line, use the Lotus 1-2-3 backslash (\) label prefix and a hyphen (-). The backslash tells Lotus 1-2-3 to repeat the next character(s) across the width of the cell.

Type: \-
Press: ⏎

A dotted line should appear in column I in the row below Total Cost of Sales. Now create the formula for Gross Margin:

Press: ↓
Press: INS
Select: **Formula**
Type: **Gross Margin**
Press: ⏎

The cell pointer is positioned for the formula to be entered. For this formula you will use a simple arithmetic formula instead of the @SUM formula. Gross Margin is equal to Net Sales minus Cost of Sales. This formula can be constructed using a plus (+) and a minus (−) sign and by pointing to the amounts you want to add and subtract.

Type: +
Move: to the amount for the Net Sales subtotal (cell I171)
Type: −

The cell pointer moves back to the cell where you are entering the formula.

Move: to the amount for Total Cost of Sales (cell I185)

Your screen should look like Figure 5-8.

This is the simple
arithmetic formula ──────→ +I171-I185

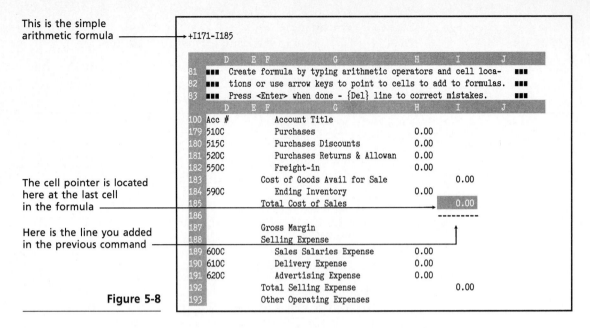

	D	E	F	G	H	I	J
81	■■		Create formula by typing arithmetic operators and cell loca-			■■	
82	■■		tions or use arrow keys to point to cells to add to formulas.			■■	
83	■■		Press <Enter> when done - {Del} line to correct mistakes.			■■	
	D	E	F	G	H	I	J
100	Acc #			Account Title			
179	510C			Purchases	0.00		
180	515C			Purchases Discounts	0.00		
181	520C			Purchases Returns & Allowan	0.00		
182	550C			Freight-in	0.00		
183				Cost of Goods Avail for Sale		0.00	
184	590C			Ending Inventory	0.00		
185				Total Cost of Sales		0.00	
186							
187				Gross Margin		--------	
188				Selling Expense			
189	600C			Sales Salaries Expense	0.00		
190	610C			Delivery Expense	0.00		
191	620C			Advertising Expense	0.00		
192				Total Selling Expense		0.00	
193				Other Operating Expenses			

The cell pointer is located
here at the last cell
in the formula ──────

Here is the line you added
in the previous command ──────

Figure 5-8

To complete the formula,

Press: (↵)

You do not need to enter parentheses when you enter a simple
formula that adds one number and subtracts another.

Insert a blank line between the formula for Gross Margin and
the heading for Selling Expense.

To review the changes you have made to the income statement,
print a dummy form.

Press: (F7)
Select: **Income**

Your printout should look like Figure 5-9. If it doesn't, use the
editing instruction keys in the top window on the screen to
change the incorrect lines or to delete and redo them.

```
Walton Electronics Detailed Income Statement 13-Oct-90 - Page 1
REVENUE
    Sales
        Sales                                    0.00
    Total Sales                                              0.00
    Deductions from Sales
        Sales Discounts                          0.00
        Sales Returns & Allowances               0.00
    Total Deductions from Sales                              0.00

    Net Sales                                                0.00
                                                         _____
TOTAL REVENUE                                                0.00
EXPENSES
    Cost of Sales
        Beginning Inventory                      0.00
        Purchases                                0.00
        Purchases Discounts                      0.00
        Purchases Returns & Allowan              0.00
        Freight-in                               0.00
    Cost of Goods Avail for Sale                             0.00
        Ending Inventory                         0.00
    Total Cost of Sales                                      0.00
                                                         _____
    Gross Margin                                             0.00

    Selling Expense
        Sales Salaries Expense                   0.00
        Delivery Expense                         0.00
        Advertising Expense                      0.00
    Total Selling Expense                                    0.00
    Other Operating Expenses
        Office Salaries Expense                  0.00
        Rent Expense                             0.00
        Supplies Expense                         0.00
        Insurance Expense                        0.00
        Utility Expense                          0.00
        Telephone Expense                        0.00
        Postage Expense                          0.00
    Total Other Operating Expenses                           0.00
    Depreciation Expense
        Depr. Exp. - Equipment                   0.00
        Depr. Exp. - Furniture                   0.00
        Depr. Exp. - Trucks                      0.00
    Total Depreciation Expense                               0.00
                                                         _____
TOTAL EXPENSES                                               0.00
NON-OPERATING ITEMS
    Interest Expense
        Interest Expense (Revenue)               0.00
    Total Interest Expense (Revenue)                         0.00
                                                         _____
TOTAL NON-OPERATING ITEMS                                    0.00

NET INCOME                                                   0.00
                                                         ===========
```

Figure 5-9

Creating a Page Break between Assets and Liabilities

The formulas and blank lines you've entered make the Balance Sheet longer. By the time you finish the exercises, the Balance Sheet will print on two pages. (The only way to check the length of the report is to print it from the Reports menu.) If the Balance Sheet is going to be two pages long, it makes sense to make the page break occur between Assets and Liabilities. Tom Walton verifies that he wants the Balance Sheet on two pages, with assets on the first page and liabilities and owners' equity on the second page.

Press: PGDN two times

Move: to the line containing the LIABILITIES heading (row 132)

Press: (F5)

Your screen should now look like Figure 5-10. The four dots that appear in column H tell Lotus 1-2-3 that you want a page break at that point in the Balance Sheet.

These four dots will tell the printer to start a new page

Figure 5-10

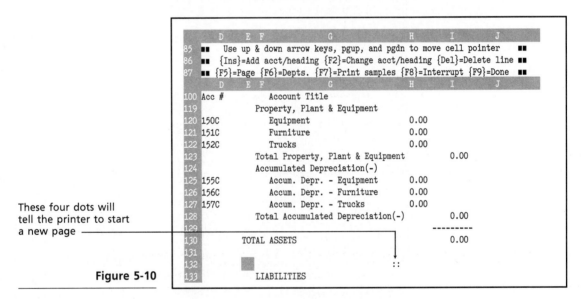

You have finished all the formatting you will do in this lab activity, but you will do some additional formatting in the exercises at the end of this lab. To save your formatting,

Press: (F9)

Select: **S**ave

RTR returns you to the Main menu.

Printing a Balance Sheet and an Income Statement

You want Tom to review the formatting you have done so far, so you want to print an initial Balance Sheet and Income Statement for Walton Electronics for period 1. These documents reflect the formatting changes you have made to the Chart of Accounts. In the exercises at the end of this lab, you will print a final Balance Sheet and Income Statement.

From the RTR Main menu,

Select: **GL Reports Statements Run**

> **Note**   If you are working on a two-diskette system, RTR prompts you to insert Program disk 2 into drive A before you select Run. After you select Statements, exchange Program disk 2 for your data disk in drive A, press ⏎, and then select Run. After you enter the period, RTR prompts you to remove Program disk 2 and re-insert your data disk.

The following prompt appears:

Enter the number of the current financial period...

Since you are running statements for January,

Type: **1**
Press: ⏎

RTR processes the transactions and adjusting entries you entered to build the financial statements. This process may take some time. As with other operations, some computers will take longer than others. When RTR finishes processing, you see the menu shown in Figure 5-11.

Figure 5-11

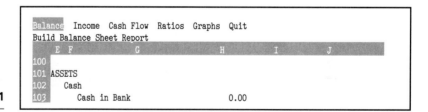

The menu has six options:

Balance	Prints the Balance Sheet.
Income	Prints the Income Statement.
Cash Flow	Prints the Statement of Cash Flows (see Lab 6).
Ratios	Prints financial analysis ratios (see Lab 6).
Graphs	Displays graphs based on the Balance Sheet and Income Statement, with a provision for printing them (see Lab 6).
Quit	Returns to the Main menu.

Building the Balance Sheet

Begin by printing the balance sheet.

Select: **B**alance

The screen shown in Figure 5-12 appears.

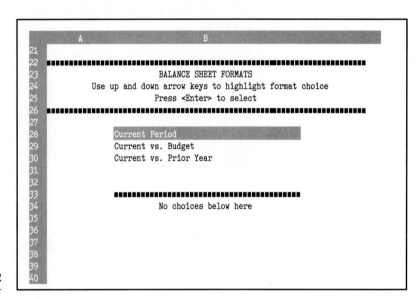

Figure 5-12

It gives you three balance sheet formats to choose from:

Current Period	Prints a balance sheet showing only current period amounts.
Current vs. Budget	Prints a balance sheet comparing current period amounts to budgeted amounts. (Budgets are covered in Lab 7.)
Current vs. Prior Year	Prints a balance sheet comparing current period amounts to the same period last year.

Since Tom Walton has just started using RTR to keep his accounting records and hasn't set up a budget yet, choose Current Period. Because the highlight is positioned on that format choice,

Press: ⏎

Again, RTR takes some time to build the balance sheet from the data files. When the balance sheet is complete, you see the menu shown in Figure 5-13.

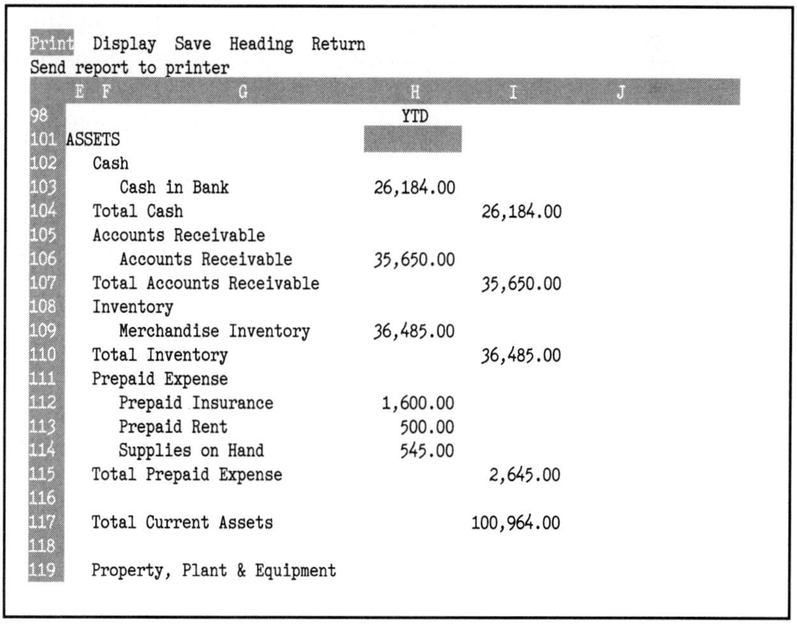

Figure 5-13

```
Print  Display  Save  Heading  Return
Send report to printer
      E  F              G                    H              I              J
 98                                         YTD
101  ASSETS
102     Cash
103        Cash in Bank              26,184.00
104     Total Cash                                     26,184.00
105     Accounts Receivable
106        Accounts Receivable       35,650.00
107     Total Accounts Receivable                      35,650.00
108     Inventory
109        Merchandise Inventory     36,485.00
110     Total Inventory                                36,485.00
111     Prepaid Expense
112        Prepaid Insurance          1,600.00
113        Prepaid Rent                 500.00
114        Supplies on Hand             545.00
115     Total Prepaid Expense                           2,645.00
116
117     Total Current Assets                          100,964.00
118
119     Property, Plant & Equipment
```

This menu is similar to the Print Options menu you saw when you printed the Trial Balance and Journals reports. It contains five options:

Print   Prints a copy of the balance sheet.

Display   Allows you to browse the balance sheet on screen.

Save   Saves the balance sheet to a file in Lotus 1-2-3 so that you can make changes to it using Lotus 1-2-3.

Heading   Allows you to change the headings on the balance sheet.

Return   Returns to the Statement Selection menu.

The top of the balance sheet appears in the screen portion of Figure 5-13. The Display and Heading commands return to this menu after they execute. However, the Print and Save commands return you to the Statement Selection menu.

Changing a Heading on a Printed Report

The heading above the amount column on the printed Balance Sheet reads "YTD," which is an abbreviation for year to date. The amounts on the balance sheets do not represent year-to-date activity, they represent a balance as of a single point in time. Tom Walton wants to see the actual date of the balance sheet, which in this case is January 31, 1992.

Select: **H**eading

Your screen should look like Figure 5-14. A window at the bottom of the screen contains the heading "YTD" along with instructions. Since there is only one heading on the Balance Sheet format you chose, the cell pointer is located on that heading.

```
      E  F            G                    H          I            J
 98  & press <Enter> when done            YTD
101  ASSETS
102     Cash
103        Cash in Bank                26,184.00
104     Total Cash                                26,184.00
105     Accounts Receivable
106        Accounts Receivable         35,650.00
107     Total Accounts Receivable                 35,650.00
108     Inventory
109        Merchandise Inventory       36,485.00
110     Total Inventory                           36,485.00
111     Prepaid Expense
112        Prepaid Insurance            1,600.00
113        Prepaid Rent                   500.00
114        Supplies on Hand               545.00
115     Total Prepaid Expense                      2,645.00
116
      E  F            G                    H          I            J
 97  Use arrow keys to move
 98  & press <Enter> when done          YTD
```

Figure 5-14

In the following command, the character you type before the date (^) is called a caret. It tells Lotus 1-2-3 that you want the information typed after it to be centered in the cell. The caret is usually the shift character on the number 6 key on the typewriter keyboard.

Type: ^**1/31/92**
Press: ⟨ ↵ ⟩

The heading cell changes to "1/31/92." Follow the instructions in the window to return to the Print Options menu:

Press: ⟨ ↵ ⟩

Displaying the Report

You want to view the entire financial statement on the screen to examine your formatting before you give Tom a printed copy. Only a portion of the balance sheet appears on the screen. To review the entire balance sheet on the screen,

Select: **D**isplay

The menu shown in Figure 5-15 appears. You have the option of choosing Summary Balance Sheet or a Detailed Balance Sheet.

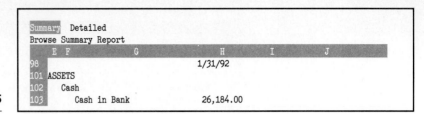

Figure 5-15

The summary balance sheet shows the totals for each summary heading in the chart of accounts, along with the blank lines and formulas you added in formatting. The detailed balance sheet shows each account within the summary headings, as well as the total for each summary heading. It also shows the blank lines and formulas you added in formatting.

To view the detailed balance sheet:

Select: **D**etailed

The message at the top of the screen tells you to use arrow keys to move around the screen and to press ⏎ when you are finished viewing the report. Use the arrow keys and PGUP and PGDN to move around the screen and look at the information. It is possible to move off the screen to the right of the balance sheet, where there are blank cells, or to move below the balance sheet where you will see what looks like an income statement. Because you selected the Balance Sheet from the Statement Selection menu, the income statement amounts are missing. If you get lost in the worksheet using the arrow keys, PGUP, and PGDN, press HOME to return to the beginning of the balance sheet.

When you finish browsing,

Press: ⏎

Printing the Balance Sheet

Print a copy of the balance sheet for Tom Walton. Be sure your printer is turned on, on-line, and that the paper is aligned properly.

Select: **P**rint

A menu similar to that shown in Figure 5-15 appears. You can choose Summary, Detailed, or Both. Print both a detailed and a summary statement so you can compare the two Balance Sheet formats.

Select: **B**oth

Choose the correct width for your printer.

Select: **Narrow** or **Wide**

RTR does not ask you to specify the type size on the financial statements. It will automatically print in condensed or regular type, depending on the printer width you chose.

When the printing is complete, the Statement Selection menu appears.

Printing the Income Statement

From the Statement Selection menu,

Select: **Income**

The screen shown in Figure 5-16 appears.

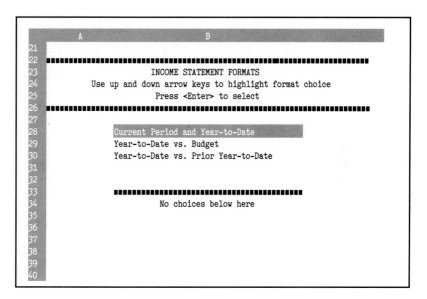

Figure 5-16

It gives you a choice of formats:

Current Period and Year-to-Date	Shows actual figures for the current month as well as cumulative amounts for the current year.
Year-to-Date vs. Budget	Compares the cumulative amounts for the current year to budgeted amounts.
Year-to-Date vs. Prior Year-to-Date	Compares the cumulative amounts for the current year to the cumulative amounts for the same time last year.

Again, since you have not yet entered budgets and since Walton Electronics started using RTR only recently, choose the first format. With the highlight on Current Period and Year-to-Date,

Press: [↵]

The Print Options menu appears. Change the heading on the report to reflect which month's income statement you are printing.

Select: **H**eading

The cell pointer should be positioned at the bottom of the screen on the heading "Current."

Type: ^**Jan 1992**
Press: [↵]
Press: [↵]   to return to the Print Options menu

Print a copy of the income statement, selecting **B**oth.

Examine the printed income statement. In addition to the amounts for January and year to date (which are the same, because January is the first period of the year), the statement shows a "% of Inc" (percentage of income) column for both the current period and the year to date. The percentage is calculated by dividing the amount on that line by the Total Revenue amount. These percentages will be helpful in performing the financial analysis to be discussed in Lab 6.

You now know how to print a copy of the primary financial statements, the balance sheet and the income statement, in either detailed or summary format. In the exercise at the end of this lab, you will print these statements again.

To return to the Main menu,

Select: **Q**uit
Select: **Y**es

Closing the Books

In your beginning accounting class, you studied closing entries. In the manual accounting exercises, you were required to write closing entries in the general journal and then post them to the general ledger. These closing entries prepared the temporary accounts to collect data for a new accounting period by zeroing out the balance. In a manual system, this process must be repeated at the end of each accounting period for which the owner or owners want financial statements.

RTR keeps a separate file for each month's transactions on the diskette. When you created the chart of accounts, RTR set up 13 period files. These files contain the audit trail information for each period in the accounting year. Since each month's data is in a separate file, you do not have to close the books at the end of each month. You have to close the books only at the end of the accounting *year*.

To demonstrate the end-of-year closing process, pretend that transactions have been recorded for all of 1992 and that you are ready to close the books at the end of that year.

Before performing the closing routine, you should back up the disk or subdirectory that contains your data files. If you are using a two-diskette system, or if you are using a hard-disk system and store your data on a separate 5¼″ or 3½″ disk, copy the files to another blank formatted disk. If you store your data on a subdirectory on your hard disk, copy the files to a blank formatted 5¼″ or 3½″ disk.

Regardless of which type of system you are using, you must exit RTR to perform the backup procedures.

Select: **Q**uit **Q**uit

You also need a new blank formatted disk to use as the backup copy of your RTR data files.

Format a new blank diskette now.

Use the procedures explained in "Getting Started" to format the diskette.

Backup on a Two-Diskette System

If you are using a two-diskette system, follow the procedures in this section. If you are using a hard-disk system, skip this section and go on to the next one.

You should have exited RTR, and you should see the A> prompt on your screen. Place the diskette containing your RTR data in drive A and the newly formatted blank diskette in drive B.

> **Note**   Be sure you put your *data* diskette in drive A, not the RTR program diskette. Also, be sure the A> prompt is on your screen. If it is not, type **A:** and press ⏎.

Type: **COPY A:*.* B:**
Press: ⏎

You will see the names of the files as the computer copies them to the new diskette.

Some of the names that appear are LEDGER.WK1, PERIOD1.WK1, and ACTIVITY.WK1. If these names do not appear, you are backing up the wrong diskette. Ask your instructor or lab assistant for help.

When the A> prompt appears again, remove the diskette from drive B and label it "Backup Data Disk, January, 1992, Walton Electronics." Keep this diskette in a safe place because you will use it later.

Now skip to the section "The Closing Procedure."

Backup on a Hard-Disk System

To back up your data using a hard-disk system, the procedures you use depend on whether you save your data on the hard disk or on a diskette. Choose the appropriate section below to back up your data.

Saving Data on a 5¼" or 3½" Diskette If your computer has two disk drives in addition to a hard disk, follow the procedures outlined in the previous section, "Backup on a Two-Diskette System."

If you have one disk drive in your computer in addition to a hard disk, begin by making sure the DOS prompt appears on your screen. It should say C> or some variation of that. Insert your RTR data disk in the disk drive.

Type: **COPY A:*.* B:**
Press: ⏎

The computer will treat the disk drive you have as both A and B. Your RTR data diskette will be the source disk and the blank formatted disk will be the target disk. The computer prompts you to place the source disk in drive A, reads a portion of the data from the RTR data disk, and then it prompts you to insert the target disk. Place the newly formatted blank disk into the drive. When it finishes writing the data it read from the source disk, the computer again prompts you to switch disks. You may have to switch disks several times because the computer cannot retain all of the data at once to copy it. When all the information is copied, the DOS prompt reappears on your screen.

Make sure that you have copied the correct diskette by listing a directory of the files on the backup diskette. With the backup diskette in drive A, at the C> prompt:

Type: **DIR A:**
Press: ⌫

A list of the files on the backup diskette should appear on the screen. The names should include LEDGER.WK1, PERIOD1.WK1, and ACTIVITY.WK1. If these filenames are not included in the directory listing, you have copied the wrong diskette. Ask your instructor or lab assistant for help.

Remove the backup disk from the drive and label it ''Backup Data Disk, January 1992, Walton Electronics.'' Keep this disk in a safe place because you will use it later.

Saving Data from a Hard-Disk Subdirectory   The instructions in this section assume that you save your data in a subdirectory entitled C:\READY\GL, which was the default subdirectory indicated by the Install program. If you save your data under a different subdirectory name, substitute the name of your subdirectory for C:\READY\GL in the following commands.

Be sure the DOS prompt appears on your screen in the format C> or some variation of that. Insert your newly formatted blank diskette into the 5¼" or 3½" drive of your computer.

Type: **COPY C:\READY\GL\ *.* A:**
Press: ⌫

The screen should show the names of the files it is copying as it copies them to the new disk. The files should include the following names: LEDGER.WK1, PERIOD1.WK1, and ACTIVITY.WK1. If these filenames are not in the list of files being backed up, you are backing up the wrong directory. Ask your instructor or lab assistant for help.

When the DOS prompt reappears, remove the diskette from the drive and label it "Backup Data Disk, January, 1992, Walton Electronics." Keep this diskette in a safe place because you will use it later.

The Closing Procedure

Now you are ready to step through the procedures to close the books for Walton Electronics at the end of 1992. To do this, you must restart Lotus 1-2-3 and RTR. If you are storing your data on a diskette, use the data diskette you have been using all along for the rest of the activities in this lab. (If you are working on a two-diskette system, RTR prompts you to insert your data diskette in drive A.)

Closing the Drawing Account In some computerized systems, including RTR, the year-end closing process *only* closes the revenue and expense accounts. It does not close the drawing account into the capital account. (In a corporation, it does not close the dividends account into retained earnings.) Because of this feature, you should record an entry in the general journal that closes the drawing account into the capital account. You *must* record this entry before you run the New-year procedure.

Record this closing entry in the General Journal. Select the appropriate commands to record entries in the General Journal using the Pairs command. You do not need to use the automatic backup system because you are recording only one entry.

Record the closing entry in period 13. Debit the Tom Walton, Capital, account and credit the Tom Walton, Drawing, account for $5,200, the balance in the drawing account. Date the entry December 31, 1992. Use JE92999 for a reference number and "CLOSE DRAWING" for the description.

If you have been completing the TWE, Inc. exercises, close the Common Dividends Declared account into Retained Earnings.

Save the entry. When you are back at the RTR Main menu, select the appropriate commands to post the entry, printing the postings reports. The Drawing (or Common Dividends Declared) account is now closed to the Capital (or Retained Earnings) account.

Print a trial balance for period 13. The printed trial balance should show the Ending Balance in Tom Walton, Drawing (or Common Dividends Declared) to be zero.

Closing the Revenue and Expense Accounts   RTR provides a special feature that closes the revenue and expense accounts to the Capital (or Retained Earnings) account automatically. From the RTR Main menu,

Select: **Files**
Select: **New-Year**

You should see the menu and screen shown in Figure 5-17. The screen warns you to make a copy of your files before you run the procedure. The menu is similar to the Run/Quit/Break menu, but the order of the commands is changed so that Quit is the default command. The warning screen and the changed order of the menu items are meant to alert you to the fact that this procedure makes irreversible changes to your data files. If you perform this procedure inadvertently, you will lose data that can take hours to replace.

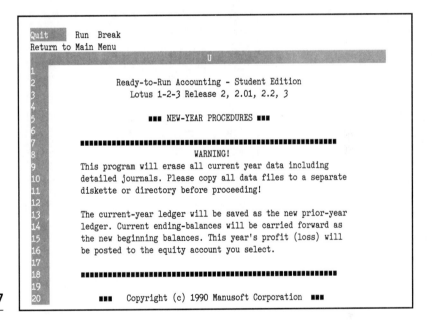

Figure 5-17

To run the New-Year procedure,

Select: **R**un

Enter your data password at the prompt. You should see the screen shown in Figure 5-18.

	C	D	E	F
	Acc #	Account Title	Beg Bal	Period 1
4	120	Merchandise Inventory	36,485.00	0.00
7	130	Prepaid Insurance	1,600.00	0.00
8	131	Prepaid Rent	500.00	0.00
9	132	Supplies on Hand	545.00	0.00
10	150	Equipment	16,500.00	0.00
11	151	Furniture	7,200.00	0.00
12	152	Trucks	4,800.00	0.00
13	155	Accum. Depr. - Equipment	(1,100.00)	0.00
14	156	Accum. Depr. - Furniture	(975.00)	0.00
15	157	Accum. Depr. - Trucks	(100.00)	0.00
16	200	Accounts Payable	(32,129.00)	0.00
17	210	Notes Payable	(2,800.00)	0.00
18	220	Interest Payable	(24.00)	0.00
19	225	Salaries Payable	(1,435.00)	0.00
20	230	Customer Deposits	(1,000.00)	0.00
21	300	Tom Walton, Capital	(84,755.00)	0.00
25		Use up/down keys to select EQUITY ACCOUNT to credit year-end		
26		income/(loss) of $5,146.00 - Press <Enter>.		

Figure 5-18

The message in the bottom window of the screen prompts you to choose the equity account to which you want to credit the net income. Since Walton Electronics is a proprietorship, the net income should be closed to the Tom Walton, Capital account. RTR highlights this account for you. (If you have been completing the TWE, Inc. exercises, you should select the Retained Earnings account. Press ⬇ until the Retained Earnings account is highlighted.)

Press: ⏎

RTR creates files to hold the transactions for each of the 13 periods in the new year. If you are *not* using a subdirectory on your hard disk for your data files, RTR prompts you to insert a disk for each of the 13 periods. Leave your data diskette in the drive and press ⏎ at each prompt. (This is the same as the procedure you followed when you set up the chart of accounts for the first time.)

You should see the RTR Main menu. To see the effect of the New-Year procedure, print a trial balance for period 1. The ending balances for the balance sheet accounts from your earlier trial balance have been transferred to the Prior Balance column. The balance in the Drawing (or Dividends) account reflects the closing entry you made and posted. Also, the revenue and expense accounts are zeroed out, and the net income has been added to the Tom Walton, Capital, or Retained Earnings account.

Restoring Your Working Data to the Original Disk or Directory

In the labs that follow, you will use the 1992 data for Walton Electronics that you backed up before you performed the New-Year procedure.

Exit RTR and Lotus 1-2-3 so that the DOS prompt appears on your screen. Restore your data by following the instructions in the appropriate section below.

Data Stored on a 5¼″ or 3½″ Diskette If you store your data on a 5¼″ or 3½″ diskette, use the *backup* diskette you created during the backup process. Cross out the word ''Backup'' on the label and use this diskette for the exercises at the end of this lab activity, as well as for future lab activities.

Write the words ''DO NOT USE'' on the label of the diskette you used during the New-Year procedure.

You may proceed to the exercises at the end of this lab.

Data Stored in a Subdirectory on a Hard Disk If you store your data in a subdirectory on your hard disk, type the following command at the DOS prompt. (These instructions again assume that your subdirectory is C:\READY\GL. If it is not, substitute your subdirectory name for C:\READY\GL.)

Place the backup diskette you just created in drive A.

Type: **COPY A:*.* C:\READY\GL**
Press: ⏎

The files are copied one at a time from the backup disk to your working subdirectory.

During the New-Year procedure, a file containing prior year balances was created on your working subdirectory. You must erase this file.

Type: **ERASE C:\READY\GL\PLEDGER.WK1**
Press: ⏎

You are now ready to proceed to the exercises at the end of this lab.

Exercises

Remember to use your backup data diskette or to restore your backed-up data to your hard-disk directory before completing these exercises.

⚡ Walton ⚡
⚡Electronics⚡

Walton Electronics

1. Make the following format changes in the balance sheet and income statement for Walton Electronics.

Balance Sheet

   a. Create a subtotal for Net Property, Plant, and Equipment after Total Accumulated Depreciation. The formula should total all of the accounts in the Property, Plant & Equipment and Accumulated Depreciation groups. Use @SUM to total all of the accounts in Column H that make up these two summary headings. (If you use simple arithmetic to add the totals of the summary headings, you must *add* — use the + sign — the total for Accumulated Depreciation because it is a negative number.)

   b. Create a subtotal for Total Current Liabilities after Total Other Current Liabilities. The formula should total all of the accounts in the Liabilities section through Other Current Liabilities.

   c. Insert blank lines before and after the two subtotals you created in numbers 1 and 2.

   d. Print a dummy form of the Balance Sheet. (Note: the dummy form will not start a new page at the page break; it will print the four dots that appear on the screen where the page break is supposed to occur.)

Income Statement

    e. Create a subtotal for Total Operating Expenses after Total Depreciation Expense. The formula should total all of the accounts in the Selling Expense, Other Operating Expense, and Depreciation Expense groups.

    f. Create a subtotal for Operating Profit after TOTAL EXPENSES. The formula should subtract TOTAL EXPENSES from TOTAL REVENUES. (Because Cost of Sales is included in TOTAL EXPENSES, this subtotal will be correct if you subtract TOTAL EXPENSES from TOTAL REVENUES.) What other formula would give you the correct result for Operating Profit?

    g. Before each of the subtotals you created in e. and f., insert a dotted line in column I (the way you did for Gross Margin in the lab). Insert a blank line after each of these two subtotals.

    h. Insert a page break in the Income Statement at Selling Expense. (Position the cell pointer *on* the Selling Expense summary heading before issuing the page break command.)

    i. Print a dummy form of the Income Statement.

2. Save the changes you have made to the Balance Sheet and Income Statement format.

3. Print summary and detailed copies of the balance sheet and income statement for period 1 showing the format changes you made in the exercises (remember to change the headings as you did in the lab activity.)

Check figures:

Net Income	$ 5,146
Total Accounts Receivable	35,650

TWE, Inc.

1. Follow the instructions for Walton Electronics.

Going Further

2. Examine the final printed copy of the detailed balance sheet. Suggest format changes that would make the statement easier to understand and/or bring the statement more in conformity with generally accepted accounting principles.

3. Examine the final printed copy of the detailed income statement. Suggest format changes that would make the statement easier to understand and/or bring the statement more in conformity with generally accepted accounting principles.

4. Assume that TWE, Inc. also had the following accounts with non-zero balances at the end of January. Indicate where these accounts would be disclosed on the RTR income statement or balance sheet and under what summary headings.

a. Allowance for Doubtful Accounts

b. 8% Bonds Payable, Due 1996

c. Discount on Bonds Payable

d. Dividend Revenue

e. Extraordinary Loss from the Early Retirement of Debt

f. Gain on the Sale of Discontinued Operations

g. Goodwill

h. Income from Discontinued Operations

i. Land Held for Resale

j. Long-term Investment in Bonds

k. Loss on Sale of Machinery

l. Retained Earnings, Appropriated for Treasury Stock

m. Treasury Stock

Lotus 1-2-3

1. Prepare a classified balance sheet.

   a. From the Reports menu, save a summary balance sheet for period 1 to a Lotus 1-2-3 file. Quit RTR to Lotus 1-2-3.

   b. In Lotus 1-2-3, retrieve the file you created from the GL subdirectory. Add a statement heading, section titles, lines, and dollar signs where appropriate. Move some account balances into column F to improve readability. Substitute a cell formula for each of the subtotals and totals. Calculate ending owner's capital or ending retained earnings. Make any other changes necessary to make the statement conform to generally accepted accounting practice.

   c. Print a copy of the balance sheet.

2. Prepare a multistep income statement, including the disclosure of percentages.

   a. From the Reports menu, save a summary income statement for period 1 to a Lotus 1-2-3 file. Quit RTR to Lotus 1-2-3.

   b. In Lotus 1-2-3, retrieve the file you created from the GL subdirectory. Delete columns G, H, and I. Add a column between columns E and F. Move some of the account balances into the new column to improve readability. Delete the headings and totals for the individual expenses and revenues. Delete the Cost of Goods Available for Sale line. Add a statement heading, section titles, lines, and dollar signs where appropriate. Substitute a cell formula for each of the subtotals and totals. Complete the percentage of sales column, using appropriate formulas. Make any other changes necessary to make the statement conform to generally accepted accounting practice.

   c. Print a copy of the income statement.

6

Financial Analysis Tools

**Ready-to-Run
General Ledger Structure**

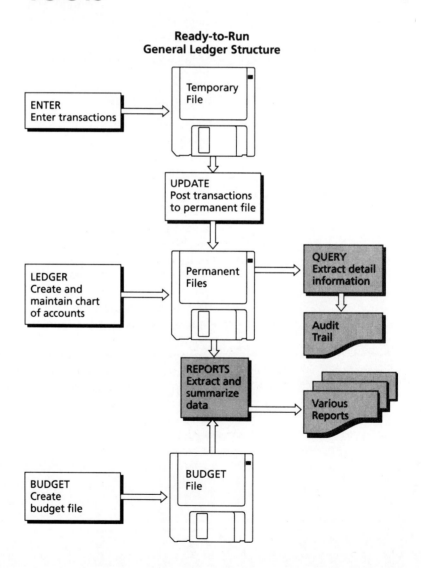

Objectives

In Lab 6, you will learn how to:

- Print a cash flow worksheet
- Print a sheet of financial ratios
- Use Ready-to-Run's graphing functions

The Cash Flows Worksheet

Because his business is growing so fast, Tom Walton has contacted his local bank about borrowing some money to expand his operations. The banker told him that he must provide a balance sheet, an income statement, and a statement of cash flows before the bank would consider his request. Tom knew when he bought the RTR software that it had a cash flows feature. He wants you to use RTR to prepare the statement of cash flows.

Most general ledger software programs cannot help with the preparation of the Statement of Cash Flows because so much of the work is analysis. Using RTR, you can print a report that allows you to identify the areas in which changes have occurred. You can use this information to help you prepare the formal Statement of Cash Flows.

Note The Ready-to-Run Cash Flows Report does not meet the specifications for the Statement of Cash Flows and should not be substituted for it.

Ready-to-Run uses the summary headings built into the chart of accounts to prepare the Cash Flows Report. Thus, it is very important for you to assign accounts to these summary headings properly when you create the chart of accounts or when you add accounts later. If you put an account into the wrong summary heading, the Cash Flows Report could be incorrect. Because of this, you must examine the Cash Flows Report carefully to be sure that each item is in the proper category for the Statement of Cash Flows.

Generating the Cash Flows Report

The Cash Flows Report is generated from the Statement Selection menu of the Statements command. From the RTR Main menu,

Select: **GL Reports Statements Run**

> **Note** If you are working on a two-diskette system, select **GL Reports Statements**, exchange Program disk 2 for your data diskette in drive A, press ⏎, and then select **R**un. After you enter the period, RTR prompts you to remove Program disk 2 and re-insert your data diskette in drive A.

At the prompt, enter the latest financial period,

Type: **1**
Press: ⏎

You should now see the Statement Selection menu, which you saw when you printed the Balance Sheet and the Income Statement. From this menu:

Select: **Cash Flow**

The next menu gives you the choice of building the Cash Flows Report from actual ledger data or from budget data. Because you have not entered budget data for Walton Electronics,

Select: **Ledger**

Printing the Cash Flows Report

A menu similar to the Statement Print Options menu you saw in Figure 5-13 appears on the screen. The options on this menu allow you to print the report, display the report, save the report to a Lotus 1-2-3 worksheet file, or return to the previous menu. The report is only one page long, so print it to examine it. Be sure your printer is on-line and the paper is properly aligned.

Select: **Print**

Because the Cash Flows Report always fits on one page even when it is printed on a narrow printer, RTR does not give you any options on how this report is printed.

> **Note** As in Lab 5, if you are completing the exercises for TWE, Inc. at the end of the labs, the figures in this lab differ from the ones you get when you complete the activity. See your instructor for the correct information to check your results.

Interpreting the Cash Flows Report

Remove the Cash Flows Report from the printer and examine it. It should look like Figure 6-1.

```
Walton Electronics          Cash Flow Report - Actual Period 1

Net Income (after tax)                    5,146.00
Plus: Depreciation & Amortization           450.00
                                        ---------------
Income Statement Cash Flow                5,596.00

Accounts Receivable-Decr.(Incr.)            630.00
Inventory-Decr.(Incr.)                   (3,985.00)
Misc. Current Assets-Decr.(Incr.)           805.00
Accounts Payable-Incr.(Decr.)             8,079.00
Accrued Liabilities-Incr.(Decr.)          1,459.00
Inc.Tax Pay. & Defer.Tax-Incr(Decr)           0.00
Other Current Liabs.-Incr.(Decr.)          (500.00)
Oth.Noncurrent Liabs.-Incr.(Decr.)            0.00
                                                        ---------------
OPERATING CASH FLOW                                        12,084.00

Marketable Securities-Decr.(Incr.)            0.00
Long Term Investment-Decr.(Incr.)             0.00
Fixed Asset-Decr.(Incr.)                 (4,800.00)
Intang.& Oth.Noncurr.A.-Decr(Incr)            0.00
                                                        ---------------
INVESTING CASH FLOW                                        (4,800.00)
                                                        ===============
CASH FLOW BEFORE FINANCING                                  7,284.00

Short Term Debt-Incr.(Decr.)              2,800.00
Long Term Debt-Incr.(Decr.)                   0.00
Subordinated Debt-Incr.(Decr.)                0.00
                                        ---------------
Debt Financing Cash Flow                  2,800.00

Capital Stock-Incr.(Decr.)                    0.00
Dividends/Drawings Paid                  (5,200.00)
Adjustment to Retained Earnings               0.00
Other Equity-Incr.(Decr.)                     0.00
                                        ---------------
Equity Financing Cash Flow               (5,200.00)
                                                        ---------------
FINANCING CASH FLOW                                        (2,400.00)


BEGINNING CASH                                             21,300.00

OPERATING CASH FLOW                                        12,084.00
INVESTING CASH FLOW                                        (4,800.00)
FINANCING CASH FLOW                                        (2,400.00)
                                                        ---------------
COMPREHENSIVE CASH FLOW                                     4,884.00

ENDING CASH                                               26,184.00
                                                        ===============
```

Figure 6-1

RTR uses the indirect method of determining cash flow from operations. The indirect method begins with net income and adjusts for those items included in net income that do not represent operating cash flows. It also adjusts for changes in other current asset and current liability accounts. (Refer to your accounting text to review the differences between the direct and indirect methods of determining cash flow from operations.) Note the categories of items used by RTR to adjust net income to arrive at operating cash flow. From what you learned about the Statement of Cash Flows in your accounting class, can you explain why Oth.Noncurrent Liabs.-Incr.(Decr.) is an adjustment to arrive at operating cash flow?

You would prepare a formal Statement of Cash Flows based on the items on this report. For example, in the INVESTING CASH FLOW section, the report indicates an increase in Fixed Assets, which represents an outflow of cash. From the transactions you entered you know that this amount represents the cost of the truck purchased during January. In the formal Statement of Cash Flows, the $4,800 should be labeled ''Purchase of Equipment.''

The Cash Flows Report gives you only the *net* change in each particular item. If Walton Electronics had sold equipment in addition to buying the truck, only the net difference between the cost of the equipment sold and the cost of the truck would show as a decrease or increase in fixed assets. On the Statement of Cash Flows, you may not net two such transactions against each other. You would have to list the proceeds of the sale of the equipment and the cost of the truck. Thus, the Cash Flows Report generated by RTR is a worksheet to help you prepare a formal Statement of Cash Flows. You will prepare a formal Statement of Cash Flows for Walton Electronics in the exercise at the end of this lab so that Tom Walton can take it to his banker along with the financial statements printed in Lab 5.

If you know how to use Lotus 1-2-3, you can prepare the Statement of Cash Flows by saving the Cash Flows Report to a Lotus 1-2-3 worksheet file. You can then make changes in wording and amounts directly on the worksheet and print it as the formal Statement of Cash Flows.

The Built-in
Ratio Analysis

Tom Walton took a continuing education class at the local college about using financial statements in a small business. He learned in class that banks usually look at certain financial ratios to help determine whether or not to loan money to a business. Tom knows that RTR has a ratio analysis calculation built into it. He wants you to print it out for him.

The ratio analysis in RTR also uses the summary heading categories that you set up in the chart of accounts. As with the Cash Flows Report, for the ratio analysis to be accurate you must assign accounts to the proper summary heading.

Printing the Ratio Analysis

To print the financial ratio analysis, from the Statement Selection menu,

Select: **R**atios

You see the same Ledger/Budget menu you saw when you selected the Cash Flows report option. Again, because you have not entered budget data yet,

Select: **Ledger**

The Statement Print Options menu appears. Again, the ratios will print on one page. Be sure your printer is on-line and the paper is properly aligned.

Select: **Print**

Interpreting the Ratio Analysis

The printed report should look like Figure 6-2.

```
Walton Electronics          Cash Flow Report - Actual Period 1

Liquidity Ratios
      Current Ratio (Cur Asst/Cur Liab)          2.70
      Quick Ratio (Cash+AR/Cur Liab)             1.65

Safety Ratios
      Debt/Worth                                 0.42
      Debt/Assets                                0.29

Balance Sheet Ratios - Annualized
      Return On Assets(Pretax%)                 48.51%
      Return On Equity(Pretax%)                 68.65%
      Asset Turnover                             5.44
      A/R Collection (Days)                     18.53
      Inventory Turnover(Days)                  27.13
      A/P Payment Period(Days)                  23.89
```

Figure 6-2

Remove the report from the printer and examine the calculated ratios. Using your accounting text's chapter on ratio analysis and the copy of Walton Electronics' financial statements from Lab 5, determine how the ratios were calculated. For example, the current ratio is calculated by dividing current assets by current liabilities. According to the balance sheet you printed in the exercises in Lab 5, Walton Electronics's Total Current Assets are $100,964 and Total Current Liabilities are $37,388. Divide $100,964 by $37,388 and you get 2.70, which is the current ratio printed on the Financial Ratios report.

The quick ratio is calculated by dividing liquid current assets by current liabilities. Normally, liquid current assets include cash, marketable securities, and accounts receivable. Since Walton Electronics does not have marketable securities, the quick ratio should be the total of cash and accounts receivable divided by total current liabilities. Cash of $26,184 and Accounts Receivable of $35,650 give you a total of $61,834. If you divide this by total current liabilities of $37,388, you get 1.65, which is the quick ratio printed on the Financial Ratios report.

Financial ratios are not meaningful by themselves. You must determine what is being measured and then have a benchmark against which to measure it. You can compare ratios to previous years' ratios, to budgeted ratios, or to industry averages. Usually some combination of the three helps the manager or owner figure out the financial stability of his or her company. Use your accounting or finance textbook to review each of the ratios included on this Financial Ratios report. You can help Tom Walton interpret them only if you understand how they are calculated and what they mean.

The current ratio tells Tom that his company has $2.70 of current assets for every dollar of current liabilities, and the quick ratio tells him that it has $1.65 of liquid current assets for every dollar of current liabilities. He thinks that his banker should be pleased with these particular ratios. He also knows that the banker will look at the other ratios. He wants you to help him understand how these ratios were calculated and what they might mean to the banker when he sees them. You will do this in the exercises.

Using the Graphing Capabilities of RTR

Tom Walton wants you to print out some of the graphs RTR can create so that he can see if they will be useful to him when he goes to see the banker.

You can use the graphing capabilities of Lotus 1-2-3 in RTR in three ways. The first is here in the Statement Selection menu, and the second is in the Query menu. A third way will be explored in Lab 7 on the Budget menu.

Graphing in the Statement Program

From the Statement Selection menu,

Select: **Graphs**

You should see a menu that offers three graphing choices.

Assets	Presents a pie chart of the composition of assets.
Debt/Equity	Presents a pie chart of the composition of liabilities and equity.
Exp/Rev	Presents a pie chart of the composition of expenses and net income.

A pie chart is a circle cut into pieces like a pie. Each piece represents a percentage of the whole. For example, the assets pie chart shows you the percentage of cash and securities in total assets. (In the pie chart, some summary headings are combined into common groupings, such as cash and marketable securities.)

After you tell Tom about the three types of graphs available in this menu, he decides that he wants to see the one that shows the composition of assets. He thinks that this graph will help him determine how much of the company's money is tied up in inventory and equipment.

Viewing the Assets Pie Chart   To view the assets pie chart,

Select: **Assets**

Because you have not entered budget data yet, you choose to see a graph based on actual ledger data:

Select: **Ledger**

The graph shown in Figure 6-3 should appear on your screen. Review it for a few minutes and note the categories represented by the pieces of the pie and what percentage of the total each piece represents.

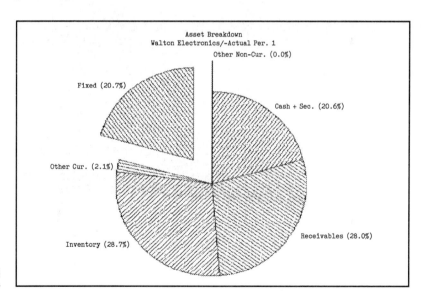

Figure 6-3

Saving the Graph for Printing   You cannot print graphs from within Lotus 1-2-3, so you cannot print graphs from within RTR. 1-2-3 comes with a separate program called PrintGraph, which prints graphs saved by Lotus 1-2-3.

To remove the graph from your screen,

Press: any key

You should see the menu shown in Figure 6-4.

Figure 6-4

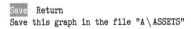

Save   Return
Save this graph in the file "A\ASSETS"

You can choose to save this graph for printing with PrintGraph or to return to the Statement Selection menu. The description line for the Save command tells you that the graph will be saved to a file called ASSETS on your data disk or in your data directory. RTR saves the file with a .PIC extension. The .PIC extension identifies a graph file that can be printed with Lotus PrintGraph. Because Tom wants a printed copy of this graph,

Select: **S**ave

The drive light on your data disk comes on while RTR saves the file ASSETS.PIC, which you can print later using PrintGraph. (The procedures for printing a file with PrintGraph are in Appendix C.) Then the prompt line shows you this message:

Graph has been saved - Use PrintGraph to print - <Enter>

Press: ⏎

to return to the Graph Selection menu.

Viewing the Debt/Equity and Exp/Rev Graphs   View the other two graphs to see how they are constructed. Note that the Exp/Rev graph shows the breakdown of expenses along with a section for net income. When there are several categories in a pie chart that each make up a small percentage of the total, the labels on the graph explaining each of those sections of the pie can overlap each other and make the graph difficult to read. For that reason, Tom does not want to have a printed copy of the other two graphs.

Graphing in the Query Program

Tom also knows that you can create bar graphs of the activity in individual accounts using the Query program in RTR. He wants to see how this graphing feature works so that he can decide whether or not to use the graphs in his visit with the banker.

Return to the RTR Main menu.

Select: **Q**uit
Select: **Yes**

From the RTR Main menu,

Select: **GL Q**uery **R**un
Select: **Black/White or Color**
Type: **1**
Press: ⏎

You should see the Query menu. Graphing is included in the Inquire command from this menu.

Select: **Inquire**

Graphing the Activity in the Cash in Bank Account   You should see the Enter/Select menu. Tom wants you to graph the Cash in Bank account first.

Select: **Enter**
Type: **100**
Press: ⏎

You should see the Inquire System Option menu. To see a bar graph of Cash in Bank,

Select: **Graph**

The graph shown in Figure 6-5 should appear on your screen.

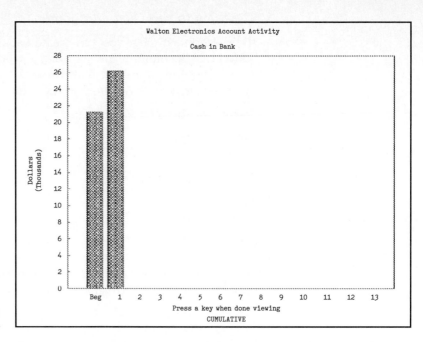

Figure 6-5

The bar on the left side of the graph shows how much cash was in the bank at the beginning of the year. The second bar shows how much cash is in the bank at the end of January. Each month, after you enter and post transactions, a bar for that month appears. By the end of the year, the graph displays 13 bars, one for the balance of the Cash in Bank account at the beginning of the year and one for the balance at the end of each month.

The instruction at the bottom of the screen says, "Press a key when done viewing." When you finish looking at the graph,

Press: any key

You should see the menu shown in Figure 6-6, which allows you to save the graph for printing with PrintGraph. After looking at this graph on the screen, Tom decides he doesn't want a printed copy of it.

Select: **R**eturn

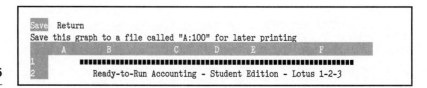

Figure 6-6

Graphing the Activity in the Sales Account Tom thinks that a graph of the Sales account is a better one to show to the banker. To return to the Query menu to select a different account,

Select: **R**eturn **I**nquire

This time use the Select command to choose the account you want to graph.

Select: **S**elect
Move to: the Sales account (use PGDN)
Press: ⏎
Select: **G**raph

The graph of the Sales account only has one bar because it is a revenue account and does not have a beginning balance. However, Tom decides that this graph is a convenient way to show the change in sales from month to month throughout the year. He wants to show it to the banker even though only one month's sales is displayed.

Press: any key
Select: **S**ave
Press: ⏎

This graph is saved under the name 400.PIC (400 is the number of the Sales account) on your data disk. Then the prompt line shows you this message:

Graph has been saved - Use PrintGraph to print - <Enter>

Press: ⏎

to return to the Graph Selection menu. To return to the RTR Main menu,

Select: **R**eturn **Q**uit

Tom wants you to graph the activity in the Merchandise Inventory and Purchases accounts also. You will complete these tasks in the exercises.

Exercises

Walton Electronics

Cash Flows Report

1. Why does short-term debt show an increase of $2,800, when Walton Electronics borrowed $4,800 to pay for the purchase of the truck?

2. Explain the $805 decrease in miscellaneous current assets that appears on the report.

3. Prepare a formal Statement of Cash Flows for Walton Electronics for the month of January.

Financial Ratios

4. Determine how RTR calculates each of the following ratios. Show supporting computations from the Walton Electronics financial statements. Note that these are annualized computations.

    a. Return On Assets

    b. Return On Equity

    c. Sales To Assets

    d. A/R Collection (Days)

    e. Inventory Turnover (Days)

    f. A/P Payment Period (Days)

5. From what you know about financial ratios in general, comment on the financial stability of Walton Electronics. As a result of this analysis, do you have any suggestions for Tom Walton when he goes to the banker to borrow money?

Graphing

6. Graph the activity for Merchandise Inventory and Purchases for Walton Electronics. Save both graphs to print later using PrintGraph.

7. Follow the instructions on using PrintGraph in Appendix C to print the graphs saved for the asset pie chart (ASSETS.PIC) and the Sales bar graph (400.PIC) in the lab activity and the graphs saved for Merchandise Inventory (120.PIC) and Purchases (510.PIC) in number 6.

TWE, Inc.

Cash Flows Report

1. Explain the $4,800 increase in Short-term Debt.

2. Explain the increase in Fixed Assets.

3. Prepare a formal Statement of Cash Flows for TWE, Inc. for the month of January using the indirect method for Cash Flows from Operating Activities

Financial Ratios

4. Complete Exercises 4 and 5 for Walton Electronics.

Graphing

5. Complete Exercises 6 and 7 for Walton Electronics.

Going Further

6. Prepare a formal Statement of Cash Flows for TWE, Inc. for the month of January using the direct method for Cash Flows from Operating Activities. Prepare a supplementary schedule to reconcile net income to cash flow from operating activities.

7. In addition to the Cash Flow Report, what other printed information available using RTR would be useful in preparing a Statement of Cash Flows? How would this information be useful?

Lotus 1-2-3

1. Prepare a statement of cash flows in good form using the indirect format for operating activities. (You must refer back to information about the original transactions in previous labs and exercises to complete this assignment.)

a. From within the Reports menu, save a cash flows report for period 1 to a Lotus file. Leave RTR and go to Lotus 1-2-3.

b. In Lotus, retrieve the file from the GL subdirectory. Add a statement heading, section titles, lines, and dollar signs where appropriate. Eliminate the categories that show no change during the periods. Substitute a cell formula for each of the subtotals and totals. Make any other changes necessary to make the statement conform to generally accepted accounting practices.

2. Print a copy of the statement of cash flows.

3. Prepare a pie graph showing how much of each sales dollar goes to the various operating expenses and interest expense.

a. From the Reports menu, save a summary income statement for period 1 to a Lotus 1-2-3 file. Leave RTR and go to Lotus 1-2-3.

b. In Lotus, retrieve the file from the GL subdirectory. Below the total revenue line, delete all the rows *except* the rows containing expenses and income after taxes.

c. Check to see if the percentages for the expenses and income after taxes equal 1.00. If they do not, recalculate them as a percentage of net sales. Move the label for the income row to column B. In column A, insert numbers from 1 to 8 in front of the expenses and income after taxes. These represent the shading designations for the pie graph. (Try using the /Data Fill command.) You may need to format column A to zero decimal places or widen it to 5 spaces.

d. Create a pie chart, designating the percentage column for the expenses and income after taxes as the A data range, the row labels as the X data range, and column A shading numbers as the B data range.

4. Save the file using the file extension .PIC for printing using PrintGraph.

7

Budgeting

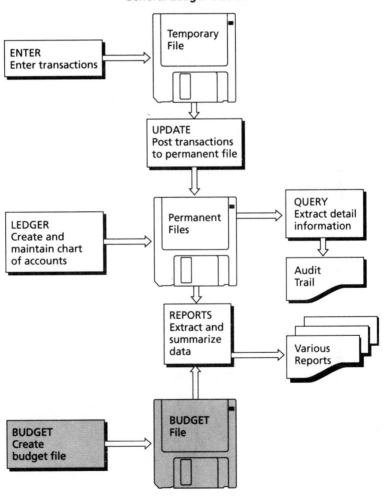

**Ready-to-Run
General Ledger Structure**

Objectives

In Lab 7, you will learn how to:

- Create a budget

- Use historical figures for a budget

- Use other features of the budget program, such as graphing and printing

Creating a Budget

During the month of January, Tom Walton developed budget projections for January of 1992. Now he wants to develop budget projections for the rest of the year. He has asked you to enter the January budget into RTR for him and produce some reports that will help him create a budget for the rest of 1992.

As you have learned in your accounting class, a budget is a financial plan for a company. It can be short-term or long-term. Long-term budgets are developed in broad general categories, but short-term budgets are more detailed. In fact, in an annual budget, each line item in the financial statements for each month must have a budget figure.

RTR creates a short-term budget. The budget module in RTR can use Walton Electronics's accounting records to compare what is actually happening with Tom Walton's plan. He can then use this information to decide whether to take action to correct problems or deviations from the plan.

Starting the Budget Program

You use the Budget command from the GL menu to access the Budget program. After you boot RTR,

Select: **GL B**udget **R**un

> **Note** If you are working on a two-diskette system, select **G**L **B**udget, exchange Program disk 2 for your data diskette in drive A, press ⏎, and then select **R**un. After you select your monitor type, RTR prompts you to remove Program disk 2 and re-insert your data diskette in drive A.

Because the Budget program contains some graphing options, you must indicate which type of monitor you have.

Select: **B**lack/White or **C**olor

You see a menu with two options: Existing and New. The Existing command allows you to change figures on a budget you've already set up during the year. Because you are creating a new budget for Walton Electronics,

Select: **N**ew

You see a menu with two options: Consolidated and Departmental. In Lab 8, you will work with the departmental feature of RTR. Since you have not yet created departments in the chart of accounts,

Select: **C**onsolidated

You see the screen shown in Figure 7-1, which contains the budgeting edit screen and the Budget menu. The screen contains the chart of accounts beginning with Cash in Bank and columns labeled Beg Bal and Period 1. The last two columns contain zeroes.

Figure 7-1

	Account Title	Beg Bal	Period 1	
	Edit/Browse Actuals Summary Graph Print Quit/Save			
	Input or change budget figures for each account			
	F	G	H	I
100	Acc #			
101	100 Cash in Bank	0.00	0.00	
102	110 Accounts Receivable	0.00	0.00	
103	120 Merchandise Inventory	0.00	0.00	
104	130 Prepaid Insurance	0.00	0.00	
105	131 Prepaid Rent	0.00	0.00	
106	132 Supplies on Hand	0.00	0.00	
107	150 Equipment	0.00	0.00	
108	151 Furniture	0.00	0.00	
109	152 Trucks	0.00	0.00	
110	155 Accum. Depr. - Equipment	0.00	0.00	
111	156 Accum. Depr. - Furniture	0.00	0.00	
112	157 Accum. Depr. - Trucks	0.00	0.00	
113	200 Accounts Payable	0.00	0.00	
114	210 Notes Payable	0.00	0.00	
115	220 Interest Payable	0.00	0.00	
116	225 Salaries Payable	0.00	0.00	
117	230 Customer Deposits	0.00	0.00	
118	300 Tom Walton, Capital	0.00	0.00	
119	310 Tom Walton, Drawing	0.00	0.00	

The Budget menu has six options:

Edit/Browse | Use this command to input or change budget figures for each account.

Actuals | Use this command to import one or more periods of actual data.

Summary | Use this command to calculate and view summary totals and cash-flow analysis.

Graph | Use this command to display graphs based on budgeted figures. You can save these graphs for printing.

Print | Use this command to print the budget.

Quit/Save | Use this command to save the budget to disk as edited or to quit without saving any work.

Importing Numbers into the Budget

Because Tom prepared his budget during the month of January, you can use the actual beginning balances as the budgeted beginning balances. To do this, use the Actuals command.

Select: **Actuals**

The prompt line should now say:

Enter period to import (0 for beginning balances - <Esc> to abort):

Because you want to import the beginning balances,

Type: **0** (zero)
Press: ⏎

You should see the Another/Done menu, which you used in Lab 4. You have the option of importing more than one period's actual figures into the budget. Because you want to import only the beginning balances,

Select: **D**one

RTR takes some time to bring the balances from the ledger file into the budget file. When it finishes, you see the screen shown in Figure 7-2. Now the Beg Bal column contains the actual beginning balances you entered in Lab 1.

These are the balances
you imported from
the ledger file

```
 Edit/Browse  Actuals  Summary  Graph  Print  Quit/Save
 Input or change budget figures for each account
            F              G                      H            I
 100 Acc #      Account Title            Beg Bal        Period 1
 101        100 Cash in Bank             21,300.00          0.00
 102        110 Accounts Receivable      36,280.00          0.00
 103        120 Merchandise Inventory    32,500.00          0.00
 104        130 Prepaid Insurance         1,800.00          0.00
 105        131 Prepaid Rent              1,000.00          0.00
 106        132 Supplies on Hand            650.00          0.00
 107        150 Equipment                16,500.00          0.00
 108        151 Furniture                 7,200.00          0.00
 109        152 Trucks                        0.00          0.00
 110        155 Accum. Depr. - Equipment  (825.00)          0.00
 111        156 Accum. Depr. - Furniture  (900.00)          0.00
 112        157 Accum. Depr. - Trucks         0.00          0.00
 113        200 Accounts Payable      (24,050.00)          0.00
 114        210 Notes Payable                 0.00          0.00
 115        220 Interest Payable              0.00          0.00
 116        225 Salaries Payable              0.00          0.00
 117        230 Customer Deposits        (1,500.00)          0.00
 118        300 Tom Walton, Capital     (89,955.00)          0.00
 119        310 Tom Walton, Drawing           0.00          0.00
```

Figure 7-2

Entering Budget Data

You are ready to enter the budget figures for January.

Select: **Edit/Browse**

You should now see the screen shown in Figure 7-3. The cell pointer is located on the beginning balance amount for Cash in Bank. According to the instructions at the bottom of the screen, you can move the cell pointer using the arrow keys, PGDN, PGUP, HOME, and END. The instructions also indicate that you can use Lotus commands to edit the budget if you know how to use them. You can also use Lotus 1-2-3 formulas to build budget numbers.

```
        F             G                      H              I
100 Acc #     Account Title              Beg Bal      Period 1
101     100 Cash in Bank                21,300.00          0.00
102     110 Accounts Receivable         36,280.00          0.00
103     120 Merchandise Inventory       32,500.00          0.00
104     130 Prepaid Insurance            1,800.00          0.00
105     131 Prepaid Rent                 1,000.00          0.00
106     132 Supplies on Hand               650.00          0.00
107     150 Equipment                   16,500.00          0.00
108     151 Furniture                    7,200.00          0.00
109     152 Trucks                           0.00          0.00
110     155 Accum. Depr. - Equipment     (825.00)          0.00
111     156 Accum. Depr. - Furniture     (900.00)          0.00
112     157 Accum. Depr. - Trucks            0.00          0.00
113     200 Accounts Payable         (24,050.00)          0.00
114     210 Notes Payable                    0.00          0.00
115     220 Interest Payable                 0.00          0.00
116     225 Salaries Payable                 0.00          0.00
                                    W
      Use cursor keys to move and Lotus commands to edit budget
            Press <Alt>+<D> when done browsing/editing
```

Figure 7-3

Balance Sheet budget figures represent the amount that you expect the account to *change* during the period, not the ending balance for the period. For example, Tom Walton expects Cash in Bank to increase during January by $5,000. Therefore you enter a positive $5,000 for Cash in Bank:

Move: to the period 1 amount for Cash in Bank
Type: **5000**
Press: ⬇

Use this entry process to enter the rest of the budget numbers for January. The cell pointer is now positioned on the period 1 amount for Accounts Receivable. Tom expects Accounts Receivable to decrease by $1,280 in January.

Type: **-1280**
Press: ⬇

Your screen should look like Figure 7-4. If it doesn't, use the ⬆ key to move back to Cash in Bank or Accounts Receivable for period 1 and correct the amount. Then position the cell pointer on the period 1 amount for Merchandise Inventory.

```
        F                 G                   H            I
100 Acc #      Account Title           Beg Bal      Period 1
101       100 Cash in Bank            21,300.00       5,000.00
102       110 Accounts Receivable     36,280.00      (1,280.00)
103       120 Merchandise Inventory   32,500.00           0.00
104       130 Prepaid Insurance        1,800.00           0.00
105       131 Prepaid Rent             1,000.00           0.00
106       132 Supplies on Hand           650.00           0.00
107       150 Equipment               16,500.00           0.00
108       151 Furniture                7,200.00           0.00
109       152 Trucks                       0.00           0.00
110       155 Accum. Depr. - Equipment  (825.00)          0.00
111       156 Accum. Depr. - Furniture  (900.00)          0.00
112       157 Accum. Depr. - Trucks        0.00           0.00
113       200 Accounts Payable       (24,050.00)          0.00
114       210 Notes Payable                0.00           0.00
115       220 Interest Payable             0.00           0.00
116       225 Salaries Payable             0.00           0.00
                                   W
1      Use cursor keys to move and Lotus commands to edit budget
2           Press <Alt>+<D> when done browsing/editing
```

Figure 7-4

Enter the rest of the budget figures for period 1 as indicated
below. The debit (positive) column should be entered as positive numbers, and the credit (negative) column should be
entered as negative numbers. Remember that increases in
assets are debits, and decreases in assets are credits, while
increases in liabilities and equity are credits and decreases in
liabilities and equity are debits. Thus, increases in liabilities
and equity accounts will appear in the credit (negative)
column, while decreases in these accounts appear in the debit
(positive) column. If an account is not listed, Tom does not
expect any change in that account during January. Check your
figures against the screens provided. Remember that you don't
include commas when you enter numbers in Lotus 1-2-3.

Account Title	Period 1 Budget	
	Debit (Positive)	Credit (Negative)
Merchandise Inventory	3,075	
Prepaid Insurance		200
Prepaid Rent		500
Supplies on Hand		150
Trucks	5,000	
Accum. Depr. – Equipment		275
Accum. Depr. – Furniture		75
Accum. Depr. – Trucks		100
Accounts Payable		5,950
Notes Payable		3,000
Interest Payable		25

Your screen should look like Figure 7-5. If it doesn't, use ⬆ and ⬇ to move around and make corrections. Fix all lines that are not correct. Then reposition the cell pointer on the period 1 amount for Salaries Payable before continuing. (If you are following the exercises for TWE, Inc., do not enter the amount for Tom Walton, Drawing.)

```
       F            G                    H           I
100 Acc #     Account Title          Beg Bal     Period 1
101      100 Cash in Bank            21,300.00     5,000.00
102      110 Accounts Receivable     36,280.00    (1,280.00)
103      120 Merchandise Inventory   32,500.00     3,075.00
104      130 Prepaid Insurance        1,800.00      (200.00)
105      131 Prepaid Rent             1,000.00      (500.00)
106      132 Supplies on Hand           650.00      (150.00)
107      150 Equipment               16,500.00         0.00
108      151 Furniture                7,200.00         0.00
109      152 Trucks                       0.00     5,000.00
110      155 Accum. Depr. - Equipment  (825.00)     (275.00)
111      156 Accum. Depr. - Furniture  (900.00)      (75.00)
112      157 Accum. Depr. - Trucks        0.00      (100.00)
113      200 Accounts Payable      (24,050.00)    (5,950.00)
114      210 Notes Payable                0.00    (3,000.00)
115      220 Interest Payable             0.00       (25.00)
116      225 Salaries Payable             0.00         0.00
                              W
1           Use cursor keys to move and Lotus commands to edit budget
2                 Press <Alt>+<D> when done browsing/editing
```

Figure 7-5

| Account Title | Period 1 Budget | |
	Debit (Positive)	Credit (Negative)
Salaries Payable		1,435
Customer Deposits	500	
Tom Walton, Drawing	5,000	
Sales		60,000
Sales Discounts	1,000	
Sales Returns & Allowances	1,250	
Beginning Inventory	32,500	
Purchases	43,000	
Purchases Discounts		500
Purchases Returns & Allowances		500
Freight-in	1,500	
Ending Inventory		35,575
Sales Salaries Expense	4,425	
Delivery Expense	300	

Now your screen should look like Figure 7-6. If it doesn't, use ⬆ and ⬇ to move around and make corrections. Then reposition the cell pointer on the period 1 amount for Advertising Expense and continue.

```
         F              G                 H            I
100 Acc #      Account Title        Beg Bal      Period 1
116       225 Salaries Payable              0.00     (1,435.00)
117       230 Customer Deposits      (1,500.00)        500.00
118       300 Tom Walton, Capital   (89,955.00)          0.00
119       310 Tom Walton, Drawing           0.00      5,000.00
120       400 Sales                         0.00    (60,000.00)
121       410 Sales Discounts               0.00      1,000.00
122       415 Sales Returns & Allowances    0.00      1,250.00
123       500 Beginning Inventory           0.00     32,500.00
124       510 Purchases                     0.00     43,000.00
125       515 Purchases Discounts           0.00       (500.00)
126       520 Purchases Returns & Allowance 0.00       (500.00)
127       550 Freight-in                    0.00      1,500.00
128       590 Ending Inventory              0.00    (35,575.00)
129       600 Sales Salaries Expense        0.00      4,425.00
130       610 Delivery Expense              0.00        300.00
131       620 Advertising Expense           0.00          0.00
                            W
        Use cursor keys to move and Lotus commands to edit budget
 1              Press <Alt>+<D> when done browsing/editing
 2
```

Figure 7-6

Account Title	Period 1 Budget	
	Debit (Positive)	Credit (Negative)
Advertising Expense	800	
Office Salaries Expense	2,750	
Rent Expense	500	
Supplies Expense	1,000	
Insurance Expense	200	
Utility Expense	500	
Telephone Expense	800	
Postage Expense	300	
Depr. Exp. – Equipment	275	
Depr. Exp. – Furniture	75	
Depr. Exp. – Trucks	100	
Interest Expense	25	

Your screen should look like Figure 7-7. Again, fix any amounts that are not correct. You have finished entering the numbers Tom gave you for January.

Press: ALT-D

Figure 7-7

```
        F              G                    H              I
100 Acc #       Account Title        Beg Bal       Period 1
128       590 Ending Inventory            0.00    (35,575.00)
129       600 Sales Salaries Expense      0.00      4,425.00
130       610 Delivery Expense            0.00        300.00
131       620 Advertising Expense         0.00        800.00
132       700 Office Salaries Expense     0.00      2,750.00
133       705 Rent Expense                0.00        500.00
134       710 Supplies Expense            0.00      1,000.00
135       715 Insurance Expense           0.00        200.00
136       720 Utility Expense             0.00        500.00
137       725 Telephone Expense           0.00        800.00
138       730 Postage Expense             0.00        300.00
139       740 Depr. Exp. - Equipment      0.00        275.00
140       745 Depr. Exp. - Furniture      0.00         75.00
141       750 Depr. Exp. - Trucks         0.00        100.00
142       800 Interest Expense            0.00         25.00
143
                                  W
1       Use cursor keys to move and Lotus commands to edit budget
2              Press <Alt>+<D> when done browsing/editing
```

Balancing the Budget

The following message appears on the prompt line:

Budget out of balance - Adjust a cash account (Y/N)?

You check with Tom Walton, who tells you that he guessed at the amount for Cash in Bank — he didn't add it up to make sure it balanced. Budget figures in RTR must balance just as an actual ledger must balance. Because Tom estimated the amount for Cash in Bank, you want to adjust a cash account.

Type: **Y**
Press: ⏎

Your screen should look like Figure 7-8.

	F	G	H	I
100	Acc #	Account Title	Beg Bal	Period 1
101	100	Cash in Bank	21,300.00	5,000.00
102	110	Accounts Receivable	36,280.00	(1,280.00)
103	120	Merchandise Inventory	32,500.00	3,075.00
104	130	Prepaid Insurance	1,800.00	(200.00)
105	131	Prepaid Rent	1,000.00	(500.00)
106	132	Supplies on Hand	650.00	(150.00)
107	150	Equipment	16,500.00	0.00
108	151	Furniture	7,200.00	0.00
109	152	Trucks	0.00	5,000.00
110	155	Accum. Depr. - Equipment	(825.00)	(275.00)
111	156	Accum. Depr. - Furniture	(900.00)	(75.00)
112	157	Accum. Depr. - Trucks	0.00	(100.00)
113	200	Accounts Payable	(24,050.00)	(5,950.00)
114	210	Notes Payable	0.00	(3,000.00)
115	220	Interest Payable	0.00	(25.00)
116	225	Salaries Payable	0.00	(1,435.00)

W

Use up/down keys to find cash account to adjust
Press <Enter> to select

5
6

Figure 7-8

The instructions in the bottom window have changed, and the cell pointer is positioned in the Acc # column on the account number for Cash in Bank. RTR has simply positioned the cell pointer at the first account in the chart of accounts. However, since this is the account that you want to adjust,

Press: ⏎

Your screen should now look like Figure 7-9. The Budget menu returns and the period 1 column contains the amounts that you entered, but the period 1 amount for Cash in Bank changes to $4,690. (The Cash in Bank amount for period 1 is $9,690 for TWE, Inc.)

Figure 7-9

```
Edit/Browse  Actuals  Summary  Graph  Print  Quit/Save
Input or change budget figures for each account
        F          G                    H           I
100 Acc #      Account Title        Beg Bal      Period 1
101      100 Cash in Bank           21,300.00    4,690.00
102      110 Accounts Receivable    36,280.00   (1,280.00)
103      120 Merchandise Inventory  32,500.00    3,075.00
104      130 Prepaid Insurance       1,800.00     (200.00)
105      131 Prepaid Rent            1,000.00     (500.00)
106      132 Supplies on Hand          650.00     (150.00)
107      150 Equipment              16,500.00        0.00
108      151 Furniture               7,200.00        0.00
109      152 Trucks                      0.00    5,000.00
110      155 Accum. Depr. - Equipment (825.00)    (275.00)
111      156 Accum. Depr. - Furniture (900.00)     (75.00)
112      157 Accum. Depr. - Trucks       0.00     (100.00)
113      200 Accounts Payable      (24,050.00)   (5,950.00)
114      210 Notes Payable               0.00    (3,000.00)
115      220 Interest Payable            0.00       (25.00)
116      225 Salaries Payable            0.00    (1,435.00)
117      230 Customer Deposits      (1,500.00)     500.00
118      300 Tom Walton, Capital   (89,955.00)       0.00
119      310 Tom Walton, Drawing         0.00    5,000.00
```

> **Note**   The Cash in Bank budget amount should be $4,690. If
> it is not, you entered one of the other numbers incorrectly.
> Select **E**dit/Browse to return to the editing screen and check
> your work. Change any incorrect amounts and then change the
> Cash in Bank budget to $4,690. Press ALT-D when you are fin-
> ished and you should balance. Make sure your screen looks like
> Figure 7-9 before you continue.

The Summary Report of the Budget

Tom wants to see the effect of the January budget on profit
and cash. The detail printout of the budget gives only a breakdown of the budget by account. The Summary command on
the Budget menu lists the budget by summary heading and also
reports the effect of each month's budget on profit and cash.

The Summary command allows you to browse or print a copy of
the budget by the summary headings in the chart of accounts.
It also allows you to graph aspects of the summary report.

Select: **S**ummary

RTR processes the budget data and summarizes it. When it finishes, you see the menu and screen shown in Figure 7-10. The summary heading descriptions from the chart of accounts replace the account titles. The amount columns display the totals for each summary heading.

Figure 7-10

```
Browse  Graph  Print  Done
Scan through summary report
      F                 G                      H             I
144                Summary Head          Beg Bal     Period 1
145                Cash                  21,300.00     4,690.00
146                Accounts Receivable   36,280.00    (1,280.00)
147                Inventory             32,500.00     3,075.00
148                Prepaid Expense        3,450.00      (850.00)
149                Other Fixed Assets    23,700.00     5,000.00
150                Accumulated Depreciation(-)  (1,725.00)    (450.00)
151                Accounts Payable      24,050.00     5,950.00
152                Notes Payable              0.00     3,000.00
153                Accrued Expense            0.00     1,460.00
154                Other Current Liabilities   1,500.00     (500.00)
155                Paid-In-Capital       89,955.00         0.00
156                Drawing (-)                0.00    (5,000.00)
157                ==============================
158                Sales                      0.00    60,000.00
159                Deductions from Revenue    0.00    (2,250.00)
160                Cost of Sales              0.00    40,425.00
161                Selling Expense            0.00     5,525.00
162                Other General & Admin.     0.00     6,050.00
163                Depreciation Expense       0.00       450.00
```

The menu on this screen has four options:

Browse   Allows you to use the arrow keys and PGUP and PGDN to move around the report.

Graph   Graphs aspects of the summary report.

Print   Prints the entire summary report.

Done   Returns to the Budget menu.

Browsing the Summary Report

Review the summary report on the screen.

Select: **B**rowse

The instructions in the bottom window of the screen tell you to use the arrow keys to move around the report. The PGDN, PGUP, and HOME keys also work in this screen.

Press: PGDN

After the last summary heading, you see lines for profit, change in cash, and cumulative cash. These are the numbers that Tom wants to review before you enter the rest of the 1992 budget.

Use the arrow keys and PGDN and PGUP to move around the report. If you use ⟶, you see additional columns for periods 2 through 13. These columns contain zeroes because you have entered budget data only for period 1.

When you finish viewing the report, return to the screen shown in Figure 7-10:

Press: ⟵

Printing the Summary Report

Tom Walton wants a printed copy of this summary report so that he can review the numbers and see if he needs to adjust them. To print the summary report,

Select: **Print**

Be sure your printer is on-line and the paper is properly aligned. You should see a menu that lets you choose to send the report to the printer or to a file on disk to be printed later or transferred to a word processing program.

Select: **Print**

You should see the menu that asks you to tell RTR whether you have a Wide or Narrow printer.

Select: **N**arrow or **W**ide

RTR prints the summary report for you. The printout should be three pages long; it should show the summary budget information for all 13 periods, as well as the beginning and ending balances. The first page should look like Figure 7-11. In the exercise for Walton Electronics, you will use a budget file that contains budget information for all 13 periods.

```
Walton Electronics              BUDGET SUMMARY REPORT                    Page 1

Summary Head         Beg Bal    Period 1    Period 2  Period 3  Period 4  Period 5
Cash                21,300.00    4,690.00       0.00      0.00      0.00      0.00
Accounts Receivable 36,280.00   (1,280.00)      0.00      0.00      0.00      0.00
Inventory           32,500.00    3,075.00       0.00      0.00      0.00      0.00
Prepaid Expense      3,450.00     (850.00)      0.00      0.00      0.00      0.00
Other Fixed Assets  23,700.00    5,000.00       0.00      0.00      0.00      0.00
Accumulated Depreciation(-) (1,725.00) (450.00) 0.00      0.00      0.00      0.00
Accounts Payable    24,050.00    5,950.00       0.00      0.00      0.00      0.00
Notes Payable            0.00    3,000.00       0.00      0.00      0.00      0.00
Accrued Liabilities      0.00   (1,460.00)      0.00      0.00      0.00      0.00
Other Current Liabilities 1,500.00 (500.00)     0.00      0.00      0.00      0.00
Paid-In-Capital     89,955.00        0.00       0.00      0.00      0.00      0.00
Drawing (-)              0.00   (5,000.00)      0.00      0.00      0.00      0.00
= = = = = = = = = = = = = =
Sales                    0.00   60,000.00       0.00      0.00      0.00      0.00
Deductions from Revenue  0.00   (2,250.00)      0.00      0.00      0.00      0.00
Cost of Sales            0.00   40,425.00       0.00      0.00      0.00      0.00
Selling Expense          0.00    5,525.00       0.00      0.00      0.00      0.00
Other General & Admin.   0.00    6,050.00       0.00      0.00      0.00      0.00
Depreciation Expense     0.00      450.00       0.00      0.00      0.00      0.00
Interest Expense (Revenue) 0.00     25.00       0.00      0.00      0.00      0.00
- - - - - - - - - - - - - -
Profit (loss)            0.00    5,275.00       0.00      0.00      0.00      0.00
= = = = = = = = = = = = = =
Change in Cash           0.00    4,690.00       0.00      0.00      0.00      0.00
Cumulative Cash     21,300.00   25,990.00  25,990.00 25,990.00 25,990.00 25,990.00
```

Figure 7-11

Graphing from the Summary Report

Tom wants to know if the graphs available in the Budget program can help him finalize his projections for 1992. He wants to make sure that related items in the financial statements make sense with the budget figures. For example, he would like to compare the budgets for Sales and Cost of Sales. The relationship between Sales and Cost of Sales should be stable, and the graph will show him whether this is true of the budget figures he asked you to enter.

The Summary part of the Budget program generates bar graphs that compare the balance in a summary heading at the end of each period, including beginning balances. Up to three summary headings can appear on a graph at one time. Using this feature, you can show Tom the graph comparing Sales and Cost of Sales.

Select: **Graph**

You should see the screen shown in Figure 7-12. The instructions in the window at the bottom tell you to select up to three summary headings by moving to the row you want to select and pressing ⏎.

	F	G	H	I
144		Summary Head	Beg Bal	Period 1
145		Cash	21,300.00	4,690.00
146		Accounts Receivable	36,280.00	(1,280.00)
147		Inventory	32,500.00	3,075.00
148		Prepaid Expense	3,450.00	(850.00)
149		Other Fixed Assets	23,700.00	5,000.00
150		Accumulated Depreciation(-)	(1,725.00)	(450.00)
151		Accounts Payable	24,050.00	5,950.00
152		Notes Payable	0.00	3,000.00
153		Accrued Expense	0.00	1,460.00
154		Other Current Liabilities	1,500.00	(500.00)
155		Paid-In-Capital	89,955.00	0.00
156		Drawing (-)	0.00	(5,000.00)
157		================================		
158		Sales	0.00	60,000.00
159		Deductions from Revenue	0.00	(2,250.00)
160		Cost of Sales	0.00	40,425.00

W

Use up/down keys and press <Enter> to select account to graph
Press D when done selecting - Up to 3 accounts maximum

Figure 7-12

Note The three summary headings you select for a graph must all be from the Balance Sheet or all from the Income Statement. Balance Sheet graphs show the balance at the end of each period, but Income Statement graphs show the change in the summary heading during each period. Also, the summary headings that appear are the "original" summary headings that come with RTR; if you changed the summary heading in the chart of accounts, your change will not be reflected on this screen.

Comparing Sales and Cost of Sales To show Tom the graph that compares Sales and Cost of Sales:

Move: to the line for Sales
Press: ⏎
Move: to the line for Cost of Sales
Press: ⏎

Follow the instructions in the window when you are finished:

Press: **D**

The graph shows two bars for each period. Only one period is displayed because data for January is the only data you entered for these summary headings. The legend at the bottom of the screen identifies which bar represents Sales and which represents Cost of Sales. Tom likes what he sees and wants you to print a copy when you have entered the budgets for the rest of the periods (in the exercise at the end of the lab). When you have finished viewing this graph,

Press: any key

You should see the Save/Return menu. Tom doesn't want you to print the graph yet, so:

Select: **Return**

Graphing the Cash Account   Tom wants to see if the graph for Cash would be useful to him in analyzing his budget projections. The Budget Summary menu should be on your screen.

Select: **Graph**

The cell pointer is on the summary heading for Cash. To view the graph for Cash,

Press: ⏎

Since you want to view only one account,

Press: **D**

The graph you see shows bars of different height for beginning balance and period 1. However, the bars for the rest of the periods are the same height as the period 1 bar because you have not entered numbers for periods 2 through 13. Tom wants you to print a copy of this graph also after you enter the remaining months' budgets for 1992 (in the exercises at the end of this lab).

Press: any key
Select: **Return**

You are finished with the Summary Report menu.

Select: **Done**

Graphing Budget Information

Tom wants to see a graph that shows the balance in the three Property, Plant, and Equipment accounts to review whether he should change the budgets in these accounts. RTR has a graphing feature on the main Budget menu that graphs individual accounts.

Select: **Graph**

You see the menu shown in Figure 7-13.

```
1.Accounts   2.Debt/Equity  3.Liquidity  4.Revenue/Expenses  Return
Graph monthly budget for selected accounts
        F              G                    H            I
100 Acc #        Account Title        Beg Bal      Period 1
101        100 Cash in Bank            21,300.00      4,690.00
102        110 Accounts Receivable     36,280.00     (1,280.00)
103        120 Merchandise Inventory   32,500.00      3,075.00
```

Figure 7-13

It contains four graphing options:

Accounts	Graphs the monthly budget for selected accounts.
Debt/Equity	Compares total liabilities to total equity in a bar graph.
Liquidity	Compares current assets to current liabilities in a bar graph.
Revenue/Expenses	Compares operating revenue to operating expenses in a bar graph.

The graphs on the menu are numbered. To select a graph, press its number rather than the first letter of its name.

Graphing Selected Accounts

The Accounts option works like the graphing feature in the Summary Report menu, and the same caution applies. Either all three accounts must be from the Balance Sheet or all three accounts must be from the Income Statement. Do not mix accounts from the two statements. Tom wants to see a graph of the budget in the Property, Plant, and Equipment accounts:

Select: **1.**Accounts

The screen is similar to the Edit/Browse screen in Figure 7-12. The lines in this screen contain the individual accounts in the chart of accounts rather than the summary headings. Thus, you can create a graph that compares the activity in individual accounts.

The instruction window at the bottom of the screen is the same as the one shown in Figure 7-12. To graph the activity in the three Property, Plant, and Equipment accounts:

Move: to the line for Equipment
Press: ⏎
Move: to the line for Furniture
Press: ⏎
Move: to the line for Trucks
Press: ⏎

When you select the third account, the graph automatically appears. (Three accounts is the maximum number you can graph at one time.)

The graph is similar to the one you saw for Cash in the previous section, except that it has three bars for each period. (Why do you think no bar for Trucks appears in the first set of bars?) Again, periods 2 through 13 show the same balance as period 1 because you have not yet entered budget data for those periods. Tom likes the way this graph looks, but he doesn't want a printed copy.

Press: any key
Select: **R**eturn

Viewing the Liquidity Graph

RTR returns you to the Budget menu. Tom is interested in viewing the Liquidity graph to see how it is constructed.

Select: **G**raph
Select: **3**.Liquidity

The liquidity graph compares Current Assets to Current Liabilities for each of the periods. Again, there is no change in the heights of the bars after period 1 because you have not entered data for periods 2 through 13. Tom wants you to print this graph after you have entered the rest of the data.

Press: any key
Select: **R**eturn

You will view these and other graphs in the exercise for Walton Electronics after you have retrieved the budget file for 1992, which has data entered for all 13 periods. Then you will print the graphs that Tom wants you to print.

Printing the Budget

When you were in the Summary Report menu, you printed a copy of the summary budget for Tom. He also wants a printed copy of the detailed budget figures to review along with that summary report. The Print command from the Budget menu prints a copy of the budget data by account.

Select: **Print**

You should see a menu that allows you to send the output to the printer or to a disk file. Send it to the printer. Be sure your printer is on-line and the paper is properly aligned.

Select: **Print**
Select: **Narrow** or **Wide**

This print program prints only the data you entered into the budget file. It does not total or summarize the data. Thus, Tom will use it to check the entry of the budget data and to provide detailed support for the summary report printed earlier. The report is three pages long, with the account numbers and titles in the left two columns on each page. The rest of the columns on each page are for the beginning balances and each of the 13 periods. The data you entered for beginning balances and period 1 should be in those columns on the first page.

Saving the Budget Data

You can return to the RTR Main menu and save the budget data you have entered while Tom reviews the printouts you have given him.

Select: **Quit/Save**

You should see a menu with the following three options:

Save   Saves the budget data and returns to the RTR Main menu.

Quit   Quits the budget program without saving your changes.

Return   Returns to the Budget menu.

Save the budget data and return to the RTR Main menu:

Select: **Save**

RTR creates the budget file from the data you entered and returns you to the Main menu.

Exercises

Walton Electronics

The disk you received with the RTR Student Edition contains a file called BLEDGER.COM. This file contains a complete budget file for Walton Electronics for 1992. To copy this file to your working data disk or directory, you must know the drive or directory where your data is located. From DOS, log on to the drive where your data is located. For example, if you are using a two-diskette system, place your data diskette in drive B and at the DOS prompt, type **B:** and press ⏎. If your data is located on a directory on your hard disk, you will need to change to that directory with the CD command. After you have logged on to the disk or directory where your data is located, place the disk you received with the RTR Student Edition in drive A. Type **A:WALTON** and press ⏎. A program confirms that your RTR data files are in the drive or directory that you are logged on to, and the program copies the BLEDGER.COM file to that drive or directory. If you get an error message, start over. Be sure that you are logged on to the correct drive or directory.

After the BLEDGER.COM file is copied to your working data disk, start RTR and complete the following exercises. Be sure to select Existing after indicating your style of monitor.

1. Print a copy of the budget detail.

2. Print a copy of the budget summary report.

3. From the Summary Report menu, graph the summary headings for Sales and Cost of Sales. Save this graph to a file to print with PrintGraph. Enter the name of the file at the prompt.

4. From the Summary Report menu, graph the summary heading for Cash. Save this graph to a file to print with PrintGraph. Enter the name of the file at the prompt.

5. From the Budget menu, graph the debt/equity ratio. Save this graph to a file for printing with PrintGraph. Enter the name of the file at the prompt.

6. From the Budget menu, graph the liquidity ratio. Save this graph to a file for printing with PrintGraph. Enter the name of the file at the prompt.

7. Print a Balance Sheet for January 1992, comparing current figures to budget figures. Print it in both detailed and summary formats.

8. Print an Income Statement for January 1992 that compares year-to-date current figures to year-to-date budget figures. Print it in both detailed and summary formats.

9. Using PrintGraph, print two of the graphs you saved in this exercise as designated by your instructor.

TWE, Inc.

The disk you received with the RTR Student Edition contains a file called BLEDGER.COM. This file contains a complete budget file for TWE, Inc. for 1992. To copy this file to your working data disk or directory, you must know the drive or directory where your data is located. From DOS, log on to the drive where your data is located. For example, if you are using a two-diskette system, place your data diskette in drive B, and at the DOS prompt type **B:** and press ⏎. If your data is located on a directory on your hard disk, change to that directory with the CD command. After you have logged on to the disk or directory where your data is located, place the disk you received with the RTR Student Edition in drive A. Type **A:TWE** and press ⏎. A program determines whether there are RTR data files in the drive or directory that you are logged on to, and the program copies the BLEDGER.COM file to that drive or directory. If you get an error message, start over. Be sure that you are logged on to the correct drive or directory.

After the BLEDGER.COM file is copied to your working data disk, start up RTR and complete the following exercises. Be sure to select Existing after indicating your style of monitor.

1. Print a copy of the budget detail.

2. Print a copy of the budget summary report.

3. From the Summary Report menu, graph the summary headings for Sales and Cost of Sales. Save this graph to a file to print with PrintGraph. Enter the name of the file at the prompt.

4. From the Summary Report menu, graph the summary heading for Cash. Save this graph to a file to print with PrintGraph. Enter the name of the file at the prompt.

5. From the Budget menu, graph the debt/equity ratio. Save this graph to a file for printing with PrintGraph. Enter the name of the file at the prompt.

6. From the Budget menu, graph the liquidity ratio. Save this graph to a file for printing with PrintGraph. Enter the name of the file at the prompt.

7. Print a Balance Sheet for January 1992 comparing current figures to budget figures. Print it in both detailed and summary formats.

8. Print an Income Statement for January 1992 that compares year-to-date current figures to year-to-date budget figures. Print it in both detailed and summary formats.

9. Use PrintGraph to print two of the graphs you saved in this exercise, as designated by your instructor.

Going Further

10. Using the information that you printed, prepare a short report for Tom Walton discussing the implications of the budgeted amounts for each of the periods in 1992. Include in your report a discussion of the financing/investing implications of the budgeted amounts.

11. Using the printed Balance Sheet and Income Statement that compares actual to budget, prepare a short report for Tom Walton discussing the results of activities for January 1992.

8

Departments and Custom Reports

**Ready-to-Run
General Ledger Structure**

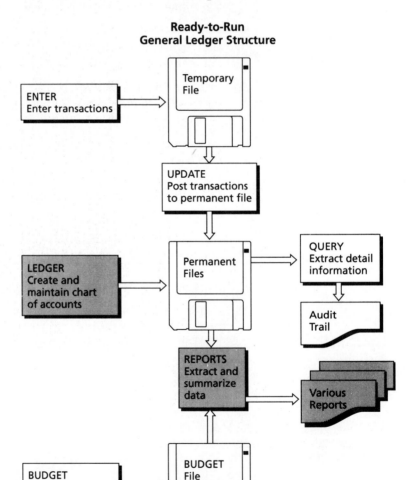

Objectives

In Lab 8, you will learn how to:

- Add departments to the chart of accounts

- Create and use custom reports

Using Departments to Obtain a Detailed Breakdown

Tom Walton wants a breakdown of Merchandise Inventory and Sales by product group. He has identified two different groups of products: base units and monitors. Ready-to-Run can add departments to existing accounts. You can use these departments to obtain a more detailed breakdown within the accounts you specify without adding more accounts. Use this feature when you want the same breakdown in more than one account.

> **Note** If you plan to use one of the Walton Electronics practice sets in the appendix, be sure to back up your data, using the backup procedure outlined in Appendix B, before you begin this lab activity. Save the backup diskette and use it when you complete the practice set.

The department feature is part of the program you used to make changes to the current chart of accounts. After you start up Lotus 1-2-3 and RTR,

Select:	**GL Ledger Ledger**
Type:	Your data password at the prompt
Press:	(↵)
Select:	**Run Backup**
Type:	**20**
Press:	(↵)
Select:	**Existing**

Adding Departments to the Chart of Accounts

The chart of accounts editing screen should appear on your monitor. The top window of this screen tells you to use (F6) for departments.

Press:	(F6)

The menu that appears has three options:

Add/Delete   Add or delete department codes.

Edit   Change existing department codes.

Return   Return to the chart of accounts editing screen.

To add departments to the chart of accounts,

Select: **Add**/Delete

You should see the screen shown in Figure 8-1. The menu allows you to add a department, delete a department, or return to the chart of accounts editing screen.

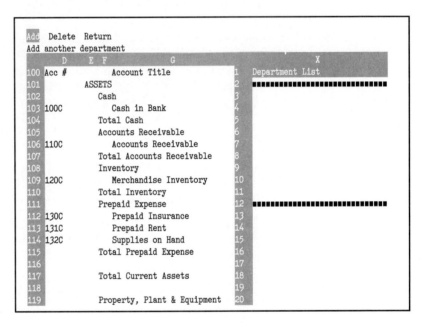

Figure 8-1

The worksheet is split into two vertical windows. The right window contains a list of current departments. Because you have not yet set up any departments, the list is blank. The lines in rows 2 and 12 indicate the limit to the number of departments you can add in RTR. You can add as many as nine departments.

Select: **Add**

The following prompt appears:

Enter a unique two-character department code:

Tom wants you to use the first two letters of each product group as the two-character department code. The first group you add is the base unit group. Its code is BA.

Type: **BA**
Press: ⏎

The screen shown in Figure 8-2 appears. The department code BA now appears in the Department List with the number 1 after it. The Add/Delete/Return menu reappears.

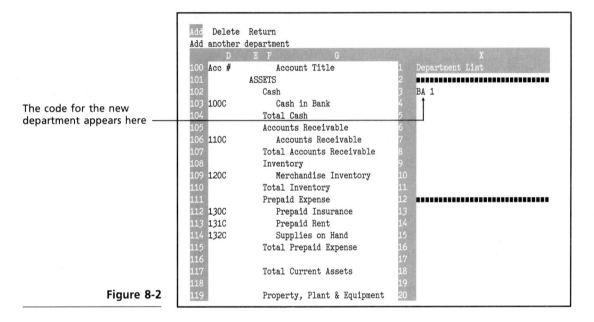

The code for the new
department appears here

Figure 8-2

Select: **A**dd

The second product group you are going to enter is monitors. Its code is MO.

Type: **MO**
Press: ⏎

The department code MO now appears in the Department List in the right window with the number 2 after it.

Select the Return command and return to the chart of accounts editing screen:

Select: **R**eturn

Adding Departments to Existing Accounts

You can now designate the accounts to which you want departments added. The first one is Merchandise Inventory, which appears on the current screen.

Move: to the line for the Merchandise Inventory account (row 109)

Press: [F2] to change the account

The following message appears on the prompt line:

Account is active - You may only change dept. status or Name - <Enter>

This message tells you that you cannot change the account number, because you have already made entries to this account.

Press: [↵]

A menu appears that lets you make this a departmental account or leave it nondepartmental. To add departments to this account,

Select: **D**epartmental

The following prompt appears:

Enter Account Title - Press <Enter> if okay:

Because you don't need to change the title of the account,

Press: [↵]

Your screen should look like Figure 8-3. The C following the account number for Merchandise Inventory has changed to a D, indicating that this account has departments added to it.

```
        D    E  F              G                H        I        J
   85  ■■    Use up & down arrow keys, pgup, and pgdn to move cell pointer   ■■
   86  ■■   {Ins}=Add menu {F2}=Change acct. {Del}=Delete line {F4}=Defaults ■■
   87  ■■   {F5}=Page {F6}=Depts. {F7}=Print samples {F8}=Interrupt {F9}=Done ■■
        D    E  F              G                H        I        J
  100  Acc #           Account Title
  101           ASSETS
  102             Cash
  103  100C        Cash in Bank               0.00
  104             Total Cash                            0.00
  105           Accounts Receivable
  106  110C        Accounts Receivable        0.00
  107             Total Accounts Receivable             0.00
  108           Inventory
  109  120D        Merchandise Inventory      0.00
  110             Total Inventory                       0.00
  111           Prepaid Expense
  112  130C        Prepaid Insurance          0.00
  113  131C        Prepaid Rent               0.00
  114  132C        Supplies on Hand           0.00
  115             Total Prepaid Expense                 0.00
```

The account number for Merchandise Inventory has a D after it instead of a C, showing that it is departmentalized

Figure 8-3

Next add departments to the Sales account:

Press: PGDN four times
Move: to the Sales account (row 165)
Press: (F2)
Press: (↵)
Select: **D**epartmental
Press: (↵)

The account number for Sales changes from 400C to 400D on your screen.

Now that you have added departments to the Merchandise Inventory and Sales accounts, you can save your work:

Press: (F9)
Select: **S**ave

This takes some time, because RTR must rebuild your chart of accounts and add the accounts with departments to all of your ledgers. When it finishes, the RTR Main menu reappears.

Adding Departments to New Accounts

You have added the departments BA and MO to the chart of accounts. Now when you add a new account to the chart of accounts, a menu appears with the options Departmental and Nondepartmental. You must indicate which you want it to be before RTR will create the new account. However, you can change an account from departmental to nondepartmental at any time.

Using Departments in Transaction Entry

Tom wants the beginning inventory for February broken down into departments. He analyzes the February beginning inventory and finds that base units made up $15,097 of the total and monitors made up $3,945 of the total. He wants you to record this breakdown as of the first of February. From the RTR Main menu,

Select: **GL Enter Run Backup**
Type: **20**
Press: ⏎

Indicate that the entry will be posted in February:

Type: **2**
Press: ⏎
Select: **Enter General**

Your entry should debit $15,097 to the base unit department for Merchandise Inventory and debit $3,945 to the monitor department for Merchandise Inventory. You should credit the original Merchandise Inventory account for the total of $19,042. Since the entry you made contains two debits and one credit, select the Single method of entering General Journal entries.

Select: **Single**

You should now see the screen shown in Figure 8-4. To see how the chart of accounts incorporates the departments you added, use (F10) to see a listing of the chart of accounts.

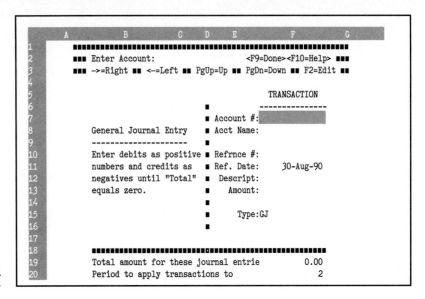

Figure 8-4

```
        A         B         C     D     E          F          G
1  ■■■■■■■■■■■■■■■■■■■■■■■■■■■■■■■■■■■■■■■■■■■■■■■■■■■■■■■■■■■■■■
2  ■■■ Enter Account:                    <F9=Done><F10=Help> ■■■
3  ■■■ ->=Right ■■ <-=Left ■■ PgUp=Up ■■ PgDn=Down ■■ F2=Edit ■■
4
5                                      TRANSACTION
6                                    ■ ---------------
7                                    ■ Account #:
8     General Journal Entry          ■ Acct Name:
9     ---------------------          ■
10    Enter debits as positive       ■ Refrnce #:
11    numbers and credits as         ■ Ref. Date:     30-Aug-90
12    negatives until "Total"        ■ Descript:
13    equals zero.                   ■   Amount:
14                                   ■
15                                   ■     Type:GJ
16                                   ■
17
18 ■■■■■■■■■■■■■■■■■■■■■■■■■■■■■■■■■■■□■■■■■■■■■■■■■■■■■■■■■■■■■■
19    Total amount for these journal entrie        0.00
20    Period to apply transactions to                2
```

Press: `F10`

The screen shown in Figure 8-5 appears, with the chart of accounts listed on the left. On rows 5 and 6, two accounts appear after account number 120, showing that Merchandise Inventory now has departments added to it. The new account numbers are also 120, but they are followed by a decimal point and a number associated with the department. The department code appears as the first part of the account name of the new accounts.

New account numbers appear for the departments added to the Merchandise Inventory account. They use the same account number with a decimal and the number associated with that code. The account title includes the code assigned to the department.

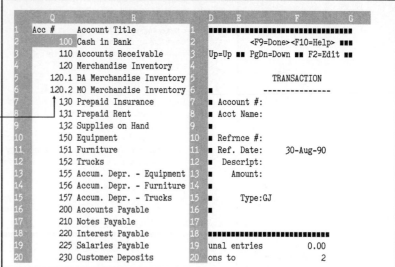

Figure 8-5

To select the BA Merchandise Inventory account,

Move: to the account number for that account (row 5)
Press: ↵

Debit this account $15,097. On the Refrnce # line,

Type: **JE92012**
Press: ↵
Type: **2/1/92**
Press: ↵
Type: **BREAKDOWN MDSE INVEN**
Press: ↵
Type: **15097**
Press: ↵

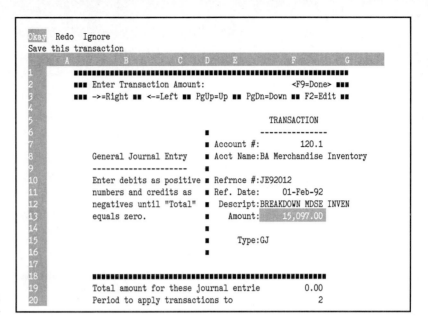

```
Okay  Redo  Ignore
Save this transaction
     A        B        C        D        E        F        G
1    ■■■■■■■■■■■■■■■■■■■■■■■■■■■■■■■■■■■■■■■■■■■■■■■■■■■■■
2    ■■■ Enter Transaction Amount:                    <F9=Done> ■■■
3    ■■■ ->=Right ■■ <-=Left ■■ PgUp=Up ■■ PgDn=Down ■■ F2=Edit ■■
4
5                                            ■          TRANSACTION
6                                            ■       ---------------
7                                            ■ Account #:        120.1
8    General Journal Entry                   ■ Acct Name:BA Merchandise Inventory
9    --------------------                    ■
10   Enter debits as positive ■ Refrnce #:JE92012
11   numbers and credits as   ■ Ref. Date:    01-Feb-92
12   negatives until "Total"  ■ Descript:BREAKDOWN MDSE INVEN
13   equals zero.             ■   Amount:    15,097.00
14                            ■
15                            ■      Type:GJ
16                            ■
17
18   ■■■■■■■■■■■■■■■■■■■■■■■■■■■■■■■■■■■■■■■■■■■■■■■■■■■■■
19   Total amount for these journal entrie        0.00
20   Period to apply transactions to              2
```

Figure 8-6

If your screen looks like Figure 8-6,

Select: **Okay**

Otherwise, select Redo and make corrections. When your screen looks like Figure 8-6, press F9 and then select Okay. To enter another debit,

Select: **A**dd

You now know that the account number for MO Merchandise Inventory is 120.2. Enter it without the help screen:

Type: **120.2**
Press: ⏎
Press: ⏎ ⏎ ⏎
Type: **3945**
Press: ⏎

Your screen should look like Figure 8-7. Select Redo if you need to make corrections, and then press F9 to return to this menu.

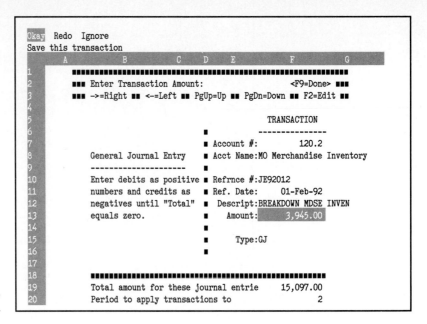

```
Okay  Redo  Ignore
Save this transaction
         A       B       C       D       E          F           G
1   ■■■■■■■■■■■■■■■■■■■■■■■■■■■■■■■■■■■■■■■■■■■■■■■■■■■■■■■■■■■■■■
2     ■■■ Enter Transaction Amount:                    <F9=Done> ■■■
3     ■■■ ->=Right ■■ <-=Left ■■ PgUp=Up ■■ PgDn=Down ■■ F2=Edit ■■
4
5                                         ■        TRANSACTION
6                                         ■      ---------------
7                                         ■ Account #:       120.2
8        General Journal Entry            ■ Acct Name:MO Merchandise Inventory
9        ---------------------            ■
10       Enter debits as positive         ■ Refrnce #:JE92012
11       numbers and credits as           ■ Ref. Date:    01-Feb-92
12       negatives until "Total"          ■ Descript:BREAKDOWN MDSE INVEN
13       equals zero.                     ■   Amount:       3,945.00
14                                         ■
15                                         ■      Type:GJ
16                                         ■
17
18  ■■■■■■■■■■■■■■■■■■■■■■■■■■■■■■■■■■■■■■■■■■■■■■■■■■■■■■■■■■■■■■
19       Total amount for these journal entrie    15,097.00
20       Period to apply transactions to                 2
```

Figure 8-7

Select: **Okay**

Credit the original Merchandise Inventory account for the total:

Select: **Add**
Type: **120**
Press: ⏎
Press: ⏎ ⏎ ⏎
Type: **− 19042**
Press: ⏎

Your screen should look like Figure 8-8. Select Redo if necessary, and then press F9 to return to this menu.

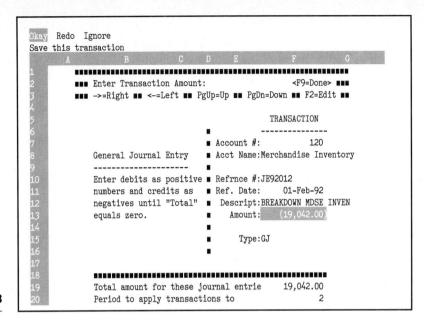

```
 Okay  Redo  Ignore
 Save this transaction
    A          B         C      D     E          F              G
 1  ■■■■■■■■■■■■■■■■■■■■■■■■■■■■■■■■■■■■■■■■■■■■■■■■■■■■■■■■■■■
 2  ■■■ Enter Transaction Amount:                  <F9=Done> ■■■
 3  ■■■ ->=Right ■■ <-=Left ■■ PgUp=Up ■■ PgDn=Down ■■ F2=Edit ■■
 4
 5                                         TRANSACTION
 6                              ■         ---------------
 7                              ■ Account #:         120
 8   General Journal Entry      ■ Acct Name:Merchandise Inventory
 9   ---------------------      ■
10   Enter debits as positive  ■ Refrnce #:JE92012
11   numbers and credits as    ■ Ref. Date:     01-Feb-92
12   negatives until "Total"   ■  Descript:BREAKDOWN MDSE INVEN
13   equals zero.              ■    Amount:    (19,042.00)
14                             ■
15                             ■       Type:GJ
16                             ■
17
18  ■■■■■■■■■■■■■■■■■■■■■■■■■■■■■■■■■■■■■■■■■■■■■■■■■■■■■■■■■■■
19   Total amount for these journal entrie    19,042.00
20   Period to apply transactions to                  2
```

Figure 8-8

Select: **O**kay

The total amount for these journal entries at the bottom of the screen should be 0.00 to indicate that your entry balances. You have finished making this entry.

Select: **D**one **D**one

You may print these entries if you want to review them. If you find errors, use the Fix command to correct them. When you are ready to return to the RTR Main menu,

Select: **S**ave

RTR saves these entries in the temporary transaction file and returns you to the RTR Main menu. Do not post the entries now.

Adding Departments to Existing Transactions

Tom's records will reflect the addition of departments from period 2 onward. However, the transactions you entered for January cannot be changed to reflect the departments. If Tom wanted his year-end figures to reflect the departments in January, you would have to analyze the balances in the accounts to which you added departments. Then you could make a General Journal entry to transfer those balances to the departments. You can make this entry in period 1 even though you have already printed the January financial statements. RTR allows you to go back to a previous period of the current year to make entries if you need to.

Creating Custom Reports

Tom Walton would like you to design three custom reports: a chart of accounts, a quarterly report of income statements reports, and an accounts receivable activity report by customer. Using RTR, you can adjust the reports from the Accounts, Journals, and Trial Reports programs on the Reports menu to fit your own specifications.

A Customized Chart of Accounts

Tom would like a printout of the chart of accounts that shows the beginning balance for each account, the net change in the account for each period, and the ending balance in each account. You can use RTR to prepare a customized Chart of Accounts report containing this information. Start at the RTR Main menu:

Select: **GL R**eports **A**ccounts

The Run/Adjust/Quit/Break menu appears. Select Adjust to make changes to the report.

Select: **A**djust

Changing the Report Headings   You now see the screen shown in Figure 8-9. The instructions in the right window tell you how to proceed. In the left window, ERASE FIELD is highlighted. Use (↑), (↓), PGUP, and PGDN to move around in the left window. In the right window, the heading "Acc #" should appear in brighter characters or in a different color from the other headings.

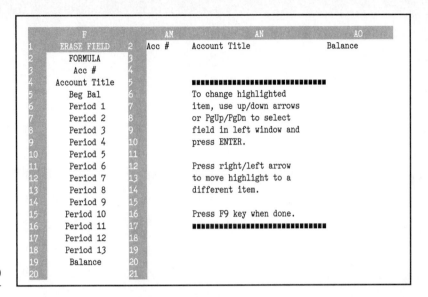

Figure 8-9

> **Note** Some monitors do not display the selected heading in the right window in brighter characters. If yours does not, you must remember without visual help which column is highlighted. The program begins with the first heading, Acc #, highlighted.

Use $\rightarrow$ or $\leftarrow$ to move from heading to heading in the right window. The headings correspond to those that appear in Ready-to-Run's standard Chart of Accounts report.

The left window gives you several options. The ERASE FIELD option deletes the column highlighted in the right window. The FORMULA option allows you to create a column containing a formula based on one or more of the other columns. The other items in the left window are the column headings you can choose for your report.

Tom Walton's report should display the following items in the columns indicated:

Column 1 (AM)   Account Number

Column 2 (AN)   Account Title

Column 3 (AO)   Beginning Balance

Column 4 (AP)   Period 1 Activity

Column 5 (AQ)   Period 2 Activity

Column 6 (AR)   Period 3 Activity

Column 7 (AS)   Period 4 Activity

Column 8 (AT)   Period 5 Activity

Column 9 (AU)   Period 6 Activity

Column 10 (AV)   Period 7 Activity

Column 11 (AW)   Period 8 Activity

Column 12 (AX)   Period 9 Activity

Column 13 (AY)   Period 10 Activity

Column 14 (AZ)   Period 11 Activity

Column 15 (BA)   Period 12 Activity

Column 16 (BB)   Period 13 Activity

Column 17 (BC)   Ending Balance

The first two columns are the same as in the standard report. Change the contents of the report beginning with the third column.

Press: → →

The Balance heading should now be highlighted. RTR uses "Balance" to refer to the ending balance for a particular account. Change the ending balance in this column to beginning balance.

Press: ↓ four times

The row Beg Bal in the left window should be highlighted by the cell pointer.

Press: ↵

Your screen should now look like Figure 8-10. The Beg Bal heading replaces Balance, and the window shifts one column to the left. Column AP is now the highlighted column, although you can't see that it is because the column has no heading. The period 1 activity should appear in this column.

The heading title for this column has been changed to the field selected from the left window

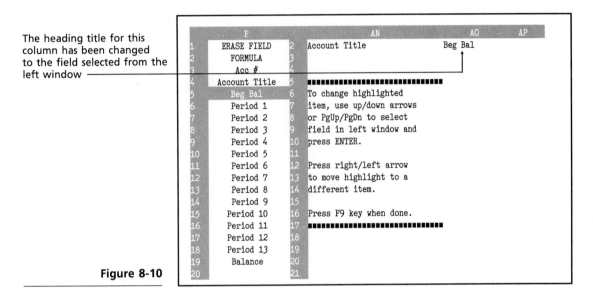

Figure 8-10

To highlight the Period 1 choice in the left window,

Press: ⬇

Press: ↵

Your screen should now look like Figure 8-11. Each time you add a column heading, the left window shifts left to the next blank column.

The Period 1 heading now appears in the next column to the right ————

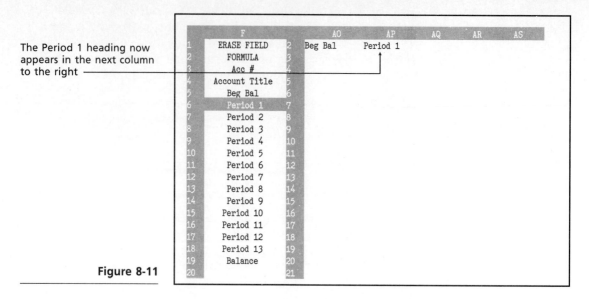

Figure 8-11

To highlight the Period 2 choice in the left window,

Press: ⬇

Press: ⏎

To highlight the Period 3 choice in the left window,

Press: ⬇

Press: ⏎

You have added two more columns to the report. Your screen should look like Figure 8-12.

Two more columns have been
added for Period 2
and Period 3 ⎯⎯⎯⎯⎯⎯⎯

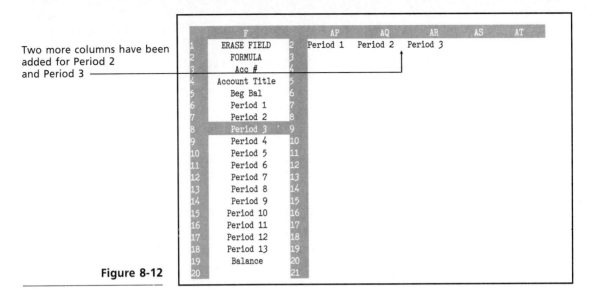

Figure 8-12

Continue to add a column to the report for each period in the
left window. After you add Period 13, you should add the
Balance column as the last column.

To highlight the Balance choice in the left window,

Press: ⬇

Press: ⏎

Your screen should look like Figure 8-13.

The last column to be
added to the report is the
Balance column ⎯⎯⎯⎯⎯⎯⎯

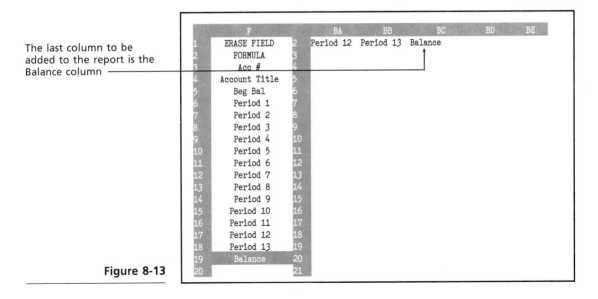

Figure 8-13

> **Note** Do not add the same choice from the left window more than once. RTR uses a Lotus 1-2-3 feature that does not allow you to have the same column appear twice in one report. If you do add the same column twice, it will be blank the second time it appears; worse yet, any subsequent columns may contain erroneous data.

When you finish editing the report,

Press:

Selecting the Accounts Criterion

You should see the menu and screen shown in Figure 8-14. On this screen, you select accounts that meet certain criteria. The current criterion, in the right window, is +A101>=0. Cell A101 contains the first account number for the Chart of Accounts. The formula includes every account, starting with cell A101, that has an account number greater than or equal to 0 (zero).

The current criterion is shown in this cell. A101 contains the account number for the first account in the chart of accounts.

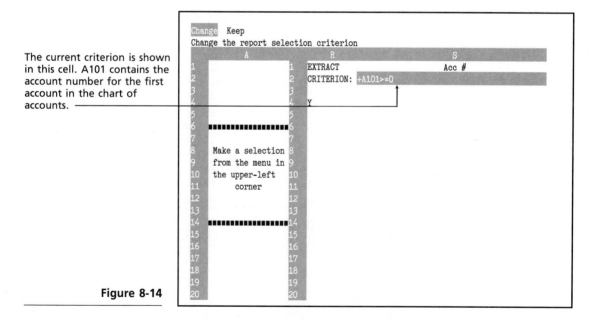

Figure 8-14

Because Tom Walton wants all of his accounts to appear on this report, you will not change the criterion.

Select: **Keep**

Specifying the Sort Order   You should see the menu and screen shown in Figure 8-15. On this screen you specify how you want the report sorted.

The report will be sorted by account number in ascending order —

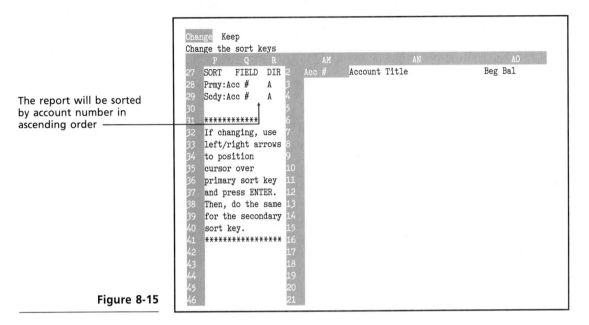

Figure 8-15

Lotus 1-2-3 and RTR can sort data using two "keys." The primary sort key indicates which column (field) to use to determine the order in which the rows (records) appear on the report. The secondary sort key tells RTR how to determine the order in which rows appear if their primary sort key is identical. Each key can be sorted in ascending or descending order. Ascending order is from lowest to highest when sorting numbers and in alphabetical order when sorting labels. Descending order is the opposite.

In the left window notice that both the primary and secondary keys are the Acc # field. Because two accounts cannot have the same account numbers, the secondary key can be the same as the primary key. The direction (DIR) for both keys is ascending order (A). Thus, the default sort format for this report is by account number in ascending order. That is what Tom wants; don't change the sort keys.

Select: **Keep**

Naming and Saving the Report You should see a menu with two choices: Adjust and Keep. If you choose Adjust, you can change the heading, or title, that appears on the report. The current title is LEDGER REPORT, which is okay with Tom.

Select: **Keep**

A menu appears that contains two commands: Save and Return. The Return command returns you to the Run/Adjust/Quit/Break menu. Select Return only if you have no need to use this report again.

Select: **Save**

A menu appears that lets you replace the existing report, save the format under a new report, or quit without saving.

> **Caution** If you choose to replace the existing report at this point, you will replace the Chart of Accounts report that comes with the RTR program. Select the New command when you create a report to be sure you don't write over another report.

Select: **New**

The screen shown in Figure 8-16 appears, with this prompt at the top:

Enter new report name (up to 8 chars):

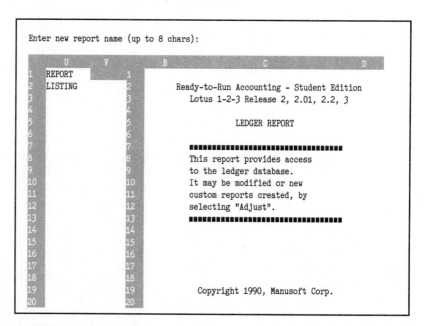

Figure 8-16

The left window of this screen contains a list of the custom report names you have already assigned. At present there are no names on the list because this is the first custom report you have created.

Type: **LEDGER1**

Press: ⟨↵⟩

The following message appears on the prompt line:

New report saved - Press ENTER

Press: ⟨↵⟩

Printing the Report   The Run/Quit/Adjust/Break menu reappears at this point. To print the report so you can look at it, after making sure your printer is on-line and the paper is properly aligned,

Select: **R**un **P**rint **N**arrow or **W**ide Condensed

When the printing finishes,

Select: **D**one

Review the printout. Periods 8 through 13 and the ending balance are printed on the second page, but the account number and title are not repeated, so you can't tell which line is which. To use this report, you would need to paste the second page to the first page.

> **Note**   If you have a wide-carriage printer and print this report in condensed print, it will fit on one page.

A Quarterly Report of Income Statement Accounts

The second report that Tom Walton wants to see is a summary of the income statement accounts for the first quarter. To create this report, use the Trial command from the Reports menu.

The RTR Main menu should be on your screen.

Select: **GL R**eports **T**rial **A**djust

Changing the Report Headings   A screen similar to Figure 8-9 appears, with some additional items at the end of the list in the left window. Tom's Quarterly Report of Income Statement Accounts should contain the following columns:

Column 1 (AM)   Account Number

Column 2 (AN)   Account Title

Column 3 (AO)   Period 1 Activity

Column 4 (AP)   Period 2 Activity

Column 5 (AQ)   Period 3 Activity

Column 6 (AR)   Total of Periods 1-3

You don't have to change the first two columns. To replace the third column (AO),

Press: ☐→ ☐→

The heading of the third column should now be highlighted. To highlight Period 1 in the left window:

Press: ☐↓ five times
Press: ☐↵

The third column heading changes to Period 1. The highlight should be on the heading in the fourth column (AP). To highlight Period 2 in the left window:

Press: ☐↓
Press: ☐↵

To highlight Period 3 in the left window:

Press: ☐↓
Press: ☐↵

Entering a Formula in a Column Head Your screen should look like Figure 8-17.

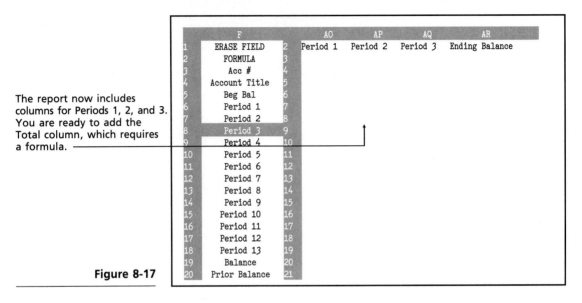

The report now includes columns for Periods 1, 2, and 3. You are ready to add the Total column, which requires a formula.

Figure 8-17

You are now ready to create a sixth column (AR) that contains a formula adding columns 3, 4, and 5. To highlight FORMULA in the left window:

Press: ⬆ six times
Press: ⏎

The prompt line displays:

Enter name for field:

You can enter a name, up to eight characters long, to appear as the heading of column 6.

Type: **Total**
Press: ⏎

The heading appears on the worksheet in column AR, and the prompt line displays:

Enter width for this column:

To accommodate potentially large numbers, you need a column that is 12 characters wide.

Type: **12**
Press: ⏎

Your screen changes to look like Figure 8-18. A list of arithmetic operators appears in the left window for you to use in constructing your formula. (The data in row 1 of the right window are formulas used by RTR to calculate what goes in those columns.)

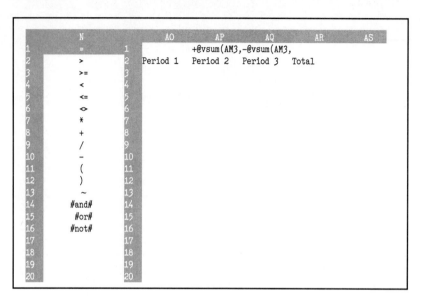

Figure 8-18

In Lotus 1-2-3, you can start a formula only with a plus sign, a minus sign, or with a left parenthesis. To highlight the plus sign in the left window:

Press: ↓ seven times
Press: ↵

Your screen should look like Figure 8-19. The cell above the Total heading in the right window contains the plus sign. The left window now lists the columns available for you to include in the report, plus an option called ENTER CONSTANT. The ENTER CONSTANT option allows you to include a fixed number or another 1-2-3 formula in your formula. For example, you might want to multiply 1.05 times the amounts for Period 1 to see the effect of a 5% increase on the accounts. The 1.05 would be a constant. However, in this case, you simply want to add the values in the columns for Period 1, Period 2, and Period 3.

The plus sign (+) has been added to the cell above the heading ———

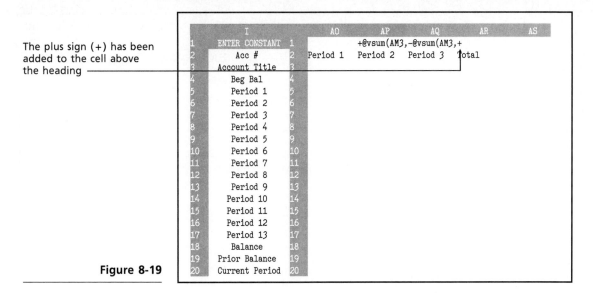

Figure 8-19

To highlight Period 1 in the left window:

Press: ↓ four times
Press: ↵

The screen shown in Figure 8-20 appears. RTR displays a menu that lets you indicate whether you have finished building the formula or whether you want to continue. The cell above the Total heading now says ''+Period 1,'' and you are ready to add Period 2.

This cell now contains the
beginning of the formula
you are building

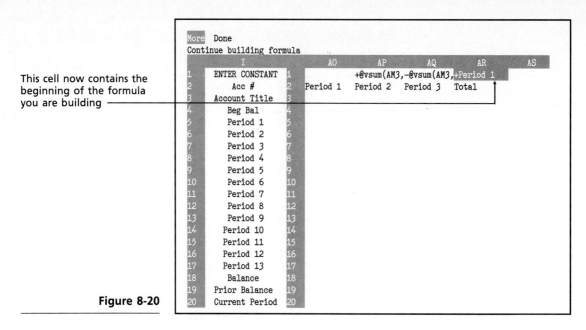

Figure 8-20

Select: **More**

The screen you see is similar to Figure 8-18, with the list of
arithmetic operators in the left window. To highlight the plus
sign in the left window:

Press: ⬇ seven times
Press: ⏎

Screen 8-20 reappears. A plus sign (+) follows Period 1 in the
formula. To highlight Period 2 in the left window:

Press: ⬇ five times
Press: ⏎

You now have added Period 1 and Period 2 and are ready to
complete the formula by adding Period 3. To select the More
command and highlight the plus sign:

Select: **More**
Press: ⬇ seven times
Press: ⏎

To highlight Period 3:

Press: ⬇ six times
Press: ⏎

The formula is now complete. Your screen should look like
Figure 8-21.

You cannot see all of
it, but the formula adds
Period 1, Period 2,
and Period 3 ————

```
More  Done
Continue building formula
                                          AO        AP        AQ        AR        AS
1   ENTER CONSTANT  1            +@vsum(AM3,-@vsum(AM3,+Period 1+Period 2+Pe
2        Acc #      2    Period 1  Period 2  Period 3  Total
3    Account Title  3
4      Beg Bal      4
5      Period 1     5
6      Period 2     6
7      Period 3     7
8      Period 4     8
9      Period 5     9
10     Period 6     10
11     Period 7     11
12     Period 8     12
13     Period 9     13
14     Period 10    14
15     Period 11    15
16     Period 12    16
17     Period 13    17
18     Balance      18
19   Prior Balance  19
20   Current Period 20
```

Figure 8-21

Select: **D**one

Because you have finished adding columns to the report,

Press: [F9]

Changing the Accounts Criterion   The Criterion Change menu
shown in Figure 8-14 appears. You do not want the Balance
Sheet accounts to appear in this report. Therefore, you must
change the report selection criterion. The report should include
all accounts with an account number equal to or greater than
the number for the Sales account (account number 400).

Select: **C**hange

A menu appears that allows you to add a criterion, start the
criterion with NOT, or select Done, which at this point would
result in no criterion being selected.

Select: **A**dd

The screen shown in Figure 8-22 appears. The left window
shows the fields that can be included in the criterion, as well
as ENTER CONSTANT.

These are printer control
codes; yours may be
different

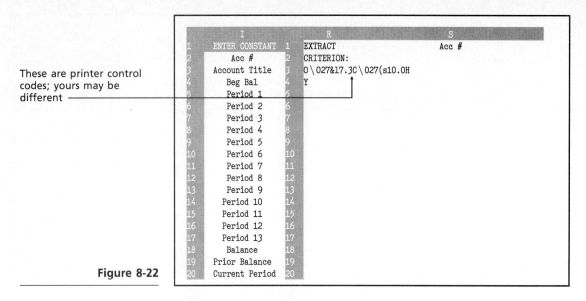

Figure 8-22

The criterion for the report is based on the account number, so
select that field to begin the criterion. To highlight Acc # in
the left window:

Press: ↓
Press: ↵

The screen shown in Figure 8-23 appears.

The criterion starts with the
field name you selected from
the first screen

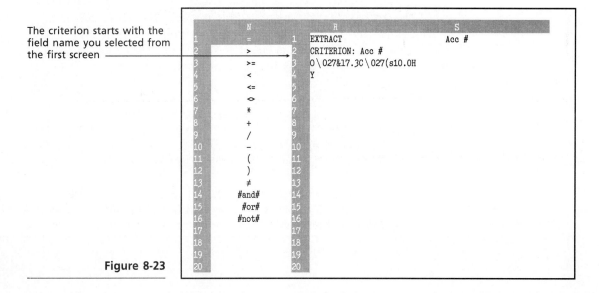

Figure 8-23

The CRITERION line in the right window contains the field name you selected: Acc #. The left window contains the listing of arithmetic operators. You want all account numbers greater than or equal to 400, so you should select the greater than or equal to sign (>=):

Press: ⬇ two times
Press: ⏎

The arithmetic operator is added to the CRITERION line in the right window. The left window changes to the one in Figure 8-22. To enter the account number 400, select the ENTER CONSTANT option. It is already highlighted.

Press: ⏎

The prompt line now displays:

Enter the value of the constant:

Enter the account number for Sales: 400.

Type: **400**
Press: ⏎

The menu shown in Figure 8-24 appears. The CRITERION line now displays: Acc #>=400. This is the complete criterion. You are finished.

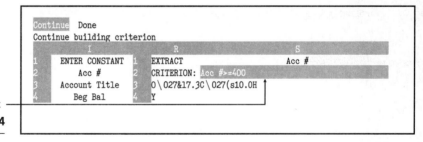

The criterion cell contains
the criterion you have built —
Figure 8-24

Select: **Done**

Completing and Saving the Report Do not change the sort keys.

Select: **Keep**

To change the report heading to "Quarter 1 Report":

Select: **Adjust**

The prompt line displays:

Enter new heading:

Type: **QUARTER 1 REPORT**
Press: ⏎

The new heading should appear in row 5 in the right window. To save the report:

Select: **S**ave **N**ew

The left window contains the name of the first report you created: LEDGER1. To add the new report:

Type: **QTR1**
Press: ⏎

Printing the Report   When RTR tells you that the report is saved,

Press: ⏎
Select: **R**un

Since you are using the Trial Balance program, a prompt asks for the current period.

Type: **1**
Press: ⏎

Be sure that your printer is on-line and the paper is properly aligned, and then select Print:

Select: **P**rint **N**arrow or **W**ide **R**egular

When the printing finishes,

Select: **D**one

Examine the report. It should contain all of the Income Statement accounts for Walton Electronics. The Period 2 and Period 3 columns contain zeroes because no data is entered for those periods.

An Accounts Receivable Activity Report by Customer

Tom Walton wants a report to help him keep track of how much each customer owes. Because he doesn't have enough business to use the Ready-to-Run Accounts Receivable module, he wants you to create a report of the activity in the Accounts Receivable account sorted by customer. Use the Journals command from the Report menu to set up this custom report.

From the RTR Main menu,

Select: **GL R**eports **J**ournals **A**djust

You should see a screen similar to the one shown in Figure 8-9.
The left window lists fields that you can select to include in the
report. The standard journals report has headings for account
number, description, reference number, reference date, special
journal code, and transaction. Tom wants all of these fields
printed in this report. To accept the fields as they are defined,

Press: (F9)

Changing the Accounts Criterion   You need to change the
criterion, because you want only activity from the Accounts
Receivable account on this report. To select the Change command and begin adding a criterion,

Select: **Change A**dd

You should see the screen shown in Figure 8-25.

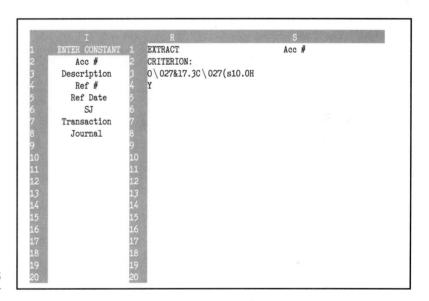

Figure 8-25

Because you want only activity from the Accounts Receivable
account, your criterion should state that you only want items
printed that contain the account number for Accounts Receivable. Use the account number field to select the data to print.

Move to: Acc #
Press: (←)

The screen is similar to the one shown in Figure 8-23. You need to choose only one account, the Accounts Receivable account, which is Account 110. The arithmetic operator to use is the equals (=) sign. The cell pointer is already positioned on that operator in the left window.

Press: ⏎

To enter the account number for Accounts Receivable, use the ENTER CONSTANT item in the left column. The cell pointer is positioned on that item.

Press: ⏎

RTR prompts you to enter the value of the constant, which is the account number for the Accounts Receivable account, 110.

Type: **110**
Press: ⏎

Your screen should now look like Figure 8-26.

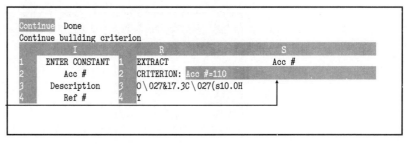

The criterion cell contains the selection criterion for this report. In order to be selected, the account number column must be equal to 110.

Figure 8-26

You have finished entering the criterion.

Select: **Done**

Changing the Sort Order   The report will be more useful to Tom Walton if the entries for each customer appear together, instead of in the order they were entered. Therefore, you want the report to sort on the Description column, where the name of the customer appears. Select the Change command from the Change/Sort/Keys menu:

Select: **Change**

You should see the screen shown in Figure 8-27.

The current sort keys are the reference date as the primary key and the account number as the secondary key. Both are sorted in ascending order.

Figure 8-27

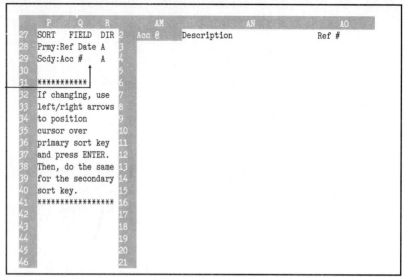

The instructions in the left window tell you to use ⟨←⟩ and ⟨→⟩ to select the primary and secondary sort key. Your primary key will be the description column, which contains the name of the customer. Tom Walton wants the receivables for each customer in order by date, so Ref Date will be your secondary key. To indicate the primary key, move the cell pointer to the Description column:

Press: ⟨→⟩
Press: ⟨↵⟩

The word Description should now appear in the left window beside the label Prmy: If it does not, you will have a chance to fix it later.

You should see a menu that offers two choices: Ascending and Descending. Alphabetical order is the same as ascending order, which is what Tom wants for this report.

Select: **A**scending

Now specify the secondary key. To move the cell pointer to the Ref Date column:

Press: ⟨→⟩ two times
Press: ⟨↵⟩

To sort the records so the oldest invoices are listed first,

Select: **A**scending

Your screen should now look like Figure 8-28, with the Change/Keep menu at the top.

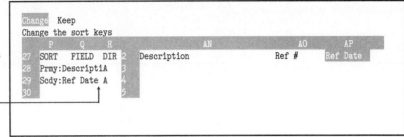

The sort keys have been changed to the description as the primary key and the reference date as the secondary key. Both will be sorted in ascending order.

Figure 8-28

Confirm that you have selected the correct columns. Compare the information in the left column on rows 28 and 29 with Figure 8-28. If the sort keys are not the same, select **C**hange and start over. When you are satisfied that the sort keys are correct,

Select: **Keep**

Changing the Report Title   To change the title that will appear on the report,

Select: **A**djust

Enter the heading for the report at the prompt:

Type: **ACCOUNTS RECEIVABLE REPORT**
Press: ⊂⤶⊃

Again, the new heading should appear in the right window on row 5. Save this as a new report with the name ACCREC:

Select: **Save New**
Type: **ACCREC**
Press: ⊂⤶⊃

When the prompt line tells you the report is saved,

Press: ⊂⤶⊃

Printing the Report   To print a copy of the report,

Select: **R**un

Enter the current period at the prompt:

Type: **1**
Press: ⊂⤶⊃

When you are prompted for the period name,

Type: **JANUARY 1992**
Press: ⏎

The Journal Selection menu appears.

> **Note**   Because you have changed the criterion for the report, *any* journal that matches the new criterion will print. However, if you select the All command from this menu, RTR erases the criterion that you set and replaces it with a different criterion. *Therefore:, when you make a selection from the Journal Selection menu for a custom report:, do not select All.*

To print Tom Walton's receivables report, select the Receivables journal. Be sure your printer is on-line and the paper is properly aligned.

Select: **R**eceivables **P**rint **N**arrow or **W**ide **R**egular
Select: **R**eturn **Q**uit

Examine the report. The code for the Accounts Receivables journal appears at the top of the report. The format is the same as that of the other journal reports except that only entries that affect account number 110 appear. This report differs from the audit trail report for account number 110 in that it is sorted by customer, making it easier to identify how much each customer still owes.

Printing a Custom Report   Tom Walton will want to see the Accounts Receivables report weekly so he can monitor whether or not each customer has paid his or her bill. To print a custom report that is already set up, from the RTR Main menu,

Select: **GL R**eports **C**ustom

A menu appears that contains three options: Select a report, Delete a report, or Return to the previous menu.

Select: **S**elect

You should see the screen shown in Figure 8-29. The left window lists the three reports you created in the order you created them.

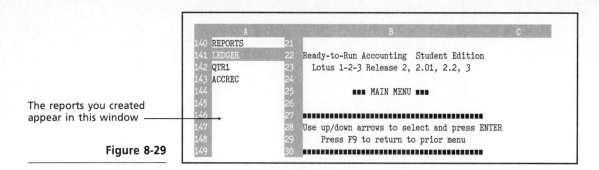

The reports you created appear in this window

Figure 8-29

To select the ACCREC report:

Press: ↓ ↓
Press: ↵

After you select the custom report, you see a menu with four options: Run, Adjust, Quit, and Break. If you want to make changes in the custom report, do so by selecting the Adjust command from this menu. Then, at the menu that lets you replace a report or save a new one, you could replace the existing report with the new version. Because you have just run and printed this report, you want to return to the Main menu:

Select: **Q**uit

You are ready to proceed to the exercises, where you will add more departments, add departments to additional accounts, and prepare additional custom reports.

Exercises

Walton Electronics

Departments

1. Tom Walton has decided to add two more departments to properly account for his sales by product group. These two departments are peripherals (code=PE) and supplies (code=SU). Add these departments to the chart of accounts.

> **Note** The accounts that already have departments added to them will automatically add these new departments when you add the new departments to the chart of accounts.

2. Tom Walton has decided that gross margin by product group would be helpful in addition to sales by product group. Add departments to all the existing Income Statement accounts through the Cost of Sales grouping.

3. Record an entry in February to allocate the balance in the Merchandise Inventory account to the two new departmental accounts for Merchandise Inventory. Debit $11,629 of the beginning February inventory to peripherals and $5,814 to supplies. Use JE92013 as the reference number.

4. Post the entries allocating the balance in Merchandise Inventory (including the ones you entered in the lab activity), and print the posting report.

Custom Reports

5. Tom Walton does not like the two-page report of the Chart of Accounts you created in the lab activity. He wants the descriptions to appear on the second page as well. Delete the existing LEDGER1 custom report by selecting GL Reports Custom Delete, highlighting the LEDGER1 report in the left window, and pressing ⏎. Design *two* new reports from the Chart of Accounts. On the first one, include the same columns as on the first page of the current LEDGER1 custom report. On the second, include the Acc # and Account Title columns first, and then periods 8 through 13 and the ending balance columns. Do not change the selection criterion, the sort keys, or the report heading. Save these reports under the names LEDGER1 and LEDGER2 respectively and print them.

6. Create a second quarter report similar to the one you created for the first quarter. Include columns for periods 4 through 6 and a total column. The report should include only Income Statement accounts. Title the report QUARTER 2 REPORT. Save this report under the name QTR2 and print it.

7. Create an activity report for Accounts Payable similar to the report you created for Accounts Receivable. List only the activity for the Accounts Payable account and sort it the same way as the Accounts Receivable report. The report heading should be ACCOUNTS PAYABLE REPORT. Save this report under the name ACCPAY and print it. (Select Payables from the Journal Selection Menu when you print this report.)

TWE, Inc.

1. Complete the exercises for Walton Electronics.

Going Further

2. You have added departments to the income statement accounts through Cost of Sales. This is the first step in providing Tom Walton with information on sales and costs of sales by product line. Describe the procedures you would use, and the reports and graphs you would produce using RTR, to provide product-line information for Tom Walton in a format that would be easy to understand and analyze.

3. Consider the income statement accounts below Cost of Sales. Choose an account that could provide additional valuable information if departments were added to it. What departments would you set up for that account?

4. You produced an Accounts Receivable report sorted by description to identify multiple transactions involving the same customer. Indicate other useful criteria for sorting the accounts receivable transactions and how the results of the sort would be helpful.

Lotus 1-2-3

1. Access the file (QTR1) containing the first quarter information on the income statement accounts that was saved during the lab activity by selecting Custom under the Reports menu, and then

Select: **Select QTR1 R**un
Type: **1**
Select: **S**ave

This saves the file QTR1.WK1 to the GL subdirectory. Quit RTR to Lotus 1-2-3, and then retrieve the QTR1.WK1 file. Clear the window and set the column widths globally to 12. Then set the width of column A to 7 and of column B to 30.

2. Format the quarterly report to show subtotals for net sales, cost of goods sold, gross margin, total operating expenses (exclusive of cost of goods sold), and net income. Insert lines and dollar signs where appropriate. Print a copy of the report.

3. Tom Walton is particularly interested in the amounts of the various selling expenses for the first quarter. Prepare a pie chart showing the selling expenses. Explode a pie slice representing one of the expenses by adding 100 to the shading code for that expense. Save the graph to a file for printing using PrintGraph.

4. Tom Walton would like a graph showing what portion of each period's net sales is cost of goods sold, total operating expenses exclusive of cost of goods sold, and net income. First change the sign on net income. Then select the Stack-Bar type of graph. Designate the column headings (Period 1 through Period 3) as the X data range. Specify data ranges A, B, and C. Create a legend at the bottom of the graph and a title at the top using the Options menu. After examining the graph, save it to a file for printing using PrintGraph.

Reference

1

Basic Skills

This chapter outlines some of the basic skills required to use RTR. Because RTR is driven by Lotus 1-2-3 macros, the chapter includes some features of Lotus 1-2-3.

Running Ready-to-Run

To run Ready-to-Run, you must have Lotus 1-2-3, Release 2.0 or higher, installed on your computer. RTR is a Lotus 1-2-3 macro-driven program and will not run without Lotus 1-2-3. You must start Lotus 1-2-3 before you start Ready-to-Run.

Starting Lotus 1-2-3

The method you use to start Lotus 1-2-3 depends on whether you have a hard-disk system or a two-disk system.

If you have a hard-disk system, you must start Lotus 1-2-3 from the directory that contains the Lotus 1-2-3 program files. Normally this directory is named 123 and is located on the C drive. From the DOS prompt, you must change to the 123 directory before starting Lotus 1-2-3. To change to the 123 directory on the C drive, type CD\123 and press ⏎ at the C> prompt. Then, to begin the Lotus 1-2-3 program, type 123 and press ⏎ at the DOS prompt.

> **Note**   Your system may have a menu that makes the required directory change for you before it starts Lotus 1-2-3. If so, simply select the menu item corresponding to Lotus 1-2-3.

If you have a two-disk system, you must start Lotus 1-2-3 from the A drive. Place the Lotus 1-2-3 System disk in the A drive. Make sure that the DOS prompt is for the A drive, then type 123 and press ⏎.

Starting Ready-to-Run

After you start Lotus 1-2-3, start RTR by retrieving the file AUTO123.WK1 from the RTR program disk or directory. Again, the procedure depends on whether you have a hard-disk system or a two-disk system.

To start RTR on a hard-disk system, you must first change the current Lotus 1-2-3 data directory to the directory containing the RTR program files. Normally, RTR will be in the READY directory on the C drive. To change to this directory, issue the following Lotus 1-2-3 command sequence: /File Directory C:\READY, and press ⏎. Then retrieve the file AUTO123.WK1 by issuing the following Lotus 1-2-3 command sequence: /File Retrieve AUTO123, and press ⏎. The RTR program begins to run.

To start RTR on a two-disk system, the current Lotus 1-2-3 data directory must be the B drive and the RTR program disk must be placed in the B drive. On a two-disk system, the default data directory in Lotus 1-2-3 is usually the B drive. To check this, issue the following Lotus 1-2-3 command sequence: /File Directory. If the drive displayed is B:\, press ⏎ to continue. If another drive or directory appears, type B: and press ⏎ to change it to the B drive. After you confirm that the data directory is the B drive, retrieve the file AUTO123.WK1 by issuing the following Lotus 1-2-3 command sequence: /File Retrieve AUTO123, and then press ⏎. The RTR program begins to run.

Making Ready-to-Run Start Automatically

When Lotus 1-2-3 starts up, it checks for a file named AUTO123.WK1 in the default directory and automatically loads it if it finds one. Therefore, if the drive or directory that contains the RTR program files is the Lotus 1-2-3 default directory, RTR starts automatically when you start Lotus 1-2-3.

To change the Lotus 1-2-3 default directory, issue the following Lotus 1-2-3 command sequence: /Worksheet Global Default Directory. Press ESC to erase the current default directory and type in the name of the directory containing RTR. On a hard-disk system, this is usually C:\READY, and on a two-disk system this is usually B:\. Press ⏎ after you type the name of the correct directory name. Then select Update from the Default menu to make the change permanent.

If you are using a two-disk system, the Lotus 1-2-3 System disk must be in drive A and must not be write-protected when you select the Update command.

If you are using a hard-disk system and change the default Lotus 1-2-3 directory, RTR will start up each time you start up Lotus 1-2-3. If you want to use Lotus 1-2-3 for other spreadsheet tasks, select the Quit command from the RTR Main menu, then select the Lotus command from the Quit menu. If you use Lotus 1-2-3 extensively for other projects, you won't want to make RTR start automatically.

Using Passwords with RTR

RTR permits you to use two passwords for security. One is a system password, and the other is a data password. You can choose to use either, both, or neither password. If you choose to use passwords, you must remember what they are, or you cannot access the RTR system or your data files.

System Password

When you install RTR and run it for the first time, after you select a printer, a prompt asks you to enter a system password. If you enter a password, it must be no more than six characters. RTR requires you to enter the password each time you start RTR.

After you enter the correct password, you can choose to change the password. You can change to no system password by pressing ⏎ at the prompt for the new password.

Data Password

RTR prompts you to enter a data password for the first time when you create a new set of books with the Files First-time command. If you enter a password at the prompt, it must be exactly six characters long. RTR then requires it each time you access the data files.

The following commands require you to use the data password:

> **GL** **L**edger **L**edger and **B**alances
>
> **F**iles **F**irst-time, **N**ew-year, and **D**ata password

Using a data password helps ensure the integrity of your data files by limiting access to them. Without the data password, other users cannot alter or destroy your data files from Lotus 1-2-3 or from Ready-to-Run.

Use the Files Data password command to change or delete the data password so that it is no longer required.

RTR Screen Messages

Because of the limitations of Lotus 1-2-3 macro menus, RTR uses either the prompt line (the second line of the screen) or the full screen to give instructions or display messages to you.

RTR uses the prompt line for brief messages that require little action on your part. The prompt line might ask you to enter data. After you enter the data, press ⏎ to continue. At other times, RTR might display a short message on the prompt line and instruct you to press ⏎ after you have read the message.

RTR uses the full screen in several ways. You must pay attention to the screen at all times to understand what the program is doing and to know what to do next.

RTR sometimes uses the full screen to give you information about the program you are running. For each program a short explanation appears, telling you what the program does and what files are affected by running the program. In some cases, these screens contain cautions you must heed to protect your data.

RTR often uses the Lotus 1-2-3 Window command to split the screen vertically or horizontally. When this occurs, one of the windows usually contains instructions as to how to proceed with the operation you are running. In some cases, such as when you edit the chart of accounts, the window contains information about the keys you can use. Other times, the window contains a listing from which you must make a choice. Use ↑ or ↓ to highlight your choice and then press ⏎ to finalize the selection.

Using Ready-to-Run Menus

To tell Ready-to-Run what to do, you select commands from menus. You can select a command either by highlighting it or by typing the first letter of the command.

Because RTR is a macro-driven program, you use menus that look similar to Lotus 1-2-3 menus to make choices in the program. The menus appear on the second line of the control panel and a rectangular highlight (called the menu pointer) highlights the first item on the menu. The next chapter, Menu Reference, contains detailed information regarding each command in RTR.

To select a menu choice in RTR, either:

1. Use $\boxed{\rightarrow}$ or $\boxed{\leftarrow}$ to highlight the menu choice and then press $\boxed{\leftarrow\!\!\!\!\rfloor}$.

2. Press the first letter of the menu choice.

For example, to select the Reports command from the GL menu, you can either press $\boxed{\rightarrow}$ two times to highlight the choice and then press $\boxed{\leftarrow\!\!\!\!\rfloor}$, or you can type R.

Selecting a command by typing is faster than the highlighting method. You will find this method useful once you are familiar with the commands in each RTR menu.

If you change your mind or realize that you have selected the wrong command, you can reverse the command in one of three ways:

1. Sometimes a menu will give you an option to return to the prior menu. If it does, simply select that option to reverse your previous selection.

2. Sometimes RTR lets you reverse your selection by pressing ESC to back up one menu-level at a time.

3. Sometimes RTR does not allow you to reverse your selection by selecting a return option or pressing ESC. In this case, you must select an option from the menu and then return to the RTR Main menu at the first opportunity via a menu selection. If you press ESC, and the same menu returns to the control panel, you must select a command on that menu to proceed.

Responding to Prompts

Sometimes when you select a command, RTR displays a prompt, or message, asking you to enter specific information in the second line of the control panel. You may have to supply this information in one of two ways:

*   If RTR suggests a response to the prompt (for example, when editing account numbers or titles), press $\boxed{\leftarrow\!\!\!\!\rfloor}$ to accept the suggested response. Alternatively, type a new response and press $\boxed{\leftarrow\!\!\!\!\rfloor}$.

*   If RTR does not display a menu or suggest a response (for example, when you first enter an account number or title), type the necessary information and press $\boxed{\leftarrow\!\!\!\!\rfloor}$.

RTR Data Entry Screens

In RTR you normally use the full screen to enter data. RTR places the cell pointer into the main portion of the screen and provides instructions either in a split-screen instruction window or somewhere on the screen itself. For example, when you enter beginning balances, the instructions appear in a window at the bottom of the screen. However, when you enter data into the journals, a separate message about each field appears at the top of the screen inside the worksheet frame. The message changes when the cell pointer moves to a new field.

After you enter data into a cell, you normally press ⏎ to complete the transaction. On some screens, when you do this, the cell pointer remains on the cell where you entered the data. To move to a different cell, use ⬆, ⬇, ⬅, or ➡. For example, when you enter budget amounts, you must move to each cell for which you want to enter a budget, enter the amount, and press ⏎. Then you must move to the next cell where you want to enter a budget.

On other screens, when you press ⏎ after typing data, the cell pointer moves automatically to the next cell for data input. For example, when you enter data in the journals, the cell pointer moves to the next cell each time you press ⏎.

Setting Up a New Company

You can use RTR to set up books for any number of companies. However, each set of books must be kept on a separate disk or in a separate directory. If you try to create a new set of books on a disk or in a directory that already contains RTR data files, the existing files are destroyed.

To set up the files for a new company, follow these three steps:

1. Create a new directory on your hard disk or format a new, blank floppy disk to store the new company's data.

2. Start Ready-to-Run.

   - **Hard-disk users:** Select Directory/Company, type the name of the directory for the new company, and select Save.

   - **Two-diskette users:** Put the new blank disk in the drive when RTR prompts for the data disk.

3. Run Files First-time to initialize the new company's files.

Closing Out a Fiscal Year

Always back up your data files before starting a new fiscal year. Procedures for backing up and restoring data files are included in Appendix B.

Use the Files New-year command to set up the books for a new fiscal year. This command creates files containing the current ledger and transfers the ending balances for Balance Sheet accounts to the beginning balances for the new year. RTR prompts you to select the account to which you want to close Net Income or Loss.

The chart of accounts may contain accounts in the Equity section that you must close out yourself at the end of a year. For example, you might close Dividends into Retained Earnings and Drawing accounts into Capital accounts. The Files New-year command does *not* close these accounts. Before you issue the Files New-year command, enter and post a general journal entry to close these Equity accounts.

Menu Reference

This section presents the RTR menus in alphabetical order. Menus with numbered selections appear first in the listing. The description beneath each menu explains where the menu appears in RTR. If a menu appears in more than one location, all appearances are explained. In most cases, a description follows that explains each of the available commands on the menu.

When you create or edit a chart of accounts in RTR, you work on an editing screen. The end of this menu reference section explains the chart of accounts editing screen and its options.

RTR Menus

1.Accounts 2.Debt/Equity 3.Liquidity 4.Revenue/Expenses Return

This menu appears when you choose the Graph command on the GL Budget menu. It allows you to select one of four graphs of the budget file for display and possible printing with PrintGraph. After the graph displays, press any key to stop viewing it.

1.Accounts

Displays a bar graph comparing the budget of up to three accounts that you select. After you choose 1.Accounts, use ⬆ and ⬇ to highlight the accounts you want to graph, and then press ⏎ to select them. To view a graph after selecting one or two accounts, press D. When you select three accounts, the graph displays automatically. The three accounts selected must all be from either the Balance Sheet or the Income Statement.

2.Debt/Equity

Displays a bar graph that compares total liabilities to total owners' equity according to the budget file.

3.Liquidity

Displays a bar graph that compares current assets to current liabilities according to the budget file.

4.Revenue/Expenses

Displays a bar graph that compares operating revenue to operating expenses according to the budget file.

This menu appears when you choose the Modules command on the Configure Redo menu. Use this command to indicate whether your version of RTR contains any of the modules listed. The Student Edition of Ready-to-Run contains only the general ledger module (GL on the menu).

Selecting an item on this menu toggles the selection on the configure screen off and on. For example, the default status of the GL module is Y (on). If you select 1.GL, the status changes to N (off). If the status is N, you cannot access the GL programs from the RTR Main menu.

If you try to select a module that is not installed, a message in the control panel indicates that the module is not included with the Student Edition.

The Return command returns you to the Configure Redo menu.

| 1.GL-DIR | 2.AP-DIR | 3.AR-DIR | 4.PAYROLL-DIR | 5.INVENTORY-DIR | Company | Save |

1, 2, 3, 4, or 5

Asks you to specify which directory contains the data files for that module. You cannot specify a directory for a module that has not been installed. If you select a module that is not installed, RTR prompts you to press ⏎ to return to the menu. These items do not appear when RTR is installed on a two-diskette system.

Company

Prompts you to enter the company name you want to appear on the reports for the data files in the current directory. The name also appears at the bottom of the RTR Main menu screen.

Save

Saves any changes made using this menu and returns you to the Main menu.

This menu appears when you choose the Options command on the Configure Redo menu. These options are available only in the commercial RTR software, not in the Student Edition. Toggle an option on and off by selecting the item from the menu.

The Return command returns you to the Configure Redo menu.

Accounts   Custom   Journals   Statements   Trial   Prior

This menu appears when you choose the Reports command on the GL menu. RTR generates the five types of reports on this menu. Three of the report commands (Accounts, Journals, and Trial) allow you to customize the report format.

Accounts

Prints a chart of accounts with the account number, account title, and current ledger balance for each account in the chart of accounts.

Custom

Prints a report you created.

Journals

Prints listings of each or all of the transaction journals.

Statements

Prints the standard financial statements for a company; namely, the income statement, the balance sheet, and a statement of cash flows worksheet. Also prints a financial analysis report and displays graphs of financial statement relationships for viewing and/or printing.

Trial

Prints a trial balance for the current period showing the beginning balance for the period, total debits for the period, total credits for the period, and ending balance for the period for each account in the chart of accounts.

Prior

Returns you to the GL menu.

Accounts Income Balance Summary

This menu appears when you press [F7] (Print samples) from
the chart of accounts editing screen. All the listings available
from this menu print in 80 columns of regular type.

Accounts

Prints the chart of accounts. If you have added departments,
you must specify whether you want to print All accounts,
including departmental accounts, or only Consolidated accounts.

Income

Prints a dummy copy of the income statement, showing
formatting.

Balance

Prints a dummy copy of the balance sheet, showing formatting.

Summary

Prints a listing of the Summary Account headings available
when editing the chart of accounts.

Add   Delete   Return

This menu appears when you press [F6] (Departments) from the
chart of accounts editing screen and select the Add/Delete
command from the menu.

Add

Adds a department to the list of departments available to those
accounts to which you have added departments. Enter a
unique two-digit code for the new department.

Delete

Deletes a department code from the list of available departments. Enter the two-digit code for the department you want
to delete or return to the chart of accounts editing screen
without deleting a department by pressing ESC.

Return

Returns you to the chart of accounts editing screen.

Add   NOT   Done

This menu appears when you select the Change command for
the criterion after selecting the GL Reports Adjust command to
customize a report.

Add

Allows you to build the criterion for your customized report.
When you select the Add command, select one of the fields in
the report or ENTER CONSTANT from the left window of the
split screen. Use ↑ and ↓ to highlight your choice and then
press ↵. Your choice appears in the right window on the
criterion line.

The left window of the split screen now displays a listing of
arithmetic operators. Use ↑ and ↓ to select the operator
you want and then press ↵. The operator appears in the
criterion in the right window.

If you select ENTER CONSTANT from the right window when
it is available, you can enter a constant or a formula at the
prompt.

When you have begun the criterion with a valid field or constant, entered an operator, and specified another field or a
constant, the Continue/Done menu appears. If you select Continue, you will again see the Add/NOT/Done menu. If you
select Done, you will proceed to the sort keys selection.

NOT

Places the criterion #NOT# in the criterion field. After you
select this command, you advance to changing or keeping the
sort keys.

Done

Checks the validity of your criterion and advances you to changing or keeping the sort keys. If you choose Done before you have finished, or if your criterion is invalid, you are prompted to begin again.

Add   Prior   Following   Done   Quit

This menu appears when you select Okay or Ignore from the confirmation menu after you enter a transaction using the GL Enter program.

Add

Lets you enter more data for the same reference number. If you are entering checks, deposits, payables, or receivables, you enter the additional data on the side of the screen that does not contain the default account number. The amount debited or credited to the default account number reflects the net of the amounts entered on the other side of the screen.

If you chose the General Pairs command, you can continue to enter any number of transactions and you can change the reference number for each screen if you want. The number of accounts debited must equal the number of accounts credited, and the total amounts entered must balance to zero.

If you chose the General Single command, choose Add to make entries until the total debit amounts equal the total credit amounts. Continue to use the Add command until all general journal entries are complete, changing the reference number as required for each one.

Prior

Displays the previous screen of data and lets you Keep, Change, or Delete the data. You cannot use this command after you have selected Done. (If you have selected Done since you entered the data, use Fix to change it.) If you select Prior at the first screen of data in the current entry sequence, you see the message: No prior transaction – Press <Enter>.

Following

Displays the next screen of data and lets you Keep, Change, or Delete the data. You cannot use this command after you have selected Done. (If you have selected Done since you entered the data, use Fix to change it.) If you select Following at the last screen of data in the current entry sequence, you see the message: No following transaction – Press <Enter>.

Done

Saves this transaction and displays the Another/Done menu. If you select Done again, you return to the Enter menu.

Quit

Returns you to the Enter menu without saving your transactions.

> **Caution** Choose the Quit command with care — it is irreversible.

Add/Delete Edit Return

This menu appears when you press F6 (Departments) from the chart of accounts editing screen.

Add/Delete

Presents the Add/Delete/Return menu so you can add another department or delete an existing department from the chart of accounts.

Edit

Lets you change the two-digit code assigned to a department.

Return

Returns you to the chart of accounts editing screen.

Adjust Keep

This menu appears when you are customizing a report from the GL Reports menu. It allows you to Adjust or Keep the current title of the report. After you select Adjust, enter the new title for the report at the prompt.

All Select

This menu appears several times in the GL Query program.

When you choose the Inquire command on the GL Query menu, you must choose an account for which you want to see activity. Then you can Print, Save, or View the activity in Summary or in Detail form. If you choose to Print, Save, or View in Detail format, the All/Select menu appears, and you can choose all periods or you can select the periods you want to see.

This menu also appears when you choose the Report command on the GL Query menu and then choose Print, Save, or View. In this case, the All/Select menu allows you to choose whether you want an audit trail report for all accounts or whether you want to select the accounts to appear on the audit trail. When you've finished choosing the accounts, the All/Select menu appears again. This time you can choose an audit trail report for all periods or for periods you select.

After you choose Select and indicate a period or account number, the Another/Done menu appears, allowing you to choose an additional period or account to appear on your report.

Another Done

This menu appears in three instances:

1. It appears when you finish entering all the debits and credits related to one transaction and select Done from the Add/Prior/Following/Done/Quit menu. If you select Another, you can enter another transaction in the same journal. If you select Done, you return to the GL Enter menu.

2. This menu appears after you choose Select from the All/Select menu in the GL Query program. If you select Another, you can choose another account or period to include in the audit trail or inquiry. If you select Done, RTR prints, saves, or displays the selected data.

3. This menu appears in the GL Budget program when you select Actuals to import data into the budget file. After you import one period, you can choose to import another. When you finish importing actual data, select Done to return to the GL Budget menu.

Ascending   Descending

This menu appears after you select Change to change the sort key when you customize a report in the GL Reports program. Select Ascending to arrange numeric data from lowest to highest. Ascending order for alphanumeric data is the same as alphabetic order. Descending sorts the key field in the opposite direction.

The menu appears twice: once for the primary sort key and once for the secondary sort key.

Assets   Debt/Equity   Exp/Rev

This menu appears when you select the Graph command on the GL Reports Statements menu. Each of the options is a pie chart you can choose to view and/or save for later printing. Once you choose the graph you want, you must indicate whether you want the graph to be based on Ledger or Budget data and whether you want the graph to be based on consolidated or on individual department data.

Assets

Shows a breakdown of total assets by major asset categories (determined by summary headings). Some of the summary headings are grouped together for the graph. If you choose to save the graph for printing, RTR saves it to the file ASSETS.PIC.

Debt/Equity

Shows a breakdown of total liabilities and owners' equity by major category. If you choose to save the graph for printing, RTR saves it to the file DEBT-EQ.PIC.

Exp/Rev

Shows expenses and profit as a percentage of total revenue. If
you choose to save the graph for printing, RTR saves it to the
file EXP-REV.PIC.

Backup   Don't

This menu appears when you run the GL Enter, the GL Ledger
Ledger, or the Files First-time programs.

Backup

Prompts you to specify an interval, in minutes, when RTR
should automatically back up your data. Automatic backup
occurs only while you enter data, not while you perform other
operations such as printing or while your computer is idle.
When RTR backs up your work, your computer beeps and the
message "PLEASE STANDBY" appears on the screen. When
the message disappears, you may continue entering data.

Don't

Does not back up your work while you are entering data.
Choose this option only if you want to perform operations that
don't require data entry (such as printing), or to make only
minor changes to data already entered.

Balance   Income   Cash Flow   Ratios   Graphs   Quit

This menu appears when you run the Statements command on
the GL Reports menu, after you enter the number of the last
financial period for which you have data.

If you have added departments to your chart of accounts, a
split screen appears, listing the departments you've added plus
the option Consolidated. Highlight the one you want and press
⏎. If you have not added departments, this split-screen menu
does not appear.

Balance

Prints, displays, or saves a worksheet file of the Balance Sheet for the current period in the format you choose. The Balance Sheet Formats available with the original RTR disk are: Current Period, Current vs. Budget, and Current vs. Prior Year. Use the cell pointer to highlight your choice of format and then press ⏎.

Income

Prints, displays, or saves a worksheet file of the Income Statement for the current period in the format you choose. The Income Statement Formats available with the original RTR disk are: Current Period and Year-to-Date, Year-to-Date vs. Budget, and Year-to-Date vs. Prior Year-to-Date. Use the cell pointer to highlight your choice of format and then press ⏎.

Cash Flow

Prints, displays, or saves a worksheet file of a Cash Flow Report for the current period, either based on actual Ledger data or on Budget data. The Cash Flow Report is not an official Statement of Cash Flows. It provides summary information from which the Statement of Cash Flows can be prepared.

Ratios

Prints, displays, or saves a worksheet file of several predetermined ratios, either based on actual Ledger data or on Budget data.

Graphs

Displays a menu that allows you to choose an Assets graph, a Debt/Equity graph, or an Exp/Rev graph.

Quit

Returns you to the RTR Main menu.

Black/White   Color   None

This menu appears when you Run either the GL Query or the GL Budget program. Both of these programs contain a graphing feature.

Black/White

Displays graphs in a single color (monochrome). If you plan to save the graphs for printing with PrintGraph and do not have a color printer, select Black/White even if you have a color monitor.

Color

Displays graphs in color.

None

Does not display graphs. Choose None if your monitor can display only text.

| Browse | Graph | Print | Done |

This menu appears when you select the Summary command on the GL Budget menu.

Browse

Allows you to view the summary report on the screen. Press ↵ when done viewing to return to the Browse/Graph/Print/Done menu.

Graph

Displays a graph comparing up to three summary headings that you select. The summary heads selected must all be from either the Balance Sheet or the Income Statement. If you select three items, the graph appears automatically. If you want to graph only one or two items, you must press D to view the graph. After you view the graph, you can save it to a .PIC file for printing with PrintGraph or return to the Browse/Graph/Print/Done menu.

Print

Sends a copy of the summary report to your printer or to a disk file called BDGT_SUM.PRN. Specify whether you have a wide- or narrow-carriage printer. The report prints in condensed print only. When printing is complete, RTR returns you to the Browse/Graph/Print/Done menu.

Done

Returns you to the Budget menu.

This menu appears when you select Adjust on the GL Reports menus. You can adjust the Accounts, Journals, and Trial reports. You can also adjust any custom report you have already created.

The Change/Keep menu first appears after you select the fields you want to include in your custom report. It allows you to Change or Keep the criteria on which the report is based.

The Change/Keep menu appears again after you have confirmed the criteria for the report. This time, it allows you to Change or Keep the sort order of the report. The left window of a split screen indicates the current sort keys and contains instructions on how to select new sort keys.

If you select Change, use (←) and (→) to highlight the column in the right window by which you want the report sorted, and then press (↵). Your first selection becomes the primary sort key, and the Ascending/Descending menu appears.

After you have selected the primary key and indicated the order, you must select the secondary key, which determines how to sort when the primary key field is the same for more than one record. The Ascending/Descending menu appears again. You can select the same field and order for both primary and secondary keys.

After you have selected the primary and secondary keys, and indicated the sort order for both of them, the Change/Keep menu appears again.

If you select Keep, either at the opening menu or after you have confirmed the criteria, the Adjust/Keep menu for the report heading appears.

Checking   Payables   Receivables   Save

This menu appears when you select the Defaults command on the GL Enter menu or when you press (F4) in the chart of accounts editing screen. It allows you to specify the default account number for the checking account, the accounts payable account, and the accounts receivable account.

Checking

Lets you specify the Cash in Bank account number for RTR to use as the default credit account for the Checks Journal and the default debit account for the Deposits Journal.

Payables

Lets you specify the Accounts Payable account number for RTR to use as the default credit account for the Payables Journal.

Receivables

Lets you specify the Accounts Receivable account number for RTR to use as the default debit account for the Receivables Journal.

Save

Saves the default account numbers.

Checks Deposits Payables Receivables General	

This menu appears when you select the Enter command on the GL Enter menu. The five selections on the menu represent the entry journals available in RTR.

Checks

Enters transactions that represent payments of cash by check. The check number is the reference number. The Checking account, which appears on the right side of the screen, is the default credit account. Enter the accounts to which the check should be distributed on the left side of the screen. Enter credit amounts, other than the credit to the default account, as negative numbers on the left side of the screen.

Deposits

Enters transactions that represent cash deposited to your bank account. The reference number is optional. The Checking account, which appears on the left side of the screen, is the default debit account. Enter the accounts to which the deposit should be distributed on the right side of the screen. Enter debit amounts, other than the debit to the default account, as negative numbers on the right side of the screen.

Payables

Enters transactions that affect the amount owed to regular vendors. Enter the vendor's invoice number as the reference number. The Payables account, which appears on the right side of the screen, is the default credit account. Enter all accounts to which the invoice or credit memo should be distributed on the left side of the screen. Enter credit amounts, other than the credit to the default account, as negative numbers on the left side of the screen.

Receivables

Use this command to enter transactions that affect the amount owed by regular customers. Enter the number of your invoice or credit memo to the customer as the reference number. The Receivables account, which appears on the left side of the screen, is the default debit account. Enter all accounts to which the invoice or credit memo should be distributed on the right side of the screen. Enter debit amounts, other than the debit to the default account, as negative numbers on the right side of the screen.

General

Enters transactions that cannot be entered into any of the four special journals. When you choose the General command, you see the Pairs/Single menu.

Condensed   Regular

This menu appears after you select the Print command on the GL Reports menu for the Accounts, Custom, Journals, or Trials report. When you have selected the carriage width of your printer, you see this menu. Indicate whether you want to print in a smaller, Condensed type size or in the Regular type size of your printer. When you highlight either command, the third line of the control panel indicates the number of pages required by the report. When you select either command, the printer starts printing the report. RTR returns you to the Main menu when printing is completed.

This menu appears in the GL Budget program, after you have designated your monitor type and indicated whether you are building a new budget or using an existing one.

Consolidated

Consolidates totals by account type in the summary report for the company as a whole.

Departments

Reports totals by department in the summary report.

Departmental   Non-departmental

This menu appears (only if you have added departments to your chart of accounts) when you add a new account (press INS and then select Account in the chart of accounts editing screen) or when you press (F2) in the chart of accounts editing screen.

Departmental

Adds departments to the account you are adding to the chart of accounts, or changes an existing account to a departmental account.

Non-departmental

Makes the account you are adding a consolidated account, or changes an existing account to a non-departmental account.

Disk   Modules   Printer codes   Options   Finished

This menu appears when you select Configure on the Main menu and then select Redo on the Redo/Okay menu. It allows you to change the configuration of your copy of RTR.

Disk

Asks you to specify whether your system is a floppy (two-diskette) or hard-disk system.

Modules

Presents a menu listing each of the modules available with RTR. Select a module to toggle that module on and off. The screen displays a *Y* for each module that is currently installed. In the Student Edition of Ready-to-Run, the General Ledger module displays a *Y*, and the other modules display an *N*.

Printer codes

Displays a list of printers supported by RTR. Press PGDN to see the rest of the list. If your printer is on the list, highlight its name using the ⬆ or ⬇ keys and then press ⏎. RTR records the codes to turn condensed print on and off for your printer. If your printer is not on the list, select NOT LISTED. RTR prompts you to enter the condensed mode ON and OFF strings for your printer and then records them.

Options

Allows you to specify whether you have the RTR Tutor or Timeslips Link, both of which are options available with RTR, but not included with the Student Edition.

Finished

Records the configuration codes you have entered and returns you to the Redo/Okay menu.

Edit/Browse   Actuals   Summary   Graph   Print   Quit/Save

This menu appears in the GL Budget program after you have indicated your monitor type, selected existing or new budget, and indicated whether you want summary data in consolidated or departments format. It is the main menu for the budget program.

Edit/Browse

Allows you to input or change budget figures. The worksheet screen is activated and you can enter numbers or 1-2-3 formulas in any of the budget columns. Press ALT-D when you are finished. If the amounts entered for any period do not balance, you cannot exit. RTR allows you to specify a cash account, and then adds or subtracts an amount for you to bring the budget into balance.

Actuals

Allows you to import one or more periods of actual data from the LEDGER file. This data can be used as the budget or can be adjusted using the Edit/Browse command. When you select Actuals, you are prompted to enter the period to import or to enter 0 (zero) to import beginning balances. After you have entered the period to import, the Another/Done menu appears. You can import additional data by selecting Another, or finish by selecting Done.

Summary

Calculates summary totals and cash flow analysis. Choosing Summary displays a menu with the options Browse, Graph, Print, and Done, allowing you to view, graph, or print the summary report.

Graph

Displays a submenu of several possible graphs to display: Accounts, Debt/Equity, Liquidity, and Revenue/Expenses.

Print

Sends a copy of the budget to the printer or to a Disk file called BDGT_SUM.PRN. The report is printed in condensed type, but you must specify whether you have a wide- or narrow-carriage printer.

Quit/Save

Displays the Save/Quit/Return menu, which allows you to save your work and return to the RTR Main menu, quit to the RTR Main menu without saving, or return to the main Budget menu.

Enter Print Fix Interrupt Defaults Save Quit

This menu appears when you Run the GL Enter program, choose an automatic backup option, and then type the number of the accounting period for which you will enter data.

Enter

Displays the journal selection menu, with the options Checks, Deposits, Payables, Receivables, and General.

Print

Prints a report of the unposted transactions in the temporary transaction file. Use this printout to look for data entry errors, which you can correct using the Fix command.

Fix

Allows you to correct errors in unposted transactions. When you select Fix, the Find/Scan/Return menu appears.

Interrupt

Allows you to stop entering transactions without saving them if you must interrupt your session. If you choose this command, the ENTER program is saved in a file called ENTER.HLD on your program disk or directory. The next time you start RTR, the message that the ENTER program was interrupted appears on the opening screen. To resume where you left off, choose GL Enter from the RTR Main menu.

Defaults

Allows you to specify default accounts for the special journals. When you select Defaults, you see a menu with the choices Checking, Payables, Receivables, and Save.

Save

Saves newly entered or corrected transactions to the temporary, unposted transactions file and returns you to the RTR Main menu.

Quit

Displays the Return/Quit menu, which returns you to the RTR Main menu without saving newly entered or corrected transactions, or returns you to the GL Enter menu.

Enter   Select

This menu appears when you select Inquire on the GL Query menu.

Enter

Allows you to type the number of the account about which you are inquiring.

Select

Displays a listing of all accounts in a split-screen window. Highlight the account you want and press ⏎.

Enter	Update	Reports	Query	Budget	Ledger	Prior

This menu appears when you select GL from the RTR Main menu. After you set up the initial chart of accounts for a set of books, you will use these commands exclusively to operate the Student Edition of Ready-to-Run, unless you add a new set of books, close the year for the current set of books, or change the data password.

Enter

Enters transactions to the general ledger. Select this command and choose Run, choose an automatic backup option, and then specify the period for which you are entering data. RTR stores transactions in a temporary transactions file until posted.

Update

Posts transactions from the temporary transactions file into the permanent ledger file. When you Run this program, the Print/ Skip menu appears. Choose to print a listing of the posting to the printer or to disk, or skip printing the report.

Reports

Displays a menu with the options Accounts, Custom, Journals, Statements, Trial, and Prior.

Query

Displays the Inquire/Report/Quit menu that lets you view or print a detail or summary of any account in the general ledger after you choose the Run command.

Budget

Creates or edits a budget file for comparison to actual results. You can import actual numbers for the budget file or prepare a graph of the budget file or summary report that includes cash flow information.

Ledger

Creates a new chart of accounts or revises an existing chart of accounts. You can select a sample chart of accounts on which to base a new chart of accounts. Also enters or revises beginning balances for the period.

Prior

Returns you to the RTR Main menu.

Existing Blank Sample

This menu appears when you run the GL Ledger program after you choose an automatic backup option. If you choose Blank or Sample and a chart of accounts already exists, a prompt asks if you want to replace the existing chart of accounts.

This menu also appears when you select Files from the RTR Main menu if no chart of accounts exists in your data files.

Existing

Allows you to edit an existing chart of accounts.

Blank

Allows you to create a chart of accounts from scratch.

Sample

Allows you to use one of the samples provided with the RTR software as a basis for a new chart of accounts. Insert the original RTR diskette into drive A of your computer at the prompt, press ⏎, and then type the name of the sample you want to use, without the COA extension.

Existing New

This menu appears in the GL Budget program after you indicate your choice of monitor. It allows you to edit an existing budget file or build a new one. If you select New and a budget file already exists, you will not be warned. However, if you then quit the budget menu without saving, the existing file is preserved.

This menu appears when you select the Fix command on the GL Enter menu. It allows you to edit transactions entered with the Enter command from the same menu.

Find

Asks you to specify the reference number of the transaction you want to edit. An edit screen appears listing the transactions and a matching reference number. Press (F9) to return to the Enter menu.

Scan

Displays all the unposted transactions on the screen. Use (↑), (↓), (←), and (→) to move around and make corrections, and then press ESC to return to the Enter menu.

To correct dates, use the Lotus 1-2-3 @DATE command. The syntax of the @DATE command is:

@DATE(YY,MM,DD)

To enter credit amounts, enter negative amounts in the edit screen.

To delete a transaction, enter * in the amount field of every row relating to that transaction.

Return

Returns you to the GL Enter menu.

First-time   New-year   Data password   Return

This menu appears when you select Files from the RTR Main menu.

First-time

Sets up data files for the first time. When you select First-time, you enter a data password if you want one, create the chart of accounts, and then enter beginning balances. If a chart of accounts already exists on the data disk, RTR displays the menu to enter beginning balances.

New-year

Set up files for a new accounting year. *Make sure you have backed up your data files prior to running this program: you cannot reverse it after you select Run.* Creates a prior year ledger file, transfers ending balances for balance sheet accounts to beginning balances, and closes out revenue and expense accounts. Enter your data password when prompted and indicate the equity account to which you want net income added.

Data password

Changes the data password for the current data files. Enter the current data password and then the new data password at the prompts. Change to using no password by pressing ⏎ at the second prompt.

Return

Returns you to the RTR Main menu.

Floppy Hard

This menu appears when you select the Disk command on the Configure Redo menu. Choose Floppy (two-diskette) or Hard (hard disk), depending on your system configuration.

GL AP/AR Inventory Payroll Directory/Company Configure Files Quit

---

This menu appears when you start RTR and enter the system password. It is the RTR Main menu.

GL

Accesses the programs that run the General Ledger portion of RTR. When you select GL, you see a menu with the options Enter, Update, Reports, Query, Budget, Ledger, and Prior.

AP/AR

Accesses the programs that run the Accounts Payable and Accounts Receivable subsidiary ledgers of RTR. Not included in the Student Edition, but available from Addison-Wesley. (See the coupon in the back of this manual.)

Inventory

Accesses the programs that run the Inventory subsidiary of RTR. Not included in the Student Edition.

Payroll

Accesses the programs that run the Payroll subsidiary of RTR. Not included in the Student Edition.

Directory/Company

Allows you to specify the disk and directory where data files are located for each of the programs in RTR. Also allows you to specify a company name to be printed on reports and on the screen.

Configure

Allows you to specify the type of hardware configuration you are using, the printer codes for condensed and regular print-ing, and the RTR programs that you have purchased.

Files

Sets up the files and beginning balances for a new company. Also allows you to create a set of files for a new year, change the data password, or return to the RTR Main menu.

Quit

Quits RTR. You can choose to quit to Lotus 1-2-3, or quit to DOS.

Inquire   Report   Quit

This menu appears when you Run the GL Query program.

Inquire

Allows you to print, save to a .PRN file, view, or graph the detail in one account for one or more periods. When you select the Inquire command, you can either enter the number of the account or select the account from a listing of the chart of accounts.

Report

Allows you to print, save to a .PRN file, or view the activity in all or selected accounts for all or selected periods. This option is primarily used to print an audit trail of all accounts.

Quit

Quits to the RTR Main menu.

Keep   Change   Delete

This menu appears when you are entering transactions in the GL Enter program. After you enter and confirm a screen, you can add screens to the transaction, access a prior or following screen, or save the transaction by choosing Done. If you select Prior or Following, this menu appears.

Keep

Keeps the current screen as part of this transaction.

Change

Lets you change the contents of the fields on the screen. When you finish, press F9 to confirm the changes.

Delete

Deletes this screen from the current transaction.

Ledger   Balances   Return

This menu appears when you select the Ledger command on the GL menu.

Ledger

Allows you to make changes to the existing chart of accounts.

Balances

Allows you to make changes to the beginning balances in the existing chart of accounts. The beginning balances must balance before you can exit from this program.

Return

Returns you to the GL menu.

```
Ledger  Budget
```

This menu appears when you select:

- The Cash Flow command on the GL Reports Statements menu. It allows you to base the cash flow worksheet on actual Ledger amounts or on Budget amounts.

- The Ratios command on the GL Reports Statements menu. It allows you base the ratios report on actual Ledger amounts or on Budget amounts.

- The Graphs command on the GL Reports Statements menu after you have designated the type of graph you want to view or print. It allows you to base the graph on actual Ledger amounts or on Budget amounts.

You must create a budget file with the GL Budget command before you can base a report or graph on budget amounts.

```
No  Yes
```

This menu appears when you:

- Select Quit on the GL Reports Statements menu. Selecting Yes returns you to the RTR Main menu. Selecting No returns you to the GL Reports Statements menu.

- Select the Quit command after you press (F9) to finish editing the chart of accounts. Selecting Yes returns you to the RTR Main menu without saving your changes. Selecting No returns you to the chart of accounts editing screen.

- Press (F9) to finish editing the chart of accounts when you are creating your chart of accounts using the Files First-time command. Selecting Yes returns you to the RTR Main menu without saving your changes to the chart of accounts. Selecting No returns you to the chart of accounts editing screen.

```
Non-Zero  Active
```

This menu appears when you select the Report command on the GL Query menu and choose to print, save, or view all accounts.

Non-Zero

Prints an audit trail for all accounts that have a non-zero beginning balance or that have activity during the period.

Active

Prints an audit trail only for accounts that have activity during the period.

Okay   Redo   Ignore

This menu appears in the GL Enter program in any of the journals. This menu appears after you have entered data into all the fields on the screen, or when you press (F9) after you complete both sides of the transaction.

Okay

Accepts the data as entered and proceeds.

Redo

Activates the cell pointer in the transaction screen so you can move to any field and make corrections. Press (F9) when you finish. The Okay/Redo/Ignore menu reappears.

Ignore

Ignores this screen of data. If you select Ignore, you cannot select Done from the next menu.

Pairs   Single

This menu appears when you select the General command on the GL Enter Journal Selection menu.

Pairs

Presents an entry screen that allows you to enter the debit on the left side of the screen and the credit on the right side of the screen. Use this command only to enter transactions that debit and credit an equal number of accounts. The amounts you enter must balance to zero before you can save the transaction.

> **Caution** If you use Pairs to enter a compound entry that debits and credits an unequal number of accounts, you may need to enter an amount of zero on either the right or left side of the screen to make the transaction balance.

Single

Presents an entry screen that allows only one account to be debited or credited at a time. Enter credit amounts as negative numbers. Use this command to enter compound entries that debit and credit an unequal number of accounts. All the amounts entered must balance to zero before you can save the transaction.

Payables Receivables Back

This menu appears when you select the AP/AR command from the RTR Main menu. It allows you to select the Payables or Receivables subsidiary program to interface with the GL program. The Back command takes you back to the RTR Main menu.

Payables Receivables Checks Deposits General All Quit

This menu appears when you run the GL Reports Journals command.

You can choose to print any or all of the journals into which you enter data. Transactions are sorted by date and then by account number. If you select the All command, the report contains all of the transactions entered for the period specified. The All command does not sort the transactions by journal.

To print a separate report for each journal, select each journal individually from this menu. After each journal prints, you return to this menu so that you can select another journal to print. Selecting Quit returns you to the RTR Main menu.

> **Note** The All command overrides the criterion for a custom report. Select an individual journal if you want to retain the extract you created.

This menu appears when you select the Accounts command or the Trial command on the GL Reports menu and then select Run.

This menu also appears when you Run a Custom report generated from the GL Reports Accounts or GL Reports Trial menus.

Print

Prints the displayed report after allowing you to select a narrow- or wide-carriage printer and regular or condensed print. Returns you to the RTR Main menu when printing is completed.

Browse

Displays a report on the screen and places the cell pointer in the report area of the worksheet. You cannot change the contents of the report on this screen. Returns you to the Print/Browse/Save/Done menu when you press ⏎ or ESC.

Save

Saves the report to a Lotus 1-2-3 worksheet file in .WK1 format. When you select this command, enter a filename for the report at the prompt. Press ESC to abandon the report without saving to a .WK1 file. Returns you to the Print/Browse/Save/Done menu when finished.

Done

Returns you to the RTR Main menu.

This menu appears when you select the Journals command on the GL Reports menu, select Run, and choose a journal from the Journal Selection menu.

This menu also appears when you run a Custom report generated from the GL Reports Journal menu.

Print

Prints the displayed report after allowing you to select a narrow- or wide-carriage printer and regular or condensed print. Returns to the RTR Main menu when printing finishes.

Browse

Displays a report on the screen and places the cell pointer in the report area of the worksheet. You cannot change the contents of the report on this screen. Returns to the Print/Browse/Save/Done menu when you press ⏎ or ESC.

Save

Saves the report to a Lotus 1-2-3 worksheet file in .WK1 format. When you select this command, enter a filename for the report at the prompt. Press ESC to abandon the report without saving to a .WK1 file. Returns you to the Print/Browse/Save/Done menu when finished.

Return

Returns you to the Journal Selection menu.

Print   Disk

This menu appears in the GL Budget program when you choose Print from the main Budget menu.

Print

Prints a copy of the budget summary or the budget file. The budget file printout contains data only, not totals. The budget summary printout shows the budget detail by summary heading and a summary of cash flows. The reports print in condensed type. Select a narrow- or wide-carriage printer.

Disk

Sends a copy of the report to a disk file called BDGT_SUM.PRN in ASCII format. Both reports are sent to the same filename.

Print   Display   Save   Heading   Return

This menu appears when you select Balance or Income on the GL Reports Statements menu.

Print

Prints the displayed report on a narrow- or wide-carriage printer. The print type is selected automatically, depending on the format of the selected report. Returns you to the RTR Main menu when printing is completed.

Display

Displays a report on the screen and places the cell pointer in the report area of the worksheet. You cannot change the contents of the report on this screen. Returns to this menu when you press ⏎ or ESC.

Save

Saves the report to a Lotus 1-2-3 worksheet file in .WK1 format. When you select this command, enter a filename for the report at the prompt. Press ESC to abandon the report without saving to a .WK1 file. Returns you to the RTR Main menu when finished.

Heading

Allows you to change the column headings that appear on the Balance Sheet or Income Statement. A horizontal split screen appears, with the headings and cell pointer in the bottom window. Move the cell pointer to the cell containing the heading, type the new heading, and press ⏎. To center the heading above the column, precede it with a caret (^). When you finish adjusting the headings, press ⏎ to return to this menu.

Return

Returns you to the Statement Selection menu.

Print   Display   Save   Return

This menu appears when you select Cash Flows or Ratios on the GL Reports Statements menu after specifying whether you want to use actual Ledger data or Budget data.

Print

Prints the report displayed. The Cash Flows and Ratios reports are printed in regular print on one page. Returns to the RTR Main menu when printing is completed.

Display

Displays a report on the screen and places the cell pointer in the report area of the worksheet. You cannot change the contents of the report on this screen. Returns to this menu when you press ⏎ or ESC.

Save

Saves the report to a Lotus 1-2-3 worksheet file in .WK1 format. When you select this command, enter a filename for the report at the prompt. Press ESC to abandon the report without saving to a .WK1 file. Returns you to the RTR Main menu when finished.

> **Note** Saving the Cash Flow Report to a worksheet file allows you to use the summary worksheet as a starting point for the Statement of Cash Flows.

Return

Returns you to the Statement Selection menu.

Print Save View

This menu appears when you select Report on the GL Query menu.

Print

Prints the audit trail you select. If you select more than one account for the audit trail, a continuous report prints, with the selected accounts printed in order by account number. If you select more than one period for the audit trail, each period begins a new page. All the selected accounts print for each period. If no transactions exist for a selected period, a page prints with the message, "No transactions found for period XX." When all the selected periods have printed, the GL Query menu appears.

Save

Creates a Lotus 1-2-3 worksheet file containing the audit trail
as it would have printed had you selected the Print command.
If you selected more than one period for the audit trail, a separate worksheet file is created for each period, with the name
filename.WK1, 2.WK1, 3.WK1, etc. (where *filename* is the
selected period). When RTR finishes saving, the GL Query
menu appears.

View

Displays the detail transactions for each period selected. The
accounts you select display in account-number order, with
each period beginning on a new screen. Use PGDN and PGUP to
browse through the report. If no transactions exist for a
selected period, a message to that effect appears in the control
panel. When you have viewed all the selected accounts, the
GL Query menu reappears.

Print   Save   View   Graph   Return

This menu appears when you select the Inquire command on
the GL Query menu.

Print

Prints the Summary or Detail for the account you select. If you
select more than one period, each period begins a new page. If
no transactions exist for a selected period, a page prints with
the message, ''No transactions found for period XX.'' When all
selected periods have printed, the GL Query menu appears.

Save

Creates a Lotus 1-2-3 worksheet file that contains the Summary or Detail as it would have printed if you had selected the
Print command. If you select more than one period, a separate
worksheet file is created for each period, with the name
ALL*period*.WK1, ALL2.WK1, ALL3.WK1, etc. (where *period* is
the number of the selected period). If no transactions exist for
a given period, no file is created. When RTR finishes saving,
the GL Query menu appears.

View

Displays the detail transactions for each period selected. Use PGDN and PGUP to browse through the report. A new screen begins for each period for which transactions exist. If no transactions exist for a selected period, a message to that effect appears in the control panel. When all selected periods have been viewed, the GL Query menu reappears.

Graph

Displays a bar graph of the activity in the selected account. A separate bar is displayed for each period of data. When you finish viewing the graph, press any key and then specify whether you want to save the graph for printing with PrintGraph or to return to the previous menu. If you select Save, the graph is saved in a file named *filename*.PIC (where *filename* is the account number in the graph).

Return

Returns you to GL Query menu.

Print   Skip

This menu appears when you run the GL Update program. It allows you to print a posting report or skip printing.

Printer   Disk

This menu appears when you select the Print command on the GL Update menu. It allows you to send the posting report to the printer or to a disk file called POSTINGS.PRN.

Quit   First-time   Beg.Balance   Stop

This menu appears when you select the Balances command on the GL Ledger menu, or when you select the First-time command on the Files menu and a chart of accounts already exists on your data disk.

Quit

Returns you to the Main menu.

First-time

Records the beginning balances when you set up a system for the first time. If you use this command and a system already exists, the existing beginning balances are zeroed out. *RTR does not warn you that a current file already exists.* Enter your data password, and an entry screen appears in which you can enter the beginning balances for each balance sheet account. You cannot enter beginning balances for income statement accounts. When you finish, press ESC. Beginning balances must balance before you can exit the entry screen. When you exit, RTR creates your new data files.

Beg.Balance

Allows you to adjust beginning balances without making any other changes to the chart of accounts or ledger files. When you finish entering beginning balances, press ESC. The Beginning balances must balance before you can exit the entry screen.

Stop

Allows you to stop execution of the RTR macros to examine or revise them. If you select this command, press ALT-S to restart this program.

```
Quit   Run   Break
```

This menu appears when you select the New-year command on the Files menu.

Quit

Quits to the RTR Main menu.

Run

Runs the program that creates the New-year files. You cannot exit the program after you select this command. Enter your data password, and a screen appears displaying the chart of accounts. Select the equity account to which you want to add the net income for the period. After you move the cell pointer to the appropriate account and press ⏎, RTR creates a prior year file that summarizes activity by period for each account. RTR then initializes the data files for the new year and returns to the RTR Main menu.

Break

Stops execution of the RTR macros so you can examine or revise them. If you select this command, press ALT-S to restart this program.

Redo   Okay

This menu appears with a screen that displays the current configuration settings when you select the Configure command on the RTR Main menu.

Redo

Allows you to make changes in the configuration settings displayed on the screen. After you make your changes and select Finished, the Okay/Redo menu reappears.

Okay

Saves the settings and returns you to the RTR Main menu.

Replace   New   Quit

This menu appears when you choose to adjust the Accounts, Journals, or Trial reports on the GL Reports menu. After you specify the fields, the criterion, the sort keys, and the report title, you can choose to Save the report or Return to the Run/Adjust/Quit/Break menu. The Replace/New/Quit menu appears when you choose to Save your custom report.

Replace

Replaces the existing report file with the custom report you have just designed and returns you to the Run/Adjust/Quit/Break menu. *If you select Replace when you have customized a standard RTR report, the RTR report is replaced.*

New

Prompts you for the name you want to use for the custom report. Press (⏎) to save the report. A message tells you that the report is saved. Press (⏎) to return to the Run/Adjust/Quit/Break menu.

Quit

Returns you to the Run/Adjust/Quit/Break menu without saving the custom report. You can then run the custom report, but the report is not saved for later re-use.

Return   Lotus   Quit

This menu appears when you select the Quit command from the RTR Main menu.

Return

Returns you to the RTR Main menu.

Lotus

Exits from RTR to Lotus 1-2-3.

Quit

Quits to DOS.

Return   Quit

This menu appears when you select Quit from the GL Enter menu. It returns you to the GL Enter menu or quits to the RTR Main menu without saving your work.

Run   Adjust   Quit   Break

This menu appears when you select Accounts, Journals, or Trial on the GL Reports menu. If you select Custom on the GL Reports menu, this menu appears after you select a report from the listing of available custom reports.

Run

Runs the report program you selected.

Adjust

Allows you to customize the report you have selected. Designate which fields you want to include in the custom report, indicate the criteria on which the report is selected, specify how you want the report sorted, and then adjust or keep the report title.

Quit

Returns you to the RTR Main menu.

Break

Stops execution of the RTR macros so you can examine or revise them. If you select this command, press ALT-S to restart the program.

Run   Quit   Break

This menu appears when you select the Enter, Update, Query, or Budget command on the GL menu. It also appears when you select the Ledger command on the GL Ledger menu.

This menu also appears if you select the First-time command on the Files menu when no chart of accounts file exists on your data disk.

Run

Runs the program you have selected.

Quit

Returns you to the RTR Main menu.

Break

Stops execution of the RTR macros so you can examine or revise them. If you select this command, press ALT-S to restart this program.

Save   Quit   Return

This menu appears when you select the Quit/Save command on the GL Budget menu or when you press F9 in the chart of accounts editing screen.

Save

Saves the changes you made to the budget or to the chart of accounts.

Quit

Quits the budget or the chart of accounts without saving the changes you made.

Return

Returns you to the Budget menu or to the chart of accounts editing screen.

Save   Return

This menu appears when you finish customizing a report by selecting Adjust for the Accounts, Custom, Journals, or Trial command on the GL Reports menu. You can save the report to a permanent file or return to the Run/Adjust/Quit/Break menu.

This menu also appears after you view any graph available in the following menus:

- GL Reports Statements

- GL Query Inquire

- GL Budget

- GL Budget Summary

After you view the graph, press any key to see this menu. You can save the graph to a .PIC file for printing with PrintGraph, or return to the menu from which you selected the Graph command.

Select   Delete   Prior

This menu appears when you select the Custom command on the GL Reports menu.

Select

Displays the names of the custom reports available in the left window of a split screen. Highlight the one you want and press ⏎. The Run/Adjust/Quit/Break menu appears. Select the Adjust command from this menu to make changes to the custom report.

Delete

Lets you delete a custom report. Displays the names of the custom reports that have been saved in the left window of a split screen. Highlight the one you want to delete and press ⏎. Returns you to the RTR Main menu.

Prior

Returns you to the GL Reports menu.

Summary   Detail

This menu appears when you select the Print or Save command from the GL Query Inquire menu.

Summary

Prints or saves the Summary screen that is displayed.

Detail

Prints or saves the Detail for the account you select. Indicate whether you want the detail for all or for selected periods. If you select Save and choose Detail, the detail for each period selected is saved to a worksheet file named ALL*period*.WK1 (where *period* is the number of the selected period). If no transactions exist for a selected period, no file is saved.

Summary   Detailed

This menu appears when you select Display or Save after selecting Balance or Income on the GL Reports Statements menu. It allows you to display or save the Summary or Detailed form of the selected financial statement.

If you selected Display to get this menu, the selected statement displays on the screen. Use ⬆, ⬇, ➡, ⬅, PGDN, or PGUP to review the report, and then press ↵ to return to the previous menu.

If you selected Save to get this menu, enter a name for the worksheet file to save the statement at the prompt. Press ESC to abandon without saving.

Summary Detailed Both

This menu appears when you select Print after selecting Balance or Income on the GL Reports Statements menu. It allows you to print the summary form, the detailed form, or both forms of the selected statement on a narrow- or wide-carriage printer.

Summary Heading Account Title Line Formula Return

This menu appears when you press INS in the chart of accounts editing screen.

Summary Heading

Presents a split-screen listing of the summary headings available for the financial statement category you are adding to. Separate listings appear for Assets, Liabilities, Owners' Equity, Revenue, Expenses, and Non-operating Items. Highlight the summary heading you want and press ↵. You can change the wording of the summary heading after you select it by using F2.

Account Title

Inserts a new account at the cell pointer. If you have added departments to your chart of accounts, you must specify whether the account is departmental or non-departmental. Enter a new account number and account title at the prompt.

Line

Inserts a blank line at the cell pointer.

Formula

Allows you to create a formula at the cell pointer. The formula determines the value printed in that cell when you generate financial statements. Enter a description of the formula at the prompt, and then create the formula using arithmetic operators and cell locations. You can also use Lotus 1-2-3 @functions to create formulas. Do not press ⏎ until the formula is complete. If you enter an incorrect formula, you must delete the line and re-create the formula.

To enter a line to indicate totals, use the formula command. Press ⏎ to skip the description and use a backslash (\ ) and either a hyphen (-) or equal sign (=) to create a single or double line at that point in the financial statement.

Return

Returns you to edit mode.

Wide   Narrow

This menu appears when you select Print on any of the following menus:

- GL Reports Accounts

- GL Reports Custom

- GL Reports Journals

- GL Reports Statements Balance

- GL Reports Statements Income

- GL Reports Trial

- GL Budget

- GL Budget Summary

It allows you to indicate whether you are printing your report on a wide- or narrow-carriage printer.

The Chart of Accounts Editing Screen

The following keys are used in the chart of accounts editing screen.

INS

Displays a menu of items you can add to the chart of accounts. The options are Summary Heading, Account Title, Line, Formula, and Return.

F2

Allows you to change an account or the wording of a summary heading. If an account is active, you can only change the title or the departmental status of the account.

DEL

Deletes the line on which the cell pointer is resting. You cannot delete an active account or a Summary Heading that contains detail accounts.

F4

Displays a menu with the options Checking, Payables, Receivables, and Save. Use these options to enter the default account numbers for the special journals.

F5

Inserts a hard page break command. When you print a financial statement, the printer advances to the top of a new page before printing the next line.

F6

Displays a menu that allows you to add, edit, or delete departments.

F7

Displays a menu that allows you to print the chart of accounts, a sample detailed income statement, a sample detailed balance sheet, or a listing of the summary account headings. When you print the chart of accounts, specify whether you want to print all accounts, including departmental accounts, or only consolidated accounts. All listings are printed in 80 columns of regular type.

`F8`

Interrupts the account editing process and saves the program in a file called NEWCOA.HLD. The next time you start RTR, the opening screen indicates that the program NEWCOA has been interrupted. Select GL Ledger. RTR retrieves the NEWCOA.HLD, and you can continue where you stopped.

`F9`

Ends editing the chart of accounts. You can save your changes, quit without saving, or return to the edit mode.

3

Troubleshooting

Situation	Solution
Your screen display shows more lines than shown in the figure in the manual.	Lotus 1-2-3 must be installed for an 80 column by 25 row screen. Reinstall Lotus 1-2-3 and select the 80×25 option for your monitor.
You can move the cell pointer around the underlying Lotus 1-2-3 worksheet. The CMD status indicator at the bottom of the screen is off.	You have left the RTR macro. Press ALT-M to return to the main menu of the routine where you were working. No data will be lost.
The computer beeps when you are starting RTR on a two-diskette system.	Be sure that your Lotus 1-2-3 System disk remains in drive A until the RTR Main menu appears.
An error message tells you that the add-in VSUM is not found.	If you are using a two-diskette system, be sure that your Lotus 1-2-3 System disk is in drive A.
	If you are using a hard-disk system, return to the installation procedure and reinstall RTR.
The following message appears on the screen: **DYN file not found; Enter ADN to Attach.**	Check to see if your Lotus 1-2-3 program files are where you said they would be during the installation procedure.
	If you are using 5¼″ disks with Lotus 1-2-3, Release 3.x, you need additional files for the installation. Send in the coupon at the end of this manual to receive a diskette with the additional files you need.
An error message appears when you are trying to save your work.	Your disk may be full; press ⏎ and try again with a blank, formatted diskette.

> **Note** If you do this, you may need to transfer files. For RTR to work properly with two data diskettes, the PERIODnn.WK1 files must be on one diskette and all other files must be on another diskette.

Continued

Situation	Solution
The program appears to print, but your printer does not respond.	Make sure your printer is correctly connected, turned on, and on-line.
	Try printing from Lotus 1-2-3. If Lotus 1-2-3 can't print, review the printer installation for Lotus 1-2-3 to see if your printer is correctly installed.
Printing starts but "printing error" message appears (with Release 3.x of Lotus 1-2-3).	Release 3 uses background printing. You do not have enough memory to continue working in RTR while printing. Wait until your report is finished printing before issuing additional commands in RTR.
Printer error message tells you to try again or abort the printing by pressing ESC.	Make sure your printer is properly connected, turned on, and on-line.
	If you press ESC, you will be allowed to save the work you have completed.
Screen goes blank during graphing.	Review Lotus 1-2-3 installation to see if monitor is installed properly for graphics.
You saved graph files for printing, but when you run PrintGraph there are no .PIC files to print.	The graphs-directory for PrintGraph must be the same as your data diskette/directory. Follow the instructions in Appendix C to print with PrintGraph.
	If you are using Lotus 1-2-3, Release 3.x, the default save mode for Graph Save is graphic metafile format. Use /Worksheet Global Default Graph to change the default save mode to .PIC format and resave your graphs.
An error message tells you to try again or abort.	A fatal error has occurred. If you try again and the same message appears, choose abort. You are returned to the RTR Main menu, but you lose the data you have entered during that session at the computer.

Continued

Situation	Solution
You see the message: **Can't run with Release 3.x files - See Manual - Press <Enter> to abort.**	You are trying to process RTR data files created with Release 3 of Lotus 1-2-3 with program files installed with Release 2 of Lotus 1-2-3. You must run a special translate program to be able to do this. Refer to the section on Using Ready-to-Run with Release 3 of Lotus 1-2-3.
You get the message: **Existing chart of accounts in Rel. 2 format - Must translate or abort.**	You are trying to process RTR data files created with Release 2 of Lotus 1-2-3 with program files installed with Release 3 of Lotus 1-2-3. If you choose to translate to Release 3 format, you must translate back to Release 2 format before you can process the files with RTR program files installed with Release 2 of Lotus 1-2-3. Refer to the section on Using Ready-to-Run with Release 3 of Lotus 1-2-3.
Your screen flashes on and off and the indicator MEM appears at the bottom of the screen, or you see the error message: **Memory Full.**	Your computer has run out of memory. Press CTRL-BREAK, and then press ESC to leave the report. You must free more computer memory (not disk space) by removing any memory-resident programs.
Your screen moves left or right instead of the cursor.	Be sure you have not engaged the SCROLL LOCK key on your keyboard.

4

Examples of Ready-to-Run Reports

```
Carron Systems                         TRIAL BALANCE                    Period 1


Acc #     Account Title        Prior Balance  Debits       Credits      Ending Balance
   111 Cash                     22,500.00     70,369.00    51,534.00    41,335.00
   112 Accounts Receivable      34,550.00     51,200.00    66,140.00    19,610.00
   121 Merchandise Inventory    37,000.00         0.00         0.00     37,000.00
   131 Prepaid Insurance         3,600.00         0.00         0.00      3,600.00
   132 Warehouse Supplies          900.00       350.00         0.00      1,250.00
   133 Office Supplies            250.00        400.00         0.00        650.00
   141 Warehouse Equipment      24,000.00         0.00         0.00     24,000.00
   142 Accum. Depr. - Warehouse  (2,400.00)        0.00         0.00     (2,400.00)
   143 Office Equipment          9,000.00       800.00         0.00      9,800.00
   144 Accum. Depr. - Office Equ  (1,800.00)        0.00         0.00     (1,800.00)
   211 Accounts Payable        (23,218.00)    42,222.00    38,393.00   (19,389.00)
   212 Salaries Payable             0.00         0.00         0.00         0.00
   213 Income Taxes Payable         0.00         0.00         0.00         0.00
   311 Common Stock          (100,000.00)         0.00         0.00  (100,000.00)
   312 Retained Earnings        (4,382.00)         0.00         0.00     (4,382.00)
   313 Dividends                    0.00      2,000.00         0.00      2,000.00
   411 Sales                        0.00         0.00     58,040.00   (58,040.00)
   412 Sales Returns & Allowance     0.00     1,490.00         0.00      1,490.00
   413 Sales Discounts              0.00      1,121.00         0.00      1,121.00
   511 Purchases                    0.00     36,358.00         0.00     36,358.00
   512 Purchases Returns & Allow    0.00         0.00       588.00       (588.00)
   513 Freight In                   0.00       878.00         0.00        878.00
   611 Sales Salaries Expense       0.00      1,100.00         0.00      1,100.00
   612 Warehouse Salaries Expens    0.00      1,000.00         0.00      1,000.00
   613 Rent Expense, Warehouse      0.00      1,400.00         0.00      1,400.00
   614 Depr. Exp. - Warehouse Eq    0.00         0.00         0.00         0.00
   615 Warehouse Supplies Expens    0.00         0.00         0.00         0.00
   616 Freight Out Expense          0.00       407.00         0.00        407.00
   617 Advertising Expense          0.00      1,385.00         0.00      1,385.00
   621 Office Salaries Expense      0.00       900.00         0.00        900.00
   622 Rent Expense, Office         0.00       500.00         0.00        500.00
   623 Depr. Exp. - Office Equip    0.00         0.00         0.00         0.00
   624 Office Supplies Expense      0.00         0.00         0.00         0.00
   625 Insurance Expense            0.00         0.00         0.00         0.00
   626 Utility Expense              0.00       216.00         0.00        216.00
   627 Telephone Expense            0.00       203.00         0.00        203.00
   628 Postage Expense              0.00       160.00         0.00        160.00
   629 Purch Discounts Lost         0.00       236.00         0.00        236.00
   631 Income Taxes Expense         0.00         0.00         0.00         0.00
   -------------------------------------------------------------------------------
                                    0.00    214,695.00   214,695.00         0.00


     Report Run: 17-Nov-90
```

Acc #	Description	Ref #	Ref Date	SJ	Transaction
111	VENDOR 3	3382	05-Jul-92	CD	(772.00)
211	VENDOR 3	0/3382	05-Jul-92	CD	772.00
111	VENDOR 2	3383	09-Jul-92	CD	(9,898.00)
211	VENDOR 2	0/3383	09-Jul-92	CD	9,898.00
111	EMPLOYEE 1	3385	12-Jul-92	CD	(550.00)
111	EMPLOYEE 2	3386	12-Jul-92	CD	(500.00)
111	EMPLOYEE 3	3387	12-Jul-92	CD	(450.00)
111	VENDOR 2	3384	12-Jul-92	CD	(6,864.00)
211	VENDOR 2	0/3384	12-Jul-92	CD	6,864.00
611	EMPLOYEE 1	0/3385	12-Jul-92	CD	550.00
612	EMPLOYEE 2	0/3386	12-Jul-92	CD	500.00
621	EMPLOYEE 3	0/3387	12-Jul-92	CD	450.00
111	PAYEE 1	3388	15-Jul-92	CD	(1,900.00)
613	PAYEE 1	0/3388	15-Jul-92	CD	1,400.00
622	PAYEE 1	0/3388	15-Jul-92	CD	500.00
111	VENDOR 4	3389	16-Jul-92	CD	(8,300.00)
211	VENDOR 4	0/3389	16-Jul-92	CD	8,140.00
629	VENDOR 4	0/3389	16-Jul-92	CD	160.00
111	PAYEE 2	3390	17-Jul-92	CD	(1,385.00)
617	PAYEE 2	0/3390	17-Jul-92	CD	1,385.00
111	PAYEE 3	3391	23-Jul-92	CD	(160.00)
628	PAYEE 3	0/3391	23-Jul-92	CD	160.00
111	VENDOR 4	3392	26-Jul-92	CD	(11,552.00)
111	EMPLOYEE 2	3394	26-Jul-92	CD	(500.00)
111	EMPLOYEE 3	3395	26-Jul-92	CD	(450.00)
111	EMPLOYEE 1	3393	26-Jul-92	CD	(550.00)
211	VENDOR 4	0/3392	26-Jul-92	CD	11,552.00
611	EMPLOYEE 1	0/3393	26-Jul-92	CD	550.00
612	EMPLOYEE 2	0/3394	26-Jul-92	CD	500.00
621	EMPLOYEE 3	0/3395	26-Jul-92	CD	450.00
111	PAYEE 4	3397	29-Jul-92	CD	(216.00)
111	VENDOR 5	3396	29-Jul-92	CD	(3,800.00)
211	VENDOR 5	0/3396	29-Jul-92	CD	3,724.00
626	PAYEE 4	0/3397	29-Jul-92	CD	216.00
629	VENDOR 5	0/3396	29-Jul-92	CD	76.00
111	VENDOR 1	3398	30-Jul-92	CD	(481.00)
211	VENDOR 1	0/3398	30-Jul-92	CD	481.00
111	BANK 1	3399	31-Jul-92	CD	(2,000.00)
111	PAYEE 5	3401	31-Jul-92	CD	(800.00)
111	VENDOR 6	3400	31-Jul-92	CD	(406.00)
143	PAYEE 5	0/3401	31-Jul-92	CD	800.00
211	VENDOR 6	0/3400	31-Jul-92	CD	203.00
313	BANK 1	0/3399	31-Jul-92	CD	2,000.00
627	VENDOR 6	0/3400	31-Jul-92	CD	203.00

- -

                                                       0.00

Report Run: 17-Nov-90

```
       1 <- Period to be posted
Acc  #   Description                 Ref #      Ref Date  SJ   Transaction
    131  INSUR EXPIRED               AJE1       31-Jul-92 GJ      (400.00)
    625  INSUR EXPIRED               AJE1       31-Jul-92 GJ       400.00
    213  ACCRUE INCOME TAXES         AJE5       31-Jul-92 GJ    (3,400.00)
    631  ACCRUE INCOME TAXES         AJE5       31-Jul-92 GJ     3,400.00
    144  DEPR ON OFFICE EQUIP        AJE4       31-Jul-92 GJ      (225.00)
    623  DEPR ON OFFICE EQUIP        AJE4       31-Jul-92 GJ       225.00
    142  DEPR ON WHSE EQUIP          AJE4       31-Jul-92 GJ      (300.00)
    614  DEPR ON WHSE EQUIP          AJE4       31-Jul-92 GJ       300.00
    133  OFFICE SUPPLIES USED        AJE3       31-Jul-92 GJ      (450.00)
    624  OFFICE SUPPLIES USED        AJE3       31-Jul-92 GJ       450.00
    132  WHSE SUPPLIES USED          AJE2       31-Jul-92 GJ      (780.00)
    615  WHSE SUPPLIES USED          AJE2       31-Jul-92 GJ       780.00
    212  ACCRUE SALARIES             AJE6       31-Jul-92 GJ      (450.00)
    621  ACCRUE SALARIES             AJE6       31-Jul-92 GJ       135.00
    612  ACCRUE SALARIES             AJE6       31-Jul-92 GJ       150.00
    611  ACCRUE SALARIES             AJE6       31-Jul-92 GJ       165.00
```

```
Carron Systems                    Balance Sheet - Period 1 (detailed)

                                  7/31/92
ASSETS
  Cash
    Cash                          41,335.00
  Total Cash                                        41,335.00
  Accounts Receivable
    Accounts Receivable           19,610.00
  Total Accounts Receivable                         19,610.00
  Inventory
    Merchandise Inventory         39,600.00
  Total Inventory                                   39,600.00
  Prepaid Expense
    Prepaid Insurance              3,200.00
    Warehouse Supplies               470.00
    Office Supplies                  200.00
  Total Prepaid Expense                              3,870.00
  Property, Plant, & Equipment
    Warehouse Equipment           24,000.00
    Office Equipment               9,800.00
  Total Property, Plant, & Equipment                33,800.00
  Accumulated Depreciation(-)
    Accum. Depr. - Warehouse Eq   (2,700.00)
    Accum. Depr. - Office Equip    (2,025.00)
  Total Accumulated Depreciation(-)                 (4,725.00)
                                                   ----------
TOTAL ASSETS                                       133,490.00

LIABILITIES
  Accounts Payable
    Accounts Payable              19,389.00
  Total Accounts Payable                            19,389.00
  Other Current Liabilities
    Salaries Payable                 450.00
    Income Taxes Payable           3,400.00
  Total Other Current Liabilities                    3,850.00
                                                   ----------
  TOTAL LIABILITIES                                 23,239.00

EQUITY
  Common Stock
    Common Stock                 100,000.00
  Total Common Stock                               100,000.00
  Retained Earnings
    Retained Earnings              4,382.00
  Total Retained Earnings                            4,382.00
  Common Dividend (-)
    Dividends                     (2,000.00)
  Total Common Dividend (-)                          (2,000.00)
  Net Income                                          7,869.00
                                                   ----------
  TOTAL EQUITY                                      110,251.00

  TOTAL LIABILITIES & EQUITY                        133,490.00

Report Run: 17-Nov-90                                  Page 1
```

```
Carron Systems              Balance Sheet - Period 1 (summary)


                                            7/31/92
ASSETS
    Cash                                  41,335.00
    Accounts Receivable                   19,610.00
    Inventory                             39,600.00
    Prepaid Expense                        3,870.00
    Property, Plant, & Equipment          33,800.00
    Accumulated Depreciation(-)           (4,725.00)
                                          ----------
TOTAL ASSETS                             133,490.00

LIABILITIES
    Accounts Payable                      19,389.00
    Other Current Liabilities              3,850.00
                                          ----------
TOTAL LIABILITIES                         23,239.00

EQUITY
    Common Stock                         100,000.00
    Retained Earnings                      4,382.00
    Common Dividend (-)                   (2,000.00)
    Net Income                             7,869.00
                                          ----------
TOTAL EQUITY                             110,251.00

TOTAL LIABILITIES & EQUITY               133,490.00



Report Run: 17-Nov-90                        Page 1
```

Income Statement - Period 1 (detailed)

	JULY 1992	% of Inc	YTD	% of Inc
REVENUE				
Sales				
Sales	58,040.00	104.71%	58,040.00	104.71%
Total Sales		58,040.00 104.71%		58,040.00 104.71%
Deductions from Sales				
Sales Returns & Allowances	(1,490.00)	−2.69%	(1,490.00)	−2.69%
Sales Discounts	(1,121.00)	−2.02%	(1,121.00)	−2.02%
Total Deductions from Sales		(2,611.00) −4.71%		(2,611.00) −4.71%
Net Sales		55,429.00 100.00%		55,429.00 100.00%
TOTAL REVENUE		55,429.00 100.00%		55,429.00 100.00%
EXPENSES				
Cost of Sales				
Cost of Goods Sold	34,048.00	61.43%	34,048.00	61.43%
Purchases	0.00	0.00%	0.00	0.00%
Purchases Returns & Allow	0.00	0.00%	0.00	0.00%
Freight In	0.00	0.00%	0.00	0.00%
Total Cost of Sales		34,048.00 61.43%		34,048.00 61.43%
Gross Margin from Sales		21,381.00 38.57%		21,381.00 38.57%
Selling Expense				
Sales Salaries Expense	1,265.00	2.28%	1,265.00	2.28%
Warehouse Salaries Expense	1,150.00	2.07%	1,150.00	2.07%
Rent Expense, Warehouse	1,400.00	2.53%	1,400.00	2.53%
Warehouse Supplies Expense	780.00	1.41%	780.00	1.41%
Freight Out Expense	407.00	0.73%	407.00	0.73%
Advertising Expense	1,385.00	2.50%	1,385.00	2.50%
Total Selling Expense		6,387.00 11.52%		6,387.00 11.52%
General & Admin. Expense				
Office Salaries Expense	1,035.00	1.87%	1,035.00	1.87%
Rent Expense, Office	500.00	0.90%	500.00	0.90%
Office Supplies Expense	450.00	0.81%	450.00	0.81%
Insurance Expense	400.00	0.72%	400.00	0.72%
Utility Expense	216.00	0.39%	216.00	0.39%
Telephone Expense	203.00	0.37%	203.00	0.37%
Postage Expense	160.00	0.29%	160.00	0.29%
Total General & Admin. Expense		2,964.00 5.35%		2,964.00 5.35%
Depreciation Expense				
Depr. Exp. - Warehouse Equi	300.00	0.54%	300.00	0.54%
Depr. Exp. - Office Equip.	225.00	0.41%	225.00	0.41%
Total Depreciation Expense		525.00 0.95%		525.00 0.95%
Total Operating Expenses		9,876.00 17.82%		9,876.00 17.82%
TOTAL EXPENSES		43,924.00 79.24%		43,924.00 79.24%
Operating Profit		11,505.00 20.76%		11,505.00 20.76%

Report Run: 17-Nov-90   Page 1

Carron Systems   Income Statement - Period 1 (detailed)

NON-OPERATING ITEMS

    Non-operating Expense (Revenue)
        Purch Discounts Lost   236.00   0.43%   236.00   0.43%
        Total Non-operating Expense (Revenue)   236.00   0.43%   236.00   0.43%
                                                 _____   _____
    Income before Income Taxes   11,269.00   20.33%   11,269.00   20.33%

    Income Taxes
        Income Taxes Expense   3,400.00   6.13% 3,400.00   6.13%
        Total Income Taxes   3,400.00   6.13%   3,400.00   6.13%
                                             _____   _____
TOTAL NON-OPERATING ITEMS   3,636.00   6.56%   3,636.00   6.56%

NET INCOME   7,869.00   14.20%   7,869.00   14.20%
                                             ========   ========

Carron Systems   Income Statement - Period 1 (summary)

	JULY 1992	% of Inc	YTD	% of Inc
REVENUE				
Sales	58,040.00	104.71%	58,040.00	104.71%
Deductions from Sales	(2,611.00)	−4.71%	(2,611.00)	−4.71%
Net Sales	55,429.00	100.00%	55,429.00	100.00%
TOTAL REVENUE	55,429.00	100.00%	55,429.00	100.00%
EXPENSES				
Cost of Sales	34,048.00	61.43%	34,048.00	61.43%
Gross Margin from Sales	21,381.00	38.57%	21,381.00	38.57%
Selling Expense	6,387.00	11.52%	6,387.00	11.52%
General & Admin. Expense	2,964.00	5.35%	2,964.00	5.35%
Depreciation Expense	525.00	0.95%	525.00	0.95%
Total Operating Expenses	9,876.00	17.82%	9,876.00	17.82%
TOTAL EXPENSES	43,924.00	79.24%	43,924.00	79.24%
Operating Profit	11,505.00	20.76%	11,505.00	20.76%
NON-OPERATING ITEMS				
Non-operating Expense (Revenue)	236.00	0.43%	236.00	0.43%
Income before Income Taxes	11,269.00	20.33%	11,269.00	20.33%
Income Taxes	3,400.00	6.13%	3,400.00	6.13%
TOTAL NON-OPERATING ITEMS	3,636.00	6.56%	3,636.00	6.56%
NET INCOME	7,869.00	14.20%	7,869.00	14.20%

Report Run: 17-Nov-90

Page 1

```
Carron Systems            Cash Flow Report - Actual Period 1


Net Income (after tax)                    7,869.00
Plus: Depreciation & Amortization           525.00
                                         _____
Income Statement Cash Flow                8,394.00

Accounts Receivable-Decr.(Incr.)         14,940.00
Inventory-Decr.(Incr.)                   (2,600.00)
Misc. Current Assets-Decr.(Incr.)           880.00
Accounts Payable-Incr.(Decr.)            (3,829.00)
Accrued Liabilities-Incr.(Decr.)              0.00
Inc.Tax Pay. & Defer.Tax-Incr(Decr)           0.00
Other Current Liabs.-Incr.(Decr.)         3,850.00
Oth.Noncurrent Liabs.-Incr.(Decr.)            0.00   _____
OPERATING CASH FLOW                                  21,635.00


Marketable Securities-Decr.(Incr.)            0.00
Long Term Investment-Decr.(Incr.)             0.00
Fixed Asset-Decr.(Incr.)                   (800.00)
Intang.& Oth.Noncurr.A.-Decr(Incr)            0.00   _____
INVESTING CASH FLOW                                    (800.00)
                                                     ==========
CASH FLOW BEFORE FINANCING                           20,835.00

Short Term Debt-Incr.(Decr.)                  0.00
Long Term Debt-Incr.(Decr.)                   0.00
Subordinated Debt-Incr.(Decr.)                0.00
                                         _____
Debt Financing Cash Flow                      0.00

Capital Stock-Incr.(Decr.)                    0.00
Dividends/Drawings Paid                   (2,000.00)
Adjustment to Retained Earnings               0.00
Other Equity-Incr.(Decr.)                     0.00
                                         _____
Equity Financing Cash Flow               (2,000.00)  _____
FINANCING CASH FLOW                                  (2,000.00)


BEGINNING CASH                                       22,500.00

OPERATING CASH FLOW                                  21,635.00
INVESTING CASH FLOW                                    (800.00)
FINANCING CASH FLOW                                  (2,000.00)
                                                     _____
COMPREHENSIVE CASH FLOW                              18,835.00

ENDING CASH                                          41,335.00
                                                     ==========



Report Run: 17-Nov-90
```

```
Carron Systems                    Financial Ratios - Actual Period 1


Liquidity Ratios
     Current Ratio (Cur Asst/Cur Liab)         4.49
     Quick Ratio (Cash + AR/Cur Liab)          2.62

Safety Ratios
     Debt/Worth                                0.21
     Debt/Assets                               0.17

Balance Sheet Ratios - Annualized
     Return On Assets (Pretax%)             101.30%
     Return On Equity (Pretax%)             132.08%
     Asset Turnover                            4.98
     A/R Collection (Days)                    10.61
     Inventory Turnover (Days)                34.89
     A/P Payment Period (Days)                17.08



Report Run: 17-Nov-90
```

5

Files Provided with Ready-to-Run

This chapter lists the files provided with RTR and explains each file's purpose.

Lotus 1-2-3 Program Files

These files have the extension .WK1 if you are running Lotus 1-2-3 Release 2.*x*; they have the extension .WK3 if you are running Lotus 1-2-3 Release 3.*x*.

AUTO123	The system main menu
BUDGET	The program that creates and edits the budget
CHANGEPW	The program that converts all data files from the old to the new password when the data password is changed
ENTER	The transaction entry and edit program
GLRPT1	The accounts (ledger) report
GLRPT2	The trial balance report
GLRPT3	The journal listing report
INQUIRE	The query program
NEWCOA	The chart of accounts customizer
NEWYEAR1	Runs the end-of-year procedure
SETCODE	The opening program for creating the configuration file
STARTUP1	The file maintenance program to adjust beginning balances and initialize files
STATE	The financial statement report generator
TRANSLAT	Used to convert data files from Lotus 1-2-3 Release 2.*x* format to Lotus 1-2-3 Release 3.*x* format and vice versa
UPDATE	Posts the TEMPDATA file to the LEDGER and period files

Lotus 1-2-3 Data Files

Each of these files except COA has a .WK1 extension, regardless of which Lotus 1-2-3 release you run. COA has a .WK3 extension if you are running Lotus 1-2-3 Release 3.x.

ACTIVITY	Lists whether there has been any activity for each account during the year (0=no, 1=yes)
BLEDGER	The yearly budget; should match the LEDGER file
COA	Contains the layout for the financial statements, including a detail Chart of Accounts with classifications
LEDGER	The ledger data file; contains each account and a summary of its activity for each period
PERIODnn	The permanent transaction files; holds the journals for each period 1 through 13
PLEDGER	Last year's LEDGER file
TLEDGER	The chart of accounts with account classifications
TEMPDATA	Holds the unposted temporary transactions

Add-In Files on the Program Disk/Directory

VSUM.ADN	Used with Release 2.x of Lotus 1-2-3
INFO.ADN	Used with Release 2.x of Lotus 1-2-3
VSUM.PLC	Used with Release 3.x of Lotus 1-2-3

Maintenance Files on the Program Disk/Directory

CODES.RTR	Contains the configuration codes
DIRCTRY.RTR	Contains a list of directories for all Ready-to-Run files in the following order: program files, GL data files, AP data files, AR data files, Payroll data files, Inventory data files
GLRPTS.RTR	Contains a listing of user-created custom reports

HOLD.RTR	Contains the running status of the program and a list of interrupted programs
REL.RTR	Contains the Lotus 1-2-3 release specified during the installation procedure

Maintenance Files on the Data Disk/Directory

ACCTS.RTR	Contains the default account numbers used by ENTER for special journals
COMPANY.RTR	Contains the company name that appears on reports
DEPTS.RTR	Contains the department codes when departments are used
PW.RTR	Contains the encrypted data password
T_PERIOD.RTR	Contains the current open period

6

Adding Transactions Using TEMPDATA.WK1

This chapter explains how you can use the TEMPDATA.WK1 file to create transactions in a Lotus 1-2-3 worksheet, then update the RTR period and ledger files with these transactions.

To do this, you must understand the format of the TEMPDATA.WK1 file. You may also need to know how to change the maintenance file T_PERIOD.RTR. The last section of this chapter describes three ways to change the contents of T_PERIOD.RTR.

The Format of the TEMPDATA.WK1 File

Figure R-1 shows the TEMPDATA.WK1 file viewed from Lotus 1-2-3.

The period counter ——————

Transactions ——————

Figure R-1

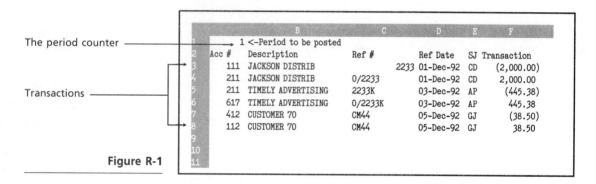

The period counter indicates the period that will receive these transactions when you run the Update program. The counter must agree with the period flag in the file T_PERIOD.RTR. The TEMPDATA file must contain transactions for only one period. Use the GL Update command to empty TEMPDATA before you enter transactions for a new period.

The data on rows 3 to 8 of the screen in Figure R-1 represent six transactions, one on each row:

Column A   Contains the account number of the ledger account to be updated by each transaction. You must enter a number that is a valid account number or the transactions will not post to the LEDGER file.

Column B   Contains the description of each transaction. It is a label.

Column C   Contains the reference field, which can be an invoice number, a check number, etc. It can be a number or a label.

Column D   Contains the date of each transaction expressed as the Lotus 1-2-3 Julian number for the date and formatted using Lotus 1-2-3 date format 1.

Column E   Contains the journal type. This is a predefined label. Use CD for cash disbursements, CR for cash receipts, AP for accounts payable, AR for accounts receivable, and GJ for general journal entries.

Column F   Contains the amount of the transaction. A positive number is a debit and a negative number is a credit.

Entering Transactions into TEMPDATA.WK1

You can enter transactions into TEMPDATA one of two ways.

First, you can enter transactions into TEMPDATA by retrieving the TEMPDATA.WK1 file with the Lotus 1-2-3 command / File Retrieve. Beginning with the first empty row at the bottom of the worksheet, enter the transaction data in the correct columns. When you finish, use the Lotus 1-2-3 command / File Save, replacing the existing file with the new one.

Second, you can create transactions using a Lotus 1-2-3 macro-driven worksheet. Before you can use this method, however, you must know how to use the following Lotus 1-2-3 commands:

/ File Combine

/ File Xtract

Create a separate row for each debit and credit that makes up a transaction. Create the columns outlined in the last section to contain the data for the transactions you enter.

If you want to validate the ledger account numbers entered into this worksheet, bring a listing of valid ledger account numbers into the worksheet using the Lotus 1-2-3 / File Combine command to combine the range name ACCOUNTS from the LEDGER.WK1 file.

After you create the transactions you want to add to TEMPDATA.WK1, use the Lotus 1-2-3 / File Combine command to bring TEMPDATA.WK1 into the worksheet. Then move or copy the new transactions to the first empty row at the bottom of TEMPDATA. Then use the Lotus 1-2-3 / File Extract command to extract the range containing both the original TEMPDATA file and the new transactions back to the TEMPDATA.WK1 file.

Remember that cell A1 holds the period for the transactions and that you may not mix transactions from different periods in the TEMPDATA file. If TEMPDATA was empty when you combined it into your worksheet, change cell A1 from 0 to the correct posting period. You must also change the maintenance file T_PERIOD.RTR to the correct posting period.

Changing the Contents of the T_PERIOD.RTR File

If you change the contents of cell A1 to reflect the period to which you want the transactions posted, you must also change the contents of the file T_PERIOD.RTR.

You can change the contents of this file in any of three ways:

1. Use COPY CON. At the DOS prompt, change to the disk or directory where your data files are stored. For example, if your data disk is in drive A, the DOS prompt should show A>. Get assistance if you do not know how to change the DOS prompt.

    Type: **COPY CON:T_PERIOD.RTR**
    Press: (↵)
    Type: (the period to which you want transactions posted)
    Press: (↵)
    Press: (F6)
    Press: (↵)

You should see a DOS message that one file has been copied. T_PERIOD.RTR now contains the posting period for your transactions. You can use this procedure any time you want to change the posting period for your transactions.

2. Use your word processing program. Start your word processing program, type the period number to which you want to post transactions, and then select the necessary options to save the document as a *text-only* file. Save the file on your data disk or directory with the filename T_PERIOD.RTR.

3. Use the Lotus 1-2-3 advanced macro commands {OPEN} and {WRITELN} if you know how to use them. Build a macro that includes the creation of a file named T_PERIOD.RTR containing the correct posting period for your transactions. (See your Lotus 1-2-3 manual for information on the {OPEN} and {WRITELN} commands.)

Appendix A Using Ready-to-Run with Lotus 1-2-3 Release 3

Installation Procedure

In the install routine for the Student Edition of Ready-to-Run Accounting, when you enter the directory containing your Lotus 1-2-3 program, the following message appears if the directory contains Lotus 1-2-3 Release 3.

Lotus 1-2-3 Release 3 has been found.
Install will save RTR in .WK3 file format.
You will not be able to run this copy of RTR using 1-2-3 Release 2, but your data files may be accessed by either release of 1-2-3. However, you will not be able to modify your chart of accounts, run financial statements, or work with a budget in Release 2 without first running a special translate program in RTR. See the manual for more details.

1. If this is the correct 1-2-3 release enter 1 to proceed.
2. To install for a different 1-2-3 release enter 2.
3. To abort the install enter 3.

If you select 1, the Ready-to-Run program files are converted to .WK3 format. Files in .WK3 format run only on Release 3; you cannot run them on Release 2 of Lotus 1-2-3.

If you install Ready-to-Run from a 5¼″ diskette on a system that has Release 3 of Lotus 1-2-3 installed, you see the following message during installation:

The RTR Student Edition uses "Add-in" technology that requires the addition of the Lotus Add-in Manager to your copy of 123.

This is available from Addison-Wesley on a separate disk at no additional charge. Please consult the manual for information on ordering this disk.

The RTR installation procedure will continue, but you will not be able to run the installed copy of RTR until the Lotus Add-in Manager is installed.

Strike a key when ready . . .

Use the coupon at the back of this manual to send for the separate disk at no additional charge. The coupon contains the address and mailing instructions.

When you have received the separate disk, place it in the 5¼″ drive of your computer. At the DOS prompt,

Type: **A:INSTALL**
Press: ⏎

Follow the instructions on the screen to install the Lotus 1-2-3 Release 3 Add-in Libraries. The Install program prompts you for the disk drive containing the installation diskette, the disk drive onto which the libraries are being installed (i.e., the drive where your Lotus 1-2-3 Release 3 system files are located), and the directory containing your Lotus 1-2-3 program. When the program finishes, the following message appears:

The Ready-to-Run Accounting Student Edition installation for 1-2-3 Release 3 Add-in Libraries has been completed. Please store the master disk in a safe place.

Printing Reports with Lotus 1-2-3 Release 3

Lotus 1-2-3 Release 3 prints reports using background printing. The printing commands are saved in the memory of the computer so that you can continue with other tasks using Lotus 1-2-3 while your reports print. After you issue a Ready-to-Run Print command, your screen returns so you can continue working in Ready-to-Run while the report prints.

However, because Ready-to-Run is macro-driven, it requires a large amount of computer memory to operate correctly. If you do not have enough memory to run both the printer and the RTR macros, a printer error occurs. Lotus 1-2-3 suspends printing until you tell it (from the Lotus 1-2-3 command line) to resume.

If you see the message "printer error," press ESC to abort. Your printer will have already stopped printing. Return to the Ready-to-Run Main menu and:

Select: **Q**uit **L**otus

You should see a blank Lotus 1-2-3 worksheet. Issue the Lotus 1-2-3 command sequence / **P**rint **R**esume. Your report should finish printing.

If you see this error frequently, you should wait until printing finishes before you proceed with other tasks in Ready-to-Run.

Saving Graphs in Lotus 1-2-3 Release 3

In Release 3 of Lotus 1-2-3 you print graphs from within the worksheet, instead of using PrintGraph. If you choose the Save command from the Graph menu, Lotus 1-2-3 assumes you intend to print the graph using another program. Ready-to-Run, because it is compatible with both Release 2.x and Release 3 of Lotus 1-2-3, saves graphs for printing with PrintGraph.

Release 3 of Lotus 1-2-3 uses the "graphic metafile" format as the default method of saving graphs. When it saves a graph, it assigns a .GMF extension. This format is not compatible with PrintGraph. Therefore, to save graphs from Ready-to-Run so you can print them with PrintGraph, you must change the default method of saving graphs in your version of Lotus 1-2-3.

To change the default graph save format, issue the Lotus 1-2-3 command sequence: / **W**orksheet **G**lobal **D**efault **G**raph. Type in the extension .PIC and press (↵). Then select **U**pdate to save this format as the default method of saving graphs. The graphs you save with Ready-to-Run can now be printed with PrintGraph.

Using Release 2 Data Files with Lotus 1-2-3 Release 3

If you attempt to use data files created by a Release 2 installation of Ready-to-Run (i.e., RTR installed with Lotus 1-2-3 Release 2) with a Release 3 installation of Ready-to-Run (RTR installed with Lotus 1-2-3 Release 3), any of several things could happen, depending on which version you are running.

Modifying the Chart of Accounts

If you try to modify the existing chart of accounts in RTR, you see the following warning message:

Existing chart of accounts in Rel. 2 format - Must translate or abort.

A menu appears that allows you to abort or translate.

If you select Abort, the existing chart of accounts remains in Release 2 format, and you return to the Main menu.

If you select Translate, the existing chart of accounts is translated into Release 3 format. However, to use it again with a Release 2 installation of Ready-to-Run, you must translate it back again using the procedures outlined in the section, "Translating Release 3 Data Files for Use with a Release 2 Installation."

Running Financial Statements

The Financial Statements program in Ready-to-Run uses the chart of accounts to build the statements. However, it does not change the chart of accounts. Therefore, if you run Financial Statements with a Release 3 installation using Release 2 data files, a message appears telling you that the chart of accounts is being *temporarily* converted into Release 3 format. In this case, your existing chart of accounts remains in Release 2 format.

Building a Budget

The Budget program in Ready-to-Run also uses the chart of accounts, but does not change it. Thus, when you run the Budget program, the chart of accounts is *temporarily* converted into Release 3 format for processing the budget menu items. The existing chart of accounts remains in Release 2 format.

Translating Release 3 Data Files for Use with a Release 2 Installation

If you want to use data files created with a Release 3 installation of Ready-to-Run on a Release 2 installation of Ready-to-Run, you must translate the chart of accounts into Release 2 format.

Start the Release 3 installation of Ready-to-Run. Be sure that the GL directory specified on the Directory/Company menu contains the chart of accounts you want to translate. (If you save your data on diskette, this should be either A: or B:.) If you change it, select Save from the Directory/Company menu before returning to the Ready-to-Run Main menu. From the Ready-to-Run Main menu:

Select: **Q**uit **L**otus

You should see a blank Lotus 1-2-3 worksheet.

Retrieve the file TRANSLAT.WK3 by issuing the Lotus command sequence / **F**ile **R**etrieve **TRANSLAT.WK3** ⏎. This is the translation program. It creates a special file in Release 2 format that you can convert to the chart of accounts in Release 2 format.

When this first step finishes, exit from Lotus to DOS.

Start the Release 2 installation of Ready-to-Run. Again check the GL directory on the Directory/Company menu. (If you are running the Release 2 installation on a two-diskette system, Ready-to-Run assumes that the data diskette is in drive A.) For the translation to proceed correctly, the GL directory on the Directory/Company menu should be *the same as* the GL directory on the Directory/Company menu for the Release 3 installation. (If you save your data on a diskette in a hard-disk installation, the GL directory should indicate the diskette drive where your data diskette is located — normally either A: or B:.) Select Save on the Directory/Company menu to save your selection and return to the Ready-to-Run Main menu.

From the Ready-to-Run Main menu:

Select: **Quit Lotus**

You should see a blank Lotus 1-2-3 worksheet.

Retrieve the file TRANSLAT.WK1 by issuing the Lotus command sequence / **File Retrieve TRANSLAT.WK1** ⏎. This program translates the special file created by Release 3 to a chart of accounts in Release 2 format.

If RTR does not start automatically,

Select: / **File Retrieve AUTO123** ⏎

Appendix B   Backing Up and Restoring Data

Whenever you store accounting data on a computer disk, you should back up the data at regular intervals. You can use the backup disk of data if something damages your regular disk. If you have entered new data for the company or made changes to data files, you should back up the data after every session at the computer.

If you use a two-diskette system, or if you are using a hard-disk system and store your data on a separate 5¼″ or 3½″ diskette, copy the files to another blank formatted diskette. If you store your data on a subdirectory on your hard disk, copy the files to a blank formatted 5¼″ or 3½″ diskette.

Regardless of the type of system you are using, you must always exit RTR to perform the backup procedures. At the RTR Main menu,

Select: **Quit Quit**

You also need at least one *new* blank formatted diskette to store the backup copy of your RTR data files. Use the procedures explained in Getting Started to format the diskette.

Format a new blank diskette now.

You can re-use a previous backup diskette for the current backup if you choose. However, you should not use the most recent backup copy. If something goes wrong during the backup process, you may need to use the most recent backup disk to restore the data.

Backup on a Two-Diskette System

If you use a two-diskette system, follow the procedures in this section. If you use a hard-disk system, skip this section and go to the next one.

You should have exited from RTR, and you should see the A> prompt on your screen. Place the diskette containing your RTR data in drive A and the newly formatted blank diskette in drive B.

> **Note** Be sure you put your *data* diskette, not the RTR program diskette, in drive A. Also, be sure the A> prompt is on your screen. If it is not, type **A:** and press ⏎.

Type: **COPY A:*.* B:**
Press: ⏎

You will see the names of the files as the computer copies them to the new diskette.

Some names that should appear are LEDGER.WK1, PERIOD1.WK1, and ACTIVITY.WK1. If you are using Release 3 or 3.1 of Lotus 1-2-3, the extension on these filenames will be .WK3. If these names do not appear, you are backing up the wrong diskette. Remove the diskette from drive A and replace it with the RTR data diskette. Ask your instructor or a laboratory assistant for help.

When the A> prompt appears again, remove the diskette from drive B and label it "Backup Data Diskette, Walton Electronics" (or TWE, Inc.). Keep this diskette in a safe place.

Backup on a Hard-Disk System

The procedures you use to back up your data depend on whether you save your data on a hard disk or on a diskette. Choose the appropriate section below.

Saving Data on a 5¼" or 3½" Diskette

If your computer has two diskette drives in addition to a hard disk, follow the procedures outlined in the previous section, "Backup on a Two-Diskette System."

If you have one disk drive in your computer in addition to a hard disk, make sure the DOS prompt (C> or some variation of that) appears on your screen. Insert your RTR data diskette into the disk drive.

Type: **COPY A:*.* B:**
Press: ⏎

The computer treats your single drive as both A and B. Your RTR data diskette is the source disk and the blank formatted diskette is the target disk. The computer prompts you to place the source disk into drive A, reads a portion of the data from the RTR data diskette, and then prompts you to insert the target disk. Place the newly formatted blank diskette into the drive. When it finishes writing the data, the computer again prompts you to switch disks. You may have to switch disks several times because the computer cannot retain all of the data in memory at once. When all the information is copied, the DOS prompt reappears on your screen.

Make sure that you have copied the correct diskette by listing a directory of the files on the backup diskette. With the backup diskette in drive A, at the A> prompt:

Type: **DIR**
Press: ⏎

A listing of the files on the backup diskette appears on the screen. The names should include LEDGER.WK1, PERIOD1.WK1, and ACTIVITY.WK1. If you are using Release 3 or 3.1 of Lotus 1-2-3, the filenames have an extension of .WK3. If these filenames are not included in the directory listing, you have copied the wrong diskette. Ask your instructor or a laboratory assistant for help.

Remove the backup diskette from the drive and label it "Backup Data Diskette, Walton Electronics" (or TWE, Inc.). Keep this diskette in a safe place.

Saving Data from a Hard-Disk Subdirectory

The instructions in this section assume that you save your data in the C:\READY\GL subdirectory, which was the default supplied by the install program. If you save your data under a different subdirectory name, substitute that name for C:\READY\GL in the following commands.

Be sure the DOS prompt (C> or some variation of that) appears on your screen. Insert your newly formatted blank diskette into the 5¼" or 3½" drive of your computer.

Type: **COPY C:\READY\GL*.* A:**
Press: ⟨⏎⟩

The screen shows the names of the files as it copies them to the new diskette. The files should include the names LEDGER.WK1, PERIOD1.WK1, and ACTIVITY.WK1. If you are using Release 3 or 3.1 of Lotus 1-2-3, the filenames will have a .WK3 extension. If these filenames are not in the list of files being backed up, you are backing up the wrong directory. Repeat the copy command using the correct directory. If you still have problems, ask your instructor or a laboratory assistant for help.

When the DOS prompt reappears, remove the diskette from the drive and label it "Backup Data Diskette, Walton Electronics" (or TWE, Inc.). Keep this diskette in a safe place.

Restoring Your Working Data to the Original Diskette or Directory

If you use a data diskette to store your data and need to use the backup data, you can use the *backup* data diskette you created as your new original diskette. If you use a directory on your hard disk to store your data, you must restore your original data to your directory.

Exit from RTR and Lotus 1-2-3 so that the DOS prompt appears on your screen.

Data Stored on a 5¼" or 3½" Diskette

If you store your data on a 5¼" or 3½" diskette, use the *backup* diskette you created during the backup process as your new original diskette. Cross out the word "Backup" on the label and use this diskette as your data diskette.

> **Note** Make a backup of this diskette before using it. Follow the procedures for making a backup diskette.

Data Stored in a Hard-Disk Subdirectory

If you store your data in a subdirectory on your hard disk, quit RTR to DOS. Place the backup diskette you want to restore into drive A and type the following command at the DOS prompt. (These instructions assume that your subdirectory is C:\READY\GL. If it is not, substitute your subdirectory name in the instructions.)

Type: **COPY A:*.* C:\READY\GL**
Press: ⏎

The files are copied one at a time from the backup diskette to your working subdirectory.

Appendix C   Using PrintGraph

To print graphs created by Lotus 1-2-3 Release 2, 2.01, or 2.2, you must use a separate program supplied by Lotus Development Corporation called PrintGraph. This program reads .PIC extension files created by Lotus 1-2-3 and prints them.

Before you can use PrintGraph, it must be properly installed for the computer and printer that you are using. Check with your instructor or a laboratory assistant to determine whether PrintGraph has been properly installed.

You can run PrintGraph from the Lotus Access menu, which you see if you type LOTUS at the DOS prompt. If you are at the Access menu,

Select: **PrintGraph**

If you have a 5¼″ two-diskette system, replace the 1-2-3 disk with the PrintGraph disk at the prompt and press ⏎.

> **Note**   To start PrintGraph directly from the DOS prompt, insert the PrintGraph disk in a drive, make that drive the current drive, and type **PGRAPH.**

In a few minutes, your screen should look like Figure C-1.

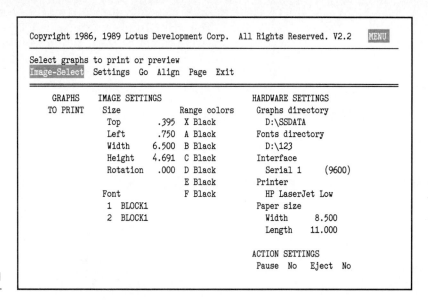

```
Copyright 1986, 1989 Lotus Development Corp.  All Rights Reserved. V2.2   MENU

Select graphs to print or preview
Image-Select  Settings  Go  Align  Page  Exit

     GRAPHS    IMAGE SETTINGS                    HARDWARE SETTINGS
     TO PRINT   Size            Range colors     Graphs directory
                 Top      .395  X Black            D:\SSDATA
                 Left     .750  A Black          Fonts directory
                 Width   6.500  B Black            D:\123
                 Height  4.691  C Black          Interface
                 Rotation .000  D Black            Serial 1     (9600)
                                E Black          Printer
                 Font           F Black            HP LaserJet Low
                 1  BLOCK1                        Paper size
                 2  BLOCK1                          Width      8.500
                                                    Length    11.000

                                                 ACTION SETTINGS
                                                 Pause  No   Eject  No
```

Figure C-1

The PrintGraph menu is automatically displayed in the third line of the control panel. You do not have to press / to display the menu. Just move the menu pointer to each command and read the short description on the line above the menu. Select commands from the menu as you do in 1-2-3 or RTR.

Printing a graph created by RTR involves four simple steps:

- Make the directory or diskette containing your RTR data files the current graphs directory

- Select the graph to be printed

- Prepare the printer

- Print

Changing the PrintGraph Graphs Directory

First, make the directory or diskette containing your RTR data files the current graphs directory. To do this, issue the following command sequence:

> **S**ettings **H**ardware **G**raphs-Directory

The default directory appears on the third line of the control panel. Tell PrintGraph where your RTR data files are located. This location depends on whether you save your data on a diskette or on a directory on your hard disk.

Data Saved on a Diskette

If you save your data on a directory on your hard disk, skip this section and proceed to "Data Saved on a Directory on Your Hard Disk."

If you save your RTR data on a diskette, that diskette should be located in drive A.

Type: **A:**
Press: ⏎
Select: **Q**uit **Q**uit

You should now see the PrintGraph main menu. Skip to "Selecting the Graph to Be Printed."

Data Saved on a Directory on Your Hard Disk

These instructions assume that you are using the default directory (C:\READY) suggested during the RTR install program and that it is located on the C drive. If these are different for your system, change the command to match your system.

Type: **C:\READY\GL**
Press: ⏎
Select: **Q**uit **Q**uit

You should now see the PrintGraph main menu. Proceed to "Selecting the Graph to Be Printed."

Selecting the Graph to Be Printed

To select the graph(s) to be printed,

Select: Image-Select

Your screen should look similar to Figure C-2. The names listed in the left column are the graphs you saved while you were running RTR. RTR names some graphs automatically and allows you to name other graphs.

```
Copyright 1986, 1989 Lotus Development Corp.  All Rights Reserved. V2.2    POINT

Select graphs to print


    GRAPH FILE  DATE     TIME    SIZE
    ------------------------------------------     Space bar marks or unmarks selection
    120         10-15-90  7:21    2998             ENTER selects marked graphs
    400         10-15-90  7:01    1852             ESC exits, ignoring changes
    510         10-15-90  7:21    1955             HOME moves to beginning of list
    ASSETS      10-15-90  6:57    3804             END moves to end of list
    CASH        10-19-90  16:45   13688            ↑ and ↓ move highlight
    DEBTEQTY    10-19-90  16:45   13968               List will scroll if highlight
    LIQUID      10-19-90  16:46   18041               moved beyond top or bottom
    SALES       10-19-90  16:45   18074            GRAPH (F10) previews marked graph








                                                                        CAPS
```

Figure C-2

When you are in PrintGraph, you cannot change any of the graph settings in the graph PIC files. However, you can preview them by using the Graph function key, (F10).

Move to: the third graph listed by pressing (↓)
Press: (F10)

Your screen should display an image of the graph you selected.

Press: SPACEBAR

to return to the list of graph files.

Use (F10) to look at the graphs you have saved and decide which one(s) you want to print.

Figure C-2 lists several graphs. Suppose you wanted to print the graphs named 120 and ASSETS.

Move to: 120
Press: SPACEBAR
Move to: ASSETS
Press: SPACEBAR

A # sign appears next to the selected graph files. To complete your selections,

Press: (←)

Your screen should look like Figure C-3.

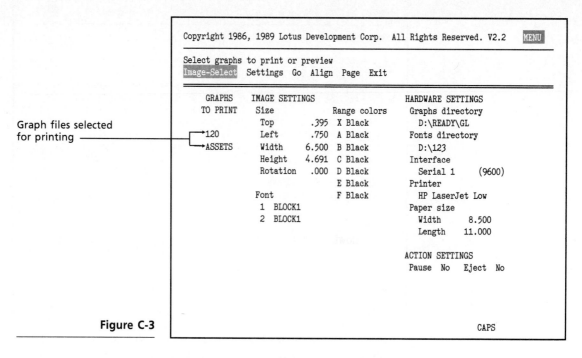

Select graphs to print or preview
Image-Select Settings Go Align Page Exit

GRAPHS	IMAGE SETTINGS		HARDWARE SETTINGS
TO PRINT	Size	Range colors	Graphs directory
	Top	.395	X Black	D:\READY\GL
120	Left	.750	A Black	Fonts directory
ASSETS	Width	6.500	B Black	D:\123
	Height	4.691	C Black	Interface
	Rotation	.000	D Black	Serial 1 (9600)
			E Black	Printer
	Font		F Black	HP LaserJet Low
	1 BLOCK1			Paper size
	2 BLOCK1			Width 8.500
				Length 11.000
				ACTION SETTINGS
				Pause No Eject No

CAPS

Graph files selected for printing —

Figure C-3

The left column of the settings sheet lists the selected graph filename.

Preparing the Printer and Printing the Graph(s)

Prepare the printer by turning it on. If you are using continuous form paper, adjust the page so that the perforation is near the first print position. Make sure the printer is on-line.

Select: **Align Go**

Align tells the printer that the paper is now at the top of a page. Go tells it to start printing. In a few moments, your printer should begin to print the graphs.

To advance the paper to the top of the next page and to leave the PrintGraph program,

Select: **Page Exit Yes**

To return to the DOS prompt (if you entered PrintGraph from the Access menu):

Select: **Exit**

Appendix D   Principles of Accounting Practice Set 1

Walton Electronics

Use the backup diskette you created at the end of Lab 7 when you complete this practice set. If you did not make a backup before you completed Lab 8, see your instructor for assistance.

The following events occurred during February 1992 at Walton Electronics.

General:

Date	Event
3	Tom Walton discovered that the payment by Excellent Hardware on January 10 included a $2,000 deposit on their next order to be shipped this month. Do not correct the January records. Prepare a correcting entry dated today.

Receivables:

Date	Event
3	Merchandise was sold to Roger's Menswear on invoice number 2042. The amount of the invoice is $6,290.
6	Merchandise was sold to Ken's Furniture Store on invoice number 2043. The amount of the invoice is $9,643.
10	Merchandise was returned by Roger's Menswear. Issued credit memo number 54 in the amount of $275.
12	Merchandise sold to Kathie's Koffee Shop on invoice number 2044. The amount of the invoice is $3,440.

14   Merchandise sold to Wally's Sportsgear on invoice number 2045. The amount of the invoice is $7,935.

18   Merchandise sold to Dean's Restaurant on invoice number 2046. The amount of the invoice is $8,241.

21   Merchandise sold to Excellent Hardware on invoice number 2047. The amount of the invoice is $13,490. Excellent Hardware made a deposit of $2,000 on this order.

24   Merchandise returned by Wally's Sportsgear. Issued credit memo number 55 in the amount of $890.

26   Merchandise sold to Julie's Pet Shop on invoice number 2048. The amount of the invoice is $15,040.

27   Merchandise returned by Julie's Pet Shop. Issued credit memo number 56 in the amount of $450.

Payables:

Date   *Event*

5   Merchandise purchased from Venus Systems. Invoice number QP75PS, dated February 3, is for $20,621, which includes $121 of freight charges.

6   Two months' advertising bill received from Today's Advertising. Invoice number QT3490, dated February 5, is for $1,500. (Record all of this bill in Advertising Expense.)

6   A freight bill from We-Haul-It for delivering merchandise to a customer on February 6. The invoice number is VVK121 and is for $125.

12   Merchandise purchased from Carron Peripherals. Invoice number HK4830-49, dated February 10, is for $7,640, which includes $140 of freight charges.

15   Received an allowance from Carron Peripherals because of merchandise damaged in the shipment. Issued debit memo number 444, dated today, in the amount of $450.

20   Merchandise purchased from J. M. Supply. Invoice number B3781, dated February 18, is for $5,200.

21   A freight bill from We-Haul-It for delivering mer-
        chandise to a customer on February 21. The invoice
        number is VVK129 and is for $400.

24   A bill from Lodico Communications for long distance
        charges. Invoice number 7293, dated February 23, is
        for $439.

24   A bill from City Power Co. for the monthly utilities.
        Tom decided to wait until the first part of March to
        pay this bill. Use STMT for the reference. The amount
        is $523.

26   A freight bill from We-Haul-It for delivering mer-
        chandise to a customer on February 26. The invoice
        number is VVK141 and is for $225.

28   Merchandise purchased from Rebco Computer. Invoice
        number Z5690, dated February 27, is for $10,500.

Checks:

Date   Event

3   Check number 1573 to Second City Bank for salaries.
        The amount is $1,435. These salaries were accrued
        at the end of January. Walton Electronics does not
        make reversing entries.

3   Check number 1574 to Venus Systems for invoice
        number QP69PR. The balance due on this invoice is
        $7,050. There are no freight charges included in the
        invoice. The terms are 2/10, net 30. Walton
        Electronics is paying it within the discount period.

5   Check number 1575 to the Postmaster. The amount
        is $300 to refill the postage meter.

6   Check number 1576 to Today's Advertising for
        invoice number QT3342. The amount due is $819.
        There is no discount.

7   Check number 1577 to Rebco Computer for invoice
        number Z5143. The balance due on this invoice is
        $6,550, which includes $250 of freight charges. The
        terms are 2/10, net 30, and the invoice is being paid
        within the discount period.

10   Check number 1578 to Second City Bank for salaries. The amount is $1,435. Sales salaries are $885 and office salaries are $550.

12   Check number 1579 to Marcia's Flower Shop for an allowance on the merchandise purchased on invoice number 2040. The amount is $300.

14   Check number 1580 to Venus Systems for invoice number QP75PS. The amount due is $20,621, which includes $121 of freight charges. The terms are 2/10, net 30, and the invoice is paid within the discount period.

14   Check number 1581 to Tom Walton for a personal withdrawal of $1,800.

17   Check number 1582 to J. M. Supply for invoice number B3559. The amount due is $16,890. There is no discount allowed.

17   Check number 1583 to Lodico Communications for invoice number 6954 recorded in January. The amount due is $558.

17   Check number 1584 to Second City Bank for salaries. The amount and distribution are the same as check number 1578.

18   Check number 1585 to Jason's Office Supplies for supplies purchased that day. The amount is $972.

21   Check number 1586 to Carron Peripherals for invoice number HK4830-49. The amount due is $7,190, which includes $140 of freight charges. Terms are 2/10, net 30, and the invoice was paid within the discount period.

24   Check number 1587 to Second City Bank for salaries. The amount and distribution are the same as check numbers 1578 and 1584.

28   Check number 1588 to Local Phone Company for telephone charges for the month of February. The amount is $249.

28   Check number 1589 to We-Haul-It for a statement received for January charges. The amount is $262.

28   Check number 1590 to Tom Walton for a personal withdrawal of $1,800.

Deposits:

Date *Event*

3   Deposit number 92012 from Marcia's Flower Shop for invoice number 2040, dated 1/24/92, in the amount of $16,500. The discount is taken and allowed.

10   Deposit number 92013 from Len's Appliance Depot for invoice number 2037, dated 1/10/92, in the amount of $12,650. No discount is allowed.

10   Deposit number 92014 from Corner Drug Store for invoice number 2041, dated 1/30/92, in the amount of $8,500. The discount is taken and allowed.

12   Deposit number 92015 from Bob's Auto Repair for invoice number 1345, representing a cash sale of $1,200.

13   Deposit number 92016 from Roger's Menswear for invoice number 2042, dated 2/3/92, which has a balance of $6,015 outstanding, which includes $65 of freight charges. A discount is taken and allowed on the balance outstanding less the freight charges.

18   Deposit number 92017 from Scott's Insurance Agency for a deposit on an order. The amount is $1,500.

19   Deposit number 92018 from Karla's Kandies for invoice number 1346, representing a cash sale of $1,860.

21   Deposit number 92019 from Kathie's Koffee Shop for invoice number 2044, dated 2/12/92, in the amount of $3,440, which includes $140 in freight charges. A discount is taken and allowed on the invoice amount less the freight charges.

24   Deposit number 92020 from Wally's Sportsgear for invoice number 2045, dated 2/14/92, which has a balance outstanding of $7,045, including $145 of freight charges. A discount is taken and allowed on the balance outstanding less the freight charges.

28   Deposit number 92021 from Dean's Restaurant for invoice number 2046, dated 2/18/92, in the amount of $8,241, including $191 of freight charges. A discount is taken and allowed on the invoice amount less the freight charges.

Required:

1. Record the transactions indicated above for Walton Electronics in the appropriate journal for February, 1992.

2. Post the entries to the permanent file, printing a copy of the posting report.

3. Print an unadjusted trial balance for Walton Electronics.

4. Record the following adjustments for Walton Electronics as of February 28, 1992:

    a. Insurance expired of $200.

    b. Rent expired of $500.

    c. Remove beginning inventory of $36,485. (The debit side of this entry should be account number 590, Ending Inventory. Otherwise, the year-to-date amounts in the Cost of Sales section of the income statement will not be correct.)

    d. Enter ending inventory of $34,200.

    e. Supplies used during February are $1,047.

    f. Record depreciation as follows:

       Equipment $275

       Furniture   75

       Trucks   100

    g. Accrue interest on the note to Del's Motors for one month. The interest rate is 12% and part of the principal was paid on January 31.

    h. Accrue a full week of salaries of $1,435.

    i. Deposits of $350 have been earned during February.

    j. Adjust Advertising Expense for the invoice received from Today's Advertising on February 6. You will need to create a Prepaid Advertising account in the Prepaid Expenses section of the Balance Sheet. Use account number 129.

5. Post the adjusting entries, printing a posting report.

6. Print the following reports for Walton Electronics for February 1992:

   a. Adjusted Trial Balance

   b. Balance Sheet

   c. Income Statement

   d. Cash Flows Report

   e. Financial Ratios Report

7. Print the following items for the audit trail:

   a. A permanent copy of each special journal

   b. A complete audit trail of the general ledger for period 1.

Appendix E   Principles of Accounting Practice Set 2

Walton Electronics

Use the backup diskette you created at the end of Lab 7 when you complete this practice set. If you did not make a backup before you completed Lab 8, see your instructor for assistance.

The following events occurred during March 1992 at Walton Electronics.

Receivables:

Date   *Event*

4   Merchandise sold to Terry's Rental Center on invoice number 2049. The amount of the invoice is $8,250.

10   Merchandise sold to Linda's Antiques on invoice number 2050. The amount of the invoice is $1,445.

13   Merchandise sold to Fred's Construction on invoice number 2051. The amount of the invoice is $4,940.

19   Merchandise sold to Scott's Insurance Agency on invoice number 2052. The amount of the invoice is $20,100. A deposit of $1,500 was made against this invoice on February 18.

24   Merchandise sold to Darin's Tax Returns on invoice number 2053. The amount of the invoice is $5,220.

25   Merchandise returned by Scott's Insurance Agency. Issued credit memo number 57 in the amount of $1,000.

26   Merchandise sold to We-Haul-It on invoice number 2054. The amount of the invoice is $7,692.

28   Merchandise sold to Kevin's Shoe Store on invoice number 2055. The amount of the invoice is $6,442.

31   Merchandise sold to Brad's Plumbing on invoice number 2056. The amount of the invoice is $8,309.

31   Merchandise returned by Kevin's Shoe Store. Issued credit memo number 58 in the amount of $210.

Payables:

Date   *Event*

4   Merchandise purchased from Venus Systems. Invoice number QP94PS, dated March 3, is for $16,500, which includes $375 of freight charges.

6   A freight bill from We-Haul-It for delivering merchandise to a customer on March 4. The invoice number is VVK152 and is for $250.

10   Returned merchandise to Venus Systems for credit. Issued debit memo number 445 in the amount of $625.

14   Merchandise purchased from Rebco Computer. Invoice number Z6004, dated March 12, is for $14,490, which includes $390 of freight charges.

19   A freight bill from We-Haul-It for delivering merchandise to a customer on March 19. The invoice number is VVK156 and is for $422.

20   Merchandise purchased from J. M. Supply. Invoice number B3999, dated March 19, is for $5,395, which includes $245 of freight charges.

24   A bill from Lodico Communications for long distance charges. Invoice number 7908, dated March 23, is for $521.

25   A freight bill from We-Haul-It for delivering merchandise to a customer on March 24. The invoice number is VVK163 and is for $193.

26   A bill from City Power Co. for the monthly utilities. Tom wants to wait until the first of April to pay this bill. Use STMT for the reference. The amount is $342.

27   A bill from Garbage Out for disposal service for the months of January through March. There is no invoice number; use STMT for the reference. The amount is for $150.

31   Received an invoice from Carron Peripherals for merchandise shipped FOB Destination. Invoice number HK4841-62, dated March 31, is for $14,500. The items on this invoice have not yet been received.

Checks:

Date   *Event*

3   Check number 1591 to Johnson Development for three months' rent in the amount of $1,575.

3   Check number 1592 to City Power Company for the statement received on February 24. The statement was recorded in payables and is for $523.

3   Check number 1593 to Second City Bank for salaries. The amount is $1,435. These salaries were accrued in total at the end of February. Walton Electronics does not make reversing entries.

5   Check number 1594 to the Postmaster. The amount is $275 to refill the postage meter.

6   Check number 1595 to Today's Advertising for invoice number QT3490. The amount due is $1,500. There is no discount.

7   Check number 1596 to Karla's Kandies for merchandise returned from the cash sale made on invoice 1346. The amount is $75.

10   Check number 1597 to Rebco Computer for invoice number Z5690. The amount due is $10,500. The terms are 2/10, net 30, and the invoice is being paid within the discount period.

10   Check number 1598 to Second City Bank for salaries. The amount is $1,435. Sales salaries are $885 and office salaries are $550.

14   Check number 1599 to Venus Systems for invoice number QP94PS. The balance due is $15,875 after the return on March 10. The amount due includes $375 of freight charges. The terms are 2/10, net 30, and the invoice is being paid within the discount period.

14   Check number 1600 to Tom Walton for a personal withdrawal of $1,800.

14   Check number 1601 to Del's Motors in payment of the balance of the note. The principal amount due is $2,800 and the check includes the interest due at 12% a month for two months. Walton Electronics does not make reversing entries; interest for January and February has been accrued. You will need to include the accrued interest plus any interest due for March.

17   Check number 1602 to Second City Bank for salaries. The amount and distribution are the same as check number 1598.

17   Check number 1603 to Lodico Communications for invoice number 7293 recorded in February. The amount due is $439.

19   Check number 1604 to Jason's Office Supplies for supplies purchased that day. The amount is $1,347.

20   Check number 1605 to J.M. Supply for invoice number B3781. The amount due is $5,200. There is no discount allowed.

24   Check number 1606 to Second City Bank for salaries. The amount and distribution are the same as check numbers 1598 and 1602.

24   Check number 1607 to Rebco Computer for invoice number Z6004. The amount due is $14,490, which includes $390 of freight charges. The terms are 2/10, net 30, and the invoice was paid within the discount period.

26   Check number 1608 to Ken's Furniture Store for return of merchandise sold on invoice number 2043. The amount is $215.

28   Check number 1609 to Local Phone Company for telephone charges for the month of March. The amount is $296.

28	Check number 1610 to We-Haul-It for a statement received for February charges. The amount is $750.
31	Check number 1611 to Second City Bank for salaries. The amount and distribution are the same as check numbers 1598, 1602, and 1606.
31	Check number 1612 to Tom Walton for a personal withdrawal of $1,800.

Deposits:

Date	Event
3	Deposit number 92022 from Excellent Hardware for invoice number 2047, dated 2/21/92, in the amount of $13,490. A deposit of $2,000 was applied against the balance. The invoice also includes freight charges of $265. The discount is taken and allowed on the full amount of the invoice less the freight charges.
7	Deposit number 92023 from Julie's Pet Shop for invoice number 2048, dated 2/26/92, which has a balance outstanding of $14,590 that includes $240 of freight charges. The discount is taken and allowed on the balance outstanding less the freight charges.
10	Deposit number 92024 from Ken's Furniture Store for invoice number 2043, dated 2/6/92, in the amount of $9,643 that includes $293 of freight charges. No discount is allowed.
10	Deposit number 92025 from Second City Bank representing the proceeds of a note payable of $5,000, borrowed from the bank for 90 days at 10% interest.
18	Deposit number 92026 from Wendell's Hair Design for invoice number 1347, representing a cash sale of $1,250.
19	Deposit number 92027 from Chet's Warehouse for invoice number 1348, representing a cash sale of $695.
24	Deposit number 92028 from Fred's Construction for invoice number 2051, dated 3/13/92, in the amount of $4,940 that includes $140 in freight charges. A discount is taken and allowed on the invoice amount less the freight charges.

26 Deposit number 92029 from Lynn's Furniture for a deposit on an order. The amount is $1,200.

31 Deposit number 92030 from Scott's Insurance Agency for invoice number 2052, dated 3/19/92, which has a balance outstanding of $20,100. A deposit of $1,500 was applied against the balance and a credit memo for $1,000 has been issued. A discount is taken and allowed on the full amount of the invoice less the amount returned.

31 Deposit number 92031 from Tom Walton for invoice number 1349, representing a cash sale of $425.

Required:

1. Record the transactions indicated above for Walton Electronics in the appropriate journal for March, 1992.

2. Post the entries to the permanent file, printing a copy of the posting report.

3. Print an unadjusted trial balance for Walton Electronics.

4. Record the following adjustments for Walton Electronics as of March 31, 1992:

   a. Insurance expired of $200.

   b. Rent expired of $525.

   c. Remove beginning inventory of $34,200. (The debit side of this entry should be account number 590, Ending Inventory. Otherwise, the year-to-date amounts for Beginning and Ending Inventory in the Cost of Sales section of the income statement will not be correct.)

   d. Enter ending inventory of $23,215.

   e. Supplies used during March are $1,221.

   f. Record depreciation as follows:

Equipment	$275
Furniture	75
Trucks	100

 g. Accrue interest on the note to Second City Bank for the number of days since it was issued. The annual interest rate is 10%. Round your accrual to the nearest dollar.

 h. Accrue one day of salaries for March 31. Use one-fifth of the salaries paid every Monday.

 i. Deposits of $225 have been earned during March.

 j. Record the expiration of the Prepaid Advertising set up in February for $750.

5. Post the adjusting entries, printing a posting report.

6. Print the following reports for Walton Electronics for March 1992:

 a. Adjusted Trial Balance

 b. Balance Sheet

 c. Income Statement

 d. Cash Flows Report

 e. Financial Ratios Report

7. Print the following items for the audit trail:

 a. A permanent copy of each special journal

 b. A complete audit trail of the general ledger for period 3.

Appendix F Manufacturing Practice Set

Use the backup diskette you created at the end of Lab 7 when you complete this practice set. If you did not make a backup before you completed Lab 8, see your instructor for assistance. The accounts you will create in this practice set do not use the departments you added in Lab 8.

Because this practice set deals with transactions in 1993, you should perform the new-year procedures outlined at the end of Lab 5. After you perform those procedures, you are ready to proceed with this practice set.

In January 1993, Tom Walton decides to expand his operation. Instead of buying completed units and then selling them to customers, he will begin to assemble some hardware. He will order the parts and hire a computer technician to assemble the units from the parts. The technician will test the assembled hardware before it is sold to a customer.

Tom needs to set aside some space where the technician can work and where the unassembled parts can be stored. These activities will require about 30% of the space currently available. Tom also needs to buy the workbench, some shelving for the unassembled parts, and tools for the technician to use.

In addition to hiring the new technician, Tom will assign one of the current shipping employees to the new manufacturing operation. The shipping employee will be responsible for receiving and stocking the unfinished parts and for moving the assembled units to a manufacturing storage area, where they are either shipped to or picked up by the customer. The shipping employee must report the time spent on these activities as a separate entry on her timecard.

To accommodate this new manufacturing operation, Tom needs to add the following accounts to the chart of accounts.

Summary Heading	Acc. #	Account Title
Inventory	125	Unassembled Parts Inventory
Inventory	126	Work in Progress Inventory
Inventory	127	Finished Goods Inventory
Property, Plant & Equipment	135	Assembly Equipment
Accumulated Depreciation	158	Accum. Depr. – Assembly Equip.
Cost of Sales	599	Cost of Assembled Units Sold

Use the Summary Heading "Other Occupancy Expense" and change the title to "Factory Overhead Expense."

Summary Heading	Acc. #	Account Title
Factory Overhead Expense	560	Indirect Labor
Factory Overhead Expense	565	Factory Supplies Expense
Factory Overhead Expense	570	Depr. Exp. – Assembly Equip.
Factory Overhead Expense	575	Rent Expense
Factory Overhead Expense	580	Utilities Expense
Factory Overhead Expense	585	Factory Overhead Applied

If you add an account to a summary heading whose accounts are included in a formula total, you may have to delete that formula total and reconstruct it based on the new accounts you have added. If you add an account in the middle of the @SUM range, you will not have to adjust the formula. If you add an account at the end of the @SUM range or before the @SUM range, you will have to delete the current formula and rebuild it including the new account(s).

Record the following summary transactions for January 1993, which involve the assembly of parts into finished units. Record all of them in the General Journal with a date of January 31, 1993. Entries should trace the flow of goods from unassembled parts to work in progress to finished goods to cost of goods sold.

1. Purchased unassembled parts on account in the amount of $15,700.

2. Used parts from inventory to assemble completed and incomplete units in the amount of $12,600.

3. Paid the technician $2,500 for his work during the month of January. The technician's work is direct labor. (Ignore payroll taxes.)

4. Paid the shipping employee $1,040 for her work during the month of January. Twenty-five percent of her time was spent on receiving and stocking unassembled parts and moving finished units to the finished goods area. (For purposes of this practice set, disregard the remainder of her time in recording the journal entry and ignore payroll taxes.)

5. Total rent for the month of January was $550. Record this amount as an adjustment crediting Prepaid Rent. Remember, 30% of total space is used in manufacturing. Record all rent. Be sure it is properly allocated.

6. Utilities for the month of January were paid in the amount of $320. Allocate utilities based on the amount of space occupied by the assembly operation. Record all the utilities. Be sure to properly allocate it.

7. Assembly equipment costing a total of $6,000 was purchased on account.

8. Depreciation for January on the assembly equipment was $125.

9. Overhead is applied to work in progress at the rate of 25% of direct labor.

10. The technician spent 175 hours working during the month of January. Of this time, 20 hours were spent on work that was not yet finished. Allocate the direct labor and the factory overhead applied between the units completed and transferred to finished goods and the units still in process. Round all computations to the nearest dollar. Materials for the units still in process cost $1,200. (See transaction number 3 for the technician's total wages.)

11. Assembled units which had been transferred to finished goods were sold to customers for $17,500. The cost of these units was determined to be $12,168.

Required:

1. Post the entries after you have recorded them.

2. Print a copy of the General Journal.

3. Print a complete audit trail for January 1993.

4. Answer the following questions (showing supporting computations):

   a. What is the cost of goods manufactured for January 1993 before considering ultimate disposition of over-applied or underapplied overhead?

   b. What is the work in progress inventory at the end of January 1993?

   c. Is factory overhead overapplied or underapplied? By how much? What should be done with this variance?

Appendix G Intermediate Accounting Practice Set

In November 1992, Tom Walton's cousin Arthur Walton decided to open a retail electronics shop, Walton's II, in a nearby metropolitan area. After discussions with Arthur, you have decided on the following chart of accounts.

Acct. #	Account Title
100	Cash in Bank
102	Petty Cash
105	Marketable Equity Securities
107	Allow. to Value Sec. at LCM
110	Accounts Receivable
112	Allowance for Doubtful Accts.
120	Merchandise Inventory
130	Supplies on Hand
140	Prepaid Advertising
145	Prepaid Insurance
150	Prepaid Rent & Lease
155	Other Prepaids
180	Refundable Deposits
200	Furniture
202	Accum. Depr. — Furniture
210	Delivery Van
212	Accum. Depr. — Van
220	Equipment
222	Accum. Depr. — Equipment

270	Organization Costs
272	Accum. Amortiz. — Org. Costs
300	Accounts Payable
310	Cur. Portion of Notes Payable
320	Income Taxes Payable
340	Interest Payable
345	Salaries & Wages Payable
355	Dividends Payable
360	Income Tax Withholding
362	FICA Taxes Payable
365	Sales Tax Payable
370	Long-term Notes Payable
410	Common Stock, $2 par
420	Add'l Paid-in Cap. — Common
450	Retained Earnings, Unappropr.
452	R.E. Appropr. for Treas. Stock
480	Treasury Stock — Common
490	Common Dividends Declared
500	Sales
510	Sales Returns & Allowances
580	Interest Revenue
585	Dividend Revenue
600	Cost of Goods Sold
610	Advertising Expense
615	Freight-out
620	Bad Debt Expense
630	Salaries & Wages Expense
635	Payroll Tax Expense
640	Rent & Lease Expense
645	Depreciation Expense

650	Amortization Expense
660	Insurance Expense
665	Supplies Expense
670	Phone & Utilities Expense
675	Miscellaneous Expense
680	Interest Expense
682	Inventory Discounts Lost
685	Loss — M. Securities Decline
690	Income Tax Expense

During November 1992, Arthur completed the following in preparation for the opening of Walton's II in December.

1. The incorporation process for Walton's II was completed. The incorporation costs (lawyer's fees, state application fees, printing costs, notary costs, etc.) totaled $2,200. Arthur has decided to allocate these costs to expense over a 10-year period.

2. Arthur took out a $50,000 personal loan from First Finance. Arthur must make ten equal annual payments of $8,136.70 to pay the principal and the interest of 10 percent per year beginning December 1, 1993. With the $50,000 and an additional $21,400, Arthur purchased 17,000 shares of Walton's II $2-par common stock. Tom Walton purchased 5,000 shares of Walton's II common stock for $21,000.

3. Arthur opened a checking account for Walton's II at First Finance Bank with the proceeds from the issuance of the common stock, minus the incorporation costs.

4. Arthur obtained a business license for Walton's II for December 1992 and all of 1993. Check number 101 to the City Treasurer is for $1,300.

5. Arthur ordered $170 of business cards and other materials from Quikprint. The materials will be paid for when they are received on December 1.

The following events occurred during December 1992 at Walton's II. Walton's II uses the perpetual inventory method.

Date   *Event*

1   Signed a 13-month lease for a building, calling for payments of $1,000 per month beginning immediately. Check number 102 to Collier Property Management is for $2,400, including a $1,400 refundable security deposit.

1   Received and paid for the business cards and other materials from the printers (invoice number R741). Check number 103 to Quikprint is for $170.

1   Arranged for three months of radio advertising to begin immediately. Check number 104 to KWZO is for $1,800 (invoice number KW405).

1   Purchased office supplies from Lucy's Office Supplies (invoice number A100-10). Check number 105 is for $778.

1   Purchased a delivery van for $19,000. Paid $5,000 down and signed a note promising to pay $659.04 every month, beginning January 1, 1993, for two years (24 payments). The nominal interest rate is 12 percent, per year on the outstanding balance. The $19,000 includes transportation costs of $400 and sales tax of $1,040. Check number 106 to Happy Trails Autos is for $5,000. (Note: The Notes Payable liability will be $7,417.58 at the end of 1993.) The van is to be depreciated using the activity method based upon a total estimated useful life of 100,000 miles. The van has an expected residual value of $2,000.

1   Invested $20,000 of the cash in a portfolio of the common and preferred stock of other companies, to be liquidated when the cash is needed for operations. Check number 107 to Drysdale Investments for $20,000 included a brokerage fee of $200.

2	Purchased office furniture from B.C. Furniture (invoice number B10745). Check number 108 is for $9,000. The furniture is to be depreciated using the double declining balance method. The estimated salvage value at the end of the 5-year useful life is $500.
2	Received merchandise from J.M. Supply. Invoice number B5322, dated December 1, is for $8,730, which includes $300 of freight charges.
2	Purchased six months of property and liability insurance coverage beginning immediately. Check number 109 to Ford Property & Casualty is for $900.
2	Received merchandise from Venus Systems. Invoice number QP35PT, dated December 1, is for $27,000, which includes $560 of freight charges. The terms are 1/10, net 30 on the full amount. Use the net method to record the discounts.
2	Created a petty cash fund. Check number 110, to Walton's II, is for $200.
3	Computer hardware and software, purchased from Venus Systems on December 2, were pulled from the sales area for use in the office. The merchandise had been purchased for $5,000, but had a listed retail price of $7,000 (Reference number JE92001). Use the straight-line depreciation method; assume a useful life of 4 years and no estimated salvage value.
4	Received merchandise from Carron Peripherals. Invoice number HK4960-70, dated December 2, is for $24,500, which includes $440 of freight charges. The terms are net 30.
5	Sold merchandise to Village Crafts on invoice number W1001. The amount of the invoice is $23,000, plus $1,380 in state sales tax. The terms of the sale are net 10. The merchandise cost Walton's II $18,000.
8	Received a freight bill from We-Haul-It for delivering merchandise to Villiage Crafts on December 5. The invoice, number VVK201, is for $356.

10	Sold merchandise to Metropolitan Utilities on invoice number W1002. The amount on the invoice is $16,300, plus $978 in state sales tax. The terms of the sale are net 20. The merchandise cost Walton's II $11,500.
11	Check number 111 to Venus Systems is for full payment of invoice QP35PT.
12	Sold merchandise to Green's Grocery on invoice number W1003. The amount of the invoice is $13,900, plus $834 in state sales tax. Green paid the entire amount (deposit number 92001). The merchandise cost Walton's II $9,700.
14	Check number 112 to Arthur's sales employee, Ken I. Sail is for sales salaries of $372. Ken is paid a gross salary of $600 every two weeks ($6.25 per hour for 96 hours), of which $180 is withheld for income taxes and $48 is withheld for social security (FICA). Walton's II is exempt from unemployment taxes, but will pay a matching amount in social security taxes.
14	Received merchandise from Rebco Computer. Invoice number Z7000, dated December 12, is for $12,900, which includes $340 of freight charges. The terms are net 15.
15	Received $24,380 from Village Crafts for invoice number W1001, dated December 5. The deposit is number 92002.
16	Returned merchandise to Rebco Computer for credit. Issued a debit memo, number D101, for $704.
19	Purchased office supplies from Lucy's Office Supplies (invoice number A176-10). Check number 113 is for $223.
22	Received merchandise from Carron Peripherals. Invoice number HK4983-70, dated December 21, is for $7,300, which includes $204 of freight charges. The terms are net 30.

23   Sold merchandise to Animal House Pets on invoice number W1004. The amount of the invoice is $2,100, plus $126 in state sales tax. The entire amount was received (deposit number 92003). The merchandise cost Walton's II $1,650.

26   Check number 114 is to Rebco Computer for full payment of invoice number Z7000, less the merchandise returned on December 16th.

27   Received notification from First Finance Bank that Animal House Pets did not have sufficient funds in its account to cover the check for $2,226. The check was returned to Walton's II. Arthur will attempt to collect the funds from Animal House Pets.

28   Check number 115 to Ken I. Sail is for sales salaries of $372. (Refer to the previous payroll transaction on December 14, 1992 for more information.)

28   Sold merchandise to Di's Beauty Supplies on invoice number W1005. The amount on the invoice is $2,300, plus $138 in state sales tax. The terms of the sale are net 20. The merchandise cost Walton's II $1,800.

28   Tom Walton sold 400 shares of common stock back to Walton's II to be held for reissuance. Check #116 was for $1,708.

29   According to the year-end statement from Drysdale Investments, the portfolio of common and preferred stocks earned $120 in dividend revenue. A check (#2004) for that amount was received with the statement and deposited in First Finance Bank (deposit number 92004).

30   Received a freight bill from We-Haul-It for delivering merchandise to Di's Beauty Supplies on December 28. The invoice, number VVK241, is for $219.

30   Declared a $.10 per-share cash dividend to be paid January 10, 1993. (Reference number JE92002.)

30   Received a bill from Metropolitan Utilities for December's utilities. Invoice number MU7890, dated December 29, for $207, is due January 10, 1993.

30   Received $17,278 from Metropolitan Utilities for invoice number W1002, dated December 10. The deposit is number 92005.

31   Merchandise was returned by Di's Beauty Supplies. A credit memo, number C101, was issued for $500. The merchandise has an inventory value of $420.

31   Received a statement from Local Phone Company for December's local and long-distance phone service. The bill, dated December 30, for $432, is due January 15, 1993.

31   Check number 117 to Arthur is for his monthly salary. Arthur earns a gross salary of $2,000, of which $600 is withheld for income taxes and $120 is withheld for social security (FICA). Walton's II will pay a matching amount in social security taxes.

31   Check number 118 to We-Haul-It for a statement received for December charges. The amount is $575.

31   Replenished petty cash with check number 119. The following receipts and cash were found in the fund.

Cash	$ 36.06
Supplies	$ 58.79
Miscellaneous Items	$105.15

31   Received the December bank statement from First Finance Bank. A reconciliation of the books and the bank revealed that deposit 10005 and checks 117, 118, and 119 were not on the bank statement. There was an unrecorded service charge of $12.80, and unrecorded interest revenue of $166.27.

31   Purchased merchandise from Rebco Computer. Invoice number Z7045, dated December 30, is for $14,310, which includes $260 of freight charges. The terms are net 15. The merchandise, shipped FOB Destination, has not been received yet.

Required:

1. Create the chart of accounts using the appropriate summary titles.

2. Record the November events in the General Journal for Period 11. Post the entries to the permanent file, printing a copy of the posting report.

3. Record the transactions for Walton's II for December 1992 (period 12). You may find it most efficient to scan the events to determine in which journal, if any, each event should be entered. Then make the entries by journal.

4. Post the entries to the permanent file, printing a copy of the posting report.

5. Print an unadjusted trial balance for Walton's II.

6. Record the following adjustments for Walton's II, as of December 31, 1992:

    a. A year-end physical count revealed that $36 of merchandise inventory was missing, and $367 of supplies were still on hand.

    b. Uncollectible customer accounts were estimated to be 2 percent of net sales.

    c. Ken I. Sail worked 16 hours since his last paycheck on December 28th.

    d. The market value of the portfolio of common and preferred stock on December 31 was $19,850.

    e. The delivery van was driven 820 miles during December.

    f. Income taxes were estimated to be $830.

    g. The state in which Walton's II is incorporated requires that retained earnings be restricted in the amount of the cost of treasury stock. To communicate this information on the financial statements, Arthur wants retained earnings appropriated for the amount of treasury stock.

    In addition, scan the events to identify any other adjustments that should be made. (Round the allocation of prepaids, interest, and depreciation to the nearest month.)

7. Post the adjusting entries, printing a posting report.

8. Format and print the following reports for Walton's II for December 1992:

   a. Adjusted Trial Balance

   b. Classified Balance Sheet

   c. Multi-step Income Statement

   d. Cash Flows Report

   e. Financial Ratios Report

9. Print the following items for the audit trail:

   a. A permanent copy of each special journal

   b. A complete audit trail of the general ledger for period 12 (December).

Index

Abort command, for quitting
  Beginning Balances without
  saving, 92
Accounting period, choosing, 49
Accounting systems
  computerized, 49–52, 193
  manual, 48–49, 52, 193
  steps in, 48–49
Account names, adding, 75
Account numbers
  adding, 75
  changing, 108
  default, function keys and, 71
Accounts
  adding to Accounts Receivables
    account, 76–78
  adding departments to, 280
  adding to existing Chart of
    Accounts, 93–95, 127, 174
  adding with GL menu, 127
  all, printing audit trail for,
    192–194
  closing, 51
  consolidation, 76
  displaying bar graphs for, 187, 326
  entering new, 72–76
  existing, adding departments to,
    278–279
  function keys and, 71
  inquiring about activity in, with
    Query program, 185–189
  interrupting entering of, 71
  specific, printing audit trail for,
    189–191
Accounts command
  for displaying a bar graph
    comparing accounts, 326
  for graphing monthly budgets,
    268–269
  menus for, 354
  for printing Chart of Accounts,
    84, 328, 329
Accounts criterion
  changing, 301–303, 305–306
  current, 292
  selecting Accounts Receivable
    items with, 305–306
  selecting menu for, 292, 301,
    330–331

Accounts/Custom/Journals/
  Statements/Trial/Prior menu, 328
Accounts/Debt-Equity/Liquidity/
  Revenue-Expenses/Return
  menu, 326
Accounts/Income/Balance/
  Summary menu, 329
Accounts Payable, debiting,
  142–147
Accounts Payable/Accounts
  Receivable (AP/AR) menu
  item, 58–59
Accounts Receivable
  adding accounts to, 76–78
  Assets Heading List, 76–78
  crediting, 151–155
Accounts Receivable activity
  report, customized, 304–310
Account Title command
  changing account titles with, 79
  entering account titles with,
    75–76, 78
  for inserting new accounts, 356
Accrual basis for preparing
  accounting financial
  statements, 173
Active option
  for printing accounts with
    activity, 193
  for printing audit trail, 351–352
Actuals command
  Budget menu, 254
  for importing data from
    LEDGER file, 343
Add/Delete/Edit/Return menu, 332
Add/Delete/Return menu, 329–330
Add-in files, provided with
  Ready-to-Run, 390
Add/NOT/Done menu, 330–331
Add option
  for adding departments, 329
  for adding more data for the
    same reference number, 331
  for building criterion for
    customized reports, 330
Add/Prior/Following/Done/Quit
  menu, 331–332

Adjust command, 167, 294
  for changing title of customized
    report, 333
  for customizing reports, 363
  for making changes in custom
    reports, 310
  for making changes to Chart of
    Accounts, 286
  menu for, 338
Adjusting entries, 166
  posting, 48
  preparing, 48, 173–179
  recording, 51
Adjust/Keep menu, 333
All/Select menu, 333
Anchoring, a range with a
  period (.), 205
Another/Done menu, 333–334
AP/AR command, 58–59, 348
  menu for, 353
Arithmetic formulas, in financial
  statements, 211–212
Arrow keys
  entering data with, 54
  for moving through reports,
    188–189
Ascending/Descending menu, 334
Ascending sort order, 293, 305
  changing to, 334
Asset accounts, entering, 79–81
Assets/Debt-Equity/Exp-Rev
  menu, 334–335
Assets graph, commands for
  creating, 334
Assets Heading List
  Accounts Receivable, 76–78
  Cash, 73–74
Assets pie chart, 242–244
Audit trail, 180–195
  accounts payable reference
    numbers and, 143
  General Ledger for, 193–194
  printing for all accounts,
    192–194
  printing journals for, 180–184
  printing posted transactions
    and, 134
  printing for selected accounts, 357

checks with one debit and no discount, 142–144
checks for a payable with a discount, 145–147
editing, 157
entering, 141–157
posting, 157
printing, 157
CD (Cash Disbursements) journal, 143
sample report, 376
Cell address, 29, 70
Cell numbers, references to, 202
Cell pointer, 70
data entry and, 323
defined, 28
movement of, 54
Change command, menu for, 330–331
Change/Keep menu, 338
Chart of Accounts
Account Title option, 72
adding accounts to, 72, 93–95, 174
adding departments to, 277–278
adding income statement accounts, 83
asset accounts, 79–81
Beginning Balances for, 87–92
Blank option, 69–70
changing an account title, 79
changing report headings on, 286–292
customized, 286–295
editing screen, 174, 368–369
entering, 69–82
equity accounts, 81–82
Formula option, 72
function keys and, 71
instruction keys for entering, 70–71
liability accounts, 81–82
Line option, 72
Lotus 1-2-3, Release 3 and, 396
menu, 69, 328
new accounts in, 72–78
preparing to enter, 66–68
printing, 83–85, 328, 329
Return option, 72
samples, 346
saving, 71, 85–86
sorting, 293
summary headings for, 72–74
Chart of Accounts editing screen
Accounts option, 84
Balance option, 84
Income option, 84
Summary option, 84
Checking option, for specifying default account numbers, 104–105, 338–339

Checking/Payables/Receivables/ Save menu, 338–339
Checks
debit and no discount, 142–144
entering, 142–150
for items expensed immediately, 147–148
multiple debits, 149–150
payable with a discount, 145–147
special journals, 101
Checks/Deposits/Payables/ Receivables/General menu, 339–340
Checks option, for entering payments of cash by check, 339
Closing procedure, 51, 222–223, 226–229
drawing account, 226
expense accounts, 227–229
revenue accounts, 227–229
CMD indicator, defined, 29
Color option, for displaying graphs in color, 337
Columns
adding to Chart of Accounts, 287–292
deleting from Chart of Accounts, 287
Commands
reversing selection of, 322
selecting, 321–322
sequences, in Lotus 1-2-3, 30
Companies, new, setting up, 323
Company name
recording with Directory/ Company, 65–66
specifying, 60, 327
Computerized accounting systems, 50–53
versus manual accounting systems, 53, 193
Condensed print, 171, 340
Condensed/Regular menu, 340
Configuration screen, 36–41
Configure command, 349
menus for, 341–342, 361
Configure Redo command, menus for, 327–328
Consolidated/Departments menu, 341
Consolidated option, for consolidating totals by account type, 341
Consolidation accounts, 76
Control panel
defined, 29
menu options on, 33
Ready-to-Run, 53

Corrections
to beginning balances, 90–91
in data entry, 54
Fix command for, 103, 131–132, 347
making before entering a cell, 54
Redo option for, 352
of typing errors, 11
to unposted transactions, 103, 131–133
Cost of Goods Available for Sale, creating a subtotal for, 209–210
Cost of sales, graphing, 266–267
CR (Cash Receipts) journal, 151
Credit balances, entering, 90
Credits
in budgets, 257
entering with debits, with Pairs command, 125–127
entering individually, with Single command, 126–127
Criterion. See also Accounts criterion
Change menu, 301
menu for, 330–331
CRITERION line, 303
Current Assets, creating a subtotal for, 202–208
Current Period format, for printing balance sheet, 217
Current Period and Year-to-Date format, for printing Income Statements, 221–222
Current ratio, calculation of, 241
Current vs. Budget format, for printing balance sheet, 217
Current vs. Prior Year format, for printing balance sheet, 217
Cursor movement, in Ready-to-Run, 54
Custom command, 167
menu for, 364–365
for printing custom reports, 328
Customers, accounts receivable activity reports by, 304–310
Custom reports
accounts receivable activity report, 304–310
Adjust option and, 363
changing accounts criterion for, 301–303
changing titles of, 308, 333
Chart of Accounts, 286–295
creating, 286–310
income statement accounts, quarterly report, 295–304
making changes in with Adjust command, 310
menus for, 364–365
naming, 294–295, 361–362
printing, 295, 308–309

Add Additional Modules to The Student Edition of Ready-to-Run Accounting

The Student Edition of Ready-to-Run Accounting is the core of the complete Ready-to-Run system. Additional stand-alone modules for **Accounts Receivable, Accounts Payable, Payroll,** and **Inventory** integrate seamlessly with the general ledger core to provide a complete accounting system. Now these modules are available* to student users of The Student Edition of Ready-to-Run Accounting at an educational price. Use this coupon to order your additional modules.

Please send me the Accounts Receivable, Accounts Payable, Payroll, and Inventory modules for The Student Edition of Ready-to-Run Accounting at the educationally discounted price of $49.95.

_____ Enclosed is my check for $49.95.

_____ Please charge my credit card:

Card No. _____

Interbank No. _____ Exp. Date _____

Signature _____

Send my modules to:

Name _____

Address/Apt No. _____

City/State/Zip _____

Telephone _____

I am a registered user. ☐ yes ☐ no

Send your completed request to:
Order Department, Addison-Wesley Publishing Company,
One Jacob Way, Reading, MA 01867.

Prices subject to change without notice.
*Available September, 1991.

Attention Lotus 1-2-3, Release 3 Users:
Free Ready-to-Run Upgrade* Request Form

If you purchased The Student Edition of Ready-to-Run Accounting in the 5¼″ disk format, you may request additional files to make your copy of Ready-to-Run compatible with Lotus 1-2-3, Releases 3 and 3.1. (If you purchased the 3½″ disk format, you don't need any additional files.) Please use the coupon below to request your free upgrade.

Yes, I would like to use my copy of The Student Edition of Ready-to-Run Accounting with Lotus 1-2-3, Release 3. Send my upgrade disk to:

Name _____

Address _____

City/State/Zip _____

Telephone _____

I am a registered user. ☐ yes ☐ no

Send your completed request to:
Educational Software Marketing, Addison-Wesley Publishing Company, One Jacob Way, Reading, MA 01867.

* The files offered here do not constitute a new version of Ready-to-Run and are offered solely as a service to our customers who may have switched to Lotus 1-2-3, Release 3 since they purchased The Student Edition of Ready-to-Run Accounting. Offer good through December, 1992.

The Student Edition of Ready-to-Run Accounting Software License Agreement

IMPORTANT: READ THIS LICENSE AGREEMENT CAREFULLY *BEFORE* OPENING THE DISK POUCH. BY OPENING THE POUCH, YOU ACCEPT THE TERMS OF THIS AGREEMENT.

REFUND

If you don't wish to follow the terms of this license agreement, you may obtain a full refund by returning this package with your receipt to your Authorized Dealer within ten (10) days provided you have not opened the sealed disk pouch. Your right to return this product for a refund for this reason expires on the eleventh day after purchase.

Addison-Wesley Publishing Company, Inc. ("Addison-Wesley") has authorized distribution of this copy of the Software to you pursuant to a license from Manusoft Corporation and retains ownership of this copy of the Software. Manusoft retains ownership of the Software itself. This copy is licensed to you for use under the following conditions.

DEFINITIONS

The term "Software" as used in this agreement means the computer programs contained in the disks in this package, together with any updates subsequently supplied by Addison-Wesley.

The term "Software Copies" means the actual copies of all or any portion of the Software, including back-ups, updates, merged or partial copies permitted hereunder or subsequently supplied by Addison-Wesley.

The term "Related Materials" means all of the printed materials provided in this package or later supplied by Addison-Wesley for use with the Software.

PERMITTED USES/YOU MAY:

- Use this Software only for educational purposes.
- Load into RAM and use the Software on a single terminal or a single workstation of a computer (or its replacement).
- Install the Software onto a permanent storage device (a hard disk).
- Make and maintain one back-up copy provided it is used only for back-up purposes, and you keep possession of the back-up. In addition, all the information appearing on the original disk labels (including the copyright notice) must be copied onto the back-up labels.
- Use the Software on a network or multiple user arrangement provided you pay for and obtain a separate licensed Software package for each terminal or workstation from which the Software will actually be accessed.

This license gives you certain limited rights to use the Software, Software Copies and Related Materials. You do not become the owner of, and Addison-Wesley and Manusoft (according to their respective interests) retain title to, all the Software, Software Copies and Related Materials. In addition, you agree to use reasonable efforts to protect the Software from unauthorized use, reproduction, distribution or publication.

All rights not specifically granted in this license are reserved by Addison-Wesley and Manusoft.

USES NOT PERMITTED/YOU MAY NOT:

- Use this Software for any purposes other than educational purposes.
- Make copies of the Software, except as permitted above.
- Make copies of the Related Materials.
- Rent, lease, sub-lease, time-share, lend or transfer the Software, Software Copies, Related Materials or your rights under this license except that transfers may be made with Addison-Wesley's prior written authorization.
- Alter, decompile, disassemble or reverse engineer the Software or make any attempt to unlock or bypass the initialization system used on the initialized disks.
- Remove or obscure the Manusoft or Addison-Wesley copyright and trademark notices.

DURATION

This agreement is effective from the day you open the sealed disk pouch. Your license continues for fifty years or until you return to Addison-Wesley the original disks and any back-up copies, whichever comes first.

If you breach this agreement, we can terminate this license upon notifying you in writing. You will be required to return all Software Copies and Related Materials. We can also enforce our other legal rights.

GENERAL

This agreement represents our entire understanding and agreement regarding the Software, Software Copies and Related Materials and supersedes any prior purchase order, communications, advertising or representations.

This license may only be modified in a written amendment signed by an authorized Addison-Wesley officer. If any provision of this agreement shall be unlawful, void or for any reason unenforceable, it shall be deemed severable from, and shall in no way affect the validity or enforceability of, the remaining provisions of this agreement. This agreement will be governed by California law.

You acknowledge that you have read every provision of this contract.

Addison-Wesley and Manusoft retain all rights not expressly granted. Nothing in this agreement constitutes a waiver of Addison-Wesley's or Manusoft's rights under the U.S. copyright laws or any other federal or state law.

Should you have any questions concerning this agreement, you may contact Addison-Wesley by writing to Addison-Wesley Publishing Company, Inc., Educational Software Division, Jacob Way, Reading, MA 01867.